D0002370

The Sociological Ambition

Theory, Culture & Society

Theory, Culture & Society caters for the resurgence of interest in culture within contemporary social science and the humanities. Building on the heritage of classical social theory, the book series examines ways in which this tradition has been reshaped by a new generation of theorists. It also publishes theoretically informed analyses of everyday life, popular culture, and new intellectual movements.

EDITOR: Mike Featherstone, *Nottingham Trent University*

SERIES EDITORIAL BOARD
Roy Boyne, *University of Durham*
Mike Hepworth, *University of Aberdeen*
Scott Lash, *Goldsmiths College, University of London*
Roland Robertson, *University of Pittsburgh*
Bryan S. Turner, *University of Cambridge*

THE TCS CENTRE
The Theory, Culture & Society book series, the journals *Theory, Culture & Society* and *Body & Society*, and related conference, seminar and postgraduate programmes operate from the TCS Centre at Nottingham Trent University. For further details of the TCS Centre's activities please contact:

Centre Administrator
The TCS Centre, Room 175
Faculty of Humanities
Nottingham Trent University
Clifton Lane, Nottingham, NG11 8NS, UK
e-mail: tcs@ntu.ac.uk
web: http://tcs.ntu.ac.uk

Recent volumes include:

The Contradictions of Culture
Cities, Culture, Women
Elizabeth Wilson

The Tarantinian Ethics
Fred Botting and Scott Wilson

Society and Culture
Principals of Scarcity and Solidity
Bryan S. Turner and Chris Rojek

Modernity and Exclusion
Joel S. Kah

Virilio Live
John Armitage

MRT-GEN
116

The Sociological Ambition

Elementary Forms of Social and Moral Life

Chris Shilling and Philip A. Mellor

University of Ottawa
BIBLIOTHÈQUES
University of Ottawa
LIBRARIES
University of Ottawa

SAGE Publications
London • Thousand Oaks • New Delhi

D.B.N. 1739940

© Chris Shilling and Philip A. Mellor 2001

First published 2001

All rights reserved. No part of this publication may be reproduced, stored in a retrieval system, transmitted or utilized in any form or by any means, electronic, mechanical, photocopying, recording or otherwise, without permission in writing from the Publishers.

SAGE Publications Ltd
6 Bonhill Street
London EC2A 4PU

SAGE Publications Inc
2455 Teller Road
Thousand Oaks, California 91320

SAGE Publications India Pvt Ltd
32, M-Block Market
Greater Kailash - I
New Delhi 110 048

British Library Cataloguing in Publication data

A catalogue record for this book is available from the British Library

ISBN 0 7619 6548 3
ISBN 0 7619 6549 1 (pbk)

Library of Congress Control Number Available

Typeset by SIVA Math Setters, Chennai, India
Printed in Great Britain by Biddles Ltd, Guildford, Surrey

HM
435
.S45
2001

This book is dedicated to

Francesca and *Max*

CONTENTS

ACKNOWLEDGEMENTS

Writing a book of this scope inevitably involves relying on the advice, support and encouragement of a number of people. The *Theory, Culture and Society* editorial group and Chris Rojek of Sage publications have been particularly supportive of our ongoing project. For reading and commenting upon various chapters of our study, we are indebted to Ross Abbinnett, Nigel Biggar, Barry Cooper, Michael Erben, Jim Ginther, Linda Hogan, Pauline Leonard, Mark Mitchell, Barry Smart and John Solomos. Mike Gane and Keith Tester read through the whole manuscript, and the book has benefited from their expertise. The ongoing support of Stephen Mennell and Eric Dunning has been invaluable, as has the intellectual stimulus provided by the University College Dublin/ University of Portsmouth link. We would like to thank the Arts and Humanities Research Board and the Universities of Leeds and Portsmouth for the funding that made this work possible. We need to emphasise, however, that responsibility for the arguments developed here, and any deficiencies in the text, is entirely ours. Finally, on a personal note, this project would have been impossible without the inspiration provided by Murielle and Debbie, Francesca, Max and Catherine.

PART I
CLASSICAL SOCIOLOGY

1
BEGINNINGS

1. Introduction

The aim of this book is to provide an analysis, comparison and overview of those classical theories central to the establishment of sociology, and those post-classical theories that have sought to reconstruct the discipline's foundations. We argue that sociology emerged during the nineteenth century with the ambition to comprehend the complex and changing relationships between *social life* and *moral life*, and that the apparently radical departures characterising its later developments nonetheless continue to *converge* around a concern for these relationships. Our identification of this convergence not only allows us to emphasise that there is greater continuity in the discipline than is often supposed, especially by those critics who argue that its classical foundations are of little relevance to current practice, but also enables us to highlight the continuing importance and vitality of the sociological ambition. Building on our analyses of the elementary forms of social and moral life outlined by the 'founding fathers' of the discipline, we make the case for an explicit, informed and creative dialogue involving the proponents of classical and post-classical theory.[1] This dialogue, we suggest, is essential if sociology is to be able to analyse productively the social, cultural and religious divisions and conflicts that continue to pervade the contemporary world.

Sociology has, from its origins, been defined by its various conceptions of social life. These have attempted to make sense of those regularities of behaviour that suggest there exists an ordered social fabric surpassing the impulses, horizons and actions of isolated individuals. Closely allied to this, however, has been the awareness that moral issues inevitably arise in relation to the constitution and development of this social fabric. As sociology has variously understood them, these moral issues refer at their most general level to those conditions under which individuals acquire a sense of responsibility towards, and act in the interests of, others, and to the distinctive matter of the capacity of individuals to construct, and act in accordance with, their own ideals in specific social contexts.[2]

In classical sociology, this interest in the relationship between social and moral life is central and explicit. It is expressed through descriptions of how social relationships shape normative values, through analyses of the problematic role of religion in modernity, and through critiques of how the 'iron cage' of capitalism exerts a deleterious effect on the capacities of individuals to determine their own moral standards. Post-classical forms of sociology are usually less explicit in dealing with this relationship, and Horowitz (1993: 227) has concluded that morality is now 'the ghost in the social science machine'. Nevertheless, moral issues frequently re-emerge in contemporary sociologists' reflections on their choice of subject, their critiques of the marginalisation of certain issues in the writings of classical theorists, and in the political thrust of their analyses of such matters as equality and difference.

This continuity can be illustrated historically with reference to Durkheim's classical interrogation of the effects of an 'abnormal' division of labour on the moral integration of individuals into industrial society, Bauman's argument that rationalised social organisations distance individuals from the moral consequences of their actions, and those contemporary theorists of sexuality who suggest that heterosexual norms stigmatise as immoral those individuals and relationships that transgress their boundaries. The subject matter of these theories is diverse, and their common concern for social and moral life should not obscure the oppositions that otherwise separate classical and post-classical sociologies. Recent theories of conflict, gender, race, and postmodernity, for example, are usually highly critical of the 'grand narratives' that have informed traditional accounts of social development. Their interest in the effects of social orders on people's moral sensibilities, identities and relationships does, however, mean that we can suggest that many forms of contemporary theory continue to pursue the sociological ambition established by the founders of sociology. As Levine (1995) suggests, moral concerns continue to shape the trajectory of sociology.

In beginning our analysis, it is important to draw attention to some important features of the social and historical circumstances in which sociology first emerged. In particular, its theological and philosophical context helps us make sense of the discipline's early interest in the relationship between social and moral life. This relationship has rarely been regarded as unproblematic: it has exercised the minds of some of the greatest philosophers since antiquity. Nevertheless, the decline of Christian notions of divine order, and the rise of a purely human centred view of the universe, heightened the sense of its problematic nature. In this context, social life and moral life were no longer inextricable dimensions of God's plan for humanity, but became objects of rational reflection and, in some cases, arenas for human design and intervention. The idea that there existed a harmonious relationship between social and moral life was further disrupted when the violence that characterised the French Revolution of 1789 – a revolution that can be seen as the political culmination of the Enlightenment – prompted a partial erosion of faith in the ability of abstract rationality to provide society with a satisfactory moral framework.

In the centuries that followed these events, theological responses to the problematisation of social and moral life characteristically sought to re-emphasise the importance of ultimate values, grounded in the will of God, as guides to a moral life. Philosophical responses took two major forms. Some continued to identify transcendent principles and ends that should govern the choices and actions of humans, while others grappled with the creative and nihilistic potentialities of the human will in the context of the 'death of God'. *Sociology* offered a distinctive approach to the problem, pursuing a middle way between transcendentalism and nihilism. It did not break completely with the tendency of religious and philo- sophical thought to associate human life with a series of 'ultimate issues'. Indeed, sociology shared with much theology, and certain philosophical perspectives, the notion that moral issues emerged as a result of people mediating issues of ulti- mate importance through this-worldly ideals and orientations towards others. This notion held that individuals and groups *necessarily* confronted such issues as the existence of life, the inevitability of death, and the experience of frailty and pain, and it expressed the belief that our survival and well-being depend upon the relationships we enter into, and the moral significance we attribute to them. Sociology departed from these traditions, however, in rejecting notions of any divine influence upon human life, and by developing an unprecedented focus on the *social contexts* in which individuals confront moral choices.

This focus immediately raises the question of why sociology chose to concern itself with moral issues and not bracket these out as concerns of theology and philosophy, pursuing an exclusive focus on social life. It did so for two reasons. First, despite its interest in the cultural and historical varieties of social life, socio- logy found itself confronted repeatedly with the question of how people attrib- uted social orders with meaning through the construction of moral frameworks and ideals. This was because these moral phenomena had always affected the symbolic character and institutional development of social orders, imparting to them particular meanings and arguably steering their overall direction (Robertson 1992). Second, sociology was concerned with the potential of moral frameworks and ideals to substitute for traditional religious justifications of social life during an era in which considerable concern was expressed about social disorder and disintegration (Nisbet 1966).

A further issue raised by sociology's focus on moral issues concerns how it was able to view morality as both associated with issues of ultimate importance and as shaped most significantly by social phenomena. Sociology pursued this dual approach by attributing an elementary significance to the capacity of particu- lar forms of social life to either *mediate* these issues into shared norms, socially patterned ethical dilemmas, and individual ideals, or to *block* this mediation of 'ultimate questions' into satisfactory moral orientations. While the former out- come provides individuals and groups with a way of orientating themselves to life's limits, the latter threatens to leave them defenceless, before a disorienting, potentially meaningless world (Berger 1967; Robertson 1992). For sociology, it is not some conception of abstract morality, nor an individual guided by the grace of God, that is primarily responsible for mediating the ultimates of life into human issues, but the form and content taken by *social life*. This is clear in Comte's notion of the positive polity, and in Durkheim's concept of the sacred. The importance of social life in this respect is such that when it is understood to *fail* to provide a context conducive to the translation of ultimate issues into moral norms and ideals, sociologists such as Weber have feared for the sanity of the individual and the future of humanity.

Instead of being marginal to the discipline, then, moral issues within sociology became inextricably entangled with social issues. Indeed, in much of the work of Parsons, the normative dimensions of societies are so significant that social and moral life become virtually synonymous. Sociology has, however, generally recognised a distinction between social coexistence and moral commitments.[3] This has enabled sociologists, in their various analyses of the money economy, of the division of labour, of ruling elites, of conflict, ideology and oppression, to illustrate the distance that can exist between social and moral phenomena, and to highlight the need to explore their various forms and relationships.

In developing our analysis of sociology, we examine how it addressed the relationship between social life and moral life through an analysis of five classical theorists and five major forms of post-classical sociology.[4] The five classical theorists we examine were arguably of most significance in establishing the early contours of sociology (Comte, Durkheim, Simmel, Weber), and in identifying and furthering the development of a vital, coherent discipline (Parsons). The five post-classical forms of theory we examine (conflict theory, feminist theory, 'racial sociology', rational choice theory and post/modern theory) are those that are of most importance in terms of their radical attempts to replace the classics with a new set of theoretical and substantive priorities.

We present these forms of sociology as systematic wholes, and seek to explicate what is at stake in the widespread amnesia of sociology's heritage that has afflicted it in recent years, the apparent fragmentation it suffered during the 1980s and 1990s, and the consequences of the much-heralded 'crisis' of sociology of the 1970s. While the age of classical sociology was characterised, in part, by a confidence in the ability of humans to create and sustain social orders imbued with moral purpose, the latter decades of the twentieth century witnessed a widespread loss of faith in people's ability to achieve such outcomes. In place of grand theoretical narratives about progress, the theories of radical sociologists attacked the heritage of sociology, while they were themselves succeeded by a proliferation of specialisms that appeared to fragment the discipline further into a series of unrelated projects. Nevertheless, it is our view that sociology is not yet ready to dissolve into abstract empiricism or a theoretical and moral tribalism that endorses as superior the experiences and viewpoint of one social group over another. Certain common problems continue to be examined across very different approaches to sociology, and it is possible to discern a renewed interest in processes elementary to the construction of social life and the relationship of these to the constitution of general moral orders. The scope of the classical ambition may have narrowed within contemporary theories, but these nevertheless provide us with the resources to formulate a more inclusive vision of social totalities.

Having outlined the purposes of this study, this introduction is divided into sections that provide more detailed accounts of our vision of the discipline. Section 2 examines sociology's social and intellectual context in relation to the philosophical legacies of the Enlightenment and Counter-Enlightenment, and in relation to those national traditions of thought that exercised most influence on the discipline. Section 3 provides an overview of the amnesia, fracture and sectarianism that has characterised much post-classical sociology. Section 4 outlines how a focus on the discipline's continuing concern with the relationship between social and moral life allows us to bring into dialogue theories that are otherwise incommensurate. Section 5 clarifies our presentation of sociology through an outline of the central features of each chapter.

2. Sociology, the Enlightenment and Counter-Enlightenment

We have already observed that sociology and the modern social sciences emerged in an intellectual context shaped by the changes that occurred in the centuries succeeding the Middle Ages, and the responses to these changes in the Enlightenment and Counter-Enlightenment. As Milbank (1990) argues, there was during the medieval period no 'secular space' waiting to be filled with the sociological conception of society as a human product. Appeals to human rather than divine judgment in a variety of areas may have been developing throughout the medieval period, and the authority of the Church was called into question by a number of secular authorities and religious reform movements, culminating in the ultimately secularising influence of the Protestant Reformation. Nevertheless, for much of the medieval period what sociologists would later call 'society' was simply the single community of Christendom; a sacred, moral order that operated through the ritual incorporation of individuals into the sacramental apparatus of the Church (Mellor and Shilling 1997).

If Protestantism mortally wounded the already fragile medieval notion of divine order, subsequent attempts to answer the question of how humans could construct social and moral orders proved problematic. This is evident in relation to Hobbes's (1651) conception of the 'problem of order' (which exerted an enduring affect on the subject matter of sociology), and the Enlightenment's and Counter-Enlightenment's philosophically opposed views of the ability of human reason to provide the means for a social order based on the moral principles of liberty, equality and fraternity.[5] The Enlightenment vested its faith in human reason, while the Counter-Enlightenment pointed to the violence of the French Revolution as evidence of both the inadequacies of rational human thought and the absolute importance of tradition. De Maistre's understanding of the Terror of the Revolution as the descent of humanity into the chaos of a Godless, anarchic existence, like Comte's description of Voltaire and Rousseau as 'doctors of the guillotine', expresses how many philosophers came to despair of the moral consequences of the Enlightenment (Nisbet 1966: 57).

The sociological response to the decline of divine order was to substitute the notion 'society' for Christendom as the milieu within which humans' social capacities are shaped and expressed. Concepts reflecting the idea that human existence and interdependence occur within the apparently secular sphere of society, such as the 'social body', replaced metaphors that connected earth with the 'kingdom of God', such as the 'king's two bodies', and justified as divinely ordained certain sources of power. This substitution removed the need to account for social and moral order in terms of traditional conceptions of the divine, although the early development of sociology was characterised by a strong interest in the social influence and character of religion, as well as 'ultimate questions' concerning the meaning of life and death. Comte, Durkheim and Weber were all interested in how Protestantism promoted an individualism and rationalism that influenced the development of modernity. These and other sociologists also had a much broader interest in the significance of religion in relation to social and moral order and human capacities, and their analyses were developed through a dialogue with Enlightenment and Counter-Enlightenment politics and philosophy.

Enlightened sociology?

It is important to bear in mind the Enlightenment's diversity, and the fact that English, French and German philosophers possessed competing conceptions of it and its historical origins (Tonelli 1997), yet it is generally acknowledged that the political culmination of the Enlightenment came with the French Revolution of 1789. This overthrew aristocratic and clerical authority and sought to institute a rational order conducive to social progress. Furthermore, the Enlightenment's various forms are united by a focus on the individual, on rationality and on progress, and by an emphasis on the need for a secular knowledge of society, nature and the human condition freed from religious authority (Gay 1973). Some Enlightenment thinkers expressed an ambivalent attitude to religion, contrary to Voltaire's increasing hostility to virtually all manifestations of religiosity, believing in its reform rather than its abolition. Nevertheless, all tended to identify science, reason and astronomy as overturning the traditional view that Christendom was the centre of the earth and the cosmos, and that human life was governed by divine order (Cassirer 1951: 136; Porter 1990: 34).

It is often suggested that these themes resonate so strongly within sociology that the discipline represents a continuation of the Enlightenment project. Hamilton (1992), for example, argues that sociology is a logical development of the 'critical rationalism' characteristic of the Enlightenment *philosophes*, and that these intellectuals would be called 'sociologists' in the present age (Brinton 1930). Enlightenment philosophy prepared the ground for sociology, according to Hamilton, by rejecting notions of divinely ordained and mediated human action whose outcomes were ultimately governed by a cosmic order. In their place, it suggested that social action could be characterised by reason, could be mediated by rational government, and could result in socially and morally progressive outcomes.

This association between sociology and the Enlightenment is common, but is only one version of the subject's origins. Commentators like Nisbet (1966) suggest that the discipline's concern with social and moral order, community and religion, makes it a product of the Counter-Enlightenment. This, like the Enlightenment, was both an intellectual and a political movement. Politically, it resulted in alliances between the Catholic Church and absolutist regimes committed to halting revolution. Intellectually, it opposed the primacy of reason as a means for organising society and took as evidence of the futility of social engineering the violence that characterised the French Revolution. As Berlin (1979: 20) elaborates, 'the organisation of life by the application of rational or scientific methods, any form of regimentation or conscription of men for utilitarian ends or organised happiness, was regarded as [its] philistine enemy'. Nevertheless, the Counter-Enlightenment adopted its own philosophical absolutes. It sought to reassert tradition by justifying 'descending' theories of earthly power – that held that earthly authority descended from God, through the sacred body of the Church, to the sacred body of the King – and opposed 'ascending' theories that held that legitimate rule was based on popular opinion.

To associate these concerns with sociology may appear surprising, but Counter-Enlightenment thought, like its Enlightenment equivalent, possessed an importance that transcended the politics of the time. Its concern with community, and with the non-rational dimensions of social order and human meaning, arguably exerted an enduring impact on the discipline and illustrate for some that sociology was 'profoundly conservative at its core' (Nisbet 1966: xii). Far from being an extension of the Enlightenment, the 'essential concepts' and 'implicit perspectives' of sociology are seen here as possessing a greater affinity with philosophical conservatism. Classical sociology's focus on the importance of religion for the construction and maintenance of social and moral orders, for example, is explained as a manifestation of conservative concerns about modern individualism and rationalism; an explanation mirrored to some extent in contemporary critiques of the 'reactionary' character of classical sociology.

Despite these arguments, it is clearly misleading to present sociology as a simple continuation of Enlightenment *or* of Counter-Enlightenment philosophy. The Enlightenment was built around the notion of free individuals able to construct their social and moral milieu, but most of its thinkers, with the possible exception of Montesquieu, failed to develop a theory of society as a 'system and objective structure' (Swingewood 1991: 33). Nevertheless, while sociology's subject matter might have been those social and moral orders that found echoes in Counter-Enlightenment philosophy, it was distinctly modern in terms of its methods. In its concern with empirical observation and the 'value-free' gathering of data and analysis, sociology built on advances in science and, in this sense, can be seen as developing certain aspects of Enlightenment thought and practice. It should also be borne in mind that the intellectual variations within these two movements mean that they might not have been as distinct as some interpreters have suggested. Some historians have noted that many Enlightenment philosophers associated with promoting a dispassionate, scientific view of humanity actually devoted considerable attention to the power of emotions in relation to problems of social order (James 1997). They have also suggested that the Enlightenment's concern with reason, intelligence and the 'faculties of the head' could not have taken shape as it did without the parallel development of 'a previously unexplored language of the heart' (DeJean 1997: 79). Furthermore, the French Revolution may have finally shattered traditional notions of divinely ordained rule, but its violent, passionate promotion of reason as a human substitute not only raised further questions about the contingency and fragility of secular social orders, but also, as Durkheim later suggested, actually blurred distinctions between rationality and emotion, the secular and the religious.

Thus, sociology drew on themes from *both* movements as well as on thinkers before and after them, but also translated these themes into its own terms. It is also important to recognise that sociology developed on the basis of different national traditions of philosophy as much as it did through a dialogue with themes raised by the Enlightenment and Counter-Enlightenment. The French and German traditions of classical sociology were of most enduring importance in laying the discipline's foundations even though it needs to be recognised that they themselves address problems formulated by a variety of other figures such as Hobbes. These two tradi-tions form a major focus of our study, and it is important in our introduction to examine their opposed approaches to the study of social and moral life. While French thought started from 'society', viewing it as possessing an inherently moral dimension and the capacity for creating moral individuals, German writers started from the 'individual' and invested this figure with the capacity and responsibility for constructing their social milieus and investing them with moral content.

Sociology, society and individuals

The French tradition of thought, from Montesquieu onwards, identifies society as a supra-individual phenomenon whose properties are irreducible to the propensi-ties of individuals. Society is the source of those moral thoughts and sentiments instilled into individuals through such institutions as the family and education. The embodied individual, in contrast, is marked by a duality consisting of egois-tic dispositions and social capacities that need to be properly harnessed if people are to join together into collectivities. In this context, as Levine (1995: 153–4) explains, normative judgments are best made by determining what enhances socie-tal well-being.[6] Morality is neither divinely ordained, nor, as the British utili-tarians and political economists argued, is it a natural expression of individual nature. Morality is socially given: what is morally appropriate depends upon a society's particular circumstances.

These assumptions about the relationship between social and moral pheno-mena informed the writings of the major French philosophers irrespective of their political or intellectual allegiances. The writings of Rousseau and de Maistre, for example, were associated respectively with the Enlightenment and Counter-Enlightenment. Rousseau idealised the human condition in the 'state of nature', but described the 'general will' as *sui generis* and not an aggregate of individual wills. The state does not arise on the basis of a contract between individuals, but as a result of the communal will (Levine 1995: 174–5). If Rousseau's search for a secular ethic culminates in a vision of societal well-being, so too does that of de Maistre. De Maistre focused on the importance of common authority and religion, but also sought to resolve the conflict between an individual's will and their social nature in favour of societal well-being.

This is the context in which the French 'inventor' of sociology, Comte, and his influential successor, Durkheim, took as their starting point an already existing 'society', a category that possessed the status of a moral absolute in their writ-ings. Critical of theories that suggested society was an aggregate of individuals entering into contracts with each other, they viewed society as analogous to an organism, as possessing parts that fulfilled needs in relation to the moral 'health' of the whole. Individuals existed in relation to, and derived their social and moral capacities from, society. Judgments concerning what was moral had to be linked to, and made from the perspective of, the social whole.

One of the major ways in which Comte and Durkheim employed this French tradition of thought to advance sociology, in a manner reducible to neither the Enlightenment nor the Counter-Enlightenment, was in their treatment of religion. They invested religion with a major role in providing society with a moral basis. This opposes the common Enlightenment view of religion as a dangerous 'superstition', but is also distinct from the Counter-Enlightenment view of religion. Comte's positivism attributed a central role to his 'Religion of Humanity', not a revitalised Catholicism, while Saint-Simon had earlier proposed a scientific 'religion of Newton'. Durkheim advanced what is probably the most far-reaching sociological conception of religion's social significance by viewing society itself as an inherently religious phenomenon.

The German tradition developed a different perspective in analysing the relationship between the social and the moral. Reflecting their own theological tradition represented in the writings of Martin Luther, German philosophers began from the social and moral capacities of the human individual instead of the moral order of society. Moral orientations were understood to derive from the inherent human capacity to distinguish between, and make choices on the basis of, good and evil. Embodied individuals were characterised by cognitive (or sometimes wilful) capacities that enabled them to transcend their immanent biological state. In this context, normative judgments were made as a result of standards constructed by individuals for themselves. Morality was not socially given, nor was it a natural expression of human nature, but could be understood by grasping the subjective meanings individuals actively attached to their actions (Levine 1995: 187). Moral social orders, then, were a construction of freely acting individuals.

These assumptions had a significant impact on the major German philosophers irrespective of their intellectual allegiances. Kant argued that the 'good' was attained when individuals transcended nature and complied with the categorical imperative. Kant (1797: 56) believed that the demand of moral reason is always clear to us as rational beings, and that the categorical imperative demands of us that we 'Act by a maxim which involves its own universal validity for every rational being'. He also suggested that this self-determination could facilitate improved principles of government (Kant 1784: 54). In contrast to Kant's focus on enlightened human reason, Herder extolled sentiment as the basis on which individuals could achieve transcendence. As Levine (1995: 187–8) explains, Herder believed that people craved spiritual self-determination, moral independence and moral salvation. He drew culturally and morally relativistic conclusions from his analysis, in contrast to Kant's universal 'categorical imperative', yet shared with Kant a concern with 'nature-transcending and self-determining subjects'.[7]

This priority accorded to the self-transcending individual, which was also developed significantly by Nietzsche in relation to the 'death of God', exerted a profound influence on Simmel and Weber. In contrast to the French founders of the discipline, these German sociologists provided a vision of sociology in which society and morality were created by individuals. They suggested that people possessed cognitive capacities that defined them as human, and made possible voluntaristic action, and argued that individuals (or, in Simmel's case, interacting individuals) possessed methodological priority over 'society'. It is this conception of the individual that possesses the status of a moral absolute in their writings.

One of the major ways in which Simmel and Weber developed this German tradition of thought was by focusing upon the *social consequences* of individual action. They examined how rational action created social structures, but were also concerned with the paradoxical outcomes of those actions. Individuals not only created rational milieus, but were also responsible for rational processes that produced *irrational* outcomes and *constrained* their subsequent capacities for rational thought and moral action. Individuals, they suggested, are perhaps ultimately fated to inhabit a world that distorts reason, marginalises moral considerations, and limits the possibilities of self-transcendence. Marking a further difference with the French tradition of sociology, the melancholy tone of Simmel's and Weber's writings in this regard is also evident in relation to religion. Both understood religion primarily in relation to the individual: Simmel recognised the deep enduring need that humans have for the experience of transcendence, while Weber associated religion with the provision of meaning for individuals. Both, however, felt there was little room for religion within modernity.

In summary, the two most influential traditions of sociological thought – the French and German – provide us with competing visions of society as a source of moral order, and as an expression of the capacities of free individuals to act with moral intent. Subsequent visions of the tradition developed in different ways, but this interrogation of the nature of, and relationship between, social life and moral life has remained a constant theme in the discipline.

3. The fracture of the 'social artifice' and the 'crisis' of sociology

Classical sociology's concern with social and moral life provided the discipline with a core focus. Some theorists, such as Weber, feared that communities based on moral principles, and actions based on fundamental values, were being undermined by an 'iron cage' of 'mechanical capitalism'. Others, such as Durkheim, looked forward to the establishment of a new moral foundation within modernity. More generally, and here we race over a substantial period in the discipline's history in order to focus on its contemporary state, sociology acquired a growing, if uneven, disciplinary identity during the early decades of its development. This was a gradual and contested process, yet the discipline became established firmly within and beyond Europe. The *American Journal of Sociology* was founded as early as 1895, for example, while Parsons (1937) did more than any other individual to construct the content and parameters of sociological theory. His vision of a discipline concerned with voluntaristic action exerted an enduring effect on the progression and contemporary reception of classical sociology.

As sociology entered the second half of the twentieth century, it was characterised by a significant degree of optimism. Theories proposing the 'end of ideology' may now appear naive, in view of those ideological disputes that later marked sociology, but they reflected a sense of the consensual moral values underpinning modern societies, and sociology's role in illuminating them. The discipline was clearly continuing to pursue the sociological ambition established by its founders. Nonetheless, sociology was soon to be subjected to two major assaults that portrayed its object, society, as an artifice in much the same way that classical sociology had conceived of notions of divine order. Heralding a period of crisis and fragmentation, critics argued that, far from constituting a shared value system, Western societies were based on oppressive foundations in which the rights of one group were established at the expense of others. This appeared to call into question the legitimacy of the classical sociological agenda.

The first assault levied against the discipline was related to the rise of 'new' social movements during the 1960s and 1970s. These included 'second wave' feminism, the development of student radicalism, and the civil rights, black power, and anti-Vietnam war movements. They were associated with a sustained critique of classical perspectives. Accused of conflating the social with the moral, sociology was condemned as a 'bourgeois' science and an apologist for the oppressions perpetuated by a world capitalist system. It was argued that the discipline occluded the interests and realities of the working classes, women, black people and others excluded from the 'power elites' of the major capitalist nations. The sociological conception of society, in short, was a normative myth that needed destroying.

These criticisms stimulated a major crisis in the discipline, heralded by Gouldner's (1970) *The Coming Crisis of Western Sociology*, and a turn to the writings of Marx in order to place conflict at the very centre of sociology. As various versions of conflict and neo-Marxist sociology and critical theory developed their own stability and respectability during the 1970s, however, they too came under attack from writers who argued that oppression and inequality were irreducible to matters of social class or economics. This was associated with a proliferation of feminist and other theories that contributed to a fragmentation of the discipline into multiple directions apparently no longer possessed of a common core.

This apparent fragmentation was made more severe by the second major assault launched against sociology in the latter half of the twentieth century. This concerned the relevance of part of its traditional subject matter, industrial society. This conception of the social was attacked as anachronistic given the rise of the service sector, the de-industrialisation of significant parts of the West, the increased importance of consumption and consumer culture, and the significance of global movements and problems. As the twentieth century drew to a close, theory after theory suggested that classical conceptions of industrial society were no longer relevant to Western societies, and that industrial forms of social stratification had been replaced by other structuring principles involving such factors as consumption and exposure to risk (e.g. Beck 1992). The widespread sense that sociology had become anachronistic, and needed radical revision if it was to remain relevant, was reflected in a multiplication of theories and sub-disciplinary areas that took little note of the discipline's heritage. Fundamentally new approaches were required to analyse the fundamentally new conditions characteristic of the 'late' or postmodern age.

The diverse and disconnected nature of these studies led many to suggest that the discipline no longer possessed identifiable content, borders or ambitions. As each new specialism developed its methods and substantive concerns, moreover, it appeared that practitioners had lost sight of the discipline's achievements. Theories of rationalisation neglected Durkheim's, Weber's and Parsons's analyses of the pre-rational foundations of rationality. Post/modern theories sought to undermine 'grand narratives' and relativise the status of knowledge in seeming ignorance of the sociologies of knowledge constructed by Durkheim and Mannheim. Theories of the emotions and sensory experience were developed without reference to Simmel's writings. Certain sociologists even argued that the discipline was never concerned with moral issues. The crisis in the discipline may have passed, at least as it was formulated in the 1970s, but the price of this appeared to be the disappearance of a readily identifiable subject or goal.

4. The future of sociology: a return to classical themes?

If recent developments raise the question of whether sociology is a coherent discipline, are the writings of the discipline's founders irrelevant to our present age? Do we need to reconstruct our vision of what sociology is and reject the agenda set by 'dead white European males'? Is there no possibility of a dialogue between classical and contemporary writings? In answering these questions, commentators have arrived at opposing conclusions. 'Radicals', such as Seidman, view the foundations of sociology as anachronistic in relation to the moral issues of the contemporary era, and its subject matter as an artificial construct. Sociology has 'lost most of its social and intellectual importance', is 'disengaged from the conflicts and public debates that have nourished it in the past' and 'has turned inward and is largely self-referential' (Seidman 1994: 119). For Seidman and other critics, these failings are associated with sociology's links with the Enlightenment, including its belief in the ability of science to discover totalising truths that can facilitate social engineering, and its nostalgia for a 'European-American world system' overturned by post-colonial developments in Asia, Africa and elsewhere (Lemert 1995).

Opposing these critics are those of a conservative temper who suggest that the loss of sociology's intellectual heritage has contributed to the shortage of ideas and ideals suitable to the contemporary era. Horowitz (1993) laments the 'decomposition of sociology' and the discipline's transformation into a 'repository of discontent' for individual political agendas. Levine's (1995) study of the sociological tradition is uncompromising in suggesting that the abandonment of our intellectual heritage has contributed to the discipline's inability to address the pressing moral issues of our time. The intellectuals 'whom Saint-Simon and Comte wanted to counterbalance the fragmentation of modern society have themselves become part of the problem. When they have not lost themselves in pursuing minute specialities, they have ... reduced the standards for truth and the vision of our common humanity to matters of gender, race, ethnicity, class, or narrow ideology' (Levine 1995: 2). For commentators like Levine, the narratives provided by classical sociology may not address all the complexities of the present, but the symbolic resources they offer can contribute to a dialogue that can develop new social ties between people in a world marked by division and conflict.

The differences between 'critics' and 'defenders' of the tradition are great, but it is revealing to identify what they share. Both recognise that contemporary socio-logical theory operates in a world very different from that of its founders, yet both seek to harness social thought to a set of moral purposes concerned with dialogue and understanding. Seidman (1994: 15) calls for a rejection of the 'grand narratives' and legislative consequences of classical sociology in favour of the construction of social theory that 'legitimates difference, expands tolerance, promotes diver-sity, and fosters understanding and communication between different groups'. From the opposing camp, Horowitz (1993: 252) argues that a universal language of social science can enable cultural differences to be preserved while enabling people to overcome 'destructive forms of particularistic credos and ideologies'. Both camps, in formulating clear moral goals for sociology, retain a sense of Weber's notion of sociology as a vocation; a profession implicated in moral issues of the utmost importance. Both camps also manifest continuity with the project classical sociology set itself. While radical critics of sociology view 'society' as just as much a contrivance as religious notions of divine order, their own prescriptions for social theory continue to search for a non-natural basis on which social and moral life may be established. Both camps, in fact, are con-cerned with the common issues of identifying what is elementary to social life and the implications of these conditions for moral existence; a concern that points a way forward for sociology.

Amongst all the apparent diversity and oppositional language, then, there is a common attempt to identify what is elementary to social and moral life; those processes and contexts that enable human relationships to be forged and main-tained within a framework that enables individuals to empathise, to identify posi-tively with, and to act in the interests of others. This centring of sociology on issues that transcend the immediate lives and experiences of individuals and groups offers hope for the emergence of a new consensus regarding the discipline, since it provides us with a basis on which to compare, and establish dialogue between classical and contemporary sociological theories. For certain 'radicals', of course, such dialogue can only come about once they have acknowledged two things: first, that the classical sociologists cannot be consigned to the 'unenlight-ened' past, but have important things to say that are of relevance to contemporary sociology; and second, that their own sociological theories are not as divorced from the classics as they imagine them to be.

We are not suggesting that the works of classical sociology reveal all we need to know about social and moral life: they are characterised by important omis-sions and marginalize certain groups that become the focus of later theories. Moreover, operating predominantly at an abstract theoretical level, they cannot provide us with ready-made solutions to the fast-changing moral issues involving families, work and care in the present era. Our engagement with these theories is a critical one. One of the most valuable things such an engagement can alert us to is the danger of replicating problems characteristic of earlier sociologies. Comte's sociology, for example, turns a deeply felt concern regarding modern threats to a genuine moral order into a religious project. Comte's attempt to sacralise his own concerns should act as a cause for reflection amongst sociologists who make single issues into objects of such reverence that alternative views or perspectives are treated as blasphemous. Re-engaging with the central theoretical concerns of classical sociology, in contrast, can cast a new light on contemporary sociological issues and problems, and point towards the future challenges facing the discipline.

5. The elementary forms of social and moral life

Each chapter that follows is devoted to a particular theoretical approach towards the discipline and consists of five sections. After a brief introduction, the second section proceeds by identifying the 'unit idea' characteristic of the approach. The notion of 'unit idea' has been used by Nisbet (1966) and Lovejoy (1942) to identify those concepts that provide continuity and substance to a discipline as a whole, but we also focus on how these ideas distinguish one vision of sociology from another. The third section examines how a sociological theory conceptualises the nature of 'the social', and its implications for 'the moral', through its own view of what is elementary to action, to the institutional media associated with this action, and to the character of those collectivities or webs of interdependency which result from this action.[8] It is possible to identify several forms of action, media and outcome within the theories we examine, but our focus is on those that most typify, and are most significant within, classical and post-classical theory. These elementary forms of social and moral life are centrally related to the ability of individuals to take notice of others, and to transcend their egoistic interests and form with others into collectivities possessed of a normative basis. The fourth section examines a major tension that is either within or explored by each theory we examine. These tensions are related to particular conceptions of the relationship between social and moral phenomena. They have sometimes had a great impact on the discipline, effectively constituting problems that sociology has struggled with repeatedly, and have sometimes formed the focal point of criticisms against a perspective. Finally, the fifth section offers a conclusion to each chapter. Our presentation of sociology, then, is based around the unit ideas of sociological theories, their competing views of what is elementary to social and moral life, and the major tensions that characterise their respective visions of the discipline.

Chapter outlines

The book is divided into two parts. Part I, 'Classical Sociology', is devoted to the major French and German theories involved in the construction and development of the discipline during the late nineteenth and early twentieth centuries, and to Parsons's consolidation of the discipline as a coherent and unified subject. We begin, in Chapter 2, with what we refer to as Auguste Comte's theory of 'Human Sociology', and examine how his vision of the discipline developed in a context marked by a series of philosophical controversies concerning 'human nature' and the proper roles of reason, emotion and religion in the governance of society. Comte is famous for establishing 'positivism' within sociology, and this approach towards sociological inquiry constitutes the unit idea of his work. He suggests that social life has the potential to be informed by moral action. Moral action involves an interdependence of emotion and reason and is prompted by feelings and ideas of empathy, altruism and self-sacrifice. Comte also analyses religion as the medium through which this action is channelled toward the outcome of an organically integrated positive polity. Comte's work, however, blurs the distinction between sociology as a scientific discipline and as a religious project. Later attempts to disentangle the two, which associated his religious project with the mental illness that afflicted him and sought to develop a positivism shorn of its non-rational dimensions, reflect a tension that shaped the subsequent history of the discipline.

Chapter 3 analyses Émile Durkheim's vision of 'Sacred Sociology'. Durkheim is best known for the importance he ascribes to the category of 'the social', and the concept of 'social facts', in his attempt to establish sociology as a distinctive discipline. It is his unit idea of 'the sacred', however, that joins together society and morality through its focus on a religiosity that Durkheim regards as a permanent feature of the constitution of societies. In analysing what is elementary to social and moral life, Durkheim differentiates social action from instinct by associating it with the effervescent energies and religious character of social life. This effervescent social action is mediated by rituals, and results in symbolic orderings of belief, morality and identity that are sacred to society. The major tension in Durkheim's work arises from his focus on the sacred as a fundamental feature of social life, and its apparent marginality in modernity.

Having examined the two main French figures in classical sociology, we turn to the major German figures who took as their starting point individuals possessed with the capacities for social and moral action. Chapter 4 analyses Georg Simmel's vision of what we refer to as 'Tragic Sociology'. Simmel competed with Durkheim in proposing a subject matter for the discipline by marginalizing the notion of a social and moral totality in favour of a focus on the development of individual personality and the diverse forms assumed by social interaction. He treated (inter)action as creative, cognitive and emotional phenomena whose outcomes are mediated by social and cultural forms. His writings on the metropolis and money economy are important here as they represent the outcomes of forms that may have been initiated by creative action but which have resulted in a stagnation of the vital contents of human life, and an eclipse of people's moral sensibilities. This leads us to the tragic tone of Simmel's analysis of the human condition and the major tension in his sociology. Individuals possess a moral soul and a religious need for coherence, he suggests, yet the levelling requirements of sociality, and the existence of an inassimilable mass of cultural forms, militates against this outcome.

Chapter 5 examines Max Weber's vision of the self-determining human subject struggling heroically to attribute their actions with meaning in a rationalised world. Rationalisation is the unit idea of Weber's 'Heroic Sociology'. The dominance of rationalising processes results eventually in the stagnation of social and moral life despite the possibility of future outbreaks of charisma. In analysing what is elementary to social and moral life, Weber identifies rational action as the most free and meaningful form of action, but suggests that 'instrumentally rational' action can erode the rational pursuit of values and human freedom. In accounting for this paradox, Weber concentrates on a major historical mediator of rational action, the Protestant ethic. By encouraging the instrumental disciplining of people's bodies and minds, Protestantism helped create conditions conducive to the emergence of a bureaucratised system of capitalism that undermined moral action. It is in this context that a main tension within Weber's sociology is one he attributes to human life: individuals are fated to either a heroic but isolated and tortuous existence directed by the rational mind and towards the search for an ethical life, or to an ignoble retreat into habits and emotions shared by others.

Chapter 6 examines Talcott Parsons's 'Normative Sociology'. This provides us with what many see as the culmination of classical sociology. Parsons identified a convergence between the analyses of action and order in the work of classical theorists, and sought to construct a new paradigm for the analysis of society. Parsons's immense influence on twentieth-century sociology rests on this characterisation of classical sociology as a convergent, consistent whole united by a common ambition, and on his bold depiction of modernity as a normative social system in which apparently divided social groups are actually united by shared value systems. He developed his unit idea of shared 'value systems' with specific reference to American society, and maintained that religious values of the type identified by Weber had an enduring importance for 'secular' society. Parsons's conception of the elementary forms of social and moral life supports this vision of moral consensus. Voluntaristic action takes place in relation to shared norms, is mediated through processes of socialisation, and results in ordered outcomes. There is a tension between Parsons's early focus on normative action and his later concern with the social system, however, and we examine how he attempted to re-conceptualise this action-system relationship through the employment of cybernetics theory.

Having detailed what Part I of our book includes, we need to comment on its exclusions. The British traditions of utilitarianism and political economy are omitted – they emerge in our later analysis of rational choice theory – as they provided negative referents for the development of sociology. From the outset, sociology opposed these individualist traditions, and the priority they placed on the economic determination of social conditions, and argued that self-interest could not account for the emergence of a morally informed social order. Our focus on the French and German traditions also means that Herbert Spencer is omitted. Spencer placed evolutionary change and the notion that society was an organism at the centre of his writings, and provides another illustration of the discipline's concern to construct a scientific basis for morality (Levine 1995: 143–5). On the other hand, he does not retain the broad influence of the continental theorists, although in rational choice theory, which we examine in Part II of this book, his influence continues to be apparent. The writings of Karl Marx are also missing from Part I, as we deal with them in Part II. Marx did not define himself as a sociologist but his writings helped establish 'society' as a viable object of study and left their imprint on Weber's writings. Many have represented him as one of the 'holy trinity' of classical sociologists, but his work has had an ambivalent relationship to the discipline, and exerted its most significant influence during the 1970s and 1980s when it informed conflict sociology and contributed to a resurgence of interest in critical theory. Marx did not enjoy the same influence in sociology's establishment as did the French and German traditions of thought, and did not enjoy the same influence as Parsons in identifying the core contours of a classical canon. There is a strong case for arguing that the placing of Marx as one of the founders of sociology is a retrospective move by late-twentieth-century sociologists. Indeed Marxists came to label sociology as a 'bourgeois science' and developed their thought in opposition to the discipline of sociology. Our treatment of Marx, then, recognises his ambivalent relationship to classical sociology but his particular significance for post-classical theory.[9]

Part II of the book, 'Post-Classical Sociology', examines approaches too diverse to be associated with a single author but which have shaped apparently radical departures from the sociological tradition. These departures attacked those versions of classical sociology that tended to pursue the sociological ambition by equating the social with the moral. In their early manifestations, they became associated with a major crisis of sociology. Chapter 7 analyses various versions of 'Conflict Sociology' that developed in the 1960s and 1970s. These were joined by a cross-disciplinary concern with conflict as a unit idea and as elementary to social life; a concern involving renewed interest in the 'critical theory' of the Frankfurt School, in Gramsci's writings, and in radical political economy. These approaches portrayed existing conceptions of morality as an ideological veneer disguising the interests of dominant elites. They represented the most significant growth of intellectual interest in conflictual action since the writings of Marx; a figure who became increasingly central to accounts of the discipline. Conflictual action was analysed variously as mediated through wage labour, through culture, and through civil society, yet its outcomes were associated with consensus and stability as much as with social change. Marx's work helps us understand this tension, which returns conflict sociology to many of the traditional concerns and assumptions of the discipline, in the sense that his analysis of morality as ideology coexists with a commitment to an authentic moral order which is prefigured by the proletariat and is to be realised within the future communist state.

'Feminist Sociology', the subject of Chapter 8, also distinguishes between the socially and morally oppressive character of existing (patriarchal) social orders, and the possibility of an alternative moral community informed by values arising from women's experiences and perspectives. Unlike conflict theories, feminist standpoints were not 'waiting to be discovered' in the writings of the classics. Sociology was accused of excluding women from its concerns by portraying them as natural rather than social, as bereft of rational faculties, and as driven by biological instincts rather than moral concerns. The unit idea of feminist theory is 'sexual otherness'. In conceptualising what is elementary to social and moral life, feminist theories view action as differentiated along a male/female divide, yet identify a variety of media through which this action is translated into patriarchal outcomes. Feminist theories injected a gendered dimension to the discipline, yet exhibit a tension concerning the issue of how far sexual identity is socially constructed. This assumed renewed urgency towards the close of the century as, under the influence of postmodernism, feminism focused on the multiple, shifting and unstable relations between difference and inequality, yet also confronted a heightened concern about the bodily bases of sexual identity and performance. Such analyses raised the possibility that there was nothing foundational to male/female action or to one's existence as a 'man' or 'woman'.

Chapter 9 examines what we refer to as 'Racial Sociology', a term that designates visions of the discipline concerned with the contexts, constructions and exclusionary outcomes associated with actions informed by 'race'. Theories of 'race', 'ethnicity' and post-colonialism raise further doubts about classical equations of social and moral orders, suggesting that the formation of strong collectivities in one part of the globe, nation or locality often facilitates the oppression and even destruction of other groups. They have much to say about the Western experience of the decline of divine order, and the anxieties white authorities displayed about the boundaries and content of a social order that could maintain a moral purpose. 'Racial otherness' tends to be the unit idea of this approach, but while theories of 'race' and 'racism' examine what is elementary to racially motivated action, they differ on the media through which this action is translated into social outcomes, and on the precise nature of these outcomes. Like feminist theories, they also confront an important tension concerning the ontological status of their subject matter.

The first three chapters in Part II of the book examine perspectives of such diversity that they cannot be associated with a single vision of the elementary forms of social and moral life. Instead, they include distinctive views of how action is mediated and results in particular outcomes. These perspectives also draw, at least in part, on *non-sociological* resources. Chapters 10 and 11 take us further in this respect by focusing on theories that seek to reconstruct sociology on the basis of different foundations, some of which have been traditionally interpreted as anti-sociological. While neither rejects completely the discipline's concern with the moral, they both ultimately restrict the scope of moral life to the individual, albeit in very different ways.

Chapter 10, 'Rational Sociology', returns to utilitarian notions of the rational individual and hence to the approach that sociology developed in opposition to, and it views individuals as a medium for rational action. Rational choice theory disregards 'society' in favour of the assumption that methodological, ontological and moral primacy is accorded to the notion of the utility-maximising, rational individual. In its minimalist conception of social life, utility-maximising action is mediated through the choices of rational individuals and results in outcomes that are simply the aggregate effects of these individual decisions. Despite its emphasis on rationality, however, this theory has not avoided completely the subject of social norms, and has made increasingly acrobatic attempts to interpret seemingly normative, value-based forms of behaviour as rational action. The question this raises is whether rational choice theory itself ultimately relies on a normative, ultimately transcendental commitment to the idea of the rational actor that cannot be justified on rational grounds.

Chapter 11 focuses on 'Post/modern Sociology', an approach that draws on developments in such areas as art history, literary and linguistic theory, and has been developed in widely different directions. Common to many sociological theorists interested in postmodernism, however, are the ideas that we live in an era which is significantly different from that suggested by conceptions of modernity, that classical notions of the social actor and the social whole are untenable, and that social 'metanarratives' are unsustainable and have historically served morally oppressive ends. The notion of the 'end of the social' constitutes the unit idea of this vision of the discipline. Action is something done by 'decentred' individuals and is mediated through the chronic reflexivity characteristic of a world in which certainties have disappeared. If post/modern theorists reject the notion of grand narratives and an overarching social totality, however, they do talk about the multiplication of social and moral worlds. Indeed, the outcome for them of reflexively mediated individual action can be seen as a plurality of 'life worlds'. This recognition of social pluralism and difference has enabled theorists to rejoin post/modern concerns to broader sociological issues concerned with shifting relationships between individual, local and even global processes. This is why we have called this chapter 'post/modern sociology', to indicate the ambivalence that sociologists who draw on postmodern themes have towards their own discipline and the scope of its ambition, and towards some of the headier theories of postmodernism. Given their concern with the fragmented individual, however, this approach to the discipline confronts a major tension concerned with identifying a viable social basis on which self–other encounters can be established and maintained as moral relationships. As such, it demonstrates that even the most radical rejections of sociology's category of the 'social' return us to the moral problems sociology sought to address from its origins.

Having detailed what Part II of the book includes, we should again comment on the exclusions. We have sought to focus on those developments that have posed the greatest challenges to classical sociology, and to provide a sense of the diversity of explanations that are contained within these approaches to sociology. This has necessitated a degree of selectivity in our coverage, but each chapter aims to capture what is distinctive about a particular body of influential theoretical work and its approach towards, and contribution to, the development of the sociological ambition. This focus on the major challenges associated with postclassical sociology also means that we have been unable to provide detailed coverage of certain theories that have developed *within* the parameters of classical theories. Thus, while recognising that Simmel provided many of the parameters in which symbolic interactionism developed, concentrating on recent developments within this area would have seriously compromised the scope of our considerations. The writings of Pierre Bourdieu and others working creatively within the heritage of the classics are similarly excluded from this particular study (see Brubaker 1985). To include them would have provided a misleading impression of the extent to which sociology has been challenged and developed by intellectual movements that originated from outside the conventional parameters of the discipline.

Chapter 12, the conclusion to this book, provides a wide-ranging evaluation of the discipline in light of our previous discussions, but focuses on one of the major factors underpinning the change in direction that characterised the shift from classical to post-classical sociological theory. Both sets of visions of sociology have been concerned with the complex relationship between social and moral life; to that extent they share the ambition for the discipline set by its founders. Their various conceptions of this relationship have, furthermore, continued to be marked by an essentially philosophical concern with the question of *how* people should live. French classical sociology tended to focus on how an overarching social order was also a moral order, while German classical sociology focused on the problematic relationship between the moral propensities of the individual and the morally ambiguous nature of society. Post-classical theory frequently gave up the focus of a totalising social order, judging that order to be morally vacuous, and took as its starting point the need to identify the authentic moral rights or moral nature of a particular group. In the case of rational choice theory, the moral social group was even replaced with the moral priority of the individual over the collective. General social relationships or orders were then evaluated in the light of this moral community, or individual. They were generally found wanting and were substituted with a narrower vision of the extent to which social orders could be directed by an authentic moral framework.

The tendency of certain contemporary theories to suggest that there is no longer a substantial overlap between social and moral life, however, raises a major question about the relevance of sociology to an age where the webs of social inter-dependency within which individuals find themselves have become more complex and globally encompassing then ever before. Nevertheless, beneath the ostensible aims and concerns of much contemporary sociology lies an implicit, if under-theorised, interest in issues convergent with those of the classical traditions. By focusing variously on the residual and latent tendencies and categories evident within contemporary theories, we identify a need for the return to the scope of the classical sociological ambition, albeit with a more inclusive recognition of the diverse groups that exist within social totalities. This becomes explicit in writings that address themselves to the global sphere of human existence. These enable us to highlight the importance of the complex interdependencies and common needs that exist within a single world dominated by a single human species.

Notes

1. This identification of a 'classical' canon of sociology has been highly contested, and there is much debate about the status and value of 'founding' texts within the discipline (e.g. see Connell 1997, Collins 1997a). Nevertheless, in its use of the term 'classical sociology' this study refers to those overarching visions of the discipline and of 'society' – and we include Simmel in this defini-tion, despite his reduction of society to interaction, for reasons that become clear in Chapter 4 – that existed within the discipline during its early decades and faded with the decline of Parsons's influ-ence. The rise of sociological forms such as 'neo-functionalism' in the 1980s, however, illustrates the continued significance of classical approaches. Those contemporary or 'post-classical' sociological theories that developed in opposition to the classics, in contrast, refer to those post-Parsonian approaches to sociology that first rejected the normative basis of social orders and then rejected as inaccurate 'metanarratives' the notion of meaningful social and moral totalities.

2. It is important for any study concerned with sociology's analyses of social and moral life to emphasise the enormous diversity characteristic of the discipline. The theories we examine often draw on different traditions of thought, express conflicting aims, and use various terminologies. In this

respect, the categories of social life and moral life are used in various ways to refer to two distinctive, if overlapping, types of actions, processes, relationships and institutions. The nature of the social has been named and investigated through such terms as the 'dyad', 'group', 'collectivity', 'structure' and 'society', while the moral has been explored through notions of 'values', 'ethics', 'norms', 'customs' and 'ultimate ends'.

3. This distinction has proved hugely important in the history of social thought. It has allowed thinkers such as Hobbes to suggest that social contracts may possibly be based on fear and a monopoly of violence, and possess minimal moral content. This distinction was also central to the priority Kant attributed to procedural rationality and Hegel's criticism of the categorical imperative as lacking substantive content. Hegel (1821: 86–104) criticised Kant's conception of morality by arguing that when it was reduced to procedural rationality (Kant's categorical imperative), it lacks any substantive content. Such a content for Hegel can only be found in the concrete relations of law, culture, state, and civil society: the relations through which individual subjects are taken up into the historical evolution of spirit (see Abbinnett 1998).

4. This focus on the major, elementary theoretical perspectives within the discipline excludes contemporary philosophical theories that have moral issues as their exclusive subject matter. It also excludes those *recent* sociological debates that focus on moral issues, and those social reforms that might contribute towards a more moral society, which are frequently derived from the elementary theories we focus on (Smart 1998). It is striking how recent discussions of communitarianism, for example, are governed by the principles underpinning Durkheim's writings.

Our focus also counteracts prevailing tendencies in contemporary theory to eschew the idea that there exists a disciplinary heritage worthy of detailed consideration. Critics of classical sociology have suggested that sociologists need to move across disciplinary boundaries and become marginal in relation to their discipline if they are to be innovative and creative (Urry 2000). However, this presupposes knowledge of sociology that is simply lacking amongst those who have been reared on a modularised, 'McDonaldised' version of the discipline. At a time when the increasing trend towards specialisation is affecting the work of scholars and students to the extent that new generations of sociologists are emerging from universities without ever having read the likes of Comte and Parsons, there is also a tendency for some of the most influential sociological theorists to be known only through a single work, or even as a result of their association with a particular concept. It is in this context that our book is designed to promote an appreciation of sociological thought as a series of systematic wholes.

5. The nihilism and despair characteristic of those philosophical and literary responses to the social and moral questions thrown up by the 'death of God', such as those expressed by the Marquis de Sade, Nietzsche and Dostoyevsky, arise out of the same context and express similar anxieties about the nature and scope of human experience in the absence of divine order.

6. This section draws on Levine's (1995) excellent account of the sociological tradition: a book that served as a major inspiration for this study.

7. Hegel's argument that an individual's ethics reflects that of their people at a particular point in history serves as a qualification of this tradition and can be interpreted as providing a bridge between the French and German traditions.

8. We are not implying that sociologists share a view of the causal relationship between action, media and outcome. Some suggest that the collectivity has causal priority, while others suggest that individual social action is most important. Furthermore, we are not implying that these theories agree about the content or outcomes of what is elementary to social and moral life, or conceptualise 'the social' and 'the moral' in the same way. Rather, their differences and disagreements define the type of theory they represent. What we are suggesting is that these different theoretical accounts of the elementary forms of social and moral life occupy an important explicit or implicit position in the broad theoretical bodies of work we examine, and that they therefore contain themes and concerns elementary to sociology itself.

9. Another omission is the work of Norbert Elias. One of the most creative and important thinkers of the twentieth century, Elias has a highly ambivalent relationship to the sociological tradition. His work is characterised by a steadfast refusal to accept the philosophical dimensions of the sociological concern with morality, although his 1985 book *The Loneliness of the Dying* provides us with a glimpse of the feasibility and potential stakes of such a refusal, and he views the moral as a code

linked with social groups and the pursuit of distinction (Elias 1989). Elias is also omitted from Part II of the book as the scope, breadth and originality of his project means that it is less a form of 'oppositional sociology' that ultimately converges with classical sociology, and more a theoretically informed programme for social research that transcends the conventional disciplinary boundaries of sociology, history and psychology. For a different view of Elias's relationship with sociology, see Kilminster (1998).

2

HUMAN SOCIOLOGY

1. Introduction

This chapter returns to the founder of sociology, Auguste Comte, and examines how the early development of the discipline took place in a context marked by a series of controversies concerning 'human nature' and the proper roles of reason, emotion, and religion in the governance of society. Students of sociology are taught that Comte sought to construct a rigorously 'positive' approach towards the acquisition of knowledge. What is less widely known is that Comte invested his positivism with two major aims that delineate the fundamental parameters of the sociological ambition: these were to gain scientifically valid data, *and* to increase the moral content of society by portraying it as a transcendent entity that embraced the intellectual and emotional capacities of humans.

In seeking to gain *scientifically valid data*, Comte's positivism embraced four fundamental methods of inquiry: observation, experiment, comparison, and history. Eschewing the unproductive methodological partisanship that characterises much contemporary sociology, Comte emphasised the importance of adopting complementary approaches towards the study of society. In seeking to increase the *moral content* of society, Comte's positivism contained a 'social imaginary', a particular moral ideal of human beings and their relationship with the world based on scientifically established possibilities rather than on theological and metaphysical speculation (Reedy 1994).

It is this 'dual approach' towards the discipline as a scientific and moral endeavour that informs our description of Comte's work as constituting a 'human sociology'. By this, we intend to highlight how his attempt to understand, nurture and maintain society as a moral order is based upon a view of specifically *human* capacities and potentialities. Comte lived at a time when social thought was confronting the question of how it was possible to conceive of society outside that traditional framework that had held it to be part of a divine order. Comte's answer to this question was not to abandon the notion of religion, as he thought that religious features of life persisted even in an apparently secular age. Indeed, a central concern of this chapter is to show how Comte's sociology revolves around assumptions concerning the relationship between the religious aspects of social life flowing from certain enduring features of human embodiment, and the development of an 'enlightened modernity'. This is key to Comte's conception of the ideal society as a thoroughly human phenomenon that is a moral order because it possesses an irreducibly religious dimension.

The chapter progresses as follows. Section 2 examines positivism as the 'unit idea' of Comte's sociology. We have noted the complex nature of this term, but explore here the different traditions and thinkers Comte drew on in formulating his conception of positive sociology. These include Enlightenment and Counter-Enlightenment philosophers, and result in his positivism incorporating within it a theory of human evolution, an appreciation of religion, and an attempt to resolve the potential conflict between human reason and emotion. Comte's attempt to resolve the conflict between reason and emotion did not only shape his positivism, but was central to his view of the elementary forms of social and moral life. Section 3 examines this view by analysing the normative conception of *moral action* implicit within Comte's sociology. Comte viewed human behaviour as founded on historically varying combinations of intellectual and emotional capacities, but promoted the notion of moral action (action prompted by feelings and ideas of empathy, altruism, and self-sacrifice) both as a means of resolving the potential conflict between these capacities and as an essential counterpart to social order (Skarga 1974). The priority Comte placed on moral action is associated with what he perceived to be the excessive secularisation, experimentation, egoism, and materialism of modern societies (Comte 1853b: 37). In response to these 'moral ravages', Comte identifies *religion* as the necessary medium for transforming moral action into a moral social order. Comte's analysis of this morally structured, organic order was contained in his utopian notion of the 'positive polity'. Once established, Comte believed that this polity could imbue individuals with moral propensities, despite the pressure of biological appetites and egoistic strivings (Levine 1995).

Comte's work was enormously important for the establishment and early development of sociology. His espousal of positivism, his view of society as what Durkheim later referred to as a 'social fact', and his strong valuation of human sentiment, resulted in an uncommonly broad appreciation of what was involved in social research and the establishment of a bold agenda for the discipline. Nevertheless, Comte's positive sociology was marked by a major tension between the requirements of science and the requirements of moral community. This tension became absorbed into the very heart of the discipline, setting the scene for divisions and debates that remain central today. Section 4 examines how Comte attempted to resolve this tension by developing a vision of the discipline as a religious project. This has been described as the 'messianic creed of a secular prophet' and 'Catholicism minus the Christianity' (Huxley 1869: 141; Simon 1963: 222). Far from making his work irrelevant, however, this vision of sociology as a religious project continues to illuminate those varieties of sociology that treat their subject matter as sacred even while opposing what they see as an 'outdated' canon of work.

2. Positivism

Comte's positivism possesses two major components. The first is concerned with the most appropriate methods for sociological study and is complemented by a view of the historical development of human knowledge. This feature of his work is highlighted in descriptions of him as 'the crucial figure in establishing the idea that the methods of the natural sciences can and ought to be applied to the study of society' (Andreski 1974: 16), and as someone who contextualised the emergence of sociology within a grand narrative about the evolution of human knowledge (Thompson 1976: 13). This evolution was characterised by a move away 'from speculative notions about occult causes to empirically grounded laws about relationships of co-occurrence and succession' (Levine 1995: 13). The second component of Comte's positivism is its concern with social and moral order. While Comte applauded the liberation of human cognition from theological and traditional forms of knowledge that accelerated during the Enlightenment, he also believed this posed a threat to the moral values underpinning the stability of society.

These two features of Comte's positivism developed as a result of his engagement with Enlightenment *and* Counter-Enlightenment thought, his interest in the positive role of emotional and religious factors in the creation of social stability, and his conception of the steady evolution of humanity towards the utopian state of the positive polity. In order to understand the overall character of his sociology, it is useful to examine each of these in turn.

The Enlightenment and Counter-Enlightenment

Comte built on important elements of Enlightenment thought by arguing that sociology should be based on observation, experimentation and comparative historical analysis rather than on 'metaphysical speculation'. Comte also viewed theory as important, however, and understood positivism to mean 'the use of theory to interpret empirical events and, conversely, the reliance on observation to assess the plausibility of theory' (Turner 1987: 156–7). Developing other aspects of Enlightenment thought, Comte also believed that sociology should facilitate a direct engagement with historical and social developments in order to bring about a new social order (Aron 1965: 61).

Comte was additionally concerned with what he saw as the unbridled individualism and rationalism of the Enlightenment, and with how this might stimulate moral disorganisation, social alienation, and a dangerous concentration of political power (Lukes 1973; Nisbet 1966: 273; Zeitlin 1981). Such fears derived from the Counter-Enlightenment reaction of the early nineteenth century and were taken up in distinctive ways by conservatives, Catholics, Saint-Simonians, Positivists, liberals and socialists: 'All agreed in condemning "l'odieux individualisme" – the social, moral and political isolation of self-interested individuals, unattached to social ideals and unamenable to social control; and they saw it as spelling the breakdown of social solidarity' (Lukes 1973: 196).

Thus, Comte's positivism cannot simply be located within the Enlightenment focus on rationality, science, and the cognitive individual, but within that *and* Counter-Enlightenment concerns about religion, social solidarity, and emotion (Comte 1853b: 23; Reedy 1994: 3). While Comte (1853a: 511) argued that modernity marked a development in aspects of intellectual life, he also suggested it was characterised by a 'monstrous' neglect of other aspects of what it is to be a human being, especially with regard to collective life (Levine 1995: 309). The early development of sociology, therefore, sought to contain, as much as explain, the cataclysmic transformations of modernity (Abrams 1972: 22; Wallerstein 1991: 126).

Positivism, religion and the emotional foundations of social order

The ambitiousness of Comte's project to reconcile Enlightenment and Counter-Enlightenment concerns becomes clear when we recognise the variety of figures upon whose work he drew. These figures examined social order, moral order, social change, Christianity, and intellectual elites, and Comte incorporated these themes into his conception of positive sociology.

In examining social order, Comte turned to Hobbes. Comte agreed with Hobbes that 'Society, conceived as a way of organising activity ... cannot help being dominated, by force', praised him as 'one of the chief precursors of the true positive polity', but argued that his thought remained tainted by a 'metaphysical' suspicion of the 'spiritual' dimensions of social life which transcended particular individuals (Comte 1853b: 350–2). In this context, Comte categorised Hobbes as an exponent of 'negative' rather than 'positive' philosophy because his individualism neglected what Comte held to be the moral dimensions of society that embrace and transform the emotional energies of its members.

In examining moral order and social change, Comte found in Montesquieu a concern with the collective, positive and negative values and emotions that form part of the non-rational basis of society (Heilbron 1995: 81), but an inability to explain social change.[1] Condorcet provided Comte with some of the resources for this task as a result of his interpretation of the development of civilisation in terms of evolutionary progress (Nisbet 1966: 8; Levine 1995: 16).[2] Comte interpreted this as involving the progressive development of human knowledge and scientific activity. These evolutionary stages were apparent in the processes of socio-cultural evolution whereby magicians and priests gave way to theologians and philosophers who, in turn, were succeeded by 'positive' scientists (Levine 1995: 16). Comte was less enamoured, however, by Condorcet's tendency to devalue the past so strongly that he was unable to appreciate how *previous* social systems had operated effectively, and to account for the major role of Christianity in developing human civilisation (Pickering 1993: 152).

In analysing the specific importance of Christianity in facilitating the operation of previous social systems, Comte turned to the work of Catholics such as de Maistre. De Maistre's analysis of Christianity and social order prioritises cohesion over rationality, and judges non-rational phenomena to be essential for social order. Institutions grounded on rationality collapse soonest according to de Maistre, while the 'dark instincts' governing individuals means that all social order is fragile and contingent (Berlin 1979: 22–3). In this context, de Maistre proposed a 'Machiavellian' endorsement of Catholicism on the basis that the real source of government power stemmed from people's attachments to superstition, to obscure saints, and to rituals. For de Maistre, anything that threatened this source of unity was pernicious, a belief which led him to condemn the Enlightenment criticism of religion (Milbank 1990: 55; Pickering 1993: 74, 263). Comte's positivism drew selectively on de Maistre. He recognised the historical role of Christianity in cementing social relationships, and the capacity of the Enlightenment to erode previous sources of authority, but extended de Maistre's insights by arguing that the Enlightenment's disintegrative potential was also due to its tendency to offer only a 'negative philosophy', rather than positively addressing the necessity of returning to an 'orderly society' (Lévy-Bruhl 1903: 297). Furthermore, Comte insisted that the emergence of the category 'religion' as a social phenomenon had to be accounted for in a detached and objective manner, reflecting the increasingly rational milieu that made the social sciences possible.[3] It could not simply be accepted as a trans-historical constant.

Each of these thinkers influenced Comte, but it was his mentor, Saint-Simon, who provided much of his general framework for sociology and a valuable resource for his thinking about the role of intellectual elites. Saint-Simon had sought to reconcile rationalism with religion by arguing that common faith was necessary to maintain a rational social order. Initially, he sought to accomplish this reconciliation through a unified theory of all phenomena based on a single law (a theory Comte rejected by arguing that different laws were needed to explain different phenomena) that could also provide the basis for a new religion of humanity called 'Physicism'. Eventually, however, Saint-Simon argued for a reaffirmation of Christianity (theism) while suggesting that an intellectual elite could adopt 'physicism' (atheism) secretly (Pickering 1993: 76).[4] Comte followed Saint-Simon in attempting to bridge the gap between rationality and the 'emotional imperatives of societal order', and recognised the need for new spiritual elites, but rejected Saint-Simon's analysis of religion by arguing that both theism and atheism belonged to the 'metaphysical' period of human development and should be abandoned.

In summary, Comte's positivism took the 'problem of order' from Hobbes (while criticising his neglect of the collective, positive emotions which can help address this problem), the idea of society as a moral, supra-individual entity with non-rational foundations from Montesquieu (while criticising his explanation of social change), and the idea of the progressive development of humanity from Condorcet (while criticising his inability to recognise the value of the past as a step to the future). Comte's concern with the importance of Christianity in facilitating social and moral integration drew from de Maistre (and also de Bonald), while his idea that new temporal and spiritual elites were needed to replace the old was indebted to Saint-Simon (Levine 1995: 161). In establishing a new discipline of positive sociology, however, Comte sought to integrate these insights into a more comprehensive account of the evolution of humanity.

The evolution of humanity

Comte's account is most famously expressed in his 'Law of Three States' that conceptualises the historical evolution of humanity through different epochs. The *theological state* refers to a period when the human mind searches for the origin and purpose of all effects and supposes that all phenomena are produced by the immediate action of supernatural beings. In the *metaphysical state*, the mind supposes that abstract forces (personified abstractions) produce all phenomena. Finally, in the *positive state* the mind gives up the vain search for absolute notions, the origin and destination of the universe, and the causes of phenomena, and studies their laws, that is, their relations of succession and resemblance. In the first state, priests are dominant, though the military rule, while in the metaphysical state churchmen and lawyers dominate, and in the positive state government would be through industrial administrators and scientific moral guides. The prototypical social unit of each state is the family, the state and, finally, the whole of humanity (Comte 1853a: 2; Thompson 1976: 13).

Mind and knowledge are prominent in Comte's evolutionary scheme, then, but are seen more generally by him to constitute part of a balance concerning what is possible for embodied human beings in terms of their science and government at a particular historical period (Ritzer 1992: 15). Indeed, Comte's writings on evolution emphasise that change occurs in both intellectual development and in the complementary stimulation of 'social feelings' (Comte 1853b: 150; emphasis added). While the progress of reason was stimulated initially by the spontaneous energies of appetites, passions, and emotions, the continuing development of humanity has also been driven by these forces (Comte 1853b: 157). Intellectual development and the stimulation of collective emotions progress *together* through the civilising process envisaged by Comte; a process that envisaged the 'interconnection of all parts of human development' (Comte 1853b: 157).[5]

As Gane (1995: 143) suggests, Comte's historical periodisation is not simply a story of human progress, but constructs a new theory of modernity. This places the modern era within the historical context of a series of processes that mark the steady evolution of humanity's ways of acquiring knowledge about and interacting with the world. Radical and postmodern theorists have accused this theory of perpetuating an 'imperial gaze' and reflecting the modern/primitive oppositions central to Europe's colonial past (Connell 1997). Modernity is not the positive stage of history in Comte's work, however, but represents a transitional period marked by the decomposition of medieval theocracy and the process of organic re-composition *towards* the positive polity. The positive society clearly lies in the *future*.

These processual features of Comte's work – his rejection of static views of eternal reason and human nature and his recognition of the situatedness and development of people, knowledge and society – are usefully emphasised in Elias's (1977: 127) writings. These clarify Comte's view that past approaches to knowledge can represent a significant advance in social thought even if they are flawed in certain respects, and emphasise that acknowledging human evolution involves rejecting the triumphalism of the Enlightenment. Instead of constructing an 'imperial gaze', then, Comte's positivism combines Enlightenment and Counter-Enlightenment concerns, is sensitive to the emotional and religious foundations of social order, and seeks to appreciate human development in the *longue durée*. Comte places events, processes and knowledge *in context*, examining how they contribute to both the advance of knowledge and to the ordering and development of society at particular historical periods.

3. The elementary forms of social and moral life

Comte's commitment to an evolutionary view of human development informs his rejection of Enlightenment attempts to reduce society to 'mythical' conceptions of rational individuals. For him, the absolutist principles of the Enlightenment were, at best, as abstract and groundless as the theological beliefs they sought to replace, and, at worst, encouraged the moral ravages of a secularism that undermines social cohesion (Nisbet 1966: 228; Pickering 1993: 263). Comte's alternative was to ground people's capacities for moral action in humanity's developing emotional capacities and predispositions. He also emphasised the importance of religious phenomena as possessing an important role in marshalling and mediating these actions towards outcomes that support his vision of the positive polity.

Moral action

Comte's normative view of moral action is informed by his understanding of the nature of humanity. Comte referred to this nature as the *tableau cérébral* and suggested that it might be regarded as twofold (consisting of the heart and mind), or threefold (consisting of two dimensions of the heart – sentiment/affection and action/will – together with the mind). It is important to elaborate on this notion of the embodied human, as it informs Comte's general analysis of action, before focusing on the specific meaning of *moral* action.

Comte's conception of humanity ensures that the interdependence of emotion, reason, and action recurs throughout his sociology. He emphasises that humans are both intelligent and inherently emotional and active, for example, and suggests that the impulse to act comes from the heart rather than the intelligence, which only guides, directs or seeks to control this emotional impulse to act (Aron 1965: 88). Furthermore, Comte associates the belief in the superiority of the intellect with the 'purely fictitious' concept of the 'I' that has dominated Western philosophy, and suggests that human experience as the 'I' is simply the result of an equilibrium, or the 'synergy', of various vital energies within the body (Comte 1853a: 462–4).[6]

Comte's analysis of action, then, is founded upon a view of human embodiment that emphasises the intersection of emotional impulses and cognitive controls. Human action of any sort possesses a relationship to emotional impulses, but these impulses can be channelled or shaped in different ways in different epochs and social contexts (Ingram 1901). In this context, *moral action* is not guaranteed for Comte. Instead, it is viewed as an ever-present potential given by the broad (emotional and intellectual) parameters in which humans evolve. When realised, however, moral action constitutes action prompted by feelings and ideas of self-sacrifice, altruism, and empathy that manifest themselves in different ways depending upon the era in which they are exercised.

The importance of moral action to Comte was such that morality became a science in his *Système de politique positive*. This science was centred on the general relationship between the emotional prompting towards action and its social shaping in the light of rational reflection. Nutritive, sexual, and maternal instincts, for example, together with emotions such as pride and vanity, tend towards egoism. Love and sympathy, in contrast, can prompt actions that foster friendship, kindness, and altruism, and facilitate social solidarity. Nevertheless, the actions resulting from the emotions and instincts were ultimately dependent on how they combined with people's intellectual dispositions. Comte also argued that people had different experiences of this relationship. Reflecting the prejudices of his time, the *Système de politique positive* suggested that different races possessed different embodied dispositions, though within the context of a common human nature. The 'black races', for example, were characterised by a propensity for affectivity which, for the later Comte at least, seemed to be associated with moral superiority (Aron 1965: 84). In the *Cours de philosophie positive*, he makes similar points about women, observing their relatively weak capacity for mental labour, while also drawing attention to their greater 'moral and physical sensibility' (Comte 1853b: 136).

Most of the time, however, Comte avoids the social polarisation of moral action, emotion, and intellect, and relates the gradual development of the emotional life of humanity *as a whole* to the broader evolution of knowledge and society. He argues that in humanity's 'social infancy' the instincts of subsistence were dominant, subordinating even sexual and domestic affections, but with the progression of the civilising process there developed social feelings that prompted moral actions such as generosity towards others. It is with the development of these morally positive social feelings and acts that society itself emerges, for these are 'the only possible basis of human association'. With the gradual improvement of the intellectual faculties brought upon by civilisation, the emotions become increasingly integrated into a moral culture. This reinforces the mutual support of intellect and emotion, and promotes moral action (Comte 1853b: 150).[7]

Religion: the medium of social action

We have emphasised that Comte possessed a normative view of moral action: it was elementary to his sociology in so far as it was central to the construction of an organic, positive polity. For the embodied basis of human behaviour to actually stimulate moral action, however, it required shaping in particular directions as part of the process of human evolution. After examining the potential of aesthetics to serve this mediating role, Comte identified *religion* as the means through which emotions are channelled towards desirable social ends. The importance of this religious mediation of action is reflected in his distinction between 'temporal' and 'spiritual' powers within a social order.

Society, for Comte, possesses non-rational foundations that transcend the concerns of isolated individuals, and whose fragmentation would threaten the continuation of social cohesion. This means that the 'temporal power' of society (its manifest institutional, contractual, or political form) is contingent upon something greater than itself (Aron 1965: 93–4). Comte discusses this transcendent basis of society in terms of 'spiritual power' and suggests that religion, seen as something that evolves both cognitively and collectively, can stimulate 'sympathetic emotions' and bind individuals into a sense of unity encompassing past and present generations (Pickering 1997: 31–2).[8] Comte ultimately proposes a Religion of Humanity that comes complete with sociologist-priests, altars, a calendar of feast days, and modes of worship. Having made this distinction between the temporal and the spiritual, which he traces to the Catholic opposition between heavenly and earthly interests, Comte's implication is that the positive polity must re-establish this distinction (shorn of any supernatural referents) in the givenness of social institutions rather than in the rationality of the mind.

Religion, for Comte, 'answers a permanent need in man. Man needs religion because he needs to love something greater than himself' (Aron 1965: 103).

The emphasis Comte places on religion as a medium of action is not a wholesale endorsement of previous forms of religion. In the *Cours de philosophie positive*, for example, Comte (1853b: 554) argues that despite admiring certain aspects of Catholic moral teaching (the sixth month of the Positivist Calendar is entirely devoted to the celebration of Catholicism), the positive polity will be the first society to truly promote collective emotions that are conducive to a pervasive and lasting moral order. As Lévy-Bruhl (1903: 16) expresses it, Comte was confident of fulfilling the Catholic programme of the Middle Ages better than Catholicism itself did.[9]

Comte's religion of humanity has been referred to as 'Catholicism minus the Christianity' and 'positivist wine poured into medieval bottles' (Nisbet 1966: 58). Rather than belief in God, however, the celebration of the human capacity for moral action was to become the focus for the spiritual power and religious devotion of the positive society. Indeed, Comte argues that this thoroughly social morality will spread along with the expansion of 'sympathetic emotions' (from individuals towards other human beings and eventually towards all sentient beings), and will culminate in the outcome of the organically ordered positive polity (Comte 1853b: 555).

Organic order: the positive polity

The positive polity represents Comte's utopian vision of the social outcome of moral action. In elaborating on what Comte means by the positive polity, we focus here on the biological analogising central to his vision of this organic social order. The influence of biology is not only consistent with the embodied concerns of Comte's sociological vision, but presents us with a very specific and highly influential version of sociology.

Comte's organic conception is derived in part from the Counter-Enlightenment's focus on society as the most important unit of analysis and its emphasis on the interdependence of the various parts of society (Zeitlin 1981), but also reflects his deep interest in biology and his sense of its close relationship to sociology. Indeed, of all Comte's discussions of the various sciences in the *Cours de philosophie positive*, it was his account of biology that was most influential. Comte was regarded as one of the leading theorists of biology in nineteenth-century France (Heilbron 1995: 246), while his biological analogising marks a critical moment in sociological theorising of society in which 'a true correspondence between Statistical Analysis of the Social Organism in Sociology, and that of the Individual Organism in Biology' could be confidently proclaimed (Turner and Maryanski 1988: 110). Comte's key concepts of crisis, organisation, consensus, and organic system all came from biological and medical models, for example, while he viewed civilisation as being like the human body, capable of spontaneously repairing itself (Pickering 1993: 208).[10]

Comte's biological analogising was important for several reasons. First, his view of society as an organism enabled him to suggest that social and moral phenomena required balancing for society to operate harmoniously and efficiently. Second, this had a lasting effect on sociology in that it encouraged what might be referred to as a methodological organicism whereby particular social pheno-mena (be they individual or collective) can be understand only in relation to their organic functioning (Comte 1853a: 27; 1853b: 113). As Turner and Maryanski (1988: 110–11) argue, 'When society is seen as an organism, it is a short analytical step to asking: What does a structure "do for" society? … While Comte never employed the word "function" nor carried his argument very far, subsequent schol-ars were to transform his ideas into an explicit form of functionalism – sociology's first theoretical perspective'. Third, Comte's view of society as a living organism was associated with his view of the importance of *interdependence* and *death* for the progression of the civilising process. In the case of interdependence, Pickering (1993: 409) suggests that Comte may have been influenced by the physiologist Broussais's notion of the sympathy that exists among organs. The death of each generation, in contrast, facilitates the steady renewal of agents able to take history forward (Comte 1853b: 153). Finally, if Comte's sociology includes physiological considerations within its concerns, it both builds upon them (just as biological study must necessarily build upon chemistry, chemistry upon physics, and physics upon astronomy), and in one sense completes them. For Comte, socio-logy is at the pinnacle of the hierarchy of the sciences, which he also refers to as a 'body', because it incorporates the rigorous investigation of all natural pheno-mena into its own focus upon the social nature of humanity (Comte 1853b: 26–8).

Comte's grand vision of positive sociology culminates in the outcome of an organically and morally integrated positive polity that is analogous to a perfectly functioning human body. A major problem with his sociology for many critics, however, is the question of whether it is simply a creative but flawed under-standing of social life arising from Comte's personal, philosophical, and religious predilections. Although Comte's positivism may have prioritised observation, experiment, comparison, and history, as well as challenging the 'metaphysical' assumptions lurking within the apparent disenchantment of Enlightenment thought, the accusation is that Comte's work was skewed by the mental illness from which he suffered and the religious obsessions it gave rise to. Indeed, the major potential tension in Comte's work, between religion as an object of posi-tivist science and religion as the vehicle through which the positive society is constituted and maintained, crystallises the issues surrounding such accusations.

4. Positive sociology: sociology as religion

We noted in the introduction to this chapter that Comte adopted a dual approach to sociology. He perceived it as a positive discipline because it embraced methods of inquiry designed to advance knowledge, and because it could undertake a con-structive role in understanding and maintaining a positive social order. In terms of the reception of his work by subsequent sociologists, however, this duality was represented as an irreconcilable dualism. Commentators saw a gulf between the 'scientifically-focused' Comte of the *Cours de philosophie positive* and the later arguments for a new religion put forward in the *Système de politique positive*

(Heilbron 1995: 249; Ritzer 1996: 106). These later writings have, largely, been rejected by contemporary sociologists, and the charge levied against Comte is that the religious medium of action came to dominate every aspect of his work. It was no longer confined to being part of the cement of the social system, but transformed his view of the positive polity from a social system amenable to scientific investigation to a metaphysical Religion of Humanity. The later Comte, the accusation continues, ignored his earlier construction of sociology and promulgated an increasingly bizarre pseudo-theology.

This view of Comte has not helped the long-term reception of his work. While it has been suggested that Comte's methodological vision was an essential source of inspiration for Marx, Spencer, Durkheim, and Weber (Andreski 1974: 18), Gane (1995: 138) notes that Comte has been 'strategically cut adrift from the formation of modern sociology' by many theorists and historians of the discipline. It is not simply Comte's later commitment to sociology as a religious project that is responsible for this reception. His engagement with phrenology, his evolutionism, and his sense of the superiority of Western societies, added to his marginalisation. Nevertheless, even when his work is recognised as being of continuing importance to the discipline, it is made clear that while the earlier Comte is a 'scientific thinker', the later is a 'mad religious reformer' (Pickering 1993: 5).[11]

It is easy to accept this division between the scientific and the religious Comte, but it might be more productive to investigate whether the gulf is as great as is now commonly accepted. In considering this question, it is useful to start with some details from Comte's biography.

The case for two Comtes

Comte's apparent transformation from a scientist to a religious advocate is often attributed to his love for Clotilde de Vaux, after his earlier, unhappy marriage to Caroline Massin (who Comte claimed, in a 'Secret Addition' to his Will, was a prostitute when he married her) (Pickering 1993: 5). Andreski (1974: 8), for example, expresses a common view of de Vaux's effect on Comte when he notes that his unconsummated passion for her, and her early death, provoked a 'sudden deterioration' of his already unstable mental condition. More generally, Comte's personal religious convictions are often seen as related to the several bouts of mental illness he suffered in adulthood.

Comte's periods of mental stability undoubtedly affected his thinking and encouraged such eccentric activities as the pursuit of 'cerebral hygiene', which involved not reading anything he thought might pollute his own ideas. Given this instability, it is easy to see how his development of a detailed series of dogmas and rituals for positive religion, together with his introduction of de Vaux as an object of worship, were seen as further evidence of insanity (Manuel 1962: 265). Nevertheless, it is important to note that his first, and perhaps most serious, illness predated the more 'scientific' arguments of the *Cours de philosophie positive*. Furthermore, Comte was proclaiming positivism a religion from a relatively early period (Pickering 1993: 695), and never advocated pure rationalism. As far as he was concerned, the scientific and the religious aspects of his project had always been united (Ducassé 1939). In this context, Aron (1965: 64) suggests that, despite some changes in style and vocabulary, Comte's thinking in the *Système de politique positive* is merely a development of ideas present in the *Cours de philosophie positive* (see also Simon 1963: 7; Reedy 1994: 11).

If the case for separating Comte into two figures is questionable, Gane (1995: 141) provides us with an illuminating connection between Comte's mental condition and the development of his thought by suggesting that Comte's madness is sociology's too, for it was out of some of his internal conflicts that the sociological project was born. In other words, Comte's attempts to achieve personal equilibrium were associated with his sociological concern with social order.

Gane (1995) begins by suggesting that Comte's own theory of his madness should be taken seriously. Shortly after his first major illness in 1826, Comte understood his own mental crisis and the crisis of modern society as analogous: both were the result of intellectual, moral, and physical forces collapsing into a disordered excess of energy (Pickering 1993: 411). In the early months of 1826, for example, Comte did much to develop his positive theory (and thus his theory of modernity, and the establishment of sociology) after 'a continuous meditation of eighty hours'. However, this theoretical development took place alongside stomach problems, his wife leaving him, accusations that his wife was a prostitute, demands for money, and, eventually, total mental and physical collapse (Gane 1995: 140–1). Taking C. Wright Mills's suggestion that we treat seriously the conjunction of private troubles and public issues, we can see here how sociology arises not from some disembodied mind, but from the embodied contradictions of Comte's own life which informed his attempts to understand a rapidly developing modern society. Comte viewed the emotional components of human action as an essential part of sociology and his analysis of 'fetishism' (which Comte associated with fundamental human dispositions but which also had the capacity to improve the moral content of social order) illustrates how this conception of human nature provided him with a means of integrating his conception of sociology as a religious science and as a religious project.

Comte's 'fetishism'

Fetishism occurs when people invest objects with values and powers that actually stem from human actions and social relationships. It is best known in sociology through Marx's analysis of how commodity production and circulation alienates people from their essential humanity. Instead of wanting to abolish fetishism, however, Comte saw in it something enduring within human nature. In the *Cours de philosophie positive*, for example, he treated fetishism as the first stage of theological philosophy (before the development of polytheism and monotheism), but also as corresponding with certain enduring aspects of humanity's emotional, intellectual, and moral nature (Pickering 1993: 634). In the early stages of the civilising process, fetishism may have been an 'empire of the passions' that endowed all types of phenomena with energy and god-like qualities, yet fetishism could also stimulate moral action as it produced in people a sense of correspondence between the universe and humanity (Comte 1853b: 190). It is the power of fetishism to take people *beyond themselves* that appealed to Comte (Scharff 1995: 77).

When Comte refers to the moral condition of fetishism as 'complete and normal' and 'permanent and universal', then, he suggests that the emotional dispositions that make it possible cannot be consigned to distant history in the way that is possible with obsolete forms of religious expression. The minds of modern persons may make it hard for us to empathise with the primitive world of fetishism, but the emotional impetus that gave it life remains powerful. As Comte (1853b: 190) argues, our 'high intellectual culture' cannot prevent us being plunged into a state of 'radical fetishism' by overwhelming hope or fear.

Comte admired the intensity and cohesive effects of religious beliefs in the fetishist stage of human development, and hoped that sociology could stimulate a new fetishism congruent with the current stage of human development that was centred on the celebration of humanity. In the *Système de politique positive*, for example, he argued that the promotion of a 'Great Fetish' would 'rejuvenate people's emotional life' (Pickering 1993: 698–9). This Great Fetish was part of a Positive Trinity that was to represent symbolically a universal order. In describing the operation of his envisaged religion, Comte (1858: 58) has the priest announce that the fundamental principle of the Religion of Humanity is the recognition of the 'existence of an order, which admits of no variation' (Wright 1986: 19). The priest explains that the 'radical sense of the word Religion' lies in its aims of 'unity' and 'synthesis', which 'bind together' humanity and the world, bringing reason, feeling, and action into harmony (Comte 1858: 46–51; Wright 1986: 20). Thus, the importance of social solidarity takes on a universal significance in the Religion of Humanity, to the point where its denial can be categorised as 'blasphemy' because it denies the essentially social nature of humans (Comte 1875–7, Vol. I: 177). It is this sociality that makes possible not only the vast processes involved in the evolution of humanity, but the most basic forms of human communication. This blasphemy is therefore not an offence against a god or an idea (the fetishism of the positive polity does not rely upon supernatural, occult, or metaphysical forces), but against *human being*.

For Comte, then, the tension between sociology as a positive science and sociology as a religious project is more apparent than real. These two aspects of his sociology are united, for while the former illuminates the true character of humanity and its destiny, the latter is the fetishistic celebration of the social nature and moral achievements of a humanity that has finally become conscious of itself. Sociology, which searches for the sources of social and moral order and seeks to understand the evolution of humanity through history, is destined to become religion as this order and evolution nears completion, as the 'sympathetic emotions' expand, and as social solidarity increases and as humanity becomes self-conscious of its true nature and place in the universal order of being. The great work of synthesis Comte set himself can be seen as complete: reason and emotion are united, the problem of order is solved, and humanity's social evolution reaches fruition in the positive polity. That, in any case, is how Comte understood it, even though some of his closest followers, such as Littré, remained unconvinced (Lévy-Bruhl 1903: 11).

Sociology may believe that the division between sociology as positive science and sociology as religion is an anachronism left behind with its move into more enlightened territory. Nevertheless, while contemporary thinkers are dissatisfied with Comte's approach to the discipline, this tension has re-emerged in the tendency for various forms of sociology to sacralise their subject matter and to treat particular human attributes as necessary foundations for the generation of 'genuine' moral orders.

5. Concluding comments

Turner (1987: 191) and Scharff (1995) have recently urged a return to Comte's vision of sociology as a science, but both ignore the religious elements of his thought. Selective approvals of Comte may eventually rescue his work from its current marginalisation in sociology, yet do nothing to alter a lack of interest in his analysis of emotions and social cohesion. According to Wright (1986: 276), for example, no one in their right mind wants to resurrect Comte's religion, and no one in their right mind would have invented it either: a judgment that adds to those previous tendencies to dismiss Comte as the 'mad philosopher'.

For Comte, however, religion *mediates* the interaction between human nature and society and facilitates the emergence of a moral order (Reedy 1994). Religion is, in fact, a unifying principle that addresses itself simultaneously to the intelligence, emotions, and will of persons, manifest in dogma, love, and the cult (Aron 1965: 91). It is central to the 'problem of order', since it encourages an intense experience of natural order and links the emotional foundations of society to the nature and evolution of humanity itself. Rather than this being a 'deranged', 'mad', or 'outrageous' idea, then, Comte's view of religion addresses a problem that has dominated the sociological tradition.

Furthermore, while the evolution of Comte's programme for sociology into the propagation of the semi-secularised Catholicism of his Religion of Humanity looks bizarre, we should remember that his era's inability to reconcile reason and emotion, and social order and morality, was a pressing problem arising from the great changes occurring within European history. Sociology's enduring concern with issues such as social solidarity, the weakening of the pre-contractual foundations of modern society, the problems of sustaining a modern moral order, and the apparent decline of religion, all testify to the significance of these changes for the development of the sociological ambition. Similarly, the contentious role of women in Comte's project reflects a set of gender issues that have gradually become more central to sociology. This feature of his work also provides us with another perspective on the (dis)continuity between the early and late Comte.

Pickering (1997: 34) has suggested that if there is a shift in Comte's work it is because he sought to present his ideas in a way that would appeal to women. Comte has been dismissed as a 'misogynist' by many feminists, but increasingly felt that the 'disorders of male reason' could best be countered by promoting the emotional, moral, and religious qualities commonly associated with women. As Manuel (1962: 290) argues, Comte was convinced of the moral superiority of women and accorded them a central place in his vision of the moral regeneration of society. Within positive religion 'Humanity' was symbolically female and, in ritual contexts, referred to as the 'Great Mother' (Thomas 1913: 133).

Anticipating some of the arguments of future feminists, Comte called for a 'feminine revolution' that would challenge the propagation of a disembodied rationality, replace the male God of Christianity with a female icon of religious Humanity, end the enforced silence of women in social affairs, and promote the values of interdependence, community, and co-operation (Dijkstra 1992: 1; Le Doeuff 1987: 182).

Comte's promotion of these values, together with his desire to revive fetishism, challenges the rather arid image of positivism often held up as Comte's theoretical system. Comte is commonly associated with the Enlightenment ideal of a 'science of ideas freed of distortion' (Lemert 1995: 74), but his attempt to create a human-centred sociology demonstrates that he was not interested in the creation of the abstract model of science that came to define positivism shorn of its 'spiritual' dimensions (Morris 1987). As Pickering (1997: 21) suggests, 'Comte asserted that objectivity was an inappropriate goal in studying society; every social theory had to depict a better society'. It is with reference to this conviction that Comte can be understood as a propagator of human sociology resulting, finally, in a sociological religion of human unity, where people are, despite social differences, united by common convictions and a single object of love (Aron 1965: 104). What he understood to be the irrefutable, universally acceptable, and 'scientific' nature of the system of ideas he offered, like his emotionally charged religious system, was intended to help provoke a new moral order characterised by consensus and social stability (Andreski 1974: 13).

If the ambitiousness of Comte's project may have been too much for him to realise satisfactorily, and it was certainly too much for those who dismissed him as a religious lunatic, subsequent attempts to make its scope more manageable led to the unproductive fragmentation of positivism (Gane 1995: 140). As Touraine (1995: 75) notes, positivism after Comte 'soon disintegrated into an appeal to science and growth on the one hand, and the dream of establishing a new Church on the other'. This is analogous to contemporary arguments concerning value freedom and scientific method on the one hand, and the socially constructed nature of all knowledge on the other. It also marks a separation of social and moral issues, contrary to Comte's wishes. This suggests that his hopes for sociology were dashed, although we would want to qualify that conclusion with regard to the discipline's *general* development. Comte's project, which was concerned with how social and moral order might be possible in the aftermath of the Enlightenment, ensured that sociology had, from its origins, to grapple with human embodiment and the role of religion in the construction and maintenance of social solidarity.

These concerns exerted a major influence on the writings of Durkheim, who also saw society as a reality transcendent of the individual and was concerned with the moral and social disintegration wrought by modernity. Contrary to Comte, Durkheim did not envisage a single evolutionary trajectory for humanity, allowing him to be more attentive to social diversity. He also refrained from advocating or inventing a specific form of religion, though he felt that a modern 'cult of the individual' might fulfil some of the functions undertaken by traditional forms of religious practice. Nevertheless, Durkheim freely acknowledged his debt to Comte, and much of the continuity between the two figures can be related to the importance of emotion in the construction of pre-contractual social bonds, and a clear sense of the limits of any sociological study concentrating on purely cognitive phenomena. It is to Durkheim's attempts to grapple with these problems that we now turn.

Notes

1. In seeking to account for differences in sensibilities in different societies, for example, Montesquieu noted the importance of climate and argued that a particular physical environment is directly responsible for the physiological, nervous, and psychological characteristics of the people who live in it. This tendency towards climactic determinism led him to believe that slavery might be inevitable for certain groups of people (Aron 1965: 36–7).

2. Condorcet's neglect of human embodiment is signalled by his conception of the scientific observer as someone located on a distant planet (Hayek 1973: 49). Heilbron (1995: 165) has called him 'the last philosophe and the first representative of a social theory founded on the natural sciences'. For him, the embodied dimensions of human existence and social life itself appear to be at best entirely secondary or, at worst, dangerous obstacles to the evolutionary development of the human mind, an evolution of cognitive processes which becomes manifest in the evolution of societies (Aron 1965: 78). Despite his individualism and narrowly cognitive concerns, which Comte rejected, Condorcet impressed upon Comte the need for a scientific explanation of progress.

3. Milbank (1990: 54) has criticised Nisbet's (1966) suggestion that Saint-Simon and Comte took aspects of the Counter-Enlightenment Catholicism of de Bonald and de Maistre and conjoined them with scientific analysis, arguing that de Bonald and de Maistre already understood their theories to be both theological and strictly scientific. Nevertheless, it is clearly the case that the danger of over-emphasising Comte's rationalism is especially evident with regard to religion.

4. As part of this debate, Saint-Simon made reference to the case of the 'Wild Boy of Aveyron' (a boy who had survived for years without human contact, discovered in 1800), suggesting that his limited reason and inability to speak emphasised society's importance in shaping the bodily potential of its members. The Wild Boy of Aveyron was the subject of much discussion in France, and there were conflicting views regarding his intelligence, his relationship with his senses, and his significance for arguments concerning the role of culture and socialisation processes. Classen's (1993: 38–9) view is that 'because the boy's sensory hierarchy differed from the culturally accepted one', he was deemed 'mentally deficient'. What Saint-Simon appears to have been reaching for, however, was not simply to assert the importance of society in creating rationality, but also its importance in drawing from, and shaping, the non-rational dimensions of human experience.

5. Levine (1995: 16) interprets Comte's analysis of the progressive development of humanity in terms of successive stages through which cognition becomes liberated from emotion, yet people are liberated from ignorance, not emotion. Emotion is an important part of what it is to be human and remains essential to the development and sustenance of society even if Comte (1853b: 156) often associates the civilisation of humanity with the increasing importance of reason in a way that is consistent with many Enlightenment thinkers.

6. This leads Comte to criticise the distinction often made between 'intellect' and 'instinct', which he accuses of fostering an insupportable distinction between humans and animals, and of failing to recognise how instinct and intellect interrelate to guide social action (Comte 1853a: 465). Drawing on the phrenological work of Gall, he argues that 'instinct' is as much a quality of highly civilised persons as it is of animals, and is in no way in conflict with intelligence (Comte 1853a: 465).

7. Comte supports this idea that social feelings are the basis of human association against the arguments of rationalists and utilitarians in two ways. First, he endorses the cerebral theories of Gall, who argues that human sociability is not the result of utilitarian considerations but is inherent within human nature. Second, he notes that the whole notion of utilitarianism did not emerge until 'after a long preparatory development of the society it was supposed to have created' (Comte 1853b: 127).

8. Heilbron (1995: 185) notes a similar concept in the work of Saint-Simon, who argued for a new 'general science' that would offer a new form of spiritual power with scientists replacing priests and

theologians. Lévy-Bruhl (1903: 297), however, suggests that Comte drew this idea of the importance of a spiritual power from de Maistre, though according to Aron (1965: 93), Comte developed his own theory of spiritual power as a counterpart to Hobbes's theory of social order. Just as the 'temporal order' of society is always dominated by force, so too there must be a 'spiritual power' underpinning it, also characterised by force. Comte's ideas about religion reflect, once again, the ambivalence of his position vis-à-vis the Enlightenment. He accepts the Enlightenment view that 'theological think-ing was a thing of the past' (Aron 1965: 68). Comte sought to extend the positive method, for exam-ple, to areas of explanation, such as those relating to the underlying and final causes of phenomena, that were still entrusted to theology. However, we have already seen how Comte was not content with purely critical, 'negative' philosophy. Earlier, Saint-Simon had developed the idea of the transition from a 'critical' to a 'positive' stage of history (Heilbron 1995: 186), and this concern to promote a 'positive' approach was even more evident in Comte's work. This is especially clear in relation to his critique of theology that did not, ultimately, lead him to reject religion.

9. Sociology has long been concerned with Protestantism's promotion of individualism and its cor-rosion of traditional social bonds, and this concern is rooted in Comte's analysis of its effects on morality (Nisbet 1966: 228–9). Comte (1853b: 344) associates Protestantism with 'moral evils' such as the endorsement of individual conscience above the concerns of the social body as a whole.

10. At certain points this concept of the social body has a recognisably vitalist character in Comte's work. After his first major period of mental illness, Comte returned to the medical studies that had interested him for many years, and suggested that positive philosophy would respect the 'vital force' within living bodies that enable them to cure themselves spontaneously when ill (Pickering 1993: 397).

11. This follows the example of Comte's pupil Littré, who believed that Comte had betrayed his own method and who sought to defend 'true positivism' against its misguided founder (Lévy-Bruhl 1903: 11). Against Littré and his followers, however, Lévy-Bruhl (1903: 12) suggests that the two works are not in contradiction, and that the *Système* frequently refers to the *Cours*, whose arguments are assumed in it. Furthermore, in correspondence with John Stuart Mill, Comte made it clear that the great work of the systematisation of philosophy he believed to be one of the major tasks of the century, and one to which he had devoted himself, should embrace, equally, ideas and feelings. Thus, the two works should be taken together and, equally importantly, it cannot be assumed that emotions have no significance in the *Cours* or ideas in the *Système*: both were part of Comte's attempt at a great systematisation (Lévy-Bruhl 1903: 12–14). Aron (1965: 64) has also supported this idea. Similarly, both Gouhier (1988) and Touraine (1995) argue that there is no decisive break between these two major works. Gouhier (1988) argues that underlying both works is the conviction that the modern triumph of individualism is temporary, and will give way to a new social integration. Touraine (1995: 74) builds upon this by noting that positivism and the search for social integration converge because the scientific spirit is hostile to subjectivism and personal interest.

3

SACRED SOCIOLOGY

1. Introduction

The complexity and richness of Durkheim's work is reflected in the diverse interpretations of his writings to be found within sociology. These have resulted in the various 'Durkheims' of anthropology, social psychology, criminology, structuralism, and education, and have prompted arguments about whether he was a materialist or an idealist, a Kantian or an anti-Kantian, a conservative or a radical. Despite these various interpretations, three features of his work recur in descriptions of his sociology. These are the centrality of the concept 'social facts', the immense importance it accords to the broad category of 'the social', and the role his conception of 'the sacred' has in establishing a close relationship between social order and moral order.

Durkheim defined sociology as the study of 'social facts' and developed this concept in order to explore the various patterns of 'the social' manifest within particular societies and religions. 'Social facts' refer to a wide continuum of phenomena, ranging from major institutional structures to the types of acting, thinking and feeling promoted by socialisation processes, and the systems of language and moral codes into which individuals are born (Durkheim 1895). In his early writings, social facts operate predominantly as a collective *constraint* on individuals. They are supra-individual phenomena – above, beyond and out of reach of those they affect – that express the power of the social and the moral over the thoughts and actions of subjects (Durkheim 1895).[1] In his later writings on social facts, however, Durkheim's emphasis on constraint is increasingly supplemented by a concern with how they represent the common symbolic and emotional processes through which individuals are *positively integrated* into social and moral order. Drawing on Mauss's and Fauconnet's definition of sociology as the scientific study of the genesis and functioning of institutions, Durkheim was concerned with how patterns of social action and thought could be both independent of particular individuals and positively embodied within these subjects (Lukes 1982: 5).

This concern with the integrative functions of social facts helps explain why the notion of the sacred became increasingly central to his work. In exploring what was common to the various forces that bound individuals to societies, Durkheim argued that this attachment occurred as a result of collective encounters with sacred objects and symbols. Society, whatever its structural or cultural specificities, was always a 'social body' and a 'moral body' reflected in, and reproduced by, the sacred symbolic orders and collective energies which integrate individuals into group life. Durkheim's fully developed notion of social facts encapsulates this transpersonal and embodied approach to the study of society. Durkheim (1912) suggests that every aspect of our lives – from the most institutional to the most intimate – is motivated by the sacred, emotional, collective effervescence of group existence. Without these deeply energising forces, as his study of suicide suggested, individuals can even lose their thirst for life itself. Instead of being one social fact and one manifestation of 'the social', then, 'the sacred' became central to the very *constitution* of these phenomena, and to the symbolic and moral order that was society. Law, ethical systems, philosophy, art, kinship and even science can all be traced back to their 'primordial' religious forms (Durkheim 1912: 1, 212; Wolff 1960: 350).[2]

In analysing Durkheim's vision of what we refer to as 'sacred sociology', this chapter proceeds as follows. Section 2 examines the sacred as the unit idea of his work, tracing its increasing centrality to his writings and his account of 'the functional indispensability of religion to society' (Nisbet 1966: 226). Section 3 examines his view of the elementary forms of social and moral life. Durkheim argued that our embodied being is internally divided between asocial impulses on the one hand and social capacities on the other. In this context, *social action* is differentiated from impulsive reaction through being stimulated by the effervescent energies associated with the religious character of social life. This effervescent social action is mediated through *rituals*, and results in *symbolic orders* of belief, meaning and identity. These are also moral orders and they constitute an integral part of Durkheim's conception of society. Section 4 explores the tensions arising from this focus on the sacred as a fundamental feature of social life, and its apparent marginality in modernity, and we conclude by examining the relevance of 'sacred sociology' to the contemporary era. Durkheim's vision of sociology has been criticised for focusing on order and stability at the expense of conflict and social change, but has proved suggestive to generations of social theorists. In a discipline that now tends to focus on difference and otherness, it highlights what is common to societies and offers an account of patterns in social and moral life that have an enduring impact upon human life and experience.

2. The sacred

The sacred is the unit idea in Durkheim's sociology as it represents the essentially 'religious' characteristics and processes through which social life is constituted, and through which individuals come to share moral dispositions and values.[3] Durkheim defines the sacred as 'things set apart and forbidden' from the mundane, profane world of daily life, and a phenomenon that is a symbolic representation of 'moral community' (Durkheim 1912: 44). Identifying moral community with the binding of individuals into social wholes, he suggests there can be no society without a sense of the sacred, calls the distinction between sacred and profane 'absolute', and argues that it is evident throughout the history of human thought (Durkheim 1912: 34–6).

This statement on the importance of the sacred is unambivalent but represents the culmination of Durkheim's thought and emerged only gradually from his studies of religion. In his first major work, *The Division of Labour in Society*

(1893), Durkheim examined the power of shared religion to bind individuals into the 'mechanical solidarity' of pre-modern societies. The *enduring* significance of religion, however, was called into question by the opposition he drew between the mechanical solidarity of primitive societies and the 'organic solidarity' of modern industrial societies. In modern societies, Durkheim argued that the *conscience collective* becomes weaker and secularised as collective emotions, beliefs and morals contract in the face of the expanding social division of labour.

The Division of Labour may initially define pre-modern and modern forms of solidarity as opposites, but Durkheim's study concludes on a more ambivalent note by suggesting that the religiously informed collective beliefs and emotions he associates with mechanical solidarity constitute the *pre-contractual foundations* for organic solidarity. In other words, the collective beliefs and emotions characteristic of mechanical solidarity are the necessary foundation if organic forms are to flourish. Having achieved this insight, the role of religion and the development of the sacred become increasingly central to Durkheim's work. It is important in *Suicide*, forms the exclusive subject of his essay 'Concerning the Definition of Religious Phenomena', and becomes central to his fully developed theory of social integration in *The Elementary Forms of Religious Life* (Durkheim 1897; 1899; 1912).

Suicide offers a specifically sociological interpretation of a phenomenon that appears to be eminently personal, and influenced by a number of 'extra-social' factors such as mental illness, alcoholism, heredity, race, ethnicity, or age. After arguing that statistics show no measurable relationship between any of these factors and different suicide rates, Durkheim outlines three major types of suicide and their *social* causes. 'Egoistic' suicide results from a lack of moral integration into society. Its polar opposite, 'altruistic' suicide, results from too much integration, while 'anomic' suicide is the product of too little regulation of the individual by society. A fourth type, 'fatalistic' suicide, is the result of too much regulation, the polar opposite of anomic suicide, and is introduced briefly in a footnote (Durkheim 1897: 276). In his discussions of 'egoistic' suicide, Durkheim concentrates on the significance of religion in terms of the various capacities of different societies to foster moral integration and thereby reduce suicide rates.

Durkheim's argument is that not only do Protestant countries exhibit higher suicide rates than Catholic ones, but also that this difference is evident within societies that contain both religious groups. Given that both religions condemn suicide equally, he argues that the only essential difference between the two is that Protestantism permits 'free inquiry' more than Catholicism, a factor Durkheim attributes to the undermining of traditional beliefs, which is itself a sign of the weakening of religious community and the sacred. In short, the higher incidence of suicide within Protestantism 'results from its being a less strongly integrated church than the Catholic Church'. Durkheim's data has come in for considerable criticism. Nevertheless, he interpreted his study as a demonstration of the continued relevance of religion to modern societies: religion remains vital if individuals are to be integrated into society through common, obligatory beliefs and practices that foster 'a sufficiently intense collective life' (Durkheim 1897: 159, 170).

This focus on the 'obligatory' nature of religion is developed further in Durkheim's 1899 essay, 'Concerning the Definition of Religious Phenomena'.

He later loosened this association of religion with obligation, just as he modified the equation of social facts with external constraint (Lukes 1973: 244). What this essay is notable for, nonetheless, is its assertion that the source of religion's power to bind individuals into collectively sanctioned ways of believing and acting lies in the 'moral power' of society itself. This power is associated with the force of 'collective sentiments' that take on a *sacred* character, in contrast to the *profane* world of the individual. By focusing on the sacred character of collective phenomena, Durkheim is drawing attention to the close association between religion and society. Religion possesses social origins, while society is a religious phenomenon. Social life, in short, is constituted through collective confrontations with the sacred: even socialisation can be understood as 'initiation into sacred things' (Durkheim 1899; Lukes 1973: 243).

The Elementary Forms of Religious Life expands on this idea, and introduces more dynamic conceptions of the spread of social feelings, ideas and beliefs, and of the ambiguous effects of the sacred on social order. Rather than suggesting that individuals are socialised through education into integrative social values, Durkheim argues that the sacred has a virus-like quality that results in a *contagious spread* of socialising influences. This conception of sacred contagion offers a more fluid and processual understanding of social integration than his earlier focus on obligation and constraint, and allows him to emphasise that sacred forces are not necessarily confined to specifically religious institutions. Sacred forces have a virulent energy that are 'always on the point of escaping the places they occupy and invading all that passes within their reach' (Durkheim 1912: 322, 327–8). Durkheim also introduces a new dimension into his account of the sacred in this study when he discusses its ambiguous effects on social order. The sacred can be benevolent, life giving and associated with moral order and the stimulation of feelings of love and gratitude. On the other hand, the sacred can produce an overflow of social energies that result in fear, violence, disorder and death (Durkheim 1912: 412, 416).[4]

In summary, the sacred becomes the unit idea of Durkheim's sociology because he feels that it encapsulates how the essential characteristics of religion symbolise and express the social processes and forms through which individuals are integrated into and excluded from the moral order of society. The forms through which social life is constituted, however, are complex and marked by ambiguity. The primary function of religion is indeed integration, stirring up collective feelings and getting individuals to identify morally with the collectivity. Nevertheless, a functionalist interpretation of Durkheim's arguments cannot easily account for the ambiguity, excess and violence he also associates with the sacred. As we shall now examine, this also applies to Durkheim's general analysis of the elementary forms of social and moral life.

3. The elementary forms of social and moral life

Durkheim's account of the origins of religion and the sacred incorporates a particular conception of social action that provides a foundation for his entire theory of society. The powers of the sacred are intimately associated with the *collective effervescence* that stimulates social action. They are also central to the *ritual* media through which social energies are channelled towards sacred objects. Finally, they are the source of the *symbolic order* that Durkheim envisages as binding individuals into moral communities through the contagious circulation of emotional energies.

Effervescent action

Durkheim's writings attribute most importance to that social action which has been stimulated by the collective effervescence of group life, yet critics have often dismissed this as a psychological theory that explains the origins of religion and society in the emotional frenzy of the crowd. Evans-Pritchard's (1965: 68) suggestion that effervescence is merely a euphemism for 'a sort of crowd hysteria' is an example of this, as is Lukes's (1982: 17) comment that Durkheim's theory 'is not only crude but highly implausible'. The essence of such criticisms is that Durkheim does not explain how these strong emotions come to have such significance for social order, and why individuals have a predilection for strong emotions. These points are somewhat unfair, however, as Durkheim does examine the social consequences of effervescent actions, and he accounts for the impact of strong emotions on individuals through his analysis of the embodied constitution of human beings.

Durkheim suggests that collective effervescence *strengthens* individual minds and actions, in the sense that they are nourished and revitalised by the heightening of emotion. This has nothing to do with people *abandoning* their reason or engaging in meaningless actions, only letting 'themselves be filled with emotion' (Moscovici 1993: 51). Crucially, this collective emotional revitalisation also gives rise to new collective ideas, ideals and values as well as to new forms of social action (Pickering 1984: 529–30). This analysis is quite different to that of the crowd psychologists. Le Bon's *Psychologie des Foules* (1895) is often cited as an unacknowledged source of Durkheim's own theories.[5] However, Le Bon, like Freud, associated the heightened emotions of the crowd with the debasement of logical thought, a 'neurotic' subjugation to emotion, and a childlike or 'primitive' lack of cognitive sophistication (Richman 1995: 61).

Durkheim's discussion of the French Revolution provides us with an example of the socially solidifying effects of these processes. In considering the 'general effervescence' that characterises particularly creative and revolutionary epochs, periods where there is a manifest revitalisation of society, he observes that the general stimulation of energies produced both sublime and savage moments, superhuman heroism and bloody barbarism, as ordinary individuals became transformed into new, more extreme beings (Durkheim 1912: 213). This implicitly acknowledges some of the potentially dangerous psychological outcomes of effervescences. Nevertheless, along with this transformation of individuals, effervescent actions transformed a range of profane phenomena into sacred things that *strengthened* revolutionary society. Despite the avowedly anti-religious character of the Revolution, notions of Fatherland, Liberty and Reason assumed a sacred quality. This resulted in a new religion 'with its own dogma, symbols, altars and feast days', that exerted a solidifying impact on the new society (Durkheim 1912: 216).

If Durkheim's account of effervescent action is associated with a strengthening of social order, it is also informed by a particular view of the embodied nature and capacities of people. Durkheim (1914) possesses a *homo duplex* conception of humanity that suggests we are internally divided between individual, egoistic, asocial impulses and social capacities for collective thought and emotion. These potentialities mean that the incorporation of individuals into a social order is never guaranteed. However, they also ensure that individuals are receptive to collectively experienced emotions that are associated with shared social practices and cognitive representations. Indeed, Durkheim argues that the part of our humanity that is social is born, and nourished, in the emotional intensity of collective effervescence. People's actions do not conform to moral obligations, for example, for rational reasons or as the result of purely utilitarian calculations, but because of their sacred quality (Durkheim 1912: 209, 221, 239, 274).

If Durkheim's conception of effervescent action addresses the issue of its social consequences for social order, and the question of why individuals have a predilection for strong emotion, it has also been criticised for its inability to explain social change. Pickering argues that Durkheim's account of these social energies does not constitute a comprehensive theory of social change because it focuses on revolution and 'fails to account for gradual social transformations which take place in society' (Pickering 1984: 413). This criticism, however, does not take account of Durkheim's concern to understand 'something eternal' in social life that is intimately related to great social transformations *and* to more subtle changes. Collective effervescence is just as evident in those small rushes of energy that affect us in our daily lives, as it is in the explosive circulations of sacred forces during periods of major change. As Pickering (1984: 386) himself recognises, effervescent action is of interest to Durkheim because of its social creativity. It arises from the gathering of individuals together in the face of what they consider to be sacred, multiplies contacts between them, makes these contacts more intimate, and enables societies to survive through periods of change as well as stability (Durkheim 1912: 213, 352).[6]

The effervescent 'stimulating action of society' does not always manifest itself in dramatic revolutions, then, but in what can be referred to as an *economy of energy* (Gane 1983a). Here, the energies generated by collective effervescence circle into and out of social life in various forms, with varying degrees of emotional impact, prompting different modes of action. In a society full of collective vitality, for example, 'surplus' energy frequently finds expression in the production of works of art and other cultural forms. On the other hand, this energy tends to fade away, and needs regular replenishing if individuals are not to retreat into their egoistic impulses and if a society is not to fall into moral decay (Durkheim 1912: 342, 385). The replenishment and mediation of this effervescent action is the essential function of *ritual*.

The ritual mediation of action

Ritual is the central medium of effervescent action. Durkheim argued that ritual intensified, regulated and directed social energies, and was a vital part of collective life: an analysis that contrasts with Freud's association of ritual with pathological obsessions and compulsions (Gane 1983b: 234). In mediating these social energies, rituals draw on the embodied capacities of individuals and construct them into a foundation for wider social relationships and the cultural ideas characteristic of society (Caillois 1950; Mauss 1904–5). Disparate rituals can be found in various segments of society, and Goffman later based his sociology around an investigation of their heterogeneous character in modern life, but Durkheim's primary interest was in those systematic patterns of ritual activity that constitute what he refers to as a *cult*. Cults are systems of rituals, which incorporate within them feasts and various ceremonies, having the essential characteristic that they recur periodically and place people in contact with what they consider to be sacred (Durkheim 1912: 60).[7]

In terms of their internal organisation, Durkheim makes a distinction between the 'negative' and 'positive' aspects of cults: a distinction that refers to the modes by which cults ritually organise and direct social energy and effervescent action. The former serve to maintain the separation of the sacred from the profane, those 'hostile and jealous rivals', through prohibitions, taboos and various ascetic rites. The latter involves a crossing of the barrier which separates people from the sacred, placing them in a potentially sacrilegious contact with what fills them with awe (Durkheim 1912: 37, 304). Both aspects of the cult, however, serve to stimulate spiritual energies in people. This maintains the social dimension of people's *homo duplex* nature: a dimension that would otherwise be 'worn away with the passage of time … in the ordinary course of events' (Durkheim 1912: 342). It also facilitates the 'expenditure of energy which revitalises society', and which enables the sacred to inspire awe and devotion. The absence of such spiritual energy would be catastrophic: it would involve the wearing away of people's social dispositions and society (Durkheim 1912: 350). The social energies and actions facilitated by the cult are therefore not merely *expressive*, but *instrumental*: they both express adherence to a group and provide the means by which that group is reproduced (Durkheim 1912: 420).

Any social or political group can assume the characteristics of a cult, but the Christian cult, at least in its Catholic form, provides a clear example of what Durkheim is talking about. The Christian cult has traditionally sought to incorporate those periods of life associated with the most intense renewal, transformation and decline of human emotion into its own ritual system. Birth, maturation into adulthood, procreation and death have all been surrounded by a ritual system centred on the sacraments (Mellor and Shilling 1997: 78). As Hertz (1922) has observed with regard to baptism, but which is also true of the sacraments of confirmation, marriage and extreme unction, such cultic activities are centred upon the harnessing and regeneration of individual and collective energy and provide a basis for particular ideas and beliefs.

In summary, the systematic rituals that constitute cults create and circulate the effervescent vitalism that informs social action and promote, maintain and express social solidarity. While this analysis has been widely criticised, once again for its emphasis on cohesion, the cyclical patterns of social life addressed by particular forms of ritual are closely bound up with Durkheim's comments on the ambiguity of the sacred as a phenomenon associated with change and exclusion as well as continuity and inclusion (Durkheim 1912: 417). The phenomenon of piacular rites (ceremonies whose purpose is to cope with a calamity), for example, allows people to symbolically confront 'evil' powers. The mourning and crying associated with such rituals gives expression to feelings of sadness, anger or distress that afflict a society, and can thereby 'restore to the group the energy that the events threatened to take away' (Durkheim 1912: 415–16). Such actions can also 'overflow', however, and be productive of violence and change within a cult. This raises the broader issue of what societal outcomes are produced by the ritual mediation of effervescent actions.

Symbolic order

Durkheim's analysis of the ritual mediation of effervescent action suggests that emotional energy has the potential to be harnessed to myths, ideas and other symbolic representations of collective thought. Durkheim refers to these as *collective representations* of social life: the forms through which 'individuals imagine the society of which they are members and the obscure yet intimate relations they have with it' (Durkheim 1912: 227). Symbols constitute a potent outcome of ritually mediated effervescent action for two main reasons. First, they express the transfigured world of sensed realities brought about through 'the hyperexcitation of intellectual forces' arising from collective effervescence, and allow a social group to become conscious of itself as a moral community (Durkheim 1912: 239). Second, they are not only representations of collective action but have 'fixed' to them the emotions originally stimulated by such action. As Durkheim (1912: 221) notes, 'the feelings a thing arouses in us are spontaneously transmitted to the symbol that represents it'. This contagious transfer of energy keeps collective emotions 'perpetually alive and fresh', serving to revive those energies that bind individuals into a social body (Durkheim 1912: 222–3). Symbols, in short, are 'evocative devices for rousing, channelling, and domesticating powerful emotions' (Turner 1969: 443), and their importance is such that Durkheim sometimes refers to society as a system of representations.

Durkheim provides many examples of occasions on which symbols perform this function. In the case of self-sacrifice, Durkheim looks to the soldier struggling to defend his country's flag on the battlefield and suggests that 'the soldier who dies for his flag dies for his country'. This sacrifice of life for the sake of the symbol, often after heroic attempts to keep the flag or territory claimed by the flag from the hands of enemies, can only be explained because the flag has become charged with the emotional power of the collective life of the country. The case of body marking can also be seen as an imprinting of the collective conscience on an individual's actions. Durkheim suggests that the symbolic marking of the body is sometimes produced by a sort of 'instinct', affirming a communion of individuals in a shared moral whole. This is illustrated by the specific ritual regulations that surround phenomena such as the shedding and distribution of blood and the cutting of hair, all of which associate the body with sacred energy and imprint upon it the identity of the group (Durkheim 1912: 222–3, 138).

For Durkheim, then, the development of symbolic order is an outcome of the processes through which collective feeling becomes conscious of itself. These processes are not only evident in collective, observable forms, however, but in the unconscious structuring of the *inner lives* of individuals. As Durkheim's more general analysis of social facts suggests, symbols exert both a constraining and socially integrating influence on individuals. They do this through a collective shaping of different layers of the individual psyche (Gane 1983a: 4). Those centred upon the idea of the 'soul' are especially significant, for the soul represents 'all the higher forms of psychic activity that society stimulates and develops in us', and is, in fact, society represented in us (Durkheim 1912: 274). The common idea of the immortality of the soul, for example, enables humanity to make sense of the 'perpetuity of the group's life' in the face of individual deaths that enfeeble collective life. It functions in this way through its association with a series of symbols and rites which reassert the idea of, and stimulate intense collective emotions associated with, group existence (Durkheim 1912: 271, 397–9).[8] Thus, the symbols associated with death serve to reinforce the symbolic orders of society through which individuals are integrated into a social and moral whole.

In summarising Durkheim's vision of the elementary forms of social life, our discussions of effervescent action and its ritual mediation emphasised his focus on social and moral order and reproduction. They have also noted the criticisms that have been made of him for not being more attentive to the social facts of conflict and change. Nevertheless, it is important to understand that Durkheim identifies several contingencies that have to be met for a society to reproduce itself. Effervescent energy has first to be channelled through the medium of ritual activity and, on top of this, needs the support of sacred collective representations of social life if this effervescence is going to bind individuals into a moral community. These comments may be interpreted as a defence of Durkheim. However, the example of death rites he uses to illustrate the reproduction of the symbolic order of society (rites which appear to have declined in modernity) lead us to question whether the 'circuit of reproduction' analysed by Durkheim has been broken in the contemporary era. This brings us to the major tension in his writings: a tension concerned with whether society and the sacred forces central to its reproduction are of continued relevance to the modern era.

4. The universality/diminution of the sacred

The apparent decline of death rituals in modern societies is just one phenomenon that raises the question of how relevant Durkheim's account of effervescent social action, ritual mediation and symbolic orders is to modern contexts. Pickering (1984) has suggested that the absolute centrality of the sacred to Durkheim's understanding of how societies arise, develop and are sustained, leads him into 'serious error' since the sacred is so marginal to modern societies. He concludes that 'Durkheim's infatuation with religion blinded him to the nature of modern society' (Pickering 1984: 516).

This opposition between the sacred and modern societies is a somewhat problematic issue in Durkheim's work, some parts of which have been used to support secularisation theories. Durkheim himself suggests that many religious forms had ceased to have the constitutive social significance he attributed to them in *The Elementary Forms of Religious Life* (Strenski 1997: 36). Nevertheless, he also believed that for 'the idea of society' to be maintained, religion would continue to be important in shaping the identities and values of individuals through their integration into the symbolic orders of the moral community (Durkheim 1914: 149). The question raised here is whether religion, morality *and* society, as a coherent symbolic domain underpinned by vital circuits of collective effervescence, have ceased to exist in the modern world.

Durkheim's ambivalence in relation to this issue is reflected in the work of his followers. The writings of Bataille, Caillois and Leiris in the *Collège de Sociologie*, for example, attribute the sacred with a precarious status in modernity. In distinguishing the vitality of the sacred from the profane devitalisation of modern societies, these writers imply that the sacred has, at least, a kind of absent-presence in modernity (Hollier 1988: xxiv). Caillois (1950: 171) doubts the significance of the sacred for modern societies. His contrast between 'primitive' and modern societies suggests it is unlikely that periods of 'stirring effervescence' could occur in the highly differentiated and rationalised contexts of modern societies. Exceptions to this modern exclusion of the sacred, he suggests, can only be found in extreme situations such as war (Caillois 1950: 225–8). Bataille (1973: 93–100) has discussed this absent-presence in terms of the paradoxical nature of the modernisation process: the more modernity's 'neutral image of life' excludes the 'invisible brilliance' of the sacred, the more it tends towards dissolution, allowing the sacred to flood back into contemporary life. Nevertheless, the question remains as to whether the sacred is absent from modern society.

The tension in Durkheim's theories between the universality and diminution of the sacred has been developed in a different direction by those who identify the strong continuation of the sacred in modernity. Bellah's (1967, 1970) notion of an American 'civil religion' is notable here in that it expresses his sense of a core set of distinctively American beliefs and values that are distinctive from the Christian churches, but which serve a 'religious' function by integrating individuals into a highly particular symbolic order. A similar argument is evident in Lloyd Warner's (1959) study of the patriotic ceremonies of Yankee City as rituals of social solidarity. Collins's (1993) attempt to translate Durkheim's theory of religion into an account of the emotional foundations of day-to-day social interactions pursues a related argument. While Collins resists the efforts of writers such as Bellah to locate an elementary social force that binds *whole* societies together, he uses Goffman's (1969) analysis of interaction to focus on the more localised rushes of emotional energy that bind individuals, through the mediation of social rituals, into segmented moral groupings.

From these above examples, it is clear that social theorists have drawn on and developed the tension in Durkheim's writings to both affirm and deny the continuance of the sacred in contemporary societies. The closest Durkheim himself comes to resolving this tension is in some of the tentative suggestions he makes regarding the continuing significance of religion for modern societies. Durkheim's conception of the 'cult of man', a *moral* rather than 'egoistic' or 'anomic' form of individualism, identifies in modernity 'a sort of religion' based on the expression of *common* values and ideals focused on what it is to be 'human' (Durkheim 1893: 172; 1897: 336). Like Comte, Durkheim notes the importance of Christianity for the emergence of this concern with the human, but sees it as expanding beyond the confines of particular religious forms to become a cult that spreads along with modernity.

These comments on the 'cult of man' as 'a sort of religion' inform Bellah's notion of a 'civil religion' centred on human rights, democracy and freedom. They also form the focus of Watts Miller's (1996) Kantian reading of Durkheim's concern with moral order as the hope for an 'ethical republic' of free persons, and Schoenfeld and Meštrović's (1991: 86) claim that Durkheim wants to distinguish between 'religious ideals that will promote cosmopolitan, humanistic aims versus narrow, ethnocentric religious ideals'. However, if Durkheim's discussion of the 'cult of man' provides us with a vision of the possible survival of the sacred in a society which has apparently turned its back on the vitalism of collective energy, his general arguments about effervescence, ritual and symbolic order ultimately remain open to competing interpretations and applications. As Mauss (1936) notes, Durkheim's theories can apply to Nuremberg rallies as much as liberal-democratic forms of the 'cult of man'. This is why Bataille (1938) can use them to support his philosophy of 'excess', while Cladis (1992) can use them to mount a 'communitarian' defence of liberalism.

This flexibility derives from the tension we have noted in Durkheim's writings between the universality and diminution of the sacred. This tension may remain only partly resolved in his work, yet Durkheim's theory of religion not only inspired the work of his immediate successors, and more recent commentators on his writings, but has become central to many accounts of 'sacralisation' in consumer culture, and notions of the 'return of the sacred'.

'Postemotional' society?

One of the interesting aspects of Durkheim's oscillation between the universality and diminution of the sacred is that it takes us to the heart of a central feature of cultural and social change in modern society. Contemporary theorists have focused repeatedly on the incidence, quality and location of eruptions of sacred energies within groups and societies. While there is considerable disagreement as to the authenticity, permanence and consequences of these eruptions, Durkheim's concern with how people's identities and experiences are forged through their encounters with the sacred continues to loom large. This is apparent in recent analyses of inauthentic collective emotions, the decline of mainstream religion, the medium of television, cultural festivals, the consecration of profane culture and revolutionary political reform.

Meštrović (1997: 105) provides us with the pessimists' reading of Durkheim's concerns in the current era. He suggests we are living in a 'postemotional society' characterised by a profane *imitation* of authentic, sacred emotion. Modern societies are simply collections of atomised individuals, without the associated collective consciousness based on the cult of the individual. Consequently, even the notion of some sort of collective past becomes fractured into competing ideological constructions, or subject to a cynical manipulation in the interests of profit, entertainment or politics. In saying that there is nothing sacred anymore in rituals incorporating emblems, celebrities, dates, battles, places and ideas, Meštrović (1997) is also arguing that there is no longer any such thing as 'society' or a moral community. It is worth noting, however, that this argument rejects the embodied basis of Durkheim's concept of the sacred. For Durkheim (1912: 639), in contrast to Meštrović, the loss of emotional energy in some social forms will be compensated for by the emotional stimulation of new forms elsewhere.

Other theorists of modernity have drawn on Durkheim to interpret the decline of mainstream forms of religion without calling into question his basic arguments about the importance of the sacred. Hertz's (1922: 71) attention to the enduring significance of emotional energy for social vitality leads him to question certain liberal theological developments. These seek to translate religion into rational, rather than ritual, systems yet risk removing 'all natural energy' from them. Similarly, Victor Turner's (1976: 525) discussion of post-Vatican II liturgical changes is underpinned by a sense of the dangers to Catholicism arising from the abandonment of the traditional ritual structures that, with their fixed symbolic content, channelled emotional energy into the life of the Church. This viewpoint is also evident in Martín-Barbero's (1997: 110) account of the decline of the Catholic Church in Latin America and the spread of emotionally vibrant forms of charismatic and Pentecostalist churches. In each case, there is the sense that Christianity can bring about a diminution of the sacred by failing to comprehend the enduring embodied basis for social and religious life.

While Durkheim's theory of religion is illuminating in relation to 'conventional' forms of religion, it is increasingly being used to help understand other cultural phenomena. Alexander's (1988) collection of essays dealing with the application and development of Durkheim's theory of religion in contemporary cultural studies is particularly notable in this respect. Covering a range of issues such as politics, relationships and media events, Alexander (1988: 15) argues that a renewed engagement with Durkheim's work 'can revitalize the practice of sociology'. Dayan and Katz (1988), for example, like Lundby (1997), argue that television not only expresses the collective values, myths and symbols that unite a society, but can reshape, or even recreate, them through the emotional power of the spectacle. Similarly, Martín-Barbero is particularly interested in the role of television as the medium through which religious energies are channelled. Contrary to Meštrović's view of televised spectacles as 'postemotional' parodies of real effervescence, Martín-Barbero (1997: 111) interprets sports contests, melodramas, and the cult of celebrity, as emotionally charged manifestations of re-enchantment, as well as visualisations of the common myths that integrate individuals into a society.

Featherstone (1991) also returns to Durkheim to make sense of the effervescent power of various collective gatherings and spectacles in modern societies, but locates the significance of these within a broader assessment of the nature of modern consumer society. Discussing music festivals of the 1960s, such as 'Woodstock', as well as televised concerts, such as the 'Live Aid' concerts of the 1980s, Featherstone (1991: 122) interprets these as the stimulation and channelling of a 'liquid emotion' that transforms the profane world of everyday life into a sacred world, transcendent of each of the individuals involved. While noting that modern societies have an unprecedented capacity for inventing traditions, manufacturing charisma, and artificially manipulating sacred symbols, Featherstone also sees in consumer culture the manifestations of a new unleashing of sacred energies, expressed as various forms of 'emotional solidarities' and the revitalisation of a sense of moral responsibility for others.

Ferguson (1992) offers a similar interpretation of contemporary consumerism and talks of a 'recovered sensuousness' in modern forms of sociality, which he interprets as a developing consecration of profane culture. Melucci's (1996) accounts of the bestowal of collective identity through collective emotional experience in various new social movements, also develops this theme. So too does Maffesoli (1996) who interprets the renewed interest in phenomena such as magic, horoscopes and nature, as well as the emergence of all sorts of new cults, as the signs of a re-enchantment of social life. He links this to the spread of an effervescent 'tribalism' that connects people to the very 'collective frameworks of memory' that Meštrović believes to have vanished. Contrary to accounts of the individualisation and atomisation of modernity, Maffesoli (1996: 38) talks of people becoming immersed in a 'fluid, nebulous world of religious sentiment'. Rather like Bataille, he suggests that the rationalisation and individualism of modernity sought to obliterate the human propensity for strong collective emotions, but that the sacred has now returned in a strong, emotionally virulent form.

Tiryakian's (1995) discussion of the 'velvet revolutions' of 1989 also draws on the concept of collective effervescence to illuminate the contagious spread of ideas of democratic reform and popular rebellion amongst the former Communist countries of Eastern Europe. Tiryakian (1995: 276) notes the rapidity of the collapse of these regimes, triggered by a series of effervescent mass demonstrations, and the spontaneous revivification of previously dormant collective symbols. More broadly, Tiryakian is interested in the unpredictability of social change; an unpredictability that cannot be accounted for easily in many sociological accounts of how social transformations arise and develop. In Durkheim's concept of collective effervescence, however, he finds a vision of the emotional dynamics of social life that can illuminate some of the vast social changes that have marked the recent history of Eastern Europe.

Most of the above writers have chosen to develop and supplement two features of Durkheim's work. First, while acknowledging the importance of effervescent energies for the recreation of social groups, they insist that basic differences exist between modern and pre-modern societies. Maffesoli's (1996) effervescent 'tribes', for example, offer collective 'warmth' *within* the 'cold winds' of modernity, while Collins (1988) emphasises that Durkheim's model of sacred groupings need not apply to a whole society, but to different forms of moral community within a broader social framework. In short, an awareness of the religious forces that circulate within significant areas of social life need not preclude an attention to the highly rationalised, profane character of other dimensions to modern societies. Second, these theorists have used Durkheim's view that societies possess an embodied, religious basis to highlight the *enduring human capacities* that underpin diverse cultural forms. Victor Turner's (1977) comparison of the leisure genres of art and entertainment in complex industrial societies with the ritual and myths of tribal cultures makes this embodied continuity especially clear. It is also evident in Csikzentmihalyi's (1975) discussion of 'flow' as a transcendent channelling of energy in a variety of social forms, from sport and art to various modes of religious experience.

5. Concluding comments

We began this chapter by noting the importance to Durkheim's sociology of 'social facts', the category of 'the social', and the close relationship he establishes between social and moral order through the conception of the sacred. Sociology, in short, should be the study of those things external to, and transcendent of, individuals, but which stimulate particular moral ways of acting, thinking and feeling (Durkheim 1895). As Jones and Kibbee (1993) note, this emphasis on the importance of 'things' defines the way in which Durkheim approaches the study of 'the social'. His unit idea of the sacred incorporates his sense of the transcendence and externality of 'things' or social facts, but is also associated with his vision of the embodied bases of social orders. It refers, in other words, to an environment of action that is both *external* to and *internal* to the individual. On the one hand, the sacred is expressed through symbols and practices that remain external to the individual and which express the power of the collective over the individual. On the other hand, it has the capacity to positively incorporate individuals into the laws, customs and practices of society through its role in the 'contagious' circulation of effervescent energies characteristic of a group.

This notion of the sacred is not, however, associated with a totally integrated model of the embodied individual. What Durkheim analyses as our *homo duplex* nature posits a fundamental tension between our asocial passions and our social capacities: a tension that can never be entirely eradicated and which provides a foundation for disruption and disorder as well as a basis for social revitalisation. Janssen and Verheggen (1997: 300) summarise this relationship between social facts of a sacred character and the body by noting that 'it is the category of "things" pertaining to the human body that become constitutive for the cultural practices of a group, including the practice of symbolising and giving meaning itself'.

This relationship between the sacred and the common embodied basis of social and moral orders has wider implications for contemporary social theory. Recent writers have 'hardened up' distinctions between pre-modern, modern, and now 'postmodern' (or even 'postemotional') societies, in a way that obscures the continuities that flow from a common human embodiment. The problems with such arguments, however, is that they are associated with a periodisation of history that conceives of adjacent ages as opposites, which analyses humans as separated by irreducible differences, and which fails to appreciate the common processes that inform the relationship between webs of interdependent individuals and the social orders they inhabit.

For Durkheim, in contrast, such oppositions are untenable as the sacred is 'a fundamental and permanent aspect of humanity' (Durkheim 1912: 1). Consequently, his reliance on ethnographic studies of totemism in *The Elementary Forms* should not obscure the fact that his study of religion was part of his attempt to grapple with pressing issues that concerned *all* societies (Strenski 1997: 154), and that were elementary to the human condition. Thus, his interest in religion cannot be read as evidence of a nostalgic, anti-modern concern with patterns of social and moral cohesion that were consigned to the past. His sociology was centred on a critical engagement with the social changes wrought by modernity, many of which he expressed deep anxieties about, but his attitude to modernity was by no means uniformly negative (Hawkins 1999: 150–1). The pattern of life, death and rebirth characteristic of society as he envisaged it in *The Elementary Forms*, together with his confidence that new effervescences would reshape modern societies, reflects this optimistic dimension of Durkheim's thought. It also proposes a model of society as a moral community that offers a continuing challenge to the disenchanted, rationalised vision of modernity central to the work of Weber.

Durkheim viewed sociology as the study of an inherently religious phenomenon, society, in contrast to Comte's perception of the discipline as a religious project. The work of Simmel, in contrast, provides us with a representative drawn from a very different, German tradition of thought. Simmel, a contemporary of Durkheim, was not interested in portraying society as inherently religious or in examining embodied action as driven by an effervescence derived from collective experience. Rather than seeking to maintain a notion of the universality of the sacred during an era in which it was apparently on the retreat, Simmel argued that while individuals possessed an inherent need for the experience of completion, modernity tended to marginalise all non-rational phenomena through the arithmetic rationalising processes central to the metropolis and money economy.

Notes

1. Whether a social fact is considered 'normal' or 'pathological', for example, is for Durkheim a statement about the degree to which it is widely spread within a society, and therefore reflects collective sentiments. It is not a value judgment about the desirability of a social phenomenon or its effects on a particular individual. Crime, for example, may appear to be a pathological social phenomenon, but it is only so when sharp fluctuations in crime rates reflect deeper disturbances in a society. In general, a certain level of crime can be 'normal' in that the criminal behaviour of individuals serves to reaffirm moral values and social integration amongst the populace.

2. Chapter 2 emphasised how religion also came to have a central role in the sociology of Comte. Durkheim had a similar sense of the historical demise of Christianity, and a similar concern for the effect of this decline on social order. Instead of inventing a new religion, however, he expressed a confidence that new religious forms would emerge of their own accord (Durkheim 1912: 429). This points to a further difference between Comte and Durkheim. Durkheim makes religion elementary to social life, and therefore central to the sociological study of society, but he does not blur the distinction between religion and sociology in the manner that Comte did. He may have referred to his sociology as 'religious sociology' but this did not involve the promotion of any particular form of religion or religion in general (cf. Strenski 1997: 152). What he meant was that all sociology should be concerned with the processes through which social life is created, maintained and renewed: processes which he saw as having a 'religious' character.

3. Lukes (1973: 417–18) has noted that Durkheim advanced at least five distinct ways of relating the 'social' and the 'moral'. First, he saw an action as moral only if it was *aimed* at a social end or interest, such as 'the common good'; second, he defined an action as moral if it was *motivated* by social, or 'altruistic', sentiments; third, he saw moral actions as *socially prescribed* in accordance with collective ideals or values; fourth, he emphasised the importance of a *social context* as a precondition

for the existence of morality, in both philosophical and empirical senses; and fifth, he stressed the *socially determined* nature of adherence to particular moral codes and deference to particular moral authorities. As Lukes (1973: 419) emphasises, it was the fifth of these that gradually came to dominate Durkheim's sociology, particularly as the links between the 'social' and the 'moral' became tied to his concept of the 'sacred'.

4. Although these two forms of the sacred give rise to other oppositions, such as those between good and bad, pure and impure, they share two essential characteristics relating to the 'contagious' nature of the sacred substance and the powerful emotional energies that carry it through a social body. First, they both have the same oppositional relationship to the profane, with resulting similarities in patterns of prohibition of contact, while the feelings aroused by each tend towards ambivalence too: horror implies a kind of respect; fear implies a kind of reverence. Second, the apparent opposition between consecration and sacrilege, which arises in relation to the two forms of the sacred and not merely between the sacred and the profane, is more ambiguous than it first appears. All contact with the sacred implies a kind of sacrilege, and in some circumstances this paradox manifests itself in an explicit sense of the *simultaneously* sanctifying and polluting consequences of contact with the sacred: 'Individuals who have communed together are, in certain cases, forced to flee one another, like carriers of a plague. It is as though they have become sources of dangerous contamination for one another. The sacred bond that joins them separates them at the same time' (Durkheim 1912: 414). This awareness of the dangers of contamination therefore applies to benevolent forms of the sacred as well as to malevolent ones (see Mellor 1998).

5. Pickering (1984: 397) seeks to distinguish collective effervescence from crowd psychology by pointing out that in *The Elementary Forms* Durkheim does not use the word '*foule*', but always the words '*rassemblement*' and '*assemblée*' in relation to effervescent social gatherings. The difference between these two words and '*foule*', according to him, is that they suggest a gathering of people that has 'a much stronger sense of "we" than has a crowd'. Richman has made the same point, adding that for Le Bon the psychological impacts of crowds are fundamentally superficial and ephemeral in terms of their influence upon social structures, while for Durkheim the '*effervescence des assemblées*' has a revolutionary potential and an enduringly significant social impact in more subtle ways (Richman 1995: 62). This is an important point, but it should be noted that Durkheim *does* use the word '*foule*' in relation to effervescence, and the creation of 'moral force', and it is probably more appropriate to say that the difference between '*foule*' and '*assemblée*' is one of degree rather than kind (see Durkheim 1912: 371, French text).

6. This idea is suggestive of Bergson's (1912) concept of the *élan vital*, or 'vital impetus'. Bergson analysed life in terms of an accumulation of energy in the face of the resistance of matter, and the 'elastic canalisation of this energy in various and indeterminate directions' (Bergson 1912: 269). The concept of the *élan vital* may have been an unacknowledged influence upon Durkheim's development of the notion of collective effervescence (Pickering 1984: 404). Bergson criticised Durkheim's inattention to the dynamic and personal factors in religion, but both approaches are underpinned by a dynamic vitalism (Bergson 1935: 85; see Pickering 1984: 199). In Bergson's (1912) work, this vitalism is of cosmic significance; all life, in fact, is analysed in terms of the accumulation and expenditure of energy within a vast evolutionary schema. In Durkheim's model, however, this vitalism is rooted specifically in society, and is stimulated through recurrent social practices (Durkheim 1912: 429).

7. The sociological significance of effervescent energy means that those writers who have emphasised the primacy of ideas and beliefs in Durkheim's thought, with the attendant charges of idealism, have misunderstood the centrality of these non-rational social forces to his understanding of society (see Parsons 1937: 441; see also Pickering 1984: 285–6, 372–3). Rejecting such accusations of idealism, Rawls (1996: 433) talks of Durkheim's 'socioempiricism', arguing that Durkheim is attentive to the apprehension of the 'real social forces' that arise from human assemblies and have a dynamic and continuous influence upon societies. Collins (1993: 208) also rejects any suggestion of idealism and bluntly states that the social significance of these emotional energies 'is simply a sociophysiological fact'. This touches upon the embodied dimensions of Durkheim's analysis that highlight the sociological significance of effervescent energies.

8. In support of his theories of the nature of the soul, Durkheim drew upon the work of Preuss (1904), who argued that 'soul and spirit are only transformations of impersonal power and force' and conceptualised these transformations in terms of spontaneous discharges of energy, which he called

'charms'. Durkheim was especially interested in Preuss's idea that this sacred energy which animates the body also has a tendency 'to escape using all available routes: mouth, nose, and every other body opening, breath, gaze, speech and so on', though he is also attentive to situations where such escape is deemed problematic and is the subject of ritual structuring (Durkheim 1912: 204). Durkheim (1912: 245) argues that 'the soul is distinct from and independent of the body', but also so intimately connected with it that it would be mistaken to conceive the body as a container for the soul. In fact, he notes that certain regions and products of the body are especially associated with the soul, noting the heart, breath, placenta and blood amongst other corporeal phenomena: 'When the blood flows, the soul escapes with it. The soul is not in the breath; it is the breath. It is inseparable from the body part in which it resides' (Durkheim 1912: 246). This can therefore explain why the mark of the group is most often imprinted upon the body (Durkheim 1912: 115).

4

TRAGIC SOCIOLOGY

1. Introduction

There are two principal features of the German contribution to the development of the classical sociological ambition that distinguish it from the French. First, in contrast to the organic models of collective life central to the work of Comte and Durkheim, the German contribution is characterised by a greater theoretical and methodological focus on individuals. Both Georg Simmel and Max Weber sought to analyse social and moral life in relation to the dispositions, decisions, and actions of individuals, though neither believed that these could be explained on the basis of utilitarian individualism. In Simmel's case, 'society' is understood to be a product of, and located within, the sociation or social interaction of individuals.[1] Sociologists, he suggests, should focus on the *forms of interaction*: the multiple patterned forms that harness individuals into unities (Simmel 1908a: 23–4). For Weber, as we examine in the next chapter, the starting point for sociological analysis should be the meaningful actions of individuals: actions which result eventually in the rationalised structures that dominate modern society. The second characteristic that distinguishes German from French classical sociology is its pessimistic outlook. Comte's sociology was shaped by his belief in the emergence of a Religion of Humanity in the 'positive' stage of human history, while Durkheim's expectation that new periods of collective effervescence would revitalise modern societies mitigated his fears about threats to social and moral order. German classical sociology, in contrast, was not marked by such optimism. Arising out of their focus on individuals, Simmel and Weber moved towards what Levine (1995: 320) has called an 'existentialist ethics in which the authentic personal decisions of each actor become the principle for directing action'. In their analyses of modern societies, however, both understood such decisions to be increasingly frustrated and problematic. For Weber, this necessitated a heroic stance in the face of the amoral rationalisations of modernity. For Simmel, the fate of individuals in modernity is a tragic one: they are surrounded by a world of objects that constrain and dominate their needs and desires, making the pursuit of meaning and authenticity increasingly hopeless (Coser 1971: 192). The social and the moral are at odds with each other, and what Simmel describes as the development of a 'moral soul' is inherently frustrated despite the autonomy and freedom associated with modernity (Simmel 1911b: 17).

This concept of a 'moral soul' provides the starting point for our consideration of Simmel's 'tragic sociology'. It is not a prominent concept in his work, yet it crystallises a range of related concerns about the development and fate of individuality, and provides a basis on which to understand his persistent focus on an individual's ability to develop an integrated personality, and his diagnosis of modernity. Simmel (1914: 91) views the soul as the property of individuals, as religious as well as moral in nature, and as expressed and developed through interaction with others. It provides people with the potential and the need to develop unique personalities, and the means by which we are able to reconcile several internal conflicts such as that between what we feel we *should* do and what we *actually* do (Simmel 1904: 43).

The ability of individuals to realise the soul's potential through the development of an integrated personality, however, is highly problematic.[2] This problem arises from the tension between the forms and the emotional and psychological contents of interaction. Personal development is dependent upon an individual's marshalling their life's contents around the core of their self, and allowing the resultant identity to find expression in appropriate forms. Forms are crystallised patterns of interaction, including the family, group relations, and relationships of economic exchange (and vary according to such factors as the distance separating individuals, and the integrative mechanisms involved in their reciprocal action), while contents are the psychological and biological phenomena that constitute the raw material of social interaction. These contents are the energies and motivations that propel individuals into being for others, with others, or against others, and include erotic, religious or aggressive drives and impulses, and motives of gain, defence, attack or instruction (Simmel 1908a: 23). There is no collective effervescence, however, that guarantees a realisation of this self within extant forms. Instead, the coherent development of self is fated to frustration amid the sociological and cultural tragedies that Simmel argues do most to blunt the moral souls of individuals.[3]

The idea that there exists a tension between the form and contents of interaction that affects the very centre of people's individuality is especially evident in Simmel's writings on the money economy and metropolis. He assumes a basic *Gemeinschaft/Gesellschaft* model of social change, but considers modernity to have harnessed and stimulated a qualitative change in human energies and senses. Pre-modern life was characterised by feelings and emotional relationships that encompassed the whole individual. Modernity, in contrast, has as its counterpart an essentially intellectualist character based on psychological foundations that must cope with the 'swift and continuous shift of external and internal stimuli' (Simmel 1903a: 325). Modern people tend to react mentally to events in a manner 'furthest removed from the depths of the personality', which involves a flight from 'direct proximity and contact with people and things' (Simmel 1903a: 326; 1907: 474). Pre-modern responses to this milieu, involving the individual's whole emotional being, would be debilitating and unsustainable.

Simmel argues that modernity releases individuals from the limits of locality, and a homogeneous culture, and *potentially* increases the opportunities for individual development. Nevertheless, modern forms also tend to congeal into stubborn structures, confronting individuals as 'social facts', prompting a general protest against their very existence (Simmel 1918a). In modernity, then, the *subjective* and *objective* dimensions of human existence are in increasing conflict. Religion, which expresses a uniquely dynamic relationship between forms and contents, has the capacity to bridge this gap, but it cannot, because its dogmatic, metaphysical claims are now held to be mere fantasy. Humans are left, therefore, with 'religious needs' to do with life's meaning, purpose and authenticity, felt more intensely than perhaps ever before, but these are left 'completely unanswered' (Simmel 1911a: 9). This subjective/objective tension expresses Simmel's sense of the ambivalent outcomes of social interaction in an extreme form: it is the means through which an authentic personality, and a 'moral soul', develops, but it can also stunt that development.

This chapter progresses as follows. Section 2 concentrates on Simmel's unit idea, social interaction, by analysing its importance to his view of society and by examining what is involved in interaction with reference to his *homo duplex* model of the individual. Section 3 focuses on the conceptualisation of the elementary forms of social and moral life central to Simmel's sociology by clarifying his treatment of (inter)actions as creative phenomena whose outcomes are mediated by the constraints associated with forms. Simmel's writings on the metropolis and money economy are important here as they identify a set of outcomes in which forms appear to have triumphed over the vital contents of human (inter)action. These writings also point towards the major tension underpinning his work. Section 4 examines this tension between life and ossification by focusing on its manifestations in the social and cultural tragedies dealt with by Simmel, and on the implications these have for his enduring concern with personality.

2. Social interaction

Simmel's writings contain a rich array of themes and concepts, but his analysis of 'interaction', or 'sociation', has exerted most influence on sociology. It is a concept Simmel makes central to sociology and elevates almost to a 'universal principle' of social life (Frisby 1981: 40). He argues that sociology has over-emphasised the importance of large-scale formations such as the state, the church, social classes and moral orders. In his view, the forms and contents of interactions *constitute* society, in the sense that its solidity, geometry and durability are completely dependent upon the numbers and cohesiveness of interactions. These interactions, furthermore, act as carriers of the most diverse impulses, passions and purposes of social life, and account for all the colour and consistency of social life that is so striking and yet so mysterious (Simmel 1908a, 1908b). For him, it is only because 'an extraordinary multitude and variety of interactions' exist at any moment that a 'seemingly autonomous historical reality' has been attributed to 'society' (Simmel 1908a: 27).

In elaborating on the importance and constitution of interaction, it is important to note that Simmel not only opposes the idea of society as a pre-structured, social totality, but also rejects the associated view that individuals are socially determined beings. In place of what later became referred to as 'over-socialised' conceptions of the subject, yet broadly in agreement with Durkheim, to this extent at least, Simmel proposes a *homo duplex* model of humans. Humans, he suggests, are characterised by a distinction between pre-social impulses and individualised mental forms on the one hand, and social emotions and reciprocated mental forms on the other. They are naturally predisposed to interact, yet are partly shaped by social interaction. This account of the constitution and development of interaction in Simmel's work can be traced by examining the factors involved in its initial facilitation, its subsequent progression, its status as a process of exchange involving individual sacrifices, and its generation of social emotions responsible for the reproduction of interaction.

Social interaction is facilitated by pre-social impulses and individualised forms. People are motivated to interact as a result of drives, purposes, or life contents that propel them towards others (Simmel 1908b). The 'dispositions' of love and affection, for example, make social closeness desirable. The precise orientation individuals adopt towards interaction, however, involves individuals employing idealised mental forms that represent to them their own and other individuals' dispositions and motivations. Forms may be created on the basis of such raw materials as physical appearance, the (dis)similarity of others to the self, or the apparent membership of a particular social organisation, and tend to be based on the perceived utility of others for the individual.

If pre-social impulses and individualised forms propel people towards particular modes of interaction, interaction progresses via the creation of reciprocal mental orientations that maintain particular modes of association. These reciprocal orientations emerge during interaction and highlight the socialised elements of human existence. Thus, individualised mental forms are modified during social interaction, combining to create a 'unity of cognition' between individuals. These reciprocated forms establish certain expectations and constraints for subsequent interaction and give individuals the idea that they are part of a larger social unity (Simmel 1908b: 8–9).

Despite the establishment of reciprocal mental orientations, however, individuals continue to lead a 'doubled' existence in Simmel's work. They are never fully incorporated into, nor estranged from, social interaction and are never fully identical to, nor separate from, their associates (Simmel 1908d: 252). This is evident in Simmel's view of interaction as a process of exchange and sacrifice. As individuals maintain their separate identity, what they offer and receive in associating with others constitutes an exchange between individuals: every conversation, every lecture, every show of affection, every game, as well as every material trade or purchase, can be regarded as an exchange (Simmel 1907: 82). These exchanges represent a giving up of something belonging to the individual, and he refers to this process as an expenditure of personal energy. Exchange within interaction does not simply involve mental frames of reference, or goods and services, but demands a bodily offering and receiving from individuals. In short, it involves a certain sacrifice (Simmel 1907: 82).

The notion of sacrifice highlights a crucial point in Simmel's account of interaction and, therefore, in his view of 'society'. Sacrifice is not simply a negative 'giving' involving a 'drain' on the individual's reserves, but enables individuals to fulfil the social dimensions of their *homo duplex* nature. Furthermore, it is these sacrificial exchanges that stimulate social emotions to bind individuals together and are indispensable for the reproduction of those interactions that determine the solidity of 'society'. This argument therefore has affinities with Mauss's notion of exchange as the development of patterns of moral obligation, though for Simmel these patterns do not imply the incorporation of individuals into a moral totality. The extent of incorporation remains ambiguous. Nonetheless, what we call society is made possible only through such exchanges. This is illustrated by Simmel's analyses of 'gratitude' and 'faith'.

'Gratitude' is an internalised, emotionally experienced 'moral memory of mankind' (Simmel 1950: 388). It originates from when an individual receives in interaction any sacrificial good – be it material or non-material – such as a complement, a gift, advice or good humour. Its significance for the binding of individuals lies in its capacity to prompt new actions by encouraging one individual to 'reach out' to, and interact with, another. Here, it acts as 'an ideal living on of a relationship which may have ended long ago' (Simmel 1950: 388–9). While gratitude may become an echo of a past relationship, however, Simmel emphasises its resilience: once an individual has received something, preceding their own action, the initial offering stays with them as a voluntary, sacrificial gift which imposes on them a moral obligation. Aside from its resilience, its absolute importance to the reproduction of interaction needs to be recognised: 'It ties together different elements of society via microscopic but infinitely tough threads to such an extent that if every grateful action, which lingers on from good turns received in the past, were suddenly eliminated, society … would break apart' (Simmel 1950: 395, 392).

'Faithfulness' is another social emotion deriving from the sacrificial character of interaction. Irrespective of the motives for establishing a relationship, its development may stimulate a deeper and pervasive inner feeling of faithfulness, making the individuals-in-relation hold fast to one another. Faithfulness is oriented to preservation and links the fluctuating motives and impulses of the individual to the form of a relationship even after the feeling or motive that initiated that relationship has ended. By virtue of it, the dualism characteristic of the individual and the form of a relationship are reconciled (Simmel 1950: 379–87). Faithfulness, like gratitude, is of great importance for the reproduction of society. Indeed, Simmel (1912: 170) argues that our 'capacity to have faith in a person or group of people beyond all demonstrable evidence … is one of the most stable bonds holding society together'. Society 'could simply not exist, as it does, for any length of time', without the existence of faithfulness to supplement and bind together the impulses, passions and interests, and the self-interest of individual members (Simmel 1950: 379).

In summary, interaction is key to Simmel's treatment of 'society', but it has to be understood in relation to his *homo duplex* model of humans. In an analysis whose complexities were often lost in the subsequent development of symbolic interactionism (Rock 1979), Simmel argues that interaction is *facilitated* by pre-social dispositions and individualised forms, *progresses* via the development of 'mental reciprocities' and is *reproduced* by social emotions stimulated by the exchanges and experiences of energy and sacrifice. These patterns are central to his distinctive account of the elementary forms of social and moral life.

3. The elementary forms of social and moral life

Simmel may be best known among theorists of social interactionism, but the 'existentialist ethics' that shapes his sociology means that his work has, in its own way, a breadth as expansive as that of Durkheim. This breadth is evident in his view of interaction as the mediator of subjective and objective dimensions of reality. These dimensions cover economic arrangements and social institutions, but also morals, religion, art and the psychological processes central to the development of personality. Within these, his theory of human action attempts to account for the processes that shape social and moral life, starting from a focus on the creativity of social action, and its mediation through those social and cultural forms that attain an 'objective' quality. Nonetheless, Simmel's consciousness of what Coser (1971: 191) has called the 'ineradicable dualism inherent in the relation between individuals and objective cultural values' ensures that his account of the outcomes of this mediation in modernity has a melancholic tone.

Creative action

Simmel suggests that human action possesses fundamentally creative capacities that can proceed, outside the realm of necessity, without fixed goals. This is in contrast to those theories that understand social action to be oriented to pre-existing rational, value-based or normative ends, and explains why his work has become a resource for theorists keen to rescue a voluntaristic notion of action (Joas 1996; Levine 1998). Simmel's opposition to such definitions of action as always rational or normative is based on his view that they elevate a mere secondary phenomenon to a positive life principle of society, and misrepresent the individual's ethical and ontological relation to the future (Frisby 1981: 47; Simmel 1918b: 356–7). In an argument that highlights the difficulties Parsons would later have in placing Simmel within a view of sociology as concerned with normative action, Simmel suggests that to view actors as dominated by pre-existing goals limits humanity to a rigidly conceived existence in the present. In contrast, Simmel's (1918b: 360) conception of creative action suggests individuals are constantly transcending themselves, their goals, and the present parameters of their existence.

Simmel identifies various sources of human creativity, all associated with the contents of human life, and suggests that these produce a 'colouring', a creativity, and a variability to the performance of social roles that sociologists later viewed as determining 'scripts'. First of all, he suggests that individuals have an inherent, cognitive creativity. The mind organises the appearances of reality, through its own categories, into its own forms, and thus actively transforms the multiple, separate and chaotic elements of the world into a series of unifying pictures, images and sentences (Levine 1971: xxxvii). Secondly, human evolution constitutes a source of creativity. Simmel examined Darwin's work early in his career, and suggests that the evolution of our physical and psychological structures repeatedly reaches stages in which available energy levels are raised to a point at which there is an 'unleashing of developmental forces' marking a period of social and cultural creativity (Simmel 1908c).

Simmel also engages with vitalistic themes in the work of Goethe, Schopenhauer, Nietzsche, and Bergson, in attributing life with an inherent generative movement that provides a foundation for human creativity. Life is borne by 'bounded' individuals, yet constitutes 'a continuous stream', a 'boundless continuity', and a 'flux without pause' whose essence is to overflow and transcend limits, barriers or forms that the organism or society places in its way (Simmel 1918b: 362). In short, life ensures there is a constant 'reaching beyond' current boundaries and limitations (Simmel 1918b: 173). This life process may become temporarily congealed in fixed forms of behaviour and expression within individuals, but its essence is too forceful, productive, and chaotic for change and creativity to be replaced by fixity and form. For example, the individual psyche, the seat of human creativity, reveals life's contents as a spontaneous and 'chaotic whirling of images and ideas' whose flow lends action an inherent creativity (Simmel 1950: 311).[4]

These sources of creativity complement Simmel's *homo duplex* model of individuals. Humans are never fully 'socialised' beings, as the vital, biological, and psychological motivating contents of human existence are pre- or extra-social (Simmel 1908a: 24; 1950: 315). Consequently, there will always be dimensions of human existence undetermined by, and a source of dynamism for, society. These add imponderables to social roles, and a creativity and unpredictability to action. As Simmel (1908b: 13) notes, our interactions would be quite different if we appeared to others 'as the mere exponent of a social role'. Instead, action is a creative phenomenon, an overcoming of boundaries faced by the individual at any moment in time (Simmel 1918b: 364). Simmel's conception of creative action is also manifest in behaviour pursued for 'its own sake'. In his analysis of forms, to which we now turn, he examines how people can develop cultural traditions and 'play forms' that they pursue for their inherent worth, apart from any instrumental consideration.

The mediation of forms

Forms emerge from individual reflection and social interaction, yet they develop structuring properties that impute a subsequent pattern to cultural knowledge and social relationships. Even highly conflictual relationships, for example, develop forms that impart a regulation to the behaviour of the participants (Simmel 1955). While Simmel develops the notion of creative social action, then, he also argues that life could be expressed only through cultural and social forms that shape and constrain this action.

Following Levine's (1971) systematisation of Simmel's analysis, the development of these forms can be described as follows. *Cultural forms* emerge in the minds of individuals when their non-reflective immersion in the world is interrupted, when the *durée* of practical activity is broken and a person becomes separated from what they have done. At this point, the experiencing self divides into a self-conscious subject and an object: an object that confronts itself with embryonic, or 'protocultural' forms in an attempt to solve the problem with which it is confronted. The origin of cultural forms, then, is associated with the development of self-consciousness (Simmel 1911a: 59): an analysis that has affinities with Mead's I/Me distinction.

Once these cultural forms are created, and despite their remaining rooted in practical purposes, they become objectified and need not be continuously reinvented. At this point, they transcend individual situations and become reciprocal mental orientations that can develop into autonomous traditions of knowledge and practice pursued not only for practical advantage but also for their own sake:

> Thus, the rhythmic and melodic variations of sound initially formed to aid human communication become transformed into music composed and played according to intrinsic canons. Knowledge of the heavens needed to grow crops or sail the seas becomes transformed into the science of astronomy. Moral regulations designed to regulate human relationships become transformed into autonomous ethical principles. This is the movement from protoforms to objective forms. (Levine 1971: xvi–xvii)

Beyond this level of objectivation, there is a third echelon of cultural forms that Simmel refers to as 'worlds'. These possess the capacity to shape the totality of life's contents 'into a self-contained, irreducible world of experience' (Levine 1971: xvii). Perhaps the most obvious of these worlds is religion, which has historically located every event and action within an overarching meaning system (Simmel 1912), but cultural worlds are not restricted and can develop in such areas as art, knowledge, and morality.

Social forms develop along three distinct, but analogous, levels. While cultural forms emerge within individual minds, social forms originate in the most elementary points of instrumental or affective contact between individuals: the points at which glances or pleasantries are exchanged, questions asked, answers given, conversations begun, and reciprocal mental orientations established. It is here that threads of social life begin to bind people together.

Social forms can be combined into larger, institutionalised forms – such as family structures, communities, military and labour organisations – that remain tied to practical or affective needs. Alternatively, they can develop into interactional forms pursued for their own sake. The best-known example of this is Simmel's (1910: 128) analysis of sociability, the 'play form' of interaction pursued for the satisfactions gained from the fact that the solitariness of the individual is resolved into togetherness, a union with others.

Social and cultural forms allow for the expression of creative action, providing media through which vital human life processes can be realised. However, these forms are also structuring principles and remain so even though they delineate modes of association that can contain the most diverse combinations of impulses and motivations. Irrespective of the motivations bringing individuals together, then, it is possible to identify forms including conflict, marriage, the family, and sociability that impose a particular patterning on individuals. While forms are initially frameworks for creative life, they soon transcend this life and acquire 'fixed identities' and 'a logic and lawfulness of their own' (Simmel 1918a: 375). This new solidity inevitably places them at a distance from the dynamic that created them.

If the forms mediating action constrain human creativity, this is not a constraint that affects everyone equally. As one of the few classical sociologists to develop a sociology of the sexes, Simmel argues that male forms of behaviour claim super-personal validity in an objective culture that is male dominated, and in which men perceive their own perspective on social life to be 'rooted in the eternal order of things' (Coser 1977). Anticipating feminist critiques of this 'male order', Simmel recognises that men seek to manage the fragmenting demands of the division of labour by developing a psychic mechanism which enables them to separate public from private life, using women as a counterweight to their own dissociative tendencies (Tijssen 1991). While Simmel possesses a highly partial view of women as more homogeneous than men, as more tied to their essential nature, and as unsuited to specialisation, he also views them as more morally 'complete' and asks whether they possess a creative potential to produce forms that might lessen the modern divide between subjectivity and objectivity. This divide, which is a recurring feature of his analysis of forms and the creative vital-ism circling in and around them, is central to his writings on modernity: writings that exemplify the morally questionable outcomes of the mediation of creative action through forms.

The metropolis and the money economy

Simmel portrays the relationship between form and content as dynamic, yet betrays a melancholic attitude to the modern outcomes of social action. This is evi-dent in his analyses of the metropolis and money economy, which constitute a syn-thesis of his views of modernity (Simmel 1903a; 1907).[5] Simmel seeks to ascertain the effects of modernity on the embodied identities and responses of humans. In terms of the identities of individuals, he highlights the opposed tendencies pro-moted by the metropolis and money economy: they allow people to experience unparalleled levels of liberty, yet simultaneously threaten their prominence, signi-ficance and individuality (e.g. Simmel 1903a: 324). In terms of the embodied responses of individuals, he charts a process of intellectualisation, based on the dislocation of humans from their natural environment, involving change from a life based on relatively full emotional engagements with people and things to one marked by a succession of shallower, rapidly oscillating psychic responses. These themes of human identity and response combine to provide us with a major analy-sis of the experience of modernity. We will elaborate on each of them in turn.

A central characteristic of modernity is its promotion of a social expansion (a growth in the number of groups individuals interact with) that increases personal liberty. Individuals may have been dependent on just one or two groups in the Middle Ages: groups that involved the whole person and allowed little room for expressions of individuality. In contrast, individuals come to depend on many groups in our economically and socially differentiated modern world – groups which involve just a segment of the person – and possess greater liberty from the demands of any one of them (Simmel 1955). Paradoxically, then, as humans become dependent on more associations, there is a growth in human liberty and individualisation. In the metropolis, for example, we are dependent for virtually every aspect of our life on a host of other people. Nevertheless, this milieu is also the 'seat of cosmopolitanism' that 'assures the individual' an unprecedented 'type and degree of personal freedom' (Simmel 1903a: 332–4).

The development of the money economy accelerates this process by allowing individuals to engage with groups purely on the basis of financial transactions liberated from the social and moral obligations that historically regulated exchange. The sale of property in ancient Greece, for example, 'was a violation of duty not only towards one's children but to a higher degree towards one's ancestors' (Simmel 1907: 353). Early German law provides another example of how wealth was tied to localised social and moral obligations: every gift could be revoked in cases of ingratitude on the part of the recipient (Simmel 1907: 333). Money, however, distances wealth from these social and moral obligations.

✳If modernity involves a social expansion and an increase in individual liberty, it is dependent on, and serves to intensify, a 'remarkable expansion of mental processes' that contrasts with 'the more impulsive, emotionally determined character of earlier epochs' (Simmel 1907: 444). There are two major factors in this expansion and intensification. First, prior modes of emotional response have become impossible as a result of the swift and continuous shift of external and internal stimuli characteristic of the metropolis. With 'every crossing of the street', with every day lived among the contrasts and varieties of the city, the individual confronts a velocity of sensory contrasts that make 'the slower, more habitual, more smoothly flowing rhythm of the sensory-mental phase of small town and rural existence' impossible to maintain. Consequently, the individual seeks to reduce the effect of the fluctuations and discontinuities of the external milieu by reacting in a rational manner, thus intensifying conscious life and withdrawing from full emotional engagement with the surrounding area (Simmel 1903a: 325–6).

2 Second, the money economy intensifies this intellectualisation. It may initially require the mental capacity to accept money as a reliable bearer of value, but intensifies this mentalisation by treating everything in the world in terms of exchange value (Simmel 1907: 444). By becoming the measure of all things, money transforms the world into an 'arithmetic problem'. People's lives become filled with 'weighing, calculating, enumerating' and reducing 'qualitative values to quantitative terms' (Simmel 1903a: 327–8)✳This promotes the domination of means over ends and, in so doing, distances people from the emotions associated with the gratifications of attaining particular ends or interacting with particular persons. Personal characteristics are pushed aside, as bonds to others are loosened, and the interests of individuals acquire 'a relentless matter-of-factness' and a 'rationally calculated economic egoism' (Simmel 1907: 429–30; 1903a: 327)✳

This intellectualisation of the individual is accompanied by a set of psychic responses central to the experience of modernity. These are associated with the decline of energy occasioned by a city life in which gaps between rest and work have shortened, and a moral relativism stimulated by a money economy in which everything is evaluated in terms of its monetary worth. They include the cynical attitude, the *blasé* attitude and its associated response of reserve (dispositions 'almost endemic to the heights of a money culture'), and their effect is to erode those social emotions and moral dispositions, such as faith and gratitude, central to the continuation of society (Simmel 1907: 255, 491, 512).✳

The cynical attitude revels in demonstrating that the finest, most ideal morals and goods are available to anyone with the money to buy them. The cynic exposes 'higher values' as equal in kind to the lowest goals, and demonstrates that respect and admiration are offered to those with money, and denied to those without it, irrespective of their moral character. What Simmel refers to as the 'nurseries of cynicism' are exemplified by metropolitan stock exchanges. It is here, where huge quantities of money are exchanged easily and regularly, that cynicism flourishes:

> The more money becomes the sole centre of interest, the more one discovers that honour and conviction, talent and virtue, beauty and salvation of the soul, are exchanged against money ... the more a mocking and frivolous attitude will develop in relation to those higher values that are for sale for the same kind of value as groceries. (Simmel 1907: 256)

The cynic is still moved by the sphere of value, however, even if only in 'the perverse sense that he considers the downward movement of values part of the attraction of life'. In contrast, those who possess the *blasé* attitude have completely lost the feeling for value differences, for distinctions, experiencing 'all things as being of an equally dull and grey hue, as not worth getting excited about, particularly where the will is concerned' (Simmel 1907: 256). The *blasé* attitude is linked to the intellectualised response to life associated with the rapidly shifting oscillations characteristic of cities. Just as overindulgence makes one *blasé*, by overwhelming the senses, exhausting them of new reactions, so too the stimuli of city life exhaust the nerves through over-stimulation. Indeed, the *blasé* individual adjusts their nerves to city life by *renouncing* the response to them, a habit that devalues the 'entire objective world' and 'drags the personality downward into a feeling of its own valuelessness' (Simmel 1903a: 329–30).

The preservation of individuals within the metropolis requires 'a no less negative type of social conduct', that of reserve, as a way of managing the sheer number of relations one is exposed to. What Goffman later referred to as 'civil inattention' is one way in which people manage their reactions to others. The related but more general strategy Simmel refers to as 'reserve' manifests 'a slight aversion, a mutual strangeness and repulsion' and even a 'flight from the present' in which people are easily offended yet lack the 'actively appropriating energies' that facilitate a positive engagement with the environment (Simmel 1903a: 331; 1907: 474–5). While reserve and indifference might be associated with metropolitan freedom, they can also promote an unprecedented feeling of loneliness: 'it is by no means necessary that the freedom of man reflects itself in his emotional life only as a pleasant experience' (Simmel 1903a: 334).

These socially produced psychic reactions have serious implications for the future of social forms. We examined earlier how Simmel sees faith and gratitude as essential for the continuation of society, yet the psychic responses promoted by the metropolis and money economy are unable to bind people together. As Moscovici (1993: 334) suggests, the fact that unifying emotions such as love have become obstacles to be removed by people seeking profit provides a reason 'for the disquiet of our age, for the melancholy that surrounds the irrevocable disappearance of a form of life drained of its substance'.[6] This signifies the gulf between the vitalistic energies of individuals and the technical and social environments of modernity. Such a gulf between form and the content is not confined to the modern milieu, however, as Simmel views it as a metaphysical problem and as the major tension examined in his writings. This tension can be examined further in relation to the two major 'tragedies' confronting humans, and their moral and developmental implications for individuals.

4. Vitality and ossification: the tragic fate of individuals

Simmel (1911a: 43) uses the term 'tragedy' in a technical sense when referring to occasions when 'the destructive forces directed against some being spring forth from the deepest levels of this very being; or when its destruction has been initiated in itself, and forms the logical development of the very structure by which a being has built its own positive form'. The tragedies that concern us here are the 'tragedy of culture', and what Simmel refers to as the 'sociological tragedy' (or what can be seen as the tragedy of sociality), and the problem these pose for the development of personality.

The tragedy of culture occurs with the increasing gulf between the development of subjective and objective culture: a gulf created by the multiplication of cultural forms produced by creative individuals. This gulf expanded in the nineteenth century and is reflected in the fact that while the eighteenth-century pedagogic ideal focused on the 'formation of man', implying the development of a personal, internal set of values, this was replaced during the following century 'by the concept of "education" in the sense of a body of objective knowledge and behavioural patterns' (Simmel 1907: 449). As a sign of this gulf, Simmel (1907: 448) argues that if one compares our culture with that of a hundred years ago, the sciences and arts are extremely refined, yet individual cultural development 'has not progressed at all to the same extent; indeed, it has even frequently declined'. This is because the increasing expansion of objective culture eventually makes it impossible for an individual to become accomplished in more than a highly specialised segment of the knowledge valued by society. The time, energies and receptive capacities of individuals to assimilate objective culture are limited by their existence as humans (Levine 1971: xx). In this situation, individuals are confronted with an insoluble dilemma. If they seek to assimilate the totality of culture they embark on an impossible task that, moreover, has negative consequences for their individual development. If they rest content with achieving a segment of cultural expertise, however, they neglect huge realms of cultural life that could be better suited for the development of their individuality.

The consequence of this gulf is that individuals confront an objective culture that rarely allows for the expression of their personal values and the development of a moral self. As Nedelmann (1991) elaborates, the more culture becomes objectified into institutions that develop according to their own trajectories, the less will individuals find their cultural demands represented. Furthermore, while the cultural system may develop according to its own systemic logic, cut off from the creative energies of individuals, individual cultural creativity tends to become either increasingly idiosyncratic, or is displaced in favour of an attachment to fashion and an enjoyment of the times (Frisby 1985).

The second major tragedy, the 'sociological tragedy', concerns the conflicting requirements associated with engaging in forms of sociality, and maintaining the integrity of individuality. While people have embodied predispositions to engage in interactions, and need to in order to develop their individualities, sociality also compromises their individuality and moral development. This is because the interactions through which individuals express themselves necessarily coalesce around what is *common* to individuals rather than what is unique in them:

> Where an area of communication is formed … in which a majority of people find understanding and common ground, the standards must be considerably closer to the person of the lowest than of the highest level. For it is always easier for the latter to descend than it is for the former to ascend. (Simmel 1907: 392)

Individuals exercise only a fragment of themselves in groups, and the more developed an individual is, the less can that person express themselves in groups (Simmel 1950: 32, 58). It is this view that explains his argument that the truly 'religious' have much less need of religion than the nonreligious; for him, religiosity, like morality, is a quality of the individual soul rather than the social group (Simmel 1911b: 17).

Drawing on Nietzsche's valorisation of the individual over and against the restrictions of group life, Simmel (1950: 32) even suggests that these conditions explain how it is possible for the 'mass' to be spoken of with contempt, and cites Schiller's formulation of the difference between individuals in and out of groups: 'Seen singly, everybody is passably intelligent and reasonable; but united into a body, they are blockheads'. From this point of view, even the most simple contacts with the masses can compromise, and are likely to 'corrupt', the proper development of an individual (Simmel 1950: 37, 33). For Simmel, like Nietzsche, the development of the individual is the 'supreme value', though his desire that individuals make their way through the world with life and strength has a clear moral dimension. With the development of the individual, a moral feeling for others can emerge that has nothing to do with objectively determined ideas (Simmel 1907: 466). Carrying 'the bold stamp of the very core of our personality in all its strength and colouring', action becomes truly free and creative, and can express a genuine moral concern for others (Simmel 1903b: 32).

Nonetheless, Simmel's conceptualisation of the tragedies of culture and sociality means that this notion of individual development remains a frustrated ideal. Individuals are not only in conflict with society, but also within themselves: society lives through individuals, confronting them with 'demands' and 'obligations' that create *internal* conflict within individual psyches (Simmel 1912: 182–3). In modernity, in particular, these external and internal conflicts are intensified. The *blasé* attitude, cynicism, reserve, and dissociation all hamper an individual's need for, and experience of, a personality that transcends itself in order to expand its own worth. Indeed, the *blasé* attitude results in a personality that is apparently free yet wishes to change its 'inner condition' (Simmel 1907: 257). The advancing division of labour no longer enables individuals to establish the 'proper relationship' between a unified personality and a unified object and makes the individual 'a single cog as over against the vast overwhelming organisation of things and forces' (Simmel 1903a: 337), while the money economy's effacing of qualitative difference can end up destroying that 'self respect that characterises the distinguished person' (Simmel 1907: 394). Individuals are fragmented into their 'particular energies' and are left with a 'lack of something definite at the centre of the soul', impelling 'a search for momentary satisfaction in ever-new stimulations, sensations and external activities' (Simmel 1907: 454, 467, 484).

The tragedies of culture and sociality and, more broadly, the tension between human vitality and its ossification in forms, return us to the *homo duplex* model of individuals underpinning Simmel's work. Individuals always have an ambiguous relationship to 'society': they need it and, in a sense, create it, but it stifles and corrupts their personal and moral development. These tragedies also highlight one of Simmel's most persistent concerns. As Levine (1995: 208) argues, the 'extent to which persons are free to choose their own actions and develop themselves in accord with their unique individualities comprises the most significant dependent variable in Simmel's widely ranging essays on social phenomena'. In this 'existentialist ethics', Simmel's ideal of personality is not concerned with normative societal criteria, such as ethical codes or systems of religious dogma, but with an individual freely developing their unique self. In social life in general, however, and in modernity in particular, this development is highly problematic, and the fate of individuals is ultimately a tragic one.

5. Concluding comments

It has been suggested that while Simmel's early work was concerned with the development of a 'social ethics', particularly in terms of the 'elements of moral consciousness', his later work, particularly *The Philosophy of Money*, exhibits a shift in focus from 'ethical' to 'aesthetic' concerns, in the sense that he becomes preoccupied with the labyrinthine patterns of interaction that constitute the 'web of society' in modernity (Frisby 1992: 16, 23). Others, however, have drawn attention to his unwavering concern for the ethical implications of the 'capacious and far-reaching collision between society and the individual' (Nisbet 1966: 98). This latter view is surely correct, given Simmel's (1907: 256) critique of the way the money economy undermines the 'higher values' of 'honour and conviction, talent and virtue, beauty and salvation of the soul', and the fact that the vast majority of his writings on religion also date from this later period. More broadly, his account of the clash between subjective and objective culture, the dangers inherent within the development of the *blasé* attitude, and his concerns about forms and contents, can all be seen as part of his enduring concern for the tension-filled relationship between social and moral life.

Simmel was aware that his own consciousness of the emptiness and oppressiveness of modern cultural forms was shared by others. He noted, in fact, that there was a developing sense that cultural forms are 'an exhausted soil which has yielded all that it could grow', despite the fact that this soil 'is still completely covered by products of its former fertility' (Simmel 1918a: 377). His discussions of subjects such as 'friendship', 'dependence', 'confidence', and 'loyalty' can be understood as examinations of those interactions where a new social and cultural fertility might become possible; where the development of moral consciousness in, and moral bonds between, individuals might emerge in a way that does not stifle individual development in the way that modernity tends to. A similar argument can also be made about his discussion of the potentialities of the 'secret society' to offer autonomy in modernity, and his exploration of sexual love as an opportunity for modern individuals to open 'the doors of the total personality' (Nisbet 1966: 101, 103, 105). It is religion, however, that Simmel views as offering the greatest potential to bridge the gap between the subjective and objective features of life, though even here his pessimism is evident.

Simmel suggests that humans possess religious needs for transcendence and completeness that stem from the vital processes and chaotic experiences of life itself, and are nourished by a longing 'for a fixed point in all the instability that surrounds us' (Simmel 1912: 142). Individual religiosity is a vital process in which the soul draws together the myriad parts of life into a coherent whole. It is realised as an ideal mode of existence when the oscillations of life are experienced 'as if they were merely the functions of different limbs bearing the life of a single organism' (Simmel 1904: 37), but it is also present in a child's devotion to their parents, a patriot's fervour for their country, and a revolutionary worker's relationship to their insurgent class. All these relationships contain a mixture of 'unselfish surrender and fervent desire, of humility and exaltation, of sensual concreteness and spiritual abstraction' (Simmel 1898: 104). Such relationships exhibit that faith Simmel views as being so important for the continuation of social forms. If social interaction is constituted by multiple tensions and conflicts, such as those residing in *homo duplex* and those promoted by modernity, it is religion that has the potential to provide a means of reconstituting these differences within a cohesive whole.

Nevertheless, Simmel's hopes for such a reconstitution are dashed by his sense that religiosity, though a 'concrete reality within the soul', is paralysed by modernity. This is not simply in the sense that the historical *religions* have been undermined by post-Enlightenment criticism, but in that the *religious impulse* itself cannot find expression, given that the gap between subjective and objective culture has become so vast (Simmel 1909: 9). This gap between the social and the religious, like that between modern ethical norms and the moral consciousness of the individual, means that Simmel's 'existentialist ethics' is, by his own account, doomed to frustration if not complete failure: as individuals we face the almost impossible task of becoming all that we could be. Simmel's distinctive contribution to classical sociology is therefore an extremely pessimistic one, eschewing the more optimistic aspects of the French tradition in favour of a focus on the tragic plight of the modern individual. This focus is also evident in the work of the better-known German 'founding father' of sociology, Max Weber.

Notes

1. Despite his intellectual importance, and in contrast to Durkheim and Weber, Simmel occupied a marginalised role within the university system until late in his life. Anti-Semitism proved an obstacle to Simmel's career in Germany, but his unorthodox writing style, his analyses of disparate phenomena, and his particular approach to sociology, all hampered his standing. Simmel's marginalisation among

contemporary sociologists is more difficult to understand. As Levine (1971) notes, the *American Journal of Sociology* published fifteen pieces from Simmel in its first seventeen years of existence, while Simmel was the best represented author in the first major published collection of sociological readings (Park and Burgess 1921). However, Parsons's (1937) enormously influential account of the tradition omitted Simmel, while recent accounts of Simmel as a sociological *flâneur*, a practitioner of bricolage, or as the first theorist of postmodernity have unintentionally contributed to this marginalisation. Fortunately, this picture has been countered by an alternative view of Simmel as indispensable to the discipline. Major contributions include Levine's analyses of the relationship between Simmelian and Parsonian sociologies, and his systematic explications of Simmel's general theoretical contribution and his considerable influence on American sociology (Levine 1971, 1980, 1991b). Frisby's (1994) three-volume collection of essays is another valuable resource and has done much to stimulate recent interest, as has the increasing amount of Simmel's work available in English translation.

2. Simmel's conception of the moral soul signals a sharp divergence from Durkheim's understanding of social and moral life. In contrast to the view that moral and religious phenomena have an inherently *collective* character, Simmel is more interested in *individual* religiosity than in religion (Simmel 1914: 91), and more concerned with the moral consciousness of the individual than with ethical systems (Simmel 1911b: 18). Like Durkheim, however, his conceptions of the religious and moral dimensions of human experience transcend their manifestation in any particular institution or ethical system (Simmel 1898: 102).

3. This notion of forms is adapted from Kant's view that there exist a priori categories of cognition that enable humans to impose order on the natural world, but differs in three main ways. Simmel's forms impose conscious order on *all* human life and its contents and not just on cognitive understanding. Instead of being fixed and immutable, they emerge and develop over time as a result of the inherent creativity of individuals. Finally, instead of being located purely in the mind of the knowing individual, they are stabilised by recurring patterns of interaction. The sociological study of forms should identify the similar elements in superficially diverse interactions in order to secure a cross-section of reality, though Simmel admits that this perspective on social life is an abstraction from reality, where forms and contents are inextricably mixed, and a one-sided exaggeration of the lines and figures evident in interaction (Simmel 1950: 200).

4. A different source of creativity is to be found in the development of technology. Human evolution sets limits to the senses, even if these limits change through time, yet Simmel (1918b: 356) examines how such developments as the telescope and microscope transform our sensible world and the previous relation thought to exist between life and its boundaries.

5. The abstract existence forced on individuals by modernity results in an alienation of individuals originating from their distance from nature and from the objective culture and society in which they live (Frisby 1985). Nevertheless, the intellectualised approach to the modern world, with all its associated dangers, remains a technically superior mode of operation within that world. Referring to Comte's placing of bankers at the head of the secular government in his utopian state, because bankers formed the class with the most general and abstract functions, Simmel (1907: 437) argues that 'the intellectual person ... has a certain power of reason, impartiality and judgment over the ... emotional, impulsive person'.

6. In this respect, *The Philosophy of Money*, in particular, has been judged to possess a stature alongside Tönnies's model of *Gemeinschaft und Gesellschaft* in mapping the transition to a capitalist society. It has also been seen as probably the most important work on the consequences of a money economy to be published since Marx's *Capital*, and as an analysis of rationalisation that serves as a model for Weber's writings on the subject (Levine 1971: 14; Turner 1986; Bottomore and Frisby 1990: 36, 22).

7. Contrary to Durkheim, it is not society *sui generis* that becomes God, but the interactive processes between human beings that become deified: it is the "dynamics of group life" that is "borne up by the momentum of religious feeling and ... projected beyond the materials and agents of those dynamics into the transcendent sphere" (Simmel 1912: 208).

5

HEROIC SOCIOLOGY

1. Introduction

Max Weber's vision of modernity is perhaps best known for its analysis of self-determining human subjects struggling to invest their actions with meaning in an increasingly rationalised world. This vision engages with, and is influenced significantly by, many of the themes raised by Simmel. It is dominated by the spectre of a capitalist order operating on 'mechanical foundations', independent of any system of meaning or religious ethic, fragmenting human existence into disconnected life-spheres. This fracturing of meaning is evident in the frequency with which capitalism promotes economic processes and human actions that are formally rational in terms of their efficiency, yet which result in outcomes that are substantively irrational. It is also associated with the promotion of cognitive thought and scientific explanation over moral valuation and emotional experience, the dominance of calculability and accountability over mystery and tradition, and the growth of relationships organised on the basis of general rules instead of on the basis of personal sentiment. These processes result in a reduction in the charismatic binding of people to normative communities, a decline in individuals' encounters with 'ultimate values', and the general 'disenchantment' of society.

Weber provides us with what is probably the most powerful account of the dominance of rationalised and mundane this-worldly phenomena to exist in sociology. While his vision of modernity is apparently driven by a bleak determinism, he rejected the methodological idea that historical 'laws' exist. Nevertheless, he acknowledged that humans had created a world that demands of them a struggle of heroic proportions if their actions and identities are to remain meaningful, and if they are to achieve or maintain any moral integrity.

These introductory comments suggest that Weber developed a very different version of sociology than that constructed by either Comte or Durkheim. Weber (1919a) saw the sociologist as a 'value free' scientist confronting an increasingly rationalised society. This not only rejected Comte's view of the sociologist as priest, but also included a methodology and diagnosis of the modern world that turned Comte's distinction between positive knowledge and emotional commitment into an almost unbridgeable chasm. Similarly, although both Weber and Durkheim advocated a scientific approach towards the discipline, Weber was more pessimistic than Durkheim about reconciling the rational and emotional capacities of humans within a moral order, and sought to prioritise the individual rather than the 'social fact' as the basic unit of explanation.

These differences may be traced in part to the variety of theoretical traditions drawn on by Weber. Sociology may have developed through a *critical* dialogue with utilitarianism, yet Weber's writings are characterised by a focus on the individual and have been viewed as a precursor to rational choice theory. In addition to the considerable influence Simmel's work had on his writings, Kant's analysis of humans as conscious, self-determining subjects clearly informed his conception of the individual. Weber's methodological use of 'ideal types' (a means of understanding predicated on the assumption that there can be no unmediated knowledge of the world) reflects an additional Kantian influence (Levine 1995). Furthermore, Weber's analysis of capitalism is influenced by a critical engagement with Marxism, while his theory of rationalisation possesses affinities with Nietzsche's writings on the 'death of God'.

These theoretical traditions also help account for how Weber has been described variously as an idealist, a conflict theorist, an interactionist, a theorist of rational choice, a 'multidimensional', and even a 'schizophrenic' thinker (Alexander 1983; Collins 1986b). A central aim of this chapter, however, is to demonstrate that Weber's work can be understood as a distinctive, coherent vision of sociology. As Bendix (1959: 481) argues, Weber attempted to combine and *reconcile* idealist and materialist approaches to human behaviour and social change, and his work was driven by a unifying concern with how the unintended products of self-determining human action can produce a rationalised world in which voluntaristic action becomes increasingly difficult. This pessimism about the 'fate' of the individual is a recurrent theme for Weber (it has done much to contribute to his reputation as a 'liberal in despair') and emerges through a series of paradoxes in his work that are central to our discussions.

This chapter is structured as follows. Section 2 analyses rationalisation as the *unit idea* in Weber's sociology by focusing on its relationship with charisma. Rationalisation assumes various meanings in Weber's work, but he insists that rationalising processes eventually result in the diminution of charisma: a development which distances people from encounters with the 'ultimate values or events' of life (Shils 1965: 199). Section 3 examines what can be identified as the elementary forms of social life in Weber's writing. If processes of rationalisation constitute the unit idea in Weber's work, *rational action* constitutes the elementary form of social action in the sense that it can be considered to reflect a quintessentially modern mode of intervening in the world. Rational action is considered to be a free and meaningful form of action by Weber, but he also suggests action that is 'instrumentally rational' can become habitual, can make problematic the human capacity to engage meaningfully with the social world, and can eventually undermine human freedom. One of the major *mediators* of rational action, which accounts for this paradox, is the Protestant ethic. Rational action is not reducible to Protestantism, and can be traced back long before the advent of the Reformation, yet Protestantism provided rational action with an ethical basis that promoted a systematic modification of people's behaviour. By encouraging the religiously informed, instrumental disciplining of people's bodies, sentiments and habits, however, Protestantism also assisted the emergence of a system of capitalism that *undermined* both the meaningful nature of rational action and the social significance of religion.

These paradoxes provide the context for Weber's analysis of personality, and it is here that we find the major substantive *tension* in his vision of sociology. Weber oscillates between assessing human behaviour as voluntaristic and meaningful on the one hand, and determined and meaningless on the other. Section 4 explores this tension by examining how Weber's sociology is permeated by a vision of the heroic individual struggling *intellectually* to construct a meaningful life and personality against the rationalisation, secularisation and disenchantment that characterises the 'iron cage' of modern capitalism. Individuals are fated in Weber's work to either a noble but isolated and tortuous life directed by the rational mind, or to an ignoble retreat into bodily habits and emotions shared by others. In contrast to Comte's and Durkheim's visions of moral orders, there is no collective reconciliation of the gap Weber suggests exists between emotional and rational action in modernity. Modernity is characterised instead by the erosion of collective values and energies.

2. Rationalisation

Rationalisation is the unit idea in Weber's sociology, the concept which provides a 'thematic unity' (Tenbruck 1980) to his writings on economy, society and world religions, and the key to understanding his work as an integrated whole. Weber nowhere provides us with a succinct definition of rationalisation, but uses the term to refer to a set of distinctive processes that exert a gradual yet seemingly unremitting pressure on social and economic life. Rationalisation develops in diverse directions, at different speeds, in separate spheres of social life, and frequently results in conflict as certain rational principles clash with those dominant in other parts of society (Collins 1986a, 1986b). Weber discusses the varied rationalisations of Confucianism, of Ancient Judaism, of Protestantism, and even of mystical contemplation, for example, and judges the instrumentally rational means of economic growth, and the value irrationality of these means for the political goals of wealth distribution, to be a major source of conflict and social problems (Weber 1951: 226–49; 1968: 112, 610–19; 1904–5; see also Parsons 1937).[1]

While Weber recognises the historically and culturally diverse character of rationalisation processes, he does attribute to them certain common features. First, rationalisation is a *universal* phenomenon in Weber's writings: it occurs in the East as well as the West. Second, it is commonly concerned with the conscious imposition of cognitive frameworks and regularised patterns of behaviour on the flux of social life: it imposes *order* on the world. Third, rationalising processes possess a systematic, recurrent and institutionalised character which distinguishes them from the various types of human action (a typology we examine in the next section) (Kalberg 1980: 1148, 1160–1). Fourth, while there is no simple beginning to rationalising processes in the West, analysts have identified distinctive stages within Weber's view of rationalisation. Tenbruck (1980: 322), for example, suggests that the vital processes of early modern rationalisation are associated with religious disenchantment that culminates in the Protestant ethic. Since that time, rationalising processes have been carried forward by new agents in science, economics and politics. Finally, Weber argues that there is a recognisable direction to rationalisation processes in the West: these have advanced those types of rationality that facilitate control and explanation at the expense of those that systematise and conserve general values.[2] This point is crucial to Weber's writing and requires elaboration.

It is in the West that rationalisation has most aggressively involved the promotion of control and explanation over meaning and value. Dominant here have been processes 'by which explicit, abstract, intellectually calculable rules and procedures are increasingly substituted for sentiment, tradition, and rule of thumb in all spheres of activity' (Wrong 1970: 26). Rationalisation 'leads to the displacement of religion by specialised science as the major source of intellectual authority; the substitution of the trained expert for the cultivated man of letters; the ousting of the skilled hand-worker by machine technology; the replacement of traditional judicial wisdom by abstract, systematic statutory codes. Rationalisation demystifies and instrumentalises life' (ibid.). In so doing, rationalisation has massively increased people's ability to control their environment. Science, for example, contributes to technological advance and helps individuals gain clarity about the means necessary to pursue a given end. Despite facilitating control, however, processes of rationalisation have also eroded the place of ultimate values in human life. Science has sought to subject values to scrutiny and testing according to its own principles of validity and found them to be wanting (Weber 1919a), yet has been unable to provide answers to the fundamental moral questions confronting humans. Science aids the advance of medicine and the systematisation of law, for example, but cannot answer the questions of when a life is worth living and whether a particular legal system is ultimately just. Instead, by helping to explain phenomena that previously appeared 'mysterious', science makes it difficult to imbue the natural and social worlds with meaning and value (Weber 1919a: 139). The world, in short, becomes disenchanted.

Rationalisation and the fate of charisma

If rationalisation is the most prominent world-transforming force in Weber's work, it is not the only process responsible for social change or for the fate of human meaning: the development of rationality is bound up with the fate of charisma. Charisma represents 'other-worldly' directed experience that has the power to inject new values into social life. It is a vehicle for human creativity, and has the potential to ignite social change (Weber 1968: 432–3). Charisma originates from the inability of mundane experience to answer problems of suffering and fortune, and provides a 'supernatural' sense of power over the inexplicable (Gerth and Mills 1948). Indeed, Weber (1968: 216) took the concept 'charisma' from Christianity where it referred to 'the gift of grace': a variety of divine gifts bestowed on the faithful.

Weber retained much of the theological meaning of charisma but in exploring its relationship with rationalisation he also used it to refer to a type of *domination* and *authority*: a typology which is central to his account of social change and the fate of meaning.[3] 'Domination' refers to the probability that a command will be obeyed by a group of persons, but implies 'voluntary compliance', while authority refers to the grounds on which a form of rule is accepted as valid (Weber 1968: 212, 946).[4] *Charismatic* domination and authority rest on a capacity to inspire 'devotion to the exceptional sanctity, heroism or exemplary character of an individual person', and to the norms and order revealed or ordained by that person (Weber 1968: 215, 954). Charisma is based on revelation, then, and remains dependent on recognition.[5] This contrasts with *traditional* domination and authority which rest on custom and established beliefs in the 'sanctity of immemorial traditions and the legitimacy of those exercising authority under them'. Finally, *rational* domination and authority rest on a system of consciously made rational rules and a corresponding belief in the legality of enacted rules, and the right of those elevated to authority under such rules to issue commands (Weber 1968: 954, 215).

Weber did not believe that society progressed through inevitable stages of domination and authority, but did analyse how charismatic, traditional and rational leadership interacted to produce social change. Traditional societies, in particular, proved vulnerable to the capacity of charisma to overturn 'all notions of sanctity and reverence for customs that are ancient and hence sacred' (Weber 1968: 1117). While traditional forms of domination and authority may be replaced by charismatic rule, charisma is *itself* subject to deterioration as a result of the establishment of bureaucratic organisation. Here, Weber highlights the paradox whereby charismatic leaders provide an impetus for the eventual establishment of rational rule by sweeping away traditional authorities (Mommsen 1974: 80), and are sometimes directly responsible for rationalisation. Jewish prophets, for example, demanded that their followers subject their lives to an 'iron law of rational social conduct'. Despite this revolutionary potential, however, charisma itself eventually becomes routinised (incorporated into this-worldly concerns that make it vulnerable to rationalisation) by forms of political and social organisation.

Several factors are responsible for this routinisation, but they are mostly related to what Weber refers to as a decisive 'striving for security' on the part of those initially associated with a revolutionary opposition to the status quo (Weber 1968: 252).[6] This routinisation of charisma is not without conflict, and particular structures such as political parties can be forced into the service of a 'charismatic hero' even in times of advanced rationalisation (Weber 1968: 1130–2), but attempts to stabilise the source and control of charisma exert an inevitable impact on its development. Weber argues that the development of rationalised structures and movements have increasingly domesticated and manipulated charisma (Weber 1968: 1121). Like Durkheim, he suggested that the Enlightenment engaged in a manipulative 'charismatic glorification' of the this-worldly power of reason while he also suggests that this eventually 'made it possible for the capitalist to use things and men freely' (Weber 1968: 1209–10). Similarly, rational, legalistic forms of domination continue to use charismatic authorities such as the monarchy to legitimise the social order. Weber (1968: 1146) suggested that this manipulation is 'the last form that Charisma has adopted in its fateful historical course', yet it is here 'much transformed' in its intensity and power, bearing little resemblance to the 'pure' form it assumed in previous manifestations. According to Weber (1968: 1148–9), the consequences of these processes are severe: the 'waning of charisma generally indicates the diminishing importance of individual action'. He recognised the possibility that new charismatic 'prophets' could arise, but was bleak about a disenchanted future which promises no 'summer's bloom ... but rather a polar night of icy darkness and hardness' (Weber 1919a).

In clarifying the status of rationalisation as a 'unit idea' in Weber's work, it is important to note that while his discussion of the relationship between rationalisation and charisma has been compared to Durkheim's analysis of the sacred and profane (Parsons and Shils 1962), it is not identical. For Weber, the decline of charisma does not affect the 'mechanical foundations' of capitalism even if it threatens the ability of individuals to pursue meaningful lives. The diminution of the sacred for Durkheim, in contrast, can entail the *breakdown* of society. Indeed, a key difference between them is that while the effervescence brought about by collective contact with the sacred was the essence of society for Durkheim, charisma rarely assumed this status in Weber's work and was relegated to a minor role in the modern world.

In summary, rationalisation and charisma are linked historically in Weber's work. Certain commentators have suggested that creative social change and human development are dependent on a balance between the two (Eisenstadt 1968), yet the this-worldly fortunes of rationalisation ultimately stand opposed to the transcendental orientation of charismatic leaders, breakthroughs and experiences.

3. The elementary forms of social and moral life

Critics have constructed a view of Weber's sociology as a fragmented project dominated by concept formation on the one hand, and various historical examinations on the other. His typology of social action, his writings on world religions, and his ideal-typical analysis of the emerging 'iron cage' of rational capitalism have all been cited as examples of what is judged to be a sprawling, unsystematic sociology. His studies assume a very different appearance, however, when viewed as distinctive parts of an overarching analysis of what was elementary to social and moral life in the development of the modern era. In his writings on the West, Weber examines a form of rational action, mediated by a religious ethic, that has done much to shape the social and moral outcomes of rational capitalism.

Instrumentally rational action

While rationalisation refers to a set of processes that influence society as a whole, and threaten the place of values in social life, Weber's analysis of social action is concerned with specific types of meaningful *individual* action (Weber defines action as meaningful if it is oriented to the behaviour of others). He identifies four ideal-types of social action that humans possess the capacity for exercising. *Instrumental* or means-ends rational action is based on judgments about how to achieve one's goals most effectively in a given environment. Here, 'the end itself is accepted beyond question' and all that matters is the effectiveness of technique (Weber 1968: 65, see also 24–6). Of the various forms of social action identified by Weber, this can be seen as the elementary form of social action in the modern world in that it is most closely associated with the dominance of rational capitalism. *Value-rational* action is when an action is seen as being *good in itself*, as governed by 'a conscious belief in the value for its own sake of some ethical, aesthetic, religious, or other form of behaviour' irrespective of its prospects of success (Weber 1968: 24–5). Conforming to the Christian ideal of 'turning the other cheek' when provoked is an example of such action that 'always involves "commands" or "demands" which, in the actor's opinion, are binding on him' (Weber 1968: 25). *Affectual* action is determined by the actor's specific feeling states, and could be manifest in an uncontrolled and violent reaction to an insult. Finally, *traditional* action is determined by ingrained habituation, without regard to the rationality of behaviour.

Weber argues that freedom and rational action go together at an individual level as long as we have *meaningful goals* to pursue or *values* to sustain. We feel most free, he suggests, when performing actions we are conscious of having rationally chosen: that is, in the absence of physical coercion, emotional reaction or accident, and in accordance with those means most efficient *in relation to our goal*. Alternatively, affectual and traditional action stand on the very 'borderline of what can be considered "meaningfully" oriented' action because they can both be simple *reactions* to events (Weber 1968: 25).

Weber's typology of social action is meant to be exhaustive of those actions humans perform, but he also suggests that pre-modern 'community' tended to be based on affectual and traditional behaviour, while modern forms of 'association' are based generally on rational action. As such, Weber would *appear* to be implying that modernity is characterised by actions that are rationally pursued and based on clearly defined values. That this is *not* the case leads us to another paradox in Weber's sociology. While initially viewing rational action as meaningful, Weber notes that over time it can become habitualised, with the subjective loss of its initial means-ends intent. Modern people prize means-ends efficiency over the actual pursuit of particular goals, to the extent that rational action becomes meaningless.

This loss of meaning does not happen automatically, but is the result of specific mediators of rational action. In this context, Weber's (1904–5) *The Protestant Ethic and the Spirit of Capitalism* demonstrates how a religious ethic served as a vital medium of meaningful rational action, but also contributed to the development of a system which demanded rational action of people while emptying this action of its subjective value.

The protestant ethic: the medium of social action

Weber argues that the emergence of rational capitalism required an appropriate ethical/motivational framework as well as an appropriate economic/institutional context. While the East possessed institutional and material foundations that could have facilitated the development of large-scale rational economic activity, its religious context did not promote a spirit of world transformation. The rise of Protestantism in the West, in contrast, promoted an ethically informed rational action that possessed a substantial affinity with the 'spirit of modern capitalism'. Protestantism established clearly-defined values that made sense of this-worldly activity in relation to God. It developed these values into a normative system that had consequences for every aspect of an individual's personal conduct, necessitating a disciplined life dedicated to hard work. Protestantism, in short, became an important mediator of rational action that harnessed individual behaviour to rationalisation processes that culminated in the development of modern capitalism.

Weber is sometimes mistakenly interpreted as suggesting that Protestantism alone transformed the ethical basis of economic life, but he highlighted a variety of other extra-economic factors conducive to the rise of rational capitalism. The development of Western European cities during the medieval era, for example, deprived kinship groups of their ritual significance and meant that people interacted as 'a confessional association of individual believers' rather than 'a ritual association of kinship groups' as they did in other parts of the world (Weber 1958). The Christian tradition, then, exerted a substantial impact on the rationalisation and individualisation of certain areas of social life centuries before the appearance of Protestantism.[7] Nevertheless, Weber insists that Protestantism crystallised and accelerated these changes. It was characterised by an ethical egalitarianism that discouraged strong emotions in relation to family or friendship, in case God's Will was compromised (Bendix 1959: 70), and provided a religious sanction for repetitive labour, long work hours, and low wages. The emphasis it placed on rational action in work becomes clear in Weber's analysis of the 'calling'.

The Protestant 'calling' was not part of Catholic theology but was introduced by Luther, who suggested that individuals were religiously obliged to fulfil their duty in worldly affairs. Work was no longer religiously neutral but a *religious duty*. There developed, however, two major versions of the calling: the Lutheran and the Calvinist. Luther's conception was relatively traditionalist, in that it emphasised that people should accept and adapt to their labours as a 'divine ordinance' (Weber 1904–5: 85). Calvin's conception of the calling, in contrast, placed priority on the *doing* of work rather than on adaptation. As Weber (1904–5: 160) emphasises, 'this calling is not, as it was for the Lutheran, a fate to which he must submit ... but God's commandment to the individual to work for the divine glory'.

These conceptions of the calling were related to other divergences in Luther's and Calvin's beliefs about God's grace and the fate of humans after death. While Christianity had, since Augustine, adopted the view that grace is the result of an objective power (not to be attributed to personal worth), Lutheranism held that grace was dependent upon an individual's worldly existence. While a sinful life lead to grace being revoked, it 'could be won again by penitent humility and faithful trust in the Word of God and in the sacraments' (Weber 1904–5: 102). Calvin, however, rejected this view: the fate of humans was predestined and it was a massive conceit to think that individuals could affect God's Will.

Weber suggests that this doctrine of predestination devastated the 'generation which surrendered to its magnificent consistency' and generated a feeling of unprecedented inner loneliness of the single individual (Weber 1904–5: 103–5). Calvinism emptied the world of positive meaning. However, Weber further argues that the psychological consequences of this doctrine proved unbearable for the broad mass of followers, and that pastoral teaching reduced its harshness by emphasising that individuals had an absolute duty to consider themselves one of the 'chosen', and to combat all doubts as temptations of the devil. This teaching also encouraged individuals to obtain confidence through an intense, rational, worldly activity that disperses 'religious doubts and gives the certainty of grace' (Weber 1904–5: 112, 180). Material success was henceforth taken to be a sign of grace.

In contrast to the relatively lax control then exerted by the Catholic Church over daily life, and the ability of individuals to gain redemption and 'reverse' their sinful lives through confession, Calvinism instituted 'a regulation of the whole of conduct' (Weber 1904–5: 36). The pastoral amelioration of the Calvinist doctrine of predestination was tied to an ascetic life that necessitated the 'infinitely burdensome' instrumental disciplining of the body, emotions and habits through incessant work. Such an ethic combined labour with abstinence in a way that suggested a transcendent engagement with disciplined work (Weber 1904–5: 53), but which also facilitated a this-worldly accumulation of capital that could be invested to increase further the scope of productive activity.

Protestantism both *promoted* action that was instrumentally rational, then, and provided this form of action with an *ethical basis*. This ethical basis is further illustrated by the fact that Protestantism's promotion of rational labour was no simple endorsement of capitalism. As Calvin's Geneva showed, numerous rules, regulations and restrictions were placed on trade in attempting to ensure that commerce remained subordinate to religion. Weber's analysis of the final outcome of this relationship between capitalism and religion, however, illustrates his argument that rational action has the capacity to erode meaningful behaviour. As instrumental action contributed to the growth of rational capitalism, this system eroded alternative means for making a living and created circumstances in which 'Whoever does not adapt his manner of life to the conditions of capitalistic success must go under' (Weber 1904–5: 72). Capitalism became 'emancipated from its old supports': it no longer needed religious justification, and felt any remaining 'attempts of religion to influence economic life ... to be as much an unjustified interference as its regulation by the state' (ibid.).

If ethically informed rational action facilitated rational capitalism, Weber was even more insistent about the eventual domination and control of capitalism than were Marxists who held onto the hope of a revolutionary subject. Protestantism helped promote a personality oriented towards disciplined work and convinced of the sinfulness of bodily being, but capitalism ruptured the link between dedication to the calling of labour and the ethic of personality and replaced it with nothing (Hennis 1988: 93). As Weber (1904–5: 182–3) concludes, while 'the Puritan wanted to work in a calling; we are forced to'.

Rational capitalism

Rational capitalism represents the eventual outcome of rational action in Weber's work even though his description of it – as a system that had yet to develop fully – is necessarily sketchy. Rational capitalism contrasts with previous types of capitalism (traditional, pariah and booty capitalism) in terms of its scope, its systematic operation, its dynamic tendency to turn into commodities all aspects of social and natural life, and its extensive adoption and development of instrumental rationality. It is further characterised by the private appropriation of the means of production, the formal freedom of labour, the minimisation of non-economic restrictions on production, and by operating within a legal system based on general rules. As Collins (1986b) notes, Weber's vision of rational capitalism is broadly in line with the neoclassical economic view of the institutional foundations of the free market. Weber progresses considerably beyond this view, however, in arguing that rational capitalism makes the pursuit of a meaningful life increasingly difficult.

One of the key features of Weber's vision of rational capitalism is rational bureaucracy: a pervasive organisational form based on the adoption of instrumentally rational rules and working practices. Alongside the spheres of politics and science, this form of bureaucracy can be seen as one of the most important contemporary mediators of rational action yet it is also far more than that in Weber's work. Bureaucracy constitutes a core characteristic of rational capitalism. Increasing areas of social and economic life were subject to the workings of rational bureaucracy, and Weber traced the advance of rational bureaucratic structures in Germany, Russia, and even America.

While Weber never provided a precise definition of rational bureaucracy, his ideal type specified those of its features that he considered particularly relevant to the future of modern societies. Modern rational bureaucracy is different from patrimonial administration (the traditional form of organisation), and presupposes a system of legal authority.[8] It is based on the formal freedom of staff appointed on the basis of contracts, and operates via general, explicit rules. It is characterised by a clear hierarchy of offices whose functions are plainly delineated. Administrative business is based upon written documents, while specialist administrative roles presuppose 'thorough and expert training' and usually constitute the official's sole occupation. Everything personal is forced out of rational bureaucracy which treats individuals as rule bound subjects and 'develops the more perfectly, the more it is "dehumanised", the more completely it succeeds in eliminating from official business love, hatred, and all … irrational, and emotional elements which escape calculation. This is appraised as its special virtue by capitalism' (Weber 1968: 975).

The development of rational bureaucracy exerted a far reaching yet ultimately stabilising influence upon society. Weber argued that bureaucracy 'reorganises everything it comes into contact with according to strictly "instrumentally-rational" principles', and that its technical efficiency (its precision, speed, continuity and uniformity) would increase its social importance (Mommsen 1974: 63–4; Albrow 1970: 45). Weber emphasised that rational bureaucracies were not guided by instrumental rationality alone, as they operated under some form of political leadership. He also insisted that technical efficiency could produce substantive inefficiencies, as rules became ends in themselves rather than the means to particular goals.

If modern bureaucracies revolutionised and then stabilised everything they came into contact with, Weber was 'haunted' by the fear that they would jeopardise individual freedom and produce 'the fully adjusted men of a bureaucratic age who no longer strive for goals which lie beyond their intellectual horizon' (Wrong 1970: 32; Mommsen 1974: 93, 20). Neither capitalism nor socialism (which Weber believed would be characterised by an even greater degree of bureaucratic organisation) looked likely to escape this fate. A future dominated by rational bureaucracy would be a future where ultimate meanings had evaporated, where the 'idea of duty in one's calling prowls about in our lives like the ghost of dead religious beliefs', and where the iron cage of mechanised, rational capitalism reigned supreme (Weber 1904–5: 182).

If Weber's analysis of rational capitalism is characterised by a deep pessimism, he sought to reinstate some hope for the future (Weber 1904–5: 182). Weber (1968) suggested that charismatic breakthroughs may be possible in the future and advocates these as a solution to the troubles facing rationalised societies. In order to reduce the stifling effects of bureaucracy, Weber invested his hope in great politicians with charismatic qualities who were able to inject meaning into the world, and advocated structures that would allow for the rise of these individuals within the framework of legal rule (Weber 1919b).[9] Given the emphasis Weber placed on the dominance of rationalising processes, however, it is less apparent how his hopes would be realised. He suggests that charismatic leaders are most likely to emerge during periods of social crises, when disadvantaged groups turn toward 'extraordinary' leaders (Turner 1996a: 146), but Weber's analysis of capitalism does not contain the self-destructive tendencies characteristic of Marx's work, and identifies no stratum in Western society able to reintroduce fundamental values into the social world (Kalberg 1980). Similarly, Weber (1919b) suggests that political bureaucracies are dependent on an electoral process in which charismatic leaders can thrive, but remains quieter when it comes to the development of such personalities. Indeed, this oscillation between the hope for creative infusions of meaning in the modern world and the seemingly inevitable march of rationalisation introduces us to the major tension in Weber's work.

4. Meaning or meaninglessness?

Weber's sociology is dominated by two features: the first is an argument about the increasing capacity of rationalising processes to erode meaning and freedom; the second involves a commitment to the meaningful actions of individuals as the basic unit of sociological explanation. The tension between these two can be examined in relation to his writings on method.

Weber's concern with the meaning of individual actions is reflected in his commitment to methodological individualism and his argument that the most appropriate method for the human sciences is *verstehen* (understanding) (Gerth and Mills 1948: 55).[10] This approach 'considers the individual ... as the basic unit, as its "atom"', and as the 'sole carrier of meaningful conduct' (Weber 1968). Consequently, it is 'the task of sociology' to reduce such concepts as 'rationalisation' and 'charisma' (as well as 'state', 'association', 'feudalism') 'to "understandable" action, that is, without exception, to the actions of participating individual[s]'. Instead of consistently employing methodological individualism, however, Weber adopts a 'structuralist' approach in his account of rationalisation by treating it as a going concern that is consequential in its own right. As Gerth and Mills (1948: 57) point out, this orientation is also evident in Weber's treatment of world religions, the state, status, bureaucracy, and the economy. Yet if these phenomena can be understood without reference to the motives of individuals, where does this leave methodological individualism?

This dual approach to method can be justified by appreciating Weber's commitment to both interpretive and *causal* explanation: sociology 'is a science concerning itself with the interpretive understanding of social action' *and* 'with a causal explanation of its course and consequences' (Weber 1968: 4).[11] Weber was insistent that adequate understanding at the level of *meaning* had to be accompanied by the observation of *empirical regularities* (Weber 1968: 12), an argument that explains his commitment to *verstehen*, on the one hand, and his employment of the 'structural principle of explanation', on the other.[12] Nevertheless, when these methodological principles need to be employed simultaneously in his work (when examining the individual in a broader 'structural' context), Weber encounters intractable problems. Indeed, Weber's analysis of individuals in rational capitalism highlights a system in which the subjective intent of the actor 'is essentially prescribed by their objective situation' (Gerth and Mills 1948: 58). Methodological individualism is marginalised here as interpretive understanding can increasingly be derived from a structuralist analysis of constraints. As Turner (1996a: 27, 45) notes, for all Weber's opposition to materialism, he focused on the importance of social action *within* a view of the increasing power of structural processes that possess a 'logic independent of the will and consciousness of individual agents', and result in a world in which 'structure dominates individual action'.

If Weber's commitment to a methodology of interpretive individualism becomes increasingly strained, the subject it encounters most difficulty with (individual existence within the 'iron cage' of modern capitalism) brings us to the major theoretical tension in his work. This involves the individual struggle to construct meaning in a rationalised world bereft of ultimate meanings.[13] Weber (1975: 192) seeks to resolve the tension in his writings – between emphasising the meaningful nature of individual action, and the development of a rational society which makes meaningful action increasingly difficult – by proposing that people should create a personality by disciplining, developing and harmonising their capacities in a manner that is rationally congruent with freely chosen values. This 'ethic of personality' rejects action driven by emotion or tradition, and imposes arduous demands on the individual: 'only through vigilant awareness and active exertion can the individual progress from ... a life governed by the chaotic impulses of ... raw, unformed, given nature to one governed by the coherent values and meanings of ... consciously formed personality' (Brubacker 1984: 97).

The division of society into proliferating life-spheres, and the increased impersonality of modern bureaucratic structures, however, make the marshalling of interior dispositions and exterior action around an ethical ideal increasingly difficult.[14] This is exemplified by the individual confrontation with life. As Weber (1919a: 140) argues, in previous eras it was possible for people to feel they had attained a pinnacle of cultural achievement and found answers to fundamental questions. In the modern age, however, meanings proliferate and change with such rapidity that it is impossible to feel assured that one's life has any fundamental worth. How, then, do people 'go on' in life? How do they establish ethical standards that inform and guide their actions as meaningful? How, in

Weber's terms, can people construct a personality that enables them to retain their humanity?

In seeking answers to these questions, Weber makes two distinctions related to his ethic of personality. The first distinguishes a 'heroic ethic' from the average ethic or the 'ethic of the mean', and recognises that the simple opposition between coherent personality and the 'given nature' of an individual is inadequate:

> All systems of ethics, no matter what their substantive content, can be divided into two main groups. There is the "heroic" ethic, which imposes on men demands of principle to which they are generally *not* able to do justice, except at the high points of their lives, but which serve as signposts pointing the way for man's endless striving. Or there is the "ethic of the mean", which is content to accept man's everyday "nature" as setting a maximum for the demands which can be made. (Weber 1978: 385–6)[15]

The second distinction contrasts an 'ethic of responsibility' with an 'ethic of ultimate ends'. All ethical conduct is informed by one of these two 'irreconcilably opposed maxims' (Weber 1919b: 120). The ethic of ultimate ends is concerned only with the righteousness of action in relation to some fundamental value (in religious terms, for example, this might be manifest in the maxim 'The Christian does rightly and leaves the results with the Lord'), but the ethic of responsibility necessitates that one contemplates the foreseeable results of one's action (ibid.).

The emphasis Weber places on the erosion of fundamental values in the modern world makes him unable to formally prioritise an ethic of responsibility over an ethic of ultimate ends. As Weber elaborates, while the follower of the ethic of ultimate ends may feel 'responsible' only 'for seeing to it that the flame of pure intentions is not quenched', it is not possible to conclude with certainty that 'the ethically good purpose "justifies" the ethically dangerous means and ramifications' (Weber 1919b: 121). The ethic of responsibility, in contrast, may weigh the consequences of alternate courses of action, but faces the danger of doubt, uncertainty and, ultimately, inactivity and a passionless stance on issues which individuals should perceive as involving matters of fundamental value (see also Weber 1919b: 126). Despite being unable to adjudicate formally between these competing ethics, Weber suggests that the heroic personality is able to combine them into a judicious mixture and, after what can be an agonising engagement with reality, take a decisive stand. In this respect, an ethic of ultimate ends and an ethic of responsibility are not *absolute contrasts* but necessary *supplements* (Weber 1919b: 127).[16]

This vision of human heroism provides the context for optimistic evaluations of Weber's work that suggest he highlights the possibility of a re-enchantment of modernity in which 'exemplary heroism, courage and integrity are still possible' (Kontos 1994: 236). Kontos suggests that Weber views the process of becoming human as implicated in the 'agonising and exhilarating' *process* of human choice, but Weber was less sanguine about the fate awaiting the average individual. Modernity was not characterised by situations in which the 'soul vibrates', but 'by rationalisation and intellectualisation and, above all, by the "disenchantment of the world"', a landscape that makes it particularly difficult for people to 'measure up to workaday existence' (Weber 1919a: 149, 154–5).

This vision culminates with the intellectually agonised heroic individual desperately struggling to live a life guided by a rational pursuit of ultimate values. But what of the charismatic breakthroughs Weber hoped for, and what of society? Weber (1968: 243) appears to have given up realistic hope for the return of affectively based 'charismatic communities' that theorists like Maffesoli (1996) and Meštrović (1994) would, at the close of the century, place as central to their respective theories of communality and conflict. Weber does identify love and eroticism as offering a form of charismatic protection from the levelling effects of rationalisation (Weber 1915: 347). It remains the case, however, that other emotionally based forms of sociability are usually evaluated as dangerous or immature flights from reality. Society itself, indeed, ultimately possesses a questionable ontology in Weber's writings. It is not simply that associations have replaced communities, but that society has been replaced by an 'iron cage' of economic rationalism without the inherent and self-destructive contradictions Marx attributed to them and without the effervescent foundations that Durkheim attributed to social orders. Individuals are left free to construct meanings but, like Weber himself, are liable to have a nervous breakdown in the process.

5. Concluding comments

Weber's vision of sociology bears the imprint of the discipline's engagement with the Enlightenment and the Counter-Enlightenment. While the former is evident in his loss of faith in religion, and in his concern to chart scientifically the advance of reason, the latter features in his recognition of the limits of scientific explanation and the impact on human life of the disenchantment of the world. The core features of his analysis of a bureaucratised world of rational capitalism were based on tendencies within the Germany of his day (Albrow 1970), while the pessimism evident in his writings is developed through a series of paradoxes we have made central to this chapter.

First, Weber associates the development of rationalisation with the systematisation of ideas but argued that once the process reached a certain stage it erodes meaning, marginalises charisma and ossifies social life. Indeed, Weber (1968: 263) argued that the link between charismatic leadership and rationalisation can be immediate, and identified instances in which the 'strictest type of bureaucracy' issued 'directly from a charismatic movement'. Second, while Weber argued that rational action is initially meaningful action, he emphasised that it is vulnerable to a loss of meaning if it becomes habituated in people's conduct or if the instrumental means of action assumes priority over the ends to be pursued. Creative individuals ultimately construct a world in which voluntaristic action becomes almost impossible. Third, Weber identifies Protestantism as a medium of ethical rational action that facilitates the emergence of a rational capitalist system that, in the end, is no longer in need of meaningful action or a religious ethic for its continuation. For Weber, the rationalising effects of ascetic Protestantism were both the basis of modern civilisation and a denial of many of the capacities that make us human (Shils 1965; Turner 1991a).[17]

These paradoxes provide the context for Weber's analysis of personality. The problems of personal coherence and meaningful existence in a world divided into various life-spheres, with their own incommensurate rules and norms, permeate Weber's sociology. Values may proliferate, but the means of arbitrating between them, or of evaluating their fundamental worth, disappear. This situation is reinforced by a culture 'that is rationally organised for a vocational, workaday life', that robs people of emotional warmth and promotes 'the world dominion of unbrotherliness' (Weber 1915: 357). Only heroic individuals are able to survive as bearers of personal integrity. They have arrived at value-judgments after exceptional deliberation, and have forged their inner and outer lives in patterns consistent with these choices. Furthermore, they have accomplished this personality without the comfort of those 'social norms' that Parsons was later to posit as an integral component of social systems transmitted to successive generations through routinised patterns of socialisation (Parsons 1951).

Weber's work is not without problems, as we have made clear, and Alvin Gouldner (1955) captures the heart of much anti-Weberian sentiment when he refers to the 'metaphysical pathos' underpinning his vision of a world characterised by rational bureaucracies. Nevertheless, Weber continues to exert enormous influence on contemporary sociology. Bryan Turner (1991a: xxvii), for example, connects Weber to an important tradition within the discipline by viewing him as 'a conservative critic of the life orders of capitalism'. These concerns have been developed in various directions by analysts of the 'emptiness' of a mass culture and commodified knowledge that is unable to transcend the present and leaves individuals bereft of a 'moral ethic' (e.g. Bell 1979; Lasch 1979).

Another source of Weber's influence can be traced to the tension between 'formal' rationality and 'substantive' irrationality. Loewith (1982), for example, argues that the irrational outcomes of rational action analysed by Weber characterise all modern culture, one that no longer bears any relation to the sensory needs of those responsible for its emergence (see also Mills 1970: 11). Wallerstein (1996) concludes that social science must engage with a moral politics that grasps this paradox. The contradiction Weber highlighted between rational action and human life and values also forms the starting point for many contemporary theories of 'risk society', and the chronic reflexivity characteristic of 'high modern' life (Beck 1992; Giddens 1991).

Other theorists have been influenced by Weber's view of personality and have suggested that contemporary individuals are dominated by a subservient 'other directedness' (Riesman 1950), a 'happy consciousness' (Marcuse 1964), a 'happy face' (Baudrillard 1993), and a 'postemotionalism' (Meštrović 1997) associated with the loss of critical thought. Weber's themes of cultural fracture, the decentring of the self and the disappearance of society have, furthermore, anticipated the work of postmodernists (Lassman and Velody 1989).

Weber's work has also been engaged with creatively by those who disagree with his analysis of modernity, especially by those who oppose his pessimism about the fate of the human condition in modern society. We have seen how Weber associated human freedom with rationally chosen action, and judged affectual and traditional action as hovering on the borders of instinctive, meaningless behaviour. Despite his frequent statements about the dominance of rationality, however, Weber also argues that his conception of rational action is not a conception of *typically* human action (Weber 1968: 21–2). If most action does *not* match these rational standards, though, traditional and affectual forms of behaviour can be seen as providing the possibility of a return of charisma and have been evaluated by critics of Weber in a more positive light. Affectual forms of behaviour are, for example, implicit within Bologh's (1990) 'ethic of sociability' which also recalls Simmel's (1910) work on the egalitarian, playful and reciprocal features of sociality which provide for the possibility of a transcendental affirmation of life.[18]

Weber provided sociology with a bleak and enormously influential view of the fate of the individual in a modern world characterised by the piercing of collective meanings, the loss of collective energies and the absence of shared morals. The twentieth century had not witnessed its last attempt to rescue a sense of the values that bound people together, however, and we now examine how the writings of Weber and others were reinterpreted within one of the most influential sociological syntheses ever constructed.

Notes

1. This potential for rationalisation to produce conflict is central to Collins's (1986a, b) view of Weber as a conflict theorist.

2. Kalberg (1980) suggests that four types of rationality are manifest in Weber's analysis of various types of rationalising processes, and that he charts the advance of practical, theoretical and formal rationality over substantive rationality. *Practical rationality* proceeds on the basis of an acceptance of given realities and involves calculating the most efficient means of realizing an individual's pragmatic interests. *Theoretical rationality* involves 'a conscious mastery of reality through the construction of increasingly precise abstract concepts' (Kalberg 1980: 1152). *Formal rationality* involves efficient action similar to practical rationality, but justifies this action with reference to rules applied universally without reference to individual personalities. In this respect, the modern bureaucracy exemplifies formal rationality. *Substantive rationality* involves the ordering of actions according to general values.

3. Weber uses the term 'ideal types', taken from debates of the time, to signify his method of abstracting from reality particularly relevant features of social life into logically precise simplifications of the world that can assist sociological understanding (Kasler 1988: 180–4). Rejecting the idea that it is possible to obtain absolute, universal knowledge, Weber (1949) recognises that ideal types are one-sided accentuations that assist the sociologist in depicting, comparing and evaluating social phenomena.

4. Domination is a special case of power (the probability that an actor 'will be in a position to carry out his own will despite resistance'), but is concerned with commands that are accepted by people who remain formally free. While Weber (1968: 53, 941–3) identifies a form of domination resulting from a 'constellation of interests' such as provided by monopoly control of resources in the free market place, he is most concerned with domination by virtue of legitimate authority (where power to command is matched by a subjectively felt duty to obey).

5. Weber's analysis of different types of authority assumes that each of these forms of rule are legitimate. A frequent criticism made of this analysis is that it provides no basis for examining *illegitimate* forms of domination.

6. First, while the leader and disciples of 'charismatic communities' usually want to extend their influence and transmit it to the next generation, this 'inescapably channels charisma into the direction of legal regulation and tradition' (Weber 1968: 1123, 265–6). Second, charisma exhibits an antipathy to, yet is unable to resist, routinised economic considerations. Charismatic leadership represents a

'calling', yet the establishment of financial structures directed towards its continuation make it vulnerable to ossifying into the structures of political office (Weber 1968: 244–5). Third, pressures for survival may lead to the systematic stratification of charisma as a commodity dispensed by some in return for the support of others (Weber 1968: 458). As Turner (1996a: 116) puts it, this can result in an 'economy of charisma' ready to be assimilated into the routines of daily life. Each of these pressures is related to the 'striving for security' by charismatic movements, yet Weber also identified the 'logic of ideas' as a further source of routinisation. Every charismatically based explanation of the world 'reaches beyond itself', requiring clarification and extension, and provides space for the development of systematised theories and analyses (Tenbruck 1980: 339).

7. So too did other factors. For example, the attempts of western European patrimonial powers to secure and extend their rule led to the centralisation and formalisation of law and administration.

8. Patrimonial administration was subject to the whims of a ruler who resisted incursions on their own authority other than those laid down by sacred tradition. Rule was exercised through a group of notables whose loyalty was secured through the granting of rights to 'own' offices which could be sold on to others. Business was conducted via personal encounter and oral communication, rather than impersonal documents, and by administrative officers who were part of the ruler's household (Bendix 1959: 424).

9. Weber advocated a 'plebiscitarian leader-democracy', an anti-authoritarian version of charismatic rule formally deriving its legitimacy from the will of the governed.

10. Social action is meaningful when oriented toward the behaviour of others. It does not, therefore, include accidents between people, action oriented solely toward inanimate objects, or the mechanical effect of a crowd on individual behaviour, but can include 'both failure to act and passive acquiescence' as long as these are 'oriented to the past, present, or expected future behaviour of others' (Weber 1968: 22). In empathising with the meaning of action, Weber (1968: 8–9) identifies two kinds of 'verstehen': direct observational understanding (*aktuelles Verstehen*), and explanatory understanding (*eklarendes Verstehen*).

11. Weber identifies two types of causation, just as he identifies two types of 'verstehen'. Adequate causation refers to a context in which any one of a number of factors may have been finally responsible for an event: the absence of a single factor would not have led to a different outcome. Chance causation, in contrast, refers to a situation in which one factor was of decisive importance for the occurrence of a particular event.

12. It also helps explain his use of the 'ideal type' in that these abstractions helped Weber ascertain those factors that might be causally responsible for the emergence of a social phenomenon. Gerth and Mills (1948), for example, summarise how Weber's use of ideal types was linked to a comparative method in his causal explanation of the rise of capitalism in the Occident. Weber examined various civilisations, and although capitalist beginnings could be observed in them, capitalism in the Western sense did not emerge. By formulating ideal types of the major factors which characterised these civilisations, Weber constructed a causal analysis which sought to uncover the necessary and sufficient conditions of capitalism (Gerth and Mills 1948: 61).

13. It is also mirrored in the fact that while Weber proposed a 'value free sociology of social action' in which the establishment of empirical facts should be kept separate from value assessments of these facts (an assessment which sociology was not qualified to make) (Parsons 1971b; Kasler 1988: 184–96), he displayed in his substantive writings a passionate concern with the fate of human personality in capitalism.

14. Simmel similarly identified the proliferation of cultural objects as a particular problem for modern people who could neither absorb the totality of culture nor be sure that what they had absorbed was worthwhile. In this context, individuals could be reduced to a 'mere cog' in the 'vast overwhelming organisation of things' and denuded of all sense of 'progress, spirituality and value' (Simmel 1903a: 337).

15. While Weber softened this opposition further, recognising a *gradation* from average to heroic ethics and the development of 'lesser' personalities operating *within* a particular life-order such as art (see Marianne Weber 1975: 378; Featherstone 1995: 63), his vision of the highest form of personality involved the individual constantly striving for heroic ethics.

16. Weber adapts this view in his normative assessment of the qualities that are decisive for a politician: 'passion, a feeling of responsibility, and a sense of proportion. This is the decisive psychological

quality of the politician: his ability to let realities work upon him with inner concentration and calmness. Hence his *distance* to things and men' (Weber 1919b: 115).

17. This is a prominent example of Weber's 'structuralist' approach towards explanation and provides a key instance of what has been referred to as the 'vanishing mediator' in his work (Jameson 1973; Turner 1996a). Furthermore, Weber's analysis of rationalisation is foreshadowed in Nietzsche's (1872) judgment that the ascetic ideal had led to a denigration of human sensuality and meaning, and a triumph of reactive over active forces (Turner 1991a). Weber, like Nietzsche, argued that 'few succeed in becoming creators of their personalities ... most remain mere creatures, mired in the meaningless flux of the merely natural' (Brubacker 1984: 98). Weber's view of the heroic individual personality, then, appears to have been influenced by the Nietzschean ideal of the 'highest exemplars' of the human species who refuse the herd mentality in order to pursue the forces of life through the 'will to power'. Yet Weber's personality is associated with a far wider set of values (Nietzsche's 'affirmation of life' is just one path for the individual; Macrae 1974: 54) and exhibits a commitment to the *cognitively directed* construction of identity in contrast to Nietzsche's endorsement of the sensual forces of life.

18. Bologh (1990) also rejects Weber's 'masculine imagery', suggesting that he constructs a view of a heroic man distancing himself from his body, his sensuality, his relationships and the temptations of the world around him. Portis (1973) and Featherstone (1995: 59) have developed this distinction by suggesting that while 'the heroic life is the sphere of danger, violence and the courting of risk', everyday life is 'the sphere of women, reproduction and care'.

6

NORMATIVE SOCIOLOGY

1. Introduction

Talcott Parsons's immense influence on twentieth-century sociology rests on his bold characterisation of modernity as a normative social system in which superficially divided social groups are united by shared values. His conception of society as a social system constituted by ordered, integrated, and subjectively meaningful roles, is notable for three main reasons. First, although, at the time Parsons was writing, secularisation was a generally accepted part of sociological visions of modernity, he drew attention to the religious origins of the values that underpin even the most 'advanced' social orders. Second, and following from this, Parsons did not suggest that charismatic leaders or heroic struggle were required to impart meaning to what Weber had characterised as a modern order of 'mechanised petrification'. Instead, he built on Durkheim's concern with the enduring significance of religion for social and moral order, and engaged critically with Weber's vision of the religious origins of modern capitalism, by conceptualising modernity as a *normative* system. Parsons argued that shared values and differentiated norms motivated all full members of a social system, and served to link individuals to the structure of a society. Third, Parsons suggested that the classical theorists had arrived at a convergence in their pursuit of the sociological ambition. They had done this by constructing a series of compatible visions of how voluntaristic action was associated with normative order.

The sociological importance Parsons (1937: 768) attributed to values and norms was such that he defined the discipline as 'the science which attempts to develop an analytical theory of social action systems insofar as these systems can be understood in terms of the property of common value integration'. Consequently, Parsons's response to concerns about the normative cohesion and possible 'crisis' of modernity was unambivalent. For him, what might look like crisis was merely a set of 'social strains' deriving from the adaptation of an evolving social system to its environment. While recognising that a fully integrated social system was an ideal, he judged suggestions of the absence of order, feared by the founders of the discipline, to be fantastic.

Parsons developed the view that normative action (action guided by norms) produces order through his overriding concern with what he referred to as the 'system of action'. This most general level of analysis consisted for Parsons (1971a) of four subsystems: the cultural, personality, biological, and social systems.[1] Each of these has its own significance, but the cultural subsystem (that which is high in information) is of most importance to Parsons. In his view, it steers, and ultimately controls, the bodily organism (that which is high in energy), as well as the personality and the social system, towards ordered outcomes. In so doing, the cultural sphere develops in Parsons's work to become the environment in which all action occurs and not simply a restricted subsystem.

Before exploring how Parsons's work can be analysed as offering *the* theory of normative social order, however, we need to distinguish his view of knowledge and his theory of the social system from his essays on modern societies. Parsons uses the term 'analytical realism' to describe his epistemology. This suggests, following what Whitehead (1925) calls the 'fallacy of misplaced concreteness', that while sociological explanations may prove scientifically adequate, they are abstractions not to be confused with reality. In one sense, then, Parsons's theory of the social system was simply an *analytical* construct of order that facilitated the examination of concrete societies (Parsons and Shils 1962: 204; Parsons 1964: 218). Parsons's recognition of the diverse and contingent factors contributing to social order was, however, compromised by his metaphysical conviction that a fully comprehensive theoretical order has its counterpart in reality (Schwanenberg 1971: 573). This is reflected in his substantive essays (especially those on American society) that mirror his analytical focus on order. In contrast to a long line of European theorists, who displayed nostalgia towards *Gemeinschaft* communities, Parsons was committed to exploring the existence of, and the positive opportunities provided by, *modern* social orders (Robertson and Turner 1991).

Parsons's view of the relationship between action, norms, values, and social order developed throughout his life. His first major study, *The Structure of Social Action* (1937), focused on *action* via a criticism of economistic solutions to the Hobbesian 'problem of order' that characterised human behaviour as the rational pursuit of self-interest. Parsons argued that such explanations could not account for order for three reasons: first, force and fraud could be 'rational' means of achieving gain yet hardly assisted social harmony; second, as Durkheim had argued, the idea of a 'contract' leaves unexplained people's pre-contractual dispositions to enter into formal agreements; and third, economistic explanations rely on 'residual categories' to explain social equilibrium (*ad hoc* categories emanating from outside the core framework of a theory). In opposing these rationalistic explanations, Parsons suggested that the founding figures of sociology converged in their conviction that adherence to the basic *values* of a society is not only necessary for consensual order but is an observable social reality, and argued that the 'state of nature' addressed by Hobbes is a theoretical artefact 'never reached by any real society' (Parsons and Shils 1962: 204). Underpinning the 'flux' of modernity subsists an enduring set of integrating values, the most deeply embedded and slowly changing of all categories of the social structure, that help order emerge from multiple individual acts. In the case of the United States, indeed, Parsons (1991: 41) perceived 'a basic stability of fundamental values from colonial times to the present'.

His later work, *The Social System* (1951), shifted attention from action to the *systems* in which action occurred. When analysing *society* as a system, Parsons (1969: 11) was concerned with a 'patterned normative order through which the life of a population is collectively organised', and which attains a high level of self-sufficiency in relation to its environment. All social systems, Parsons suggested, were marked by a structure whose survival depended on fulfilling the functions of *Adaptation* to the external environment, setting and achieving *Goals* in that environment, accomplishing the internal *Integration* of the system's various elements, and maintaining the *Latent* processes motivating people to maintain the value patterns of a social order. It is this 'AGIL' formulation that became associated with the term 'structural functionalism': the structural perspective examining the relatively stable patterned relationships of roles within a system, and the functional perspective examining the conditions needing to be fulfilled for the system to be a 'going concern' (Parsons 1964: 214–19).

This shift from action to structure is often held to be contradictory. Nevertheless, Parsons's concern to integrate positivist and idealist approaches to action, his consistency in analysing action as a *system*, and his commitment to the importance of common values for understanding both the parts of action and the structures and functional needs of action systems, has contributed to a view of his work as a relatively coherent whole. Cultural values, in particular, were of enduring importance to Parsons. They infused social roles and personalities, and helped integrate, and ultimately steer, the social system (Parsons 1978).

In assessments of his contemporary importance, Parsons is frequently depicted as a sociological dinosaur, yet he is responsible for the most ambitious synthesis of modern sociology and has been hailed as 'setting the scene' for all that followed in the twentieth century (Scott 1995). Sociologists concerned with socialisation, social roles, organisations, and social differentiation, work within traditions shaped by Parsons. Furthermore, there was a revival of interest in his work in the 1980s under the 'banner' of neo-functionalism (Alexander 1998), and even his sternest critics suggest that 'no theory of society can be taken seriously today if it does not … situate itself with respect to Parsons' (Habermas 1981b). Parsons's focus on normative orders also provides us with a challenge to postmodern assertions that modernity promotes the absence of such collectivities. While theorists like Lemert (1998) and Meštrović (1997) identify an absence of consensual social orders in the contemporary world, Parsons urges sociologists to look beneath the complex patterns of differentiation and social organisations that characterise modern societies, and to uncover those pre-contractual forms of moral consensus that still bind individuals into collectives.

This chapter progresses as follows. Section 2 examines the unit idea of Parsons's work, *value systems*, by tracing the historical development of the American value system. Section 3 focuses on Parsons's view of the elementary form of social life. *Normative action* is neither a purely cognitive nor a wholly emotional form of action. It stands Janus-faced to the effervescence motivating Durkheim's collective subjects and the rational engagements with the world characteristic of Weber's individuals. For Parsons, action is mediated through processes of *socialisation* that instil into individuals the norms that motivate them to act in relation to particular ends. This normative shaping of action results in *ordered outcomes* because of the contribution it makes to the structural parts of the social system, such as the maintenance of social roles. Section 4 then focuses on the tensions between Parsons's writings on social action and social systems, and analyses his final attempt to achieve a resolution of this action-system relationship through the employment of cybernetics theory (the science of systems). This suggests that both individual action and social systems operate within a wider cultural environment shaped by values that are ultimately religious in origin. In concluding, we look at the significance of Parsons's work for contemporary approaches to the sociological ambition.

2. Value systems

Value systems are the most deep-rooted, generalised expression of the normative patterns of a culture. They constitute the principles from which less general norms and expectations can be applied and institutionalised within a social system. The American Constitution, for example, incorporates an 'assertion of value commitments', but also includes many derivative, lower level norms concerning the conduct of government in relation to civil society dealt with by the legislature (Parsons 1969: 21, 481; 1991: 39). Parsons further distinguishes between cultural, social and personal value systems: a cultural value system addresses issues of 'ultimate concern' confronting all societies and individuals; a social value system defines 'a desirable state or direction for a society'; and a personal value system defines this direction for an individual' (Parsons 1991: 44).

In examining the Western *cultural value system*, Parsons offers his own particular interpretation of Weber's and Durkheim's writings on the non-rational value foundations of modern society. Instead of depicting a post-religious, meaningless world, for example, Weber is interpreted as revealing how apparently 'secular' values possess religious foundations, and how freedom from tradition is replaced by individuals' choosing between culturally prescribed alternatives. Instead of being concerned with the effervescent foundations of society, Durkheim is interpreted as analysing the values underpinning collective orders. Parsons also insists that even if Durkheim and others have demonstrated the social significance of emotions, these somatic responses are subordinate to cognitive values. Emotions are 'necessarily integrated with cognitive patterns; for without them there could be no co-ordination of action in a coherently structured social system' (Parsons 1978: 54–9, 171, 221–5, 241, 320; 1991: 54; 1964: 209).

Religion occupies a prime place in the co-ordination of action through values. Disagreeing emphatically with the contention that 'the Protestant Ethic is dead' Parsons analyses Christian values as informing the cultural value system of modern America. He is not talking about church membership, nor even about the commitment of individuals to a particular religious expression, but suggesting that the Protestant heritage of America continues to provide a 'pre-contractual' foundation for the development of modern life in the sense that its 'secular' orders still approximate to the normative models provided by religion (Parsons 1978: 168, 240).

Parsons also discusses the role of religion in terms of the *social value system*, suggesting that Protestantism continues to normatively pattern the direction of society through providing seemingly secular roles with meaning and purpose. Ascetic Protestantism, in particular, imbued people with 'a strong sense of responsibility for achievements in this-worldly callings, the obverse of which was the ambition to "succeed"' (Parsons 1978: 202–3). This pursuit of success did not support 'anarchic individualism', but *institutionalised individualism* that encouraged people to contribute 'to the building of the holy community on Earth'. The religious foundations of secular values, in short, resulted in a 'worldly instrumental activism' at the social level dedicated to improving the capacity and productivity of the social system (Parsons 1991: 53). Parsons suggests that the provision of education and health systems, and even the ideal of 'equal opportunities', are valued for these reasons.

Finally, at the level of *personal value systems*, Parsons suggests Protestantism has made worldly activity the basis of individual moral standing. Human action is treated not as a search for individual fulfilment, but instrumentally in relation to a task imposed from outside. Similarly, individual freedom is valued not for its own sake, but because it became a necessary condition of acting responsibly in relation to cultural values (Parsons 1978: 54, 59; 1991: 54). In Durkheim's terms, what Parsons is talking about is the individual internalisation of the 'conscience collective', the normative patterning of individual decisions and choices through the incorporation of collective values into the personal identities of individuals. Without this incorporation, which in Weber's terms can also be referred to as a 'calling', Parsons (1978: 320) holds that the 'instrumental apparatus of modern society' could not function.

The evolution of the American value system

Parsons suggests that while Puritanism has stimulated a worldly instrumental activism at the social and individual levels, the American value system has undergone further evolution since the 1960s. The development of Calvinist values initially produced a situation in America whereby certain groups, such as the Jews and Catholics, were only 'tolerated negatively' and were deprived of membership of the 'full social community' (Parsons 1966a: 132). As the twentieth century progressed, Parsons suggests the American value system has operated at a higher level of generality and inclusion at the social level, but has also undergone a privatisation at the personal level. Both trends have resulted in the desire for, and in many respects the achievement of, greater social inclusion and tolerance (see Herberg 1956).

At the social level, religious affiliation has been reconciled with secular citizenship and freedom of opportunity, and the American community has become an ecumenical Judaeo-Christian community (Parsons 1978: 203). Parsons cites a number of reasons for this, including American revulsion at the Nazi policy of genocide toward the Jews during the Second World War, and the national mourning following the assassination of the first Catholic President, John F. Kennedy. These events mitigated situations in which Jews had served as 'the prototype of "foreignness" in the sense that they are diffusely attached to a community separate from, and alien to, the American', and in which Catholics had suffered from the image of their Church as 'a kind of state within a state' (Parsons 1969: 269–71).

If the religious values underpinning the American social value system have become more generalised, Parsons also observes a privatisation of religion at the *personal* level as society becomes more differentiated and specialised. These tendencies are complementary rather than contradictory, and have their most important link in what Parsons terms 'conscience': the individual manifestation of what Bellah (1967) calls 'civic religion'. Conscience is an individual's definition of their 'moral obligations in this life', and is a 'moral currency' involving trust in a shared commitment to such abstract, fundamental commitments as 'freedom, with its implication of toleration, justice, certain basic equalities of status, high achievement, [and] responsibility not only for others, but in collective affairs' (Parsons 1966a: 136).

This picture may be interpreted as supporting those who accuse Parsons of possessing an 'over-socialised' view of the individual and an over-integrated model of society (Wrong 1961; Dawe 1978), but his analysis of the translation of cultural values into the social system identifies resistances to these developments manifest in such episodes as McCarthyism (Parsons 1969). Parsons refers to these 'social strains' as deriving from America's altered global position following the Second World War and the Korean War. By placing national issues of 'adjustment' and 'disturbance' in their international contexts, he anticipates contemporary sociological concerns with globalisation. Parsons raises the issue of Islam's importance to the world as a whole, and points to the tensions likely to arise in the relationship between modernisation and differentiation, and the traditional role of religion in Islamic societies. Within America, he views the treatment of Afro-Americans and other 'racial' minorities as major social strains and a problem for the 'inclusiveness' of the American value system, and recognises the importance of arguments viewing the situation of 'racial minorities' in the USA as one of American imperialism (Parsons 1969: 276–81).

While recognising such strains, Parsons did not go along with those critics of American society dominant in the 1960s. He opposed theorists of 'mass culture' who argued that cultural standards had declined and that people were being dislodged from meaningful social ties and made vulnerable to authoritarianism. Instead, Parsons (1969: 250) suggested that increases in communication systems could result in 'a proportionately greater spread of higher levels of culture'. Parsons was equally critical of C. Wright Mills's (1956) analysis of 'the power elite'. First, he suggested Mills neglected the balances built into American politics, and the institutionalised character of individualism in the modern world; second, he ignored the fact that in an advanced, differentiated society 'a relatively well-defined elite ... should be expected to develop in the business world'; and third, he held a 'zero-sum' conception of power that ignored elite contributions to raising the overall capacity of the social system (Parsons 1969: 193). Nevertheless, Parsons saw neither radical Left programmes nor capitalism as 'the answer' to problems of societal capacity and adaptation. He focused instead on the similarities of capitalism and communism, particularly in terms of their common 'religious origins', on how cold-war conflict might proceed in a legitimised framework, and on how both systems faced pressures which might lead to a common 'third type' of world system (Parsons 1969: 292–310; 1979; Nielson 1991).

Values and medical instrumentalism

Parsons's discussion of the religious bases of value systems has been accused of being empirically meaningless (Mills 1970), but his essay on the 'Gift of Life' illustrates how religious values underpin many modern 'ethical complexes'. He notes that police activity serves to protect life, that education aims to develop individual 'gifts', and even that the regulation of automobile traffic can be assessed in terms of the protection of life. Parsons is, though, particularly interested in the religious underpinnings of medical instrumental rationality.

Parsons suggests medical instrumentalism is associated with the Christian notion of life as a gift from God: a 'gift' which became central to the development of American civil religion. As Bellah (1967) argues, after the 'tremendous national trauma of the Civil War and its culminating symbolic event, the assassination of Lincoln, a new note of martyrdom and sacrifice entered into the symbolisation of the community, which brought the civil religion nearer to Christian patterns, in that Lincoln was frequently conceived of as having died that the nation might live' (Parsons 1978: 220; Bellah 1967). Parsons further suggests this 'gift of life' has come to form the basis for the ethical patterning of professionalism. This is discussed through the apparently secular 'protection' of life that 'involves practical efforts to control the causes of unnecessary and premature death' (Parsons 1978: 279). According to Parsons, the grief engendered by 'early' deaths involving the termination of a promising career is directly related to the religious concern of a 'calling' cut short.

Medical instrumentalism is frequently criticised by contemporary sociologists (who suggest doctors take insufficient notice of the emotional issues associated with care), but Parsons views this instrumentalism as dependent on the 'existence of congruent religious orientations in the broader society'. The exclusion of 'emotional reactions' from medics acting in the face of death 'add to the extent to which *underlying* commitments must be profoundly *serious*, in the sense of Durkheim's definition of religion as belonging to "the serious life"' (Parsons 1978: 278, 280). Thus, although many people have a tendency to make a sharp distinction between the modern 'scientific' and the 'mystical' approaches towards life, illness, and death, this misconceives the extent to which the two are related.

3. The elementary forms of social and moral life

We have discussed how value systems are central to Parsons's theoretical and substantive writings, but in order to understand his conception of the elementary form of social life, which is implicit in his work, we have to consider how common values become deployed in action. Normative action is channelled through the medium of socialisation processes and results, in the maintenance of social roles, ordered through what Parsons refers to as 'pattern variables', and an overarching normative social order.

Normative action

Parsons (1968: 14) examines action as 'a system of the behaviour of living organisms', 'organised – and hence controlled – in relation to systems of cultural meaning at the symbolic level'. This is quite different from philosophical conceptions of action as the expression of 'free will' (which is why his term the '*voluntarist* theory of action' is somewhat misleading). Instead, action involves the connection of the actor to cultural values through *social norms*.

Parsons uses the term 'unit act' to describe his deconstruction of action into its constituent parts. The unit act involves an actor, with a specified goal or end, who employs the means perceived to be available, within the constraints of the situation or conditions they are in, but who also acts with reference to certain social norms in order to achieve their end (Parsons 1937: 44). The unit act is not directed predominantly towards 'the physiological processes internal to the organism but rather to the organisation of an actor's orientation to a situation ... Action has an orientation when it is guided by the *meaning* which the actor attaches to it in its relationship to his goals' (Parsons and Shils 1962: 4, emphasis added). Parsons acknowledges that individuals possesses biologically-driven needs, but points out that these can usually be satisfied in various ways with a variety of objects. When individuals approach these variations as meaningful, and do not just react to them, they must employ some *evaluative criteria* for deciding between them. This evaluation rests on 'cognitive standards of truthfulness, appreciative standards of appropriateness, or moral standards of rightness' (Parsons and Shils 1962: 5), and it is these standards that are shaped by the norms of a society.

Moving from normative action to normative *interaction*, Parsons views the most basic social system as maintained on the basis of a 'complementarity of expectations' between 'ego' and 'alter'. The actions of each person in a dyadic encounter are oriented in part to the expectations of the other, and the presence of this orientation implies the existence of elementary norms (e.g. of trust) and the possibility of building further norms of interaction. When normative expectations become accepted by enough people across enough chains of interaction, they become emergent structures institutionalised into roles.

This account of action and interaction presupposes at the heart of Parsons's scheme a competent and cognitively skilful actor, yet this is not an actor driven by abstract reason or 'rationality'. As noted previously, norms stand Janus-faced to the passionate effervescence motivating Durkheim's subjects and Weber's cognitively driven rational individuals. Parsons's writings on personality, for example, seek to explain the complex sources of information and energy that dispose people to act in relation to norms, but it is the *information high* personality that ultimately exercises control over the *energy high* organism. Drawing on Freud, Parsons views personality as an emergent system appearing at the conflict-ridden meeting place of 'motivation and energy, the roots of which are ultimately biological' and 'the values and norms of the socio-cultural environment' (Parsons 1961: 106). With the resolution of psychic crises, such as the Oedipal complex, infant levels of bodily and emotional dependency are overcome. As development reaches the stage when 'autonomous' action becomes possible, people assume the capacity to be motivated by social norms rather than drives. The actor may not be exclusively cognitively driven, then, but it is information, symbols, and codes that steer action. Even erotic impulses become transformed into cultural signs in Parsons's (1951: 138–9) suggestion that the 'superego' dominates the 'id' and 'ego'.

Socialisation as the medium of action

Having established that individuals have the *capacity* to act in relation to norms, it remains to be seen how people are actually motivated to engage in normative action, and how normative action results in ordered outcomes. In this respect, socialisation is a crucial medium of action. It is through socialisation that norms come to shape the identities of individuals and motivate them to act in specific ways. Socialisation, furthermore, helps solve 'the fundamental problem which arises from the interaction of two or more actors': the impossibility of providing enough objects and services to satisfy every actor (Parsons and Shils 1962: 197).

Parsons (1978: 332) argues that what distinguishes humans from animals is the fact that humans use symbols, particularly linguistic ones, to communicate with others and to understand themselves. This ability to comprehend and use symbols is not born with the human organism, but develops in the socialisation process. Here, the social actor is immersed in learning patterns of relationships, of language, and of the rules orientating individual action to the environment. Agents of socialisation, such as teachers, tend to have acquired a high level of internalisation of a culture's general normative characteristics in order to assist the less socialised, such as children, to become adept at the use of symbols and to form personalities in accordance with the dominant social and cultural values.

Socialisation usually proceeds, in modern industrial societies, with the mother–infant dyad, the family, the school, the peer group and the workplace. At each stage, the actor is expected to assume a new role within a collectivity and to become motivated less by the sensual needs of the body and more by norms derived from the cultural value system. As Parsons (1968: 18) continues, socialisation means that 'The child becomes oriented to the wishes which embody for him the values of the adult, and his viscerogenic needs become culturally organised needs'. The embodied being develops a personality that steers, rather than is steered by, the 'drives' of the organism. As this occurs, external coercion is replaced by internalised control as socialisation promotes the absorption of 'the standards and ideals' of the social group as motivating forces for conduct (Parsons 1964: 230–1).

The importance of socialisation for moulding conduct is such that Parsons even views the 'affects' as a primary 'integrative medium', resulting from interaction between the social system and the personality system, rather than sensual products of the body. In his discussion of sex roles, for example, Parsons (1978: 424) suggests that while erogenous zones are components of the human organism, the development of sexual identities and roles are part of a complex pattern of socialisation that begins at birth and proceeds, through the gradual repression of infantile eroticism, to transform the human organism into the member of a social collectivity. Successful socialisation engages with this 'affective economy' of people and results in a personality that achieves 'high levels of gratification' from full participation in a social system (Parsons 1970: 860). It therefore contributes towards the maintenance of social roles that are integral to the maintenance of an overarching normative order.

Social order as the outcome of normative action

The outcome of normative action, for Parsons, is an ordered social system. Social roles, structured by 'pattern variables' reflecting the priorities of that system, are key components of this outcome. Parsons (1951, 1962) analysed social roles as functionally integrated parts of a normative social system sustained, in part, by appropriately motivated individuals. Social roles have functional significance both for the *internal relationships* within a social system (they incorporate rights and responsibilities which may provide for consensual interaction between, for example, employer and employee), and for the system's relationship with its *wider environment* (the contribution doctors make to maintaining the health of the population, for example, contributes toward economic productivity). Roles provide people with specific responsibilities in relation to the social system, they consist of the 'normative behaviour ... associated with the holding of a particular social position' (Scott 1995: 43), and they link actors as 'psychological' entities to the wider social structure.

This analysis is illustrated in his view of the school class as a socialising agent. As modern societies became increasingly differentiated, the education system played a growing role in developing within individuals 'the commitments and capacities which are essential prerequisites of their future role-performance' (Parsons 1959: 86). By emancipating the child from primary emotional attachment to the family, and facilitating the internalisation of more general societal values and norms, the school not only socialises the individual, as we discussed above, but assists in the internal integration of the social system. By differentiating pupils relative to 'ability', justifying this differentiation, and thereby channelling individuals towards future roles, the school also assists the social system in meeting its goals and adapting to its environment (Parsons, Bales et al. 1955; Parsons 1959). If this sounds unambiguously functionalist – providing an explanation based solely on the needs of a social system – those sympathetic to Parsons argue that the *contingencies* of socialisation mean that the 'functional needs' of a social system have no independent causal role in his writings, but can explain action only when 'they are taken into account in the subjective orientations of individual actors' (Scott 1995: 44).

Parsons's sensitivity to the varieties of these social roles, and the social orders to which they contribute, is illustrated by the emphasis he places on the 'pattern variables'. By separating Tönnies's *Gemeinschaft/Gesellschaft* dichotomy into a series of contrasting variables, rather than a single binary opposition, Parsons highlighted how supposedly traditional values could coexist with values associated with modernity. These variables come to form 'a peculiarly strategic focus of the whole theory of action', forming the 'most important thread of continuity' in his work, and mediating the transition of norms 'from the cultural system to that of a concrete system of action, the social system' and onto the personalities of actors (Parsons and Shils 1962: 49; Parsons 1970: 842; 1991: 53).

The pattern variables refer both to a set of fundamental choices that all actors have to make (implicitly or explicitly) before they can act, and to a series of fundamental alternatives confronting social and cultural systems. These consist of *Affectivity vs. Affective Neutrality; Self-Orientation vs. Collective Orientation; Universalism vs. Particularism; Ascription vs. Achievement;* and *Specificity vs. Diffuseness.* The best illustration of how pattern-variables structure social roles, and link the individual to the social system, is Parsons's analysis of the sick role and the doctor-patient relationship.

Given the 'worldly instrumental activism' central to American culture, being sick was, in a certain sense, being deviant. Sickness, involving withdrawal from work and an inability to fulfil 'normal' social roles, constituted a potential threat to the individual organism and the social system (Parsons 1951: 431). The sick person/doctor roles, however, are structured by pattern variables aimed at restoring the established order. While the sick role temporarily exempts an individual from normal duties, it imposes on them an obligation to seek out and co-operate with a doctor who is charged with facilitating reintegration into 'normal' life and conducting an important role of social control (Parsons 1951: 451, 477).

The pattern variables structuring this doctor's role are crucial to the doctor-patient relationship. The role needs to be *achievement* driven, as it involves the application of scientific knowledge by technically competent, trained personnel. It is characterised by *universalism*, as recruitment needs to draw on the widest possible constituency and would not be helped by nepotism, since the doctor must treat patients equally. Functionally, the role is *specific*: the doctor is a highly trained specialist who helps legitimise certain claims made on the patient (e.g. to take a particular medicine). The role is *affectively neutral*, which helps keep the doctor-patient relationship on a professional level. Finally, the doctor role has a *collective orientation* that places the interests of others over the personal interests of the doctor. This contrasts with the role of the businessman for whom a self-interested orientation towards financial gain is socially accepted (Parsons 1951: 463).

In summary, Parsons's vision of the elementary forms of social and moral life moves via a series of value homologies from the actions of individuals, to the media structuring action, to ordered outcomes. As Turner (1991b: xxix) suggests, Parsons's work can be seen 'as an attempt to develop a general sociology of values' by deriving the 'principal components of a social system from the structure of social action' via the underlying *pattern variables* they express. Cultural patterns exist both in people's minds and in the social system (Parsons 1961: 362; Rocher 1974: 35–6), and, on this basis, Parsons's work can at least be seen as possessing an internal coherence. Whether it accurately reflects the 'real world' is another question, and one that has been frequently answered negatively.

4. Action theory or systems theory?

In developing his general framework for sociology, Parsons wanted to overcome the partiality and dualism of existing approaches. He suggested that positivism emphasised material conditions at the expense of human thought, while idealism emphasised human voluntarism at the expense of the concrete circumstances contextualising social life. Parsons (1937) criticises such partial approaches by evaluating theoretical schemes in terms of their positive and negative, or 'residual' categories. While positive categories emanate from the core features of a theory, *ad hoc*, residual categories emerge to account for observations at odds with the main explanatory framework. As Holmwood (1996) notes, residual categories are significant for Parsons as their existence suggests a theory is flawed. In the case of positivistic and idealistic theories, neither can theoretically account for both human voluntarism and the material world, yet both find themselves having to employ residual categories to protect their accounts from criticism. For Parsons, this signals the need for theory reconstruction in order to turn residual categories into the affirmative categories of a truly comprehensive theory.

Parsons wanted to incorporate positivist and idealist approaches (which have come to be discussed by sociologists in terms of a structure-agency dualism) into one theory dealing with both the material contexts of action and voluntarism. The response to his attempt has been mixed. Theorists like Wrong (1961) and Sorokin (1966) argued that Parsons viewed social relations as structured according to the imperatives of the social system, and suggested that this resulted in his abandoning the voluntaristic actor and constructing an 'oversocialised' conception of the agent. Habermas (1981b) suggests that the only alternative to this criticism is to see Parsons as having constructed a Kantian 'moral imperative' whereby individuals freely adopt and dutifully follow social norms. Alexander (1984) counters this view by seeing Parsons's critics as focusing on selective aspects of his work, and by arguing that his action theory was never voluntaristic in the manner in which that term came to be understood. Instead, it was always a systems theory of action as evident in the systemic structure of the 'unit act' (Adriaansens 1980). Even Parsons's strongest supporters, however, recognise he is not always successful in combining voluntaristic human action with social order (Alexander 1984). As Holmwood (1996) notes, as soon as action is conceptualised *in relation to* an integrated system, it is difficult to maintain human voluntarism:

> Parsons began his analysis of "unit acts" with a commitment to the "openness" of human action, but this position cannot be maintained once the requirements of the 'total system of action' are addressed. Action is organised in relation to processes of the system where ends are mutually consistent. Thus, in systems which are integrated, the individual appears as the expression of structures, despite the initial perception that structures should be seen as a *product* of action. (Holmwood 1996: 71)

This lack of 'openness' or creativity of action highlights another criticism frequently levelled at Parsons's work: it cannot deal with conflict or radical social change. Parsons emphasises that his model of the social system is an ideal, never reached in practice, and discusses 'social strains', 'disturbances', and, as we have seen in the case of the 'sick role', 'deviance'. Yet these divergences from social and moral order are references to what obtains empirically and do not emanate from Parsons's analysis of the integrated social system. Having criticised others for this manoeuvre, Parsons resorts 'to residual categories ... not theoretically integrated with the positive categories of the scheme' (Holmwood 1996: 71).

To describe Parsons as a theorist of static systems would, however, be wrong. He has been accused of not possessing a *sociological* theory of social change (Haines 1987), but did construct a theory of social *evolution* that provides a fresh dimension to his view of the action-structure relationship. This theory of evolutionary change rests on an account of the heightened informational basis of modern life in which the cognitive element of human action, and of cultural values, grows increasingly important. Drawing on Norbert Wiener's (1948) study of cybernetics, Parsons's later writings on the agent and social system suggest that information in general, and 'ultimate values' in particular, become more dominant than ever in steering individual behaviour and social development.

The evolution of humans and social systems

The status of culture changes for Parsons from being an element within the social system to an overarching environment in which change takes place (Alexander 1998). The physical world and the biological organism are also environments for social systems, but act simply as constraining factors and constitute a 'unit point of reference' whose study belongs to the natural sciences or psychology (Parsons 1951: 541–2, 547–8). The cultural system, in contrast, is of most positive importance as it 'structures commitments *vis-à-vis* ultimate reality into meaningful orientations toward the rest of the environment and the systems of action, the physical world, personalities, and social systems' (Parsons 1966b: 9–10). This structuring operates, in part, because just as humans need to make sense of 'ultimate questions', so too do they need to make related sense of everyday values and goals: the tendency towards integrating these two levels of understanding 'seems to be inherent in human action' (Parsons 1964: 209).

Culture assumes this importance for Parsons as a result of an evolutionary perspective suggesting that 'strains' or 'disturbances' in the relationship between social action and the social system should lessen as each develop within a *common cultural environment*. The structure-agency relationship, in other words, cannot be analysed adequately as a dualism. Instead, actions and systems must be located in their wider, more important, relationship to culture. This has been demonstrated, for Parsons (1964: 209), by Weber's analysis of how 'variations in socially sanctioned values and goals in secular life correspond to the variations in the dominant religious philosophy of the great civilisations', but Parsons's own 'solution' to this relationship requires some elaboration.

Starting with his model of the human actor as a system, Parsons (1978: 366) shares with a number of sociologists the view that *symbolic meanings* constitute the essential dividing line between *human* being and mere organic being (e.g. Elias 1991; Lévi-Strauss 1966). This dividing line emerged when evolution made it possible for culture to become more important to human adaptation than further genetic change, and informs his view of personality (Parsons 1967a: 494–5). It resulted in a situation whereby humans oriented themselves to their surroundings by 'treating the world, including ... action itself, as composed of entities that have symbolically apprehendable *meaning* to human actors' (Parsons 1978: 366). Consequently, *language* becomes privileged because of its status as a '*medium* through which knowledge may be acquired from an indefinite range of categories of objects' (Parsons 1978: 368). This human capacity to 'learn and use symbols and their meanings' is why Parsons (1978: 364) suggests 'ultimate questions' or 'telic problems' are 'internal to the human condition' and are important to sociology.

Parsons argues that societies, as well as human beings, have gone through changes that have increased the importance of cultural symbols. Societies have passed through three fundamental evolutionary stages – primitive, intermediate, and modern – each of which involves developments in its capacities of symbolisation. *Primitive* societies are marked by a weakly developed language system resulting in only minor differentiation between their social and cultural systems. *Intermediate* societies are characterised by the development of a written language, containing an elaborated and formal system of codes. The symbolic contents of a culture can, with the development of writing, be stored separately from specific action contexts. This allows for the separate development of the social and cultural systems, and assists people in reflecting on, stabilising, and standardising the social system. Finally, *modern* societies are distinguished from their intermediate predecessors by the development of a legal system: a process of formalisation that facilitates a more stable and sophisticated social division of labour (Parsons 1966b: 26; Savage 1981).

This evolutionary view of human beings and societies helps explain Parsons's emphasis on the importance of information-based values. As a result of distinctive evolutionary developments, societies and individuals become more reflexive, more concerned with codifying and assessing their environments. Contemporary sociologists suggest this can result in a 'chronic reflexivity' in which knowledge becomes destabilised (e.g. Giddens 1991), but Parsons argues this development highlights the importance to humans of 'ultimate questions'. This is why Parsons has been characterised as one of 'the very few sociologists in the classical tradition to develop an interest in religion in industrial society' and to keep alive 'the analysis of the sacred as a central aspect of analytical sociological enquiry' (Robertson and Turner 1991: 12).

This evolutionary narrative is closely associated with Parsons's use of cybernetics theory and his model of the *cybernetic hierarchy*. In analysing the modern social system Parsons (1978: 375) notes that science has established that systems high in information and low in energy can, under properly defined conditions, control other systems low in information and high in energy (he illustrates this with the example of a thermostat that controls, using minimal physical energy, the temperature of an enclosed space by turning a heating apparatus on and off in response to deviations from the required degree of warmth). In analysing the human action system, Parsons (1978: 376) additionally notes that physiologists have substituted the idea of the human organism as a 'heat engine' with the view of it as an 'information processing system'.

The importance of the cybernetic hierarchy, is that it connects Parsons's writings on cultural values, religion, and the human condition with his enduring concern with *systems*. In so doing, it provides us with one account of the means by which individuals and social systems are integrated in the modern world, thus providing Parsons's 'solution' to the structure-agency relationship. There is a clear congruence between Parsons's view of the social system as 'controlled by cultural *symbol[s]*' and his view of the human action system as controlled by the internalisation of '*information* received from the external environment' (Parsons 1978: 377, emphasis added). Indeed, Parsons's late formulations of his 'voluntaristic theory' define action as 'those aspects of human behaviour … involved in or controlled by culturally structured symbolic codes' (Levine 1991b: 192).

This fit between social system and individual does not satisfy realist social theorists who emphasise the importance of recognising differences between the stratified layers of social life. Indeed, Parsons's later writings appear to collapse both individuals and structures into culture, and he once referred to himself as a 'cultural determinist' (Toby 1977: 8). As Alexander and Colomy (1998) note, when Parsons developed his theory of the social system through the cybernetic model, he raised the normative dimension of his scheme to a position of unparalleled importance, and also tended to conflate the model of a cybernetic system with empirical societies. Neither would this elevation of culture answer those critics who accuse Parsons of an 'over-socialised' and 'over-integrated' view of the individual. Furthermore, in relegating the body from sight, Parsons raises the question of why it is that cultural codes, or information, should be considered more important than the organism that limits and provides a context for their significance (Craib 1984: 55). Despite these problems, it is difficult not to admire the scope of Parsons's synthesis and his bold statement of the sociological ambition. His analysis of the transmutation of bodily drives and effervescent emotions into information-based values relied on a creative appropriation of the sociological classics, and a selective incorporation of psychology (Parsons 1981: 192).

5. Concluding comments

Much nineteenth-century thought held that religious bases of social cohesion were becoming irrelevant in an era of rapid social change and industrial development. In light of this concern, Turner and Maryanski (1988: 110) suggest 'it is little wonder that the emergence of sociology as a self-conscious discipline would ask the question: what can social structures "do for" and "contribute to" the construction and maintenance of social order?' Parsons prolongs this classical concern into the twentieth century and does so by restoring the status of religion to the centre of the discipline via his interrogation of the 'ultimate values' and normative action guiding human life. If Durkheim gives us a view of the relationship between the sacred, moral communities, and the emotional embodiment of people, Parsons's focus on values envisages a different stage in the anthropological development of what it means to be an embodied being in modernity. Religion does not have the fundamentally *emotional* power it does for Durkheim, but is important as a symbolic codification of the values that shape apparently secular cultures. In this respect, Parsons's discussion of the religious basis of modern instrumentalism provides us with a view of modernity quite different from Weber's vision of the 'iron cage' of human existence.

Parsons's totalising analysis of society as an ordered social system reached back to the foundations of sociology for its inspiration, and was opposed to what he referred to as 'factor theorising': theories which elevated one explanatory variable such as class or conflict to a position of absolute primacy. From a substantive perspective, Parsons used his approach to combat what he perceived to be 'ideological distortions' in academic understandings of American society (Lidz 1991). Themes of social, political, and moral malaise had been explored in publications such as *The Lonely Crowd* (Riesman 1950), *The Power Elite* (Mills 1956), *The Sane Society* (Fromm 1956), *Yankee City* (Warner 1963), *America as a Civilization* (Lerner 1957), *The Authoritarian Personality* (Adorno et al. 1950), and *The Eclipse of Community* (Stein 1960). Parsons provided detailed critiques of the methods and conclusions of such studies, suggested they mistook the evolution of a social system within a changing global context for a more fundamental crisis, and was to have written a major study of American society. While this was never finished, Parsons emphasised the enduring values that provided an important integrating function for the American social system (Lidz 1991: 31). Critics suggested that his ultimate optimism about racial inclusion underestimated the deep roots of racial division in the United States. Nevertheless, Parsons suggests that people are able to be outraged and protest against such issues as poverty and inequality, as well as racial oppression, precisely because they have internalised the same basic value system:

> Thus, high standards in the economic, health and education fields, certain fundamental patterns of equality, notably of citizenship and opportunity, and certain aspects of freedom for individuals and associational groups are almost universally valued. Conversely ... [m]any of the intrasocietal and intersocial problems that distress the modern world owe much of their salience and form of statement to the processes of institutionalisation of Christian values ... The distress over them is not so much a measure of the irrelevance of the historic impact of Christianity as a measure of the incompleteness of institutionalisation; a conception which implies that there has been in the past significant *relative* success. (Parsons 1978: 207)

This focus on an ordered social system seemed particularly appropriate immediately prior to the 1960s when the dominant sociological view was that Western societies had entered a period characterised by the 'end of ideology' and consensus over basic social values. For Parsons, it was this 'maturation' of modern society that presaged the real age of sociology, and not the more frequently cited earlier inception of 'secular' industrial society (Holmwood 1996: 4–5). With the spread of military, industrial, and social conflict in the 1960s and 1970s, however, Parsons was seen as an apologist for capitalism's excesses (Gouldner 1970), and as someone whose theories were based on a conservative ideological justification of American values in the period of Cold War between the superpowers (Hacker 1961). Underpinning this was his theory of social evolution that is commonly perceived as implausible and obsolete, and as making 'Parsons seem complacent about the present' (Habermas 1981b: 203; Toby 1977: 20).

Parsons remains vulnerable to the accusation that he dealt inadequately with issues concerning power and conflict, despite his attempt to do so through the notion of 'social strain' (Parsons 1962). His writings have also been viewed as religiously reductionist (stemming from the fact that the values ultimately determining the direction of social systems belong to the 'non-empirical' world which is not open to substantive scrutiny) (Robertson 1991: 142). His comparison of social systems and organic systems has been criticised for slipping from being metaphoric to a metaphysical statement of the world (Craib 1984). In opposition to suggestions that he was complacent about social tensions and conflicts, however, Nielson (1991) has highlighted Parsons's support of the Civil Rights movement, his concerns about poverty, and his criticisms of the radical right. Nevertheless, Parsons's interest in the enduring significance of religious values for modern social systems meant he was fundamentally optimistic about the future of society.

This optimism did not just contrast with the assessments of his radical contemporaries, however, but with the German foundations of the discipline. For Weber (1904–5: 181–2), 'victorious capitalism, since it rests on mechanical foundations' no longer needs the support of human values. Parsons, in contrast, disagreed with Weber about the 'disenchantment' of the modern world, and suggested that the instrumentalism of the most advanced modern society, the United States, be evaluated in relation to *extra*-societal bases of value *outside* itself (Parsons 1982; see also Lechner 1991). The need for instrumentalism to justify itself with reference to values was, moreover, unlikely to disappear given Parsons's view that collectivities and individuals have a periodic need to revitalise their culture by addressing themselves to questions of 'ultimate meaning' which can only be described as religious in nature (Robertson 1992: 43). Conflict and disagreement may be rife within modern social orders but, in countries such as America, Parsons would not interpret this as a broader 'Balkanisation of the West' (cf. Meštrović 1994). Instead, the relative rarity of breakdown in modern societies would be judged as an indicator of just how much value consensus exists in social systems.

Parsons remains *the* theorist of social order whose work depicted normative action as the elementary form of social life. He supported this view by arguing there was a direct parallel between Weber's conception of a value system, Freud's conception of the super-ego, and Durkheim's conception of the conscience collective (Parsons 1981). The strong emphasis Parsons placed on order, however, prepared the ground for the 'one-sided' sociologies of conflict and disorder that followed his writings. If the post-1960s generation in sociology marched against Parsons's grand theory (Lemert 1998: x), it also turned away from issues concerned with social integration, and spent much of the next four decades focusing on such matters as 'difference', 'deconstruction' and the 'virtual realities' of postmodernism. The 'social system', in the sense Parsons understood this term, had, for a while at least, had its day. The classical concern with 'the society of humanity' was displaced by a more focused, if potentially sectarian, analysis of particular social groups and identities.

Note

1. With regard to human embodiment, Parsons recognised a system of 'viscerogenic needs' grounded in the bodily organism-environment relationship, and wrote about the major existential predicaments of the human condition such as sickness and death (Parsons 1969, 1970). Nevertheless, his real interest was in how the social *mediation* and *transformation* of bodily needs contributes to social order. This is clear in his appropriation of psychoanalysis, which distinguishes the bodily organism from the personality on the basis that personality consists of *culturally given codes*.

Part II

POST-CLASSICAL SOCIOLOGY

7

CONFLICT SOCIOLOGY

1. Introduction

If the Parsonian concern with values, norms, and roles left an indelible mark on the discipline, so too did the emergence of 'conflict sociology'. This focus on conflict developed during the 1960s and 1970s and constituted, in part, a direct reaction against Parsonian orthodoxy. It was also associated with a far wider cross-disciplinary concern with conflict that drew on the 'critical theory' of the Frankfurt School, on the writings of the Italian Marxist, Antonio Gramsci, and on radical political economy.[1] For all their differences, these perspectives represented the most significant growth of intellectual interest in conflict since the writings of Marx. In the case of sociology, their aim was to offer a radical departure from the classical sociological concern with consensual social and moral order. This was exemplified by the influence of Marx, a figure whose work previously served as a negative referent rather than a direct source of guidance for the discipline's development, yet who was now seen to highlight themes that should be central to the sociological imagination. Under his influence, a focus on social conflicts, divisions, and the 'ideological' veils that obscured them, displaced the classical interest in religion, ultimate values and normative consensus. An implicit concern for moral issues remained, but this was confined largely to issues of social injustice as the scope of the 'social' and the 'moral' became focused on class conflicts. Nonetheless, many of these approaches never moved as far away from classical sociological themes as they often claimed and, in some instances, a re-engagement with the breadth of the classical sociological ambition soon became explicit.

The sub-discipline of conflict sociology constituted a thoroughly *sociological* reaction to Parsonian priorities rather than being driven by the philosophical or political concerns of critical theory. The theoretical frameworks proposed by Lewis Coser (1956) and Ralph Dahrendorf (1959), for example, opposed the emphasis sociology had previously placed on shared values and moral communities by emphasising the importance to modern industrial societies of struggles over power, authority, and resources. Marx was recognised as *the* classical theorist of conflict (Coser 1967: 137), and a creative engagement with his writings was central to the development of this perspective even if the roots of conflict theory were located in the work of classical military and political writers concerned with the 'enduring realities' of war and struggle (Collins 1974). Indeed, conflict theorists have been described as 'post-Marxists' or 'left-Weberians' whose biographical experiences of war, economic depression, and the rise of Fascism and Stalinism, led them to feel that Parsons's work neglected historical reality (Wrong 1994).

Emerging from a different tradition were those intellectuals associated with the 'New Left' and responsible for a revival of interest in the critical theory of the Frankfurt School, and the political theory of Gramsci.[2] The Frankfurt School developed in Germany of the 1920s and 1930s before going into exile during the Nazi era. Its leading figures included Max Horkheimer, Theodor Adorno, and Herbert Marcuse, and its traditions continue in the work of Jürgen Habermas. Critical theory was influenced by Marx's analysis of capitalism as a system characterised by exploitation and struggle, was directly indebted to his early philosophical writings on human alienation, but also drew on Freud's work in analysing the personality types characteristic of competitive and monopoly capitalism. Its interest in the apparent stability and moral consensus achieved by capitalism, however, led critical theory to be more concerned with traditional sociological and cultural issues than Marx. There is also a pessimism pervading many of its writings that echoes Weber's concern with the 'fate of our times' rather than Marx's revolutionary optimism (Turner 1996b). This pessimism is also evident, as we shall see, in Gramsci's distinctive account of the hegemonic containment of conflict: a containment effected by the conservative effects of bourgeois culture and morality.

This chapter progresses as follows. Section 2 focuses on 'conflict' as a unit idea. It does this by examining how theorists associated with the sub-discipline of conflict sociology challenged Parsons's emphasis on normative orders, but nonetheless maintained a strong interest in the relationship between conflict *and* consensus. Section 3 examines how this interest was central to the work of even the most radical classical theorist, Marx. Here, we analyse how the ambiguities within Marx's vision of the elementary forms of social and moral life help us to understand both the heterogeneity of conflict sociology and the preoccupations and problems associated with the writings of twentieth-century neo-Marxists. While Marx provided a vastly influential account of conflictual change in capitalism, he was also concerned with the formation of an authentic moral community. Section 4 examines how this relationship between conflict and consensus developed into an increasing theoretical tension within conflict sociology and critical theory. It employs Lockwood's (1956) distinction between 'social integration' and 'system integration' in order to highlight the need for social theory to distinguish carefully between the sources, scope and impact of different conflicts. In concluding, we examine how, despite their ostensible aims, these visions of sociology can be viewed in retrospect as a representing a continuation of, as much as a break from, the scope and concerns of Parsonian sociology.

2. Conflict

Obserschall (1978) has suggested that conflict sociology is a hugely diverse set of methodologies and techniques that cannot be summarily designated as one theoretical school. What unites many conflict sociologies, however, is that, while they are clearly interested in a diverse range of overt or latent antagonisms, they rarely reject the concerns of normative sociology. Despite its frequent appeals to Marx, then, conflict sociology is often preoccupied by issues of value consensus and moral solidarity as well as the functional consequences of conflict.

In this context, the tendency to analyse conflict and consensus as opposites, associated with separate theorists and linked with different national traditions of sociology, is misleading. Instead, it is possible to differentiate 'stronger' and 'weaker' versions of conflict sociology. There are those that view conflict as laying bare inauthentic, ideological forms of value consensus and generating social transformation (e.g. Rex 1961), those that view conflict as being constrained by social differentiation and broader forms of moral consensus (e.g. Dahrendorf 1959), and those that view conflict as leading to new forms of value consensus and reinvigorated moral communities (e.g. Coser 1956, 1967).

Conflict overcoming consensus
Of the major conflict sociologists, John Rex (1961) presents us with an unusually strong version of this approach that draws on the writings of Marx and Weber and rejects those of Durkheim and Parsons. Emphasising how the aims of capitalist society are outcomes of contests between different groups and classes and not, as Parsons would have it, the result of shared values, Rex (1961: 187; 1981: 3) defines conflict as action carried out against the resistance of other parties. Having reinterpreted 'norms' as the *outcome* of conflict, Rex also deconstructs exchange theory. Exchange theory suggests that free-market transactions can benefit all individuals involved and lead to the maximum satisfaction of needs and wants. Rex (1981: 104), in contrast, argues that what *appears* to be 'a mutually beneficial [market] exchange', is actually characterised by 'elements of compulsion and exploitation that appear as normative only because the oppressed and the exploited do not have the power to resist them'.

Having highlighted the prevalence of power and exploitation, Rex makes social class and social change central to his concerns. Class struggle was the 'motor force' of history for Marx, and Rex (1961: 187) argues that 'the study of class conflict' will always be an 'essential preliminary' to the analysis of social institutions, and to the changes in power relations which lead to reform or revolution. Shifts in the source of one class's power over another can lead to a destruction not only of the domination of the ruling class, but the very basis of its existence.

Rex's vision of sociology is informed by Marx's analysis of class, but extends the meaning of conflict through a Weberian analysis of social stratification. Focusing on how people's life chances are determined by class, status, and politics, Weber identified multidimensional bases to social stratification. Rex adopts this approach in examining conflicts over housing opportunities and racial residential patterns, and maintained a Weberian dimension to his writings on race and ethnicity (Rex 1973, 1986). The criticisms he makes of other conflict sociologies, however, suggest his is not the most representative example of this genre. Rex (1961: 115), for example, states that no contemporary conflict theorist has 'taken their criticisms of "integrationist" and "functionalist" theory far enough'. This is because they view conflict as functional for social order (in revitalising social norms), or, as we shall see with Dahrendorf, because they suggest it is confined by the segmented nature of modern society.

Conflict constrained by social differentiation and consensus

Dahrendorf's (1959: 162, 208) *Class and Class Conflict in Industrial Society* views conflict and coercion as 'social facts' of industrial society, as central to 'all that is creativity, innovation, and development in the life of the individual, his group and his society'. Nevertheless, it is *authority* and not the mode of production that is the ultimate source of classes, conflict, and change: *'there are as many social classes as there are authority relations'* (Dahrendorf 1959: 271). Marx may remain important but, according to Dahrendorf, his writings have become dated. It is to Weber that we must turn.

Dahrendorf begins with Weber's suggestion that the bureaucratisation and rationalisation of capitalist society is accompanied by a proliferation of institutional arrangements characterised by internal relations of legitimate authority which produce dominant and subordinate groups with opposing interests. Each of these institutions is legitimate in its own right, but they produce distinctive patterns of hierarchy in separate sections of society. In this context, class conflict results from multiple bases rather than simply revolving around the ownership of property. Classes follow 'the distribution of authority in social organisations', and are present 'wherever authority is distributed unequally over social positions', while individuals become members of a class by virtue of holding a social role which does or does not involve the exercise of authority (Dahrendorf 1959: 201, 207, 148–9). In this context, and in contrast to Rex, the identification of authority roles and their particular capacities becomes 'the first task of conflict analysis' (Dahrendorf 1959: 165).

Dahrendorf's conflict theory is reliant on his argument that the class structure of advanced capitalism has radically changed since Marx's time: authority roles have proliferated with the growth of parliamentary and industrial democracies and the spread of managers, bureaucracies, and property ownership. This proliferation increases the consensual legitimacy accorded to the social system by ordinary people and diminishes the systemic importance of social class. In this respect, Dahrendorf is particularly critical of C. Wright Mills's identification of a 'power elite': a dominant class overlapping the spheres of industry, politics, and society. In its place, Dahrendorf argues that the class structure is characterised by social mobility, and that class conflicts encompass only parts of society and rarely extend into, or overlap with, political struggles (Dahrendorf 1959: 245–57). Industry, politics, and society have become 'dissociated', which means that conflicts deriving from production remain institutionally isolated, and 'robbed of their influence on other spheres of society' (Dahrendorf 1959: 268). Class conflicts may occur 'wherever authority is distributed unequally over social positions', but can be regulated effectively because of their location within rationalised authority structures. These characteristics mean we have now entered a 'post-capitalist society' (Dahrendorf 1959: 201, 247).

In a conclusion that is as reminiscent of Durkheim's view of moral solidarities as it is of Marx's view of conflict, Dahrendorf argues that industrial conflict has 'found a stable and definite place' within society, while the subjective images people may have of a 'dichotomous view of social stratification' do not derive from capitalism but from the more permanent 'myths and religions of mankind' (Dahrendorf 1959: 288; Ossowski 1956: 19). If authority relations are ubiquitous in Dahrendorf's liberal view of industrial society, however, he provides no thoroughgoing explanation of the source of these relations' legitimacy, and has been accused of constructing a de-contextualised view of the ways in which they work (Binns 1977: 87). Dahrendorf's vision of conflict sociology provides us, in short, with a deliberately restricted view of the societal scope of social conflicts.

Conflict as a source of consensus

If Rex's and Dahrendorf's theories engage with Marx, as well as Weber, Coser constructs a 'weaker' vision of conflict sociology. While Coser (1967: 137, 156) identifies conflict sociology with Marx, and criticises the discipline's 'conservative' concern with social cohesion, he also states that social conflict and moral consensus are connected and should be *complementary* interests (Coser 1967: 8–9). This has been demonstrated by the reformist concerns of American sociology, and by Simmel's view of conflict as a form of sociation that creates unity between antagonistic groups (Coser 1956; Simmel 1955: 23).

Coser's (1956) *The Functions of Social Conflict* starts by criticising sociology's preoccupation with the Parsonian themes of 'tensions', 'strains', and 'psychological malfunctioning'. Instead of pursuing issues of conflict central to its founders, the discipline has followed the leads given by Elton Mayo's study of management and Lloyd Warner's anthropologically informed community study, works which attributed conflict with 'overwhelmingly negative connotations' (Coser 1956: 15, 20, 24). Coser (1956: 31) then proceeds, via a close exegesis of Simmel's (1955) essay, to argue that 'conflict is an essential element in group formation and the persistence of group life'. Nevertheless, it is the language of *integration* rather than the language of social change that dominates Coser's study. Conflict maintains relationships by 'setting free pent-up feelings of hostility', by resolving tensions between antagonists, by uniting a group against its enemies, by leading to the establishment of new norms, and by acting as a unifying agent of socialisation for antagonistic parties (Coser 1956).

Coser repeats Cooley's (1918) point that conflict and co-operation are two sides of the same coin, suggests that conflict 'prevents the ossification of the social system by exerting pressure for innovation and creativity', and ultimately adopts a form of functionalism that is consistent with a Durkheimian approach. Seeking support for his argument that conflict unifies, for example, Coser cites Durkheim's (1893) statement that 'Crime brings together upright consciences and concentrates them' as evidence of another major theorist who recognises the 'integrative function of antagonistic behaviour' (Coser 1956: 127). Coser (1956: 157) concludes by arguing that conflict is only dysfunctional for a social structure when 'there is no or insufficient toleration and institutionalisation of conflict'.

Despite the apparent centrality of conflict to his analysis, Coser's treatment of the subject neglects the argument made by Rex and Dahrendorf that conflict can set the *direction of change* to a social system. As such, Coser's work is only a partial rejection of consensual sociology and, despite his protestations to the contrary, of Parsons. For Coser, conflict is studied in relation to its capacity for creating *new* forms of consensus. Duels, ritual revenge, and the scapegoating of ethnic and religious minorities, for example, are viewed in terms of a Durkheimian channelling of hostility on to particular targets in order to stabilise relationships *within* moral groups (Coser 1956: 68; Scott 1995: 124).[3]

The influence of Durkheimian themes within this 'weak' form of conflict sociology raises the question of whether there is anything that radically differentiates this theory from normative sociology. This can be illustrated with reference to Durkheim's *The Division of Labour in Society* (1893). Here, conflict is one prominent theme, but it is judged to be 'abnormal' or 'pathological', or regulated by a deeper moral solidarity. Opposing Marx, Durkheim views the institution of class arising from the division of labour as capable of producing *solidarity*. Class conflict has become common in modernity only because of the development of an abnormal division of labour which has resulted in anomie and a mismatch between people's natural abilities and their work (Durkheim 1893: 304, 311).[4]

The point of this brief summary of Durkheim is to illustrate that 'consensual sociologies' are fully capable of incorporating reflections on conflict into a normative conception of social order. 'Weak' versions of conflict sociology, therefore, may be seen as representing a qualification of, rather than an alternative to, theories of social order. Collins's (1975) conflict sociology recognises this by insisting that a Durkheimian model of the individual (emphasising the social bases of emotion and cognition) can be combined with an overarching view of conflict taken from Weber and Marx. Conflict exists, for Collins, because of a scarcity of social and material goods and 'because violent coercion is always a potential resource' used in obtaining these goods. Individuals pursue their interests in groups, however, and it is the emotionally energising processes of ritual interaction, analysed by Durkheim, that shape individual goals and norms, but that also pitch competing groups against each other.

Conflict sociologies may be distinct from the normative sociologies they oppose, but even strong versions of conflict theory have been unable to jettison a concern with shared values and social orders. Furthermore, conflict theories have been unable to overcome difficulties and contradictions when seeking to explicate the embodied bases of social antagonism. In contrast to Durkheim's vision of the effervescence underpinning group cohesion, only Collins possesses any explicit analysis of the physical motivations that predispose people towards conflictual relationships. Ironically, these problems concerning the relationship between conflict and consensus and the embodied basis of conflictual relationships can be traced to the enduring influence of Marx's writings (Marshall 1950; Glass 1954; Schelsky 1956; Dahrendorf 1959: 72–116; Bendix 1964; Binns 1977). This becomes clear when we examine the tensions contained within Marx's vision of the elementary forms of social life.

3. The elementary forms of social and moral life

The sub-discipline of conflict sociology drew on, debated with, and recognised the importance of Marx's analysis of class conflict as an elementary form of social action. Marx was an essential figure in the sociological tradition, according to writers such as Gouldner, because he was *the* theorist of conflict. Indeed, the tendency for conflict sociology to place Marx at the centre of the discipline both contrasted with Parsons's account of the subject and was one of the reasons Marxism reached a high point in its academic influence during the 1960s and 1970s. If Marx was one figure indispensable to the analysis of social conflict, though, why was this area characterised by such ambivalence about the final consequences of conflict? Why, furthermore, did the wider analysis of conflict that developed during this period have difficulties constructing an adequate vision of the embodied basis of human life conducive to the transformation of social systems?

In this section we suggest that a significant source of these problems resides in two features of Marx's own writings. First, even though Marx is heralded as a theorist of social action as conflictual, conflict is closely tied to implicit conceptions of consensual moral order in his work. Second, there is a significant tension in Marx's analysis of the medium of class struggle, labour. On the one hand, he suggests that humans are an embodied species whose nature is socially constructed by the collective conditions surrounding economic production. On the other hand, he makes the completely different argument that labour is itself governed by a rationality that transcends immediate economic contexts and which provides a cognitive motivation for class conflict. Having examined Marx's view of the elementary forms of social and moral life, we then turn to the distinctive explanations of these forms to be found in the work of the Frankfurt School and in the writings of Gramsci.

Marx and class struggle

In conceptualising class struggle as the elementary form of social action, Marx was working both within and against the sociological tradition. Like Comte, Durkheim, and Parsons, Marx insisted on recognising the *collective* and *social* bases of human action, and rejected the utilitarian view of the autonomous individual. Humans can individuate themselves 'only in the midst of society', Marx argued, while the idea of individuals being able to survive economically outside society 'is as much of an absurdity as is the development of language without individuals living together and talking to each other' (Marx 1973: 84). In opposition to sociology, however, Marx elevated class conflict to a position of unparalleled importance as a determinant of collective action. Class conflict is *the* principle of history in Marx's philosophy, 'comparable in scope to Comte's law of three stages, to Tocqueville's political centralisation, to Weber's rationalisation' (Nisbet 1966: 202). In Marx's words, 'the history of all hitherto existing society is the history of class struggles' (Marx 1848: 35).[5]

For all its apparent focus on conflict, however, moral consensus assumes a prominent role in Marx's writings on class struggle. For Marx, conflict serves certain ordering functions even within capitalism in that it creates class consciousness and solidarity by promoting loyalty and group consciousness (Aron 1965: 163; Marx 1956: 489). In developing this argument, Marx anticipates Simmel's and Coser's point that conflict can be approached as a form of sociation that facilitates unity. Lockwood (1992: 161) goes further, suggesting that Marx's analysis of the polarisation of classes implies an almost Durkheimian view of the separation that can exist between different but internally unified moral communities. Indeed, there is a sense in which class conflict is as 'pathological' for Marx as it is for Durkheim. In comparison with the conflict-free conditions of 'primitive communism' and those that will prevail in a future communist state, Marx argued that capitalist society is pathological in being an alienating social form (Aron 1965: 145, 171). As Holton (1996: 27) notes, although the Marxist account of class takes as its starting point the economic relationships of *Gesellschaft* capitalist society, it is actually underpinned by a *Gemeinschaftlich* view of class as a (moral) community of the proletarian class triumphing over the individualism and atomisation of capitalism. This implies that Marx does not oppose normative, consensus-based sociologies with an unambivalent focus on conflict, but provides an analysis of the relationship between conflict and consensus that is not as radically different from conventional sociology as is often assumed.

If Marx displays a certain ambivalence about the dominance of conflict over consensus in his analysis of class struggle as the elementary form of social action, there exists a complementary tension in his view of how this action is shaped through the medium of *labour*. On the one hand, the form taken by labour is *socially constructed* by humans who transform themselves by transforming their environment through work. As Arthur (1970: 21) notes, the most fundamental idea running through Marx's *1844 Manuscripts, The German Ideology*, and *Capital*, is that classes produce themselves through the collectively determined conditions surrounding economic labour. On the other hand, Marx suggests elsewhere in his writings that the form taken by labour is an expression of a rationality that ultimately transcends people's immediate circumstances. Marx's (1906) view of the capitalist class, for example, is underpinned by a conception of the 'rational miser' devoted to accumulating profit, while his analysis of the proletariat is associated with two forms of rationality. The short-term aim of the proletariat involves maximising its wages, but the proletariat is also associated with a 'higher-order rationality' that recognises its interests can only be fully realised by the abolition of capitalism (Lockwood 1992: 205). This 'higher-order' rationality is a transcendent rationality in that it can only be realised when the proletariat moves from being a class-in-itself to a class-for-itself which is cognisant of its interests and which seeks the inception of a communist state.[6] Such analysis expresses a foundational, rationalistic concept of humanity that allows Marx, for example, to evaluate workers as alienated from their species-being within capitalism.

Marx's writings on labour, then, contain contrasting emphases on the collective determination of human species-being and on the identification of a human rationality that is able to transcend its immediate social context and recognise interests that can only be realised by economic transformation (Geras 1983; McLellan 1985). This shifting between two positions is why theorists are able to come to such different conclusions about Marx's writings on human nature.[7] Thus, Coser (1971: 44) claims that 'Marx was a relativising historicist'. Nisbet (1966: 286–7), in contrast, argues that Marx expresses 'an unwavering acceptance of the stability and reality of the human being'. As Levine notes, such contrasting interpretations stem from the fact that Marx's philosophy is part of a contradictory 'effort to anchor the quest for transcendent freedom in worldly realities'. Yet this 'bequeaths a gaping contradiction' between the idea that there is something essentially rational about human nature and the idea that humans are malleable, socially constructed beings (Levine 1995: 221–2). Sociology usually sees these competing visions of humanity as mutually exclusive options: 'Rational man and socialised man are not congenial companions' (Lockwood 1992: 233).[8]

These two related sets of tensions within Marx's work (involving the relationship between conflict and consensus, and the contrasting views of labour as a socially constructed medium and as a rational medium of action) help explain the heterogeneity of conflict sociology. This heterogeneity is further evident in Marx's analysis of the *outcomes* of conflict.

Marx's analysis of class, expressed through the medium of labour, is contained within a vision of capitalism as a conflict-filled system whose internal contradictions would ultimately produce economic crisis: a vision developed by the radical political economists who carried Marx's legacy into the 1970s.[9] Nevertheless, despite Marx's suggestion that class conflict would necessarily overcome constraining patterns of consensus (his assumption of the 'inevitability' of revolution), he was also concerned with how the structural and ideological features of a capitalist system could contain conflict.

The outlines of a concept of ideology are evident in Marx's early critique of religion. While his writings on this subject changed over time, Marx generally treated ideology as a system of ideas reflecting the interests of the ruling class yet presented as incorporating the moral interests of the whole community. If there is one all-embracing 'dominant ideology' in each particular epoch, however, it is difficult to explain how any significant conflict arises (Abercrombie, Hill and Turner 1980). Indeed, the Marxist idea that 'religious ideologies unite divergent classes behind the garment of religious institutions and beliefs' has parallels with the Durkheimian understanding of religion as a means of integrating individuals into the group and reinforcing common values (Turner 1991c: 78). Even if we accept the 'inevitability' of revolution, it is also worth nothing that Marx interpreted communism as presiding at the end of history as a conflict-free state.

Despite being portrayed as *the* theorist of conflict, then, Marx's analysis of the elementary forms of social life provide us with a contradictory and ambivalent view of the scope, embodied basis, and impact of class struggle. Because of this, the very divergent forms and developments of conflict sociology can all draw some sustenance from Marx's theories. For example, the close association conflict sociology draws between conflict and consensus (e.g. Coser 1956) can be justified in part on the basis of Marx's work. Alternatively, conflict theorists have sometimes taken from Marx the argument that modern societies are marked by collective action (even if the character of that collective action is sometimes redefined using Weber's writings on stratification), and have simply assumed people pursue their self-interests in economically unequal social contexts. Finally, conflict theorists have tended either to avoid the issue of the embodied basis of class conflict or have developed one or other aspects of Marx's vision of the species-being (e.g. Collins 1975). Such theoretical pluralism leaves us with disparate versions and developments of collective economic action, however, and with the continued question of whether conflict theories are radically distinctive from normative visions of social theory. We can pursue this question further by looking at how the Frankfurt School of critical theory developed Marx's ideas.

The Frankfurt School and the problem of consciousness

The Frankfurt School was formed long before this interest in conflict developed during the 1960s and 1970s. Nevertheless, this sociological development contributed towards a revival of interest in its past and present products. The Frankfurt School confronted the fact that the development of class conflict into revolutionary consciousness and social transformation had not occurred as Marx envisaged. In this context, as Horkheimer noted, critical theorists became preoccupied by the question of how 'tensions between social classes ... impelled toward conflict because of the economic situation, can remain latent?' (Honneth 1987: 353). In seeking answers to this question, the Frankfurt School supplemented Marxism with three disciplines that it thought could assist analysis of what had clearly become a 'post-liberal' phase of capitalism. Political economy was meant to facilitate analysis of whether National Socialism in particular was based on a new set of economic organising principles. Psychology helped explore the integration of personality into the economic system, and cultural analysis assisted the examination of mass culture's central role in mediating this integration (Honneth 1987). These developments provided a vision of the elementary forms of social life that blurred further the difference between theories of conflict and theories of consensus, and which placed increased emphasis on rationalist conceptions of humanity.

The critical theorists associated with the Frankfurt School did not jettison in its entirety Marx's view of social action as class struggle. Nevertheless, while acknowledging that it remained integral to advanced modern societies, and could explode into revolution at any time, writers like Marcuse (1964) and Adorno (1966) also argued that the effects of class struggle could be managed and contained indefinitely (Held 1980: 70–3). Indeed, Honneth (1987) has suggested that the picture of capitalist domination that critical theory proposed often seemed total, and that the transformation of liberal capitalism into a 'one-dimensional' society meant that the possibility of class conflict as Marx envisaged it was no longer possible. Conflict faded into the background and the Frankfurt School turned its attention to the '*problem of consciousness*' (Flacks and Turkel 1978).

This shift from conflict to consensus is also evident in the Frankfurt School's vision of the cultural media through which consciousness was forged. Mass culture operated to blunt people's critical faculties and to foster social and moral order.[10] As Adorno (1975: 19) argued, mass culture 'impedes the development of autonomous, independent individuals who decide and judge consciously for themselves'. Mass culture was able to exert such significance because of the prominence of an instrumental reason, based on the principles of technological domination, which had emptied society of moral values (Connerton 1976: 27). Another factor responsible for its ideological influence was the changing structure of the family. The loss of traditional authority relations in the family removed the means by which moral values were transmitted between generations and facilitated the psychological adjustment of individuals to cultural domination. In an analysis that draws more on Marx's view of the rational capacities of people than on their social determination, the Frankfurt School places its hopes for social change in the transformation of consciousness. In mediating consciousness, then, the cultural industry plays a major role in producing *outcomes* of order and consensus rather than the revolutionary change predicted by Marx. While the Frankfurt School develops Marx's notion of ideology through a focus on consensus and rationality, however, Gramsci's account of the stabilisation of capitalism exhibits a greater concern for the non-rational features of human being.

Gramsci and class action

Gramsci (1971) does not dispense with the idea of class conflict, but focuses on the role of *hegemonic action* as elementary to social life. This notion of hegemony refers to the domination of one class over the other through the combination of political force and ideology. However, ideology is no longer a matter of the indoctrination of fetishistic cognitive orientations into subordinate classes, but involves the circulation of *non-rational* sentiments and values. Gramsci's 'hegemony' resonates with Durkheim's 'collective conscience' and Weber's concern with the social ethic of a religion in making sense of both the 'spontaneous', 'religious' consent of the masses to the prevailing social order, and the generation of social and moral solidarity (Lockwood 1992: 325). If hegemonic action is elementary to social life for Gramsci, intellectuals are central to the exercise of this action. They produce the philosophic elements of ideology, but, in order to be effective, representatives of a social class must connect these to 'common sense' (the taken-for-granted assumptions of the masses grounded in faith) and 'folklore' (the beliefs and superstitions stemming from tradition) (McLellan 1987: 115). For class conflict to be directed toward successful forms of oppositional action, for example, 'organic intellectuals' must emerge from the masses and assist in the diffusion of 'critical forms of truth': a process of moral, intellectual and symbolic re-education (Lockwood 1992: 330).

One aspect of Gramsci's writings that made them so popular with Western neo-Marxists in the 1970s was their concern with civil society, an area of social life perceived as under-theorised in Marx's own work yet which had assumed increasing importance in advanced capitalist states. Gramsci suggested that revolutionary activity might breach the defences of the state, but these defences were themselves underpinned by the immensely resilient foundations of civil society. Civil society was the medium through which hegemonic action was channelled. It is through the diffusion of culture in the institutions, values, beliefs, and intellectual systems of civil society that class conflict is either neutralised in favour of consensus, or is translated into actions productive of social transformation (Bobbio 1979: 40). In exercising hegemonic action, then, intellectuals have to operate in and through civil society.

In examining the *outcomes* of hegemonic action, Gramsci emphasises the contingencies associated with social order and change. Given the supposedly immense hold of civil society on the beliefs, emotions, and values of the masses, however, Gramsci's analysis of hegemony remains vague about the precise mechanisms involved in social change. Seeking to clarify these mechanisms, Lockwood (1992: 334) notes that even 'the conversion of the masses to new beliefs' is not solely dependent on the actions of organic intellectuals alone, but on what is described in almost Durkheimian terms as an 'organic crisis' where the hegemony of the ruling class is disturbed by a sudden discontinuity in social life (Gramsci 1971: 210). The precise processes leading to such a crisis, however, still remain vague. Just as some of Durkheim's followers have been accused of using 'collective conscience' to develop an over-integrated view of society and an over-socialised view of the individual, then, Gramsci's analysis of 'hegemony' has enabled Marxist theorists concerned with explaining the lack of proletarian revolution to espouse an 'equally questionable view of global ideological domination' (Lockwood 1992: 337). Instead of being on the precipice of disaster, as in Marx's major writings on economics, capitalism becomes capable of generating normative support of a kind never envisaged by Weberian visions of the 'iron cage' of rational capitalism: a support which comes close to Parsons's vision of social order.

The distinctive visions of the elementary forms of social life associated with Marx, the Frankfurt School, and Gramsci, help explain the various and sometimes contradictory analyses of conflict within sociology and social theory. The problem with visions of conflict and incorporation associated with such concepts as 'ideology', 'the culture industry' and 'hegemony', however, is that they rob conflict sociology of its unit idea. If people are assimilated into a system maintained by ruling ideas, there seems little place left for the issues of conflict and social change that Parsons was condemned for neglecting. This is evident even in the work of the radical figure who has been rehabilitated as 'the American sociologist who has come to grips most forcefully with the macrostructure of organised power in the United States', C. Wright Mills (Collins and Makowsky 1978: vii–viii).[11]

In 1943 Mills identified organised labour as the collective agent able to promote genuine democracy, yet later retreated from identifying any class as having the potential to instigate social change. In place of a vision of class struggle leading to revolutionary change, Mills depicted a picture of society informed by a 'Weberian-influenced model of organised, bureaucratic capitalism, securely founded on a stable technical and administrative basis and reinforced by a systematic and effective political order' (Binns 1977: 133). The media, in particular, plays a major role in (mis)representing the world to people, and in creating a mass society no longer guided by moral ideals but populated by 'cheerful robots' with little control over their lives (Mills 1951, 1956). It filters into our experiences of 'external realities' and into 'our very experience of our own selves'. It bestows identities upon people, and provides them with aspirations and subjective forms of 'escape' when material success proves illusory (Mills 1956: 314).[12]

4. Social integration and system integration

The major theoretical tension underpinning conflict theory is how to analyse the relationship between conflict and consensus. Lockwood (1956, 1992) provides us with an influential perspective on this tension. In opposing sociological theories that portray society as either permanently consensual or crisis ridden, or that veer between the two, Lockwood argued that the differentiated character of modern social systems means there are two major areas in which conflict can arise and spread, or even be contained. In identifying them, Lockwood uses the term 'social integration' to refer to the degree of conflict or cohesion characteristic of *social and moral relationships* in a society.[13] 'System integration', in contrast, refers to the degree of conflict or cohesion characteristic of the *institutional and economic parts* of a society. According to Lockwood, then, there can be no single form of conflict sociology or, indeed, of consensus sociology. Instead, it is necessary to examine how the forms of action and media relevant to the social and systemic parts of society interact to produce particular outcomes.

On the basis of his insistence that social relationships and the structural parts of a society are distinctive, Lockwood criticises Parsons for equating order with normative social relations and for overlooking an important source of potential conflict in the economic system which might disrupt these relationships. According to this analysis, Marx might also be criticised for emphasising the significance for social change of conflicts at the systemic level, the 'contradictions' inherent within the capitalist system, at the expense of events relevant to social integration. Nevertheless, Lockwood (1992: 405) is favourably disposed toward Marx for clearly differentiating between social and system integration. In view of this, Lockwood (1992: 404) suggests that Dahrendorf's and Rex's use of Marx in conflict sociology to interpret social change in terms of the shifting balance of power between conflict groups is a misreading of Marx, and a conflation of patterns of social and system integration. The 'cultural' Marxism of the Frankfurt School and Gramsci, in contrast, remain true to Marx's focus on class, but attribute far more importance to patterns of social integration in explaining why the working class failed to develop revolutionary consciousness despite the 'contradictions' inherent within the capitalist system (Lockwood 1992: 322; Bobbio 1979). While this rejects the simple systemic determinism of Marx, it also prepares the ground for a radical rejection of the idea of the economic category of social class as an elementary form of social life. This rejection is exemplified by one of the most influential theorists of the late twentieth century: Jürgen Habermas.

Habermas's theory of consensus

Habermas sought to reinvigorate the Frankfurt School's promotion of critical reason, and Marx's view of social theory as committed to the promotion of human freedom, in an analysis that contains one of the most rationalistic views of society and the embodied person, and one of the most consensually based theories, in the entire Marxist tradition.

Habermas elevates rational communicative interaction to the status of a normative form of social action central to human liberation. He does this through a critique of Marx's exclusive concern with labour as medium of class action. The material reproduction of society is significant for Habermas, but so too is the reproduction of the communicatively structured life-worlds of individuals concerned with cultural knowledge, socialisation, and identity. This dual approach towards the media of social action resembles the distinction Lockwood makes between social/system integration, and engages not only with Marx's analysis of the capitalist system but with Durkheim's, Mead's, and Schutz's accounts of everyday (inter) subjectivity. Habermas suggests that while social integration is achieved by communicatively achieved value consensus, system integration requires impersonal media such as money and power that stretch beyond the immediate contexts of interaction in co-ordinating states and markets.

Habermas (1981b: 117) refines this social integration/system integration distinction into a conception of the life-world and the system, and it is these that mediate communicative interaction. Both are subject to increasing rationalisation in Habermas's writings on the evolution of society, but this is initially a less pessimistic view of rationalisation than that characteristic of the Frankfurt School. Whereas the system is indeed associated with instrumental, means–ends rationality, linguistic interaction in the life-world is associated with a *communicative rationality* geared toward mutual understanding. The high point of this rationality emerges in what Habermas refers to as the 'ideal speech' situation involving dialogue between free and equal individuals dominated by the merits of argument. Pessimism re-emerges, though, in his suggestion that *the rationalisation of the life-world becomes colonised by the rationalisation of the system-world*. The regulation of everyday interaction occurs increasingly through media associated with the organisation of politics, bureaucracy, and labour and no longer has to be justified on the basis of mutual understanding and adjustment.

In identifying the causes of this colonisation, Habermas turns to Marx's analysis of commodities and his theory of value, but class struggle fades from view (Mészáros 1985: 35). As Habermas (1982: 225) argues, 'in the developed capitalist societies there is no identifiable class, no clearly circumscribed group which could be singled out as the representative of a general interest that has been violated'. Class antagonism no longer dominates the life-worlds of the citizens of modern welfare states: people perceive their identities in a more differentiated manner as consumers as well as producers of public and private goods, while the fragmentation of consciousness accompanying this differentiation means that there is no basis on which a struggle for a culturally unified ideology can proceed (Outhwaite 1994: 99; Habermas 1981a: 352). Conflict is effectively displaced from the system and is confined within the life-world to a diverse range of moral issues revolving around the spread of instrumental reason concerning rights, quality of life, the integrity of communities, and issues relating to health and education (Habermas 1985; Berger 1991: 168; Seel 1991).

In considering even these life-world issues, however, Habermas is still as interested in consensus as much as he is in conflict. His analysis of the evolution of the life-world as a liberating process points to the expansion of a morally consensual, democratic public realm (Seidman 1998: 197) and, while Coser (1956, 1967) argued that conflict creates consensus, Habermas sees social conflict as possible only when adversaries have common cultural references. Thus, conflict itself presupposes consensus in a manner that is strongly reminiscent of Parsons's stress on the importance of the maintenance and reproduction of cultural norms, social values and mechanisms of socialisation (Touraine 1995: 337). Indeed, while Marx's theory of conflict has been interpreted as a theory of how to change society, Habermas's analysis of positive social change rests on the concept of 'rational consensus'.

One of the great attractions of Habermas's work is its vast scope and apparent coherence in an age characterised by fragmentation in sociology. It is also politically attractive to many in its endorsement of democratic talk and in its rejection of non-rational, collective forces (which Habermas tends to associate with phenomena such as Nazism). Nevertheless, there are problems with his work that suggest he has not escaped from the issues that continue to trouble those drawing on the Marxist tradition. Habermas leaves us with a disembodied view of social actors defined by their capacity for talk. Social class fades from view, and we can question whether the term 'conflict' retains any sociological import if it is confined to a life-world characterised by a communicatively achieved moral consensus. The notion of an 'ideal speech' situation and, more broadly, the consensual theory of truth informing Habermas's work have been identified as philosophically and practically dubious (Delanty 1997), but their sociological value is surely questionable too in terms of their helpfulness in building a theory of conflict.

Lockwood distinguished social and system integration in order to understand conflict in terms of the *interplay* between them (Archer 1988: xiv); Habermas's analogous life-world/system distinction not only restricts conflict to one of these dimensions, but assesses it in terms of pre-existing, emerging, and consequent patterns of consensus. This represents a culmination of the marginalisation of conflict within the Marxist tradition. Habermas's theory is as thoroughly focused on consensus as any within the Durkheimian and Parsonian traditions, and is distinguished from these in terms of its underlying rationalism rather than because of any analytical priority accorded to the issue of conflict.

5. Concluding comments

In terms of their theoretical treatment of conflict, the twin developments of conflict sociology and critical theory follow remarkably similar patterns. Conflict sociology emerged as a reaction to Parsonian visions of value consensus, and sought to make social struggle, antagonism, and conflict central to sociology. With few exceptions, however, it returned its focus to consensus, and diluted the significance of class conflict for social change.[14] As Holmwood (1996: 97) argues, 'The pathos of post-Parsonian social theory – especially its Marxist variants – is that it is brought back to the very problems of Parsons's own approach' (see also Scott 1995: 250). Indeed, conflict studies quickly appeared to lose their disciplinary identity in dealing with such issues as international conflict, strikes, race riots, and guerrilla war (Obserschall 1978). If the early Marxist interest in 'conflict' was symbolic of the fragmentation of sociology, however, this renewed interest in 'consensus' might have symbolised a new desire for synthesis. A particularly significant aspect of Habermas's project, for example, is the idea that it is possible to establish a grand theoretical basis for a synthetic sociology that will end the fragmentation characterising contemporary analyses of social relations. Given Parsons's (1937: 774) own rejection of the fact that 'there are as many systems of sociological theory as there are sociologists', and his consequent attempt to establish a sociological synthesis, Habermas's project is not so different. As Bryant (1990: 76) expresses it, 'Could it not be said that the wheel has turned full circle? *Plus ça change, plus c'est la même chose?*'

In conclusion, although Parsons's account of the discipline may have marginalised Marx, developments of the Marxist tradition increasingly converged around some of the concerns Parsons identified as central to sociology. Conflict sociology's apparent challenge to the classical theorists therefore ends up reinforcing the significance of many central classical themes, and calling into question the idea that 'conflict' must be a unit idea for sociology: the more this narrowing of the scope of the social and the moral is pursued, the more it necessarily widens out again as issues of consensus and order reassert themselves. This is evident even in the fact that Gramsci and Habermas return to the issue of religion as a source of social and moral order. If 'the wheel has turned full circle' in this respect, however, the development of feminist sociologies and sociologies of 'race' appear to offer a more radical and extensive challenge to classical sociology. They too are as concerned with consensus as well as conflict, developing their own 'communities' of accepted theories and norms in opposition to what they perceive to be the conventionalism of traditional sociology, but they do not generally advocate building new forms of sociological synthesis rooted in a re-engagement with classical sociology.

Notes

1. The growth of radical political economy was opposed to visions of societal order, but exerted most impact in disciplines such as politics. Some accounts of sociology have classified political economy as 'radical sociology', but such a view disguises the extent to which such developments represented a *rejection* of sociology as concerned with social action and a return to extreme economistic visions that make society and social relationships epiphenomenal to production and the market place.

2. The emergence of what became known as the 'New Left' (a loose and informal alliance of groups linked, in the United States, with civil rights, student protest, and opposition to the war in Vietnam) formed an important part of the context for these developments by exerting considerable influence on intellectual trends of the time. Its representatives condemned sociology as 'a conclave of high and low priests, scribes, intellectual valets, and their innocent victims' engaged in research that reinforced an exploitative social system (cited in Gouldner 1970: 10). The force of such condemnations may be tempered by the realisation that they often came from young activists enjoying entry to, and success within, the discipline. Nevertheless, they revealed a major gap between new radical sociological sentiments and more conventional sociological theories. This was highlighted by Wright Mills (1970) and Gouldner (1970), who viewed Parsonian theory as being detached from the struggles of

contemporary societies, and argued for the abolition of sociology's 'conservative' assumptions as a way of connecting with new social movements intent on transforming Western societies.

3. Similar things can be said of Max Gluckman's (1956, 1963) influential anthropological studies of how conflicts in African tribal societies lead to the re-establishment of social cohesion.

4. Lockwood (1992: ix, 7) suggests that Durkheim's account of conflict implies the logical possibility of a polarisation of society into 'two totally opposed moral communities'. For Lockwood (1992: 152), however, Durkheim does not allow us to account for this development and presents us with a 'problem of disorder'. By according an analytical priority to normative elements in his analysis of the structuring of social action, Durkheim cannot deal with disorder except by treating it as the total normlessness of anomie.

5. The notion of 'social class' as the principal form of collective action emerged as part of the Enlightenment's criticism of traditional hierarchy, and assumed increasing importance with the growth of industrialism and the spread of democracy in the nineteenth century. As Nisbet (1966: 200) notes, 'It would be hard to find any social concept possessed of more pivotal importance after 1849 than the concept of class'. In this context, Marx denied any credit for having invented the concept of 'social class' or 'class struggle'. What Marx did lay claim to was the idea that class conflict would eventually result in the dictatorship of the proletariat and the establishment of a communist state free from basic antagonism. For all its importance to his writings, however, Marx's discussion of the concept of class is full of ambiguity and frequently appears, in common with the usage of the time, as a synonym for a faction or group (Giddens 1981: 42; McLellan 1980: 18–20). Nevertheless, Marx initially identified three classes (wage labourers, capitalists, and landowners) but recognised this was complicated by intermediate strata, and also considered the intelligentsia and lumpenproletariat as classes. Social classes, however, remained defined by their relationship to the mode of production. Hence, there are two fundamental classes in capitalism, the bourgeoisie (the owners of the means of production) and the proletariat (those who have only their labour power to sell), and it is these that face each other in a final conflict when economic crises have eradicated all intermediate strata (Marx 1849).

6. While Marx's view of class conflict clearly rejects the utilitarian view of the isolated actor, his identification of labour as the medium of this action shares certain similarities with utilitarianism insofar as rational economic action sometimes motivates collective conflict. In this context, Gouldner (1980: 110) has argued that 'Marx's critique of utilitarianism centers on its limited bourgeois form', and Lockwood goes even further in holding that Marx's theoretical system is not only consistent with the utilitarian idea of the 'rational actor', but actually rests on it (Lockwood 1992: 205).

7. In opposition to this interpretation of Marx as a rationalist, Synnott (1991: 73) suggests Marx stands out from the entire Western philosophical tradition, from Plato to Hegel, in emphasising the biological and sensory dimensions of humanity as well as its cognitive components. What Synnott does not discuss, however, is the ambiguity of Marx's account of these sensory aspects.

8. This shifting view of man is clearly associated with other Enlightenment views of humanity. Nisbet (1966: 286–7) notes that Marx's view of the proletarian is strongly suggestive of Calvin's man of God (since it implies an elect, 'invisible community' of self-sufficing individuals moving inexorably through a vale of sorrow to eventually take up residence in the realm of the righteous), but that his view of 'communist man' is also suggestive of Rousseau's view of 'natural man'. Within this interpretation, Marx's socialism replaces Rousseau's notion of the 'general will' as 'the means whereby men could be liberated from the fragmenting, corrupting influence of institutions' (Nisbet 1966: 288). More broadly, Marx was strongly committed to the Enlightenment's belief in the perfectibility of humanity (Coser 1971: 71). The non-antagonistic, post-capitalist society Marx envisaged was the goal of mankind's search for itself (Aron 1965: 139). His account of the development of this perfectibility through socialism is, however, drawn from a number of philosophical sources.

9. Despite the centrality of 'social class' to conflict sociology in the 1960s and 1970s, Marxists and Weberians engaged in vitriolic exchanges concerning the meaning of class, whether status and political groups might be equally important media of collective action, and whether the conditions in which class conflict occurred constituted a challenge to the status quo. Dahrendorf (1959) anticipates some of these debates in commenting that the 'history of the concept of class ... is surely one of the most extreme illustrations of the inability of sociologists to achieve a minimum of consensus'. In the current context, though, where class and even capitalism have become unfashionable concepts

substituted by postmodern theorists for notions suggestive of multiplicity and fragmentation, Marxist and Weberian perspectives seem to share far more in common than they did forty years ago. In particular, they are both concerned with the major structural features of capitalism, and with the factors able to extend the life of this system.

10. The attempt to remain faithful to Marx's core concerns, while developing an analysis of advanced modern societies that is more sensitive to their complexities, is evident in a number of developments of the Marxian tradition we have not looked at in any detail here. E.O. Wright's (1985) analysis of class relations is an example, though just as the Frankfurt School has been accused of slipping back into Kantian idealism Wright has been accused of reverting to a Weberian approach.

11. Mills was not alone in his conclusions and a number of interdisciplinary studies provided empirical support for his thesis that the state and major corporations were controlled by an overlapping stratum of privileged elites. Instead of providing moral direction to American society, Mills (1956, 1959) argued that the power elite was characterised by a 'higher immorality' characterised by institutionalised corruption and a 'crackpot realism' that threatened a third world war.

12. In response to this vision of seemingly inescapable order and consensus, unintentionally promoted by critical theorists, it is possible to endorse a strong version of Marxist economic determinism, suggesting that economic processes, working behind the backs of people, will eventually precipitate a crisis itself productive of conflict and change. Writers like O'Connor (1973) and Gough (1979) focused on the 'fiscal crises' facing the state in its provision of economic infrastructure and welfare services. The basic premise of their work was that the state in capitalist society had for its own survival to ensure the profitability of capital (by meeting collective expenditures for goods and services such as roads, education, and training), but was increasingly unable to meet such responsibilities. This was because its very source of funding (taxes on profits and wages) threatened the continued profitability of capital during times of economic crisis. The development of radical political economy in the 1970s expresses this view (Flacks and Turkel 1978). This can hardly be called conflict *sociology*, however, as it makes social relations epiphenomenal to economic forces.

13. Lockwood's discussion of social integration tends to conflate social order and moral order, and can itself be criticised for being unable to analyse adequately the difference between various degrees of social and moral integration.

14. According to various sociological currents, the concept of class was on the retreat because of its limited practical utility, the discrediting of Marxism following the collapse of the Soviet Union, and new patterns of stratification associated with the de-industrialisation and 'informationalisation' of modernity.

8

FEMINIST SOCIOLOGY

1. Introduction

As we saw in the last chapter, sociology has long been subject to claims that the interests of the powerful have been translated into some of the key concerns of sociology. In offering a critique of existing social orders, and sociological complicity in their maintenance, this type of argument implies a sharp distinction between social and moral orders, and rejects social scientific notions of value neutrality in favour of a morally concerned engagement with perceived inequalities and patterns of social exclusion. Some proponents of this view have abandoned sociology altogether in favour of alternative traditions of thought. Others have attempted to 'write themselves' into the discipline and thereby reconstruct it in a form more reflective of their concerns. In rejecting value neutrality, often having an overtly political intention, and yet also drawing on critical resources, methods and theories provided by the discipline, such developments enjoy an ambivalent relationship to classical sociology. This chapter focuses on feminist theory, one of the most influential forms of this sociological development.[1] Some expressions of feminist theory have explored how certain issues, such as 'race', cannot be reduced into male/female oppositions (Carby 1982; Amos and Parmar 1984; Sinha 1987). Historically, however, its major aim has been to highlight what it perceives to be the oppression of women, and to promote alternative visions of social existence that are informed by women's experiences and insights. In this respect it has a Janus-faced attitude to classical sociology.

Some feminists have sought to transform what have been termed 'malestream' theories into analytical tools suitable for their own purposes, utilising them as valuable theoretical resources in accounting for the exclusion of women from 'patriarchal' communities. Of particular importance in this respect are sociological and anthropological writings on family, kinship and taboo. Lévi-Strauss (1961) drew on Durkheim's (1898b) analysis of the incest taboo, as a social mechanism that binds people into a community transcendent of the biological mother-child bond, to develop a comprehensive theory of how men come to construct communities through the regulation and exchange of women. Gayle Rubin (1975) utilises Lévi-Strauss's work to explore how social systems are maintained on the basis of taboos that divide the sexes into two mutually exclusive corporeal categories and justify the exogamous circulation of women as gifts. By focusing on the taboo-driven exchange of women, Rubin also provides an influential interrogation of the sex/gender division. This distinguishes between biology and sexuality, on the one hand, and a system of socially instituted relations and moral norms, on the other, and emphasises that there is nothing natural about women's biology that justifies their social subordination. Thus, Durkheim's work can be criticised for offering an analysis of social and moral order that marginalises women (Gane 1983b), but Rubin draws on it, via Lévi-Strauss, to develop an influential analysis of how socially constructed models of sexual otherness can be seen as foundational to the establishment of social and moral orders.

This use of classical sociological resources is not characteristic of feminist theories in general. Many forms of feminist theory have not, like conflict sociology or feminists such as Rubin, found resources for its critique of sociology 'waiting to be discovered' in the writings of the classics. On the contrary, the discipline has been accused of reinforcing patriarchal assumptions about women. Bologh's (1990: 2) study of Weber, for example, argues that his 'social and political thought epitomises modern patriarchal masculine thinking'. Similarly, Jay (1992: 136) argues that, for Durkheim, 'true social life ... takes place among men only'. Consequently, feminist theories appear to offer a more robust challenge to classical sociology than conflict or critical theories. The extent to which they converge on themes central to the classics is also more questionable, since explicit, positive reassessments of classical figures, such as Habermas's late discovery of the merits of Durkheim or Parsons, do not tend to characterise this form of theory (but see Lehmann 1993, 1994). Nevertheless, feminism's engagement with the constraints and potentialities of human bodies, issues of meaning and identity, and the ethical dimensions of relationships between men and women, manifests an implicit convergence with core classical themes. The importance of its contribution to sociological reflection on these themes rests on its concern with the exclusionary processes through which embodiment, identity and meaning come to be contained within *male* patterns of social and moral order.

This chapter progresses as follows. Section 2 examines the notion of sexual otherness as the unit idea of feminist sociology, and analyses the general sociological importance of this concept with reference to Klaus Theweleit's (1977, 1978) study of fascism and masculinity and Simone de Beauvoir's (1949) *The Second Sex*.[2] Feminism complements the focus on sexual otherness with the view that social action is differentiated along a male/female divide, yet has identified a variety of media through which this action is translated into patriarchal outcomes. Section 3 focuses on several feminist visions of the elementary forms of social and moral life that trace the exclusion of women from male culture and thought. Radical feminism emerged in the 1960s and became influential in the 1970s. Psychoanalytic feminism grew in the 1970s and flourished in the 1980s, and deconstructive approaches to sexual difference multiplied from the 1980s and were accompanied by metaphysical conceptions of 'women as fluid' during the 1990s. The theories we examine offer distinctive visions of male/female relationships as elementary to social action and the structure of society. They also illustrate the gulf between feminist theories of the 1970s and 1990s, and the enduring theoretical tension that underpins feminist writings on difference. Section 4 focuses on this tension which involves the issue of whether sexual identity is 'natural' or socially constructed, and which assumed particular urgency towards the close of the twentieth century. Poststructuralists and postmodernists focused on the multiple, shifting and unstable relations between difference and inequality, yet also confronted a renewed concern about the bodily bases of sexual identity and performance (Nicholson 1990). These analyses suggested otherness might be subject to fragmentation and raised the possibility that sexual otherness might no longer be elementary to social action or human identity. In concluding, we analyse whether this tension dilutes the clarity and effectiveness of feminism's continuing challenge to sociology's classical concerns.

2. Sexual otherness

Feminist analyses have engaged creatively with classical theories concerning the origins of society by highlighting how social orders are characterised by a system of ideas reflecting the interests of men, yet presented as incorporating universal moral interests. The very forces that stimulate patterns of male order, indeed, are based on the marginalisation and oppression of women who might otherwise threaten that order. Durkheim, Lévi-Strauss, Freud, and Bataille all associated sexual difference with the establishment of social order, and understood women to have a marginal status, and even a destructive potential, with regard to the reproduction of social systems.

Central to these accounts of order is the role taboos play in facilitating the structuring of society in terms of a sexed bodily order. The term 'taboo' is derived from the Polynesian term *tapu*, meaning 'forbidden', though the concept has other associations including prohibition, sacredness, uncleanness and contagion (Radcliffe-Brown 1952). Taboo has also been understood as a response to the threat of danger. Freud (1950: 21), for example, notes how certain prohibitions are perceived to be necessary 'because certain persons and things are charged with a dangerous power, which can be transferred through contact with them, almost like an infection'. These threats have often been associated with women. As Durkheim (1912: 404) notes, women's inferior status is signalled by the fact that in religious cults they are 'more readily singled out to fill the function of the scapegoat'. Taboos separating the sacred from the profane also separate men from women: men are associated with goodness, creativity, strength, life and purity, while women are associated with maleficent powers, weakness, death and impurity (Hertz 1973: 12). The Hebrew Bible, for example, states that when a woman is in a state of 'menstrual pollution' she makes 'unclean' anything she touches, and anyone who touches anything she has touched will also be unclean and must wash their clothes and body (Leviticus 15: 24).

Male social order, in short, is maintained on the basis of taboos that locate women on the borders of culture, that classify their bodies as a threat to the boundaries of moral communities, and that can therefore turn them into surrogate victims who must bear the costs of 'civilisation' (Girard 1972: 307). The potential consequences of such a threat for women's and men's bodies is examined in a particularly illuminating manner in Theweleit's study of fascism, masculinity, and the German *Freikorps*.

Women, Floods, Bodies, Taboos

The *Freikorps* were volunteer armies formed to defeat revolutionary activity in Germany in 1918 some of whose members were subsequently prominent within

Hitler's regime. It is Theweleit's thesis that the fascism of these troops was forged through the development of 'armoured' bodies, constructed on the basis of taboos against femininity and interdependence. While the fleshy exteriors of these soldiers were experienced as masculine, solid and individuated, Theweleit suggests that their 'unreliable interiors' threatened this integrity because of their cultural and emotional associations with an other, dedifferentiating and forbidden femininity, that was also associated with fears of societal and moral dissolution. The archetypal threat to this bodily and social order was the Red Flood of communism, symbolised through the bodies of, and acts of sexual violence against, women (Theweleit 1977: 191, 405, 409). Such attacks represented 'a dread, ultimately, of dissolution – of being swallowed, engulfed, annihilated (Ehrenreich 1987: xiii; Theweleit 1977: 244).

The socialisation of armoured bodies inculcated in boys a disgust with bodily fluids, 'negativized to such an extent that they became the physical manifestation of all that was terrifying' (Theweleit 1977: 410). This taboo extended to warmth, and to any dedifferentiating relationship that might blur the skin's boundaries. Theweleit argues that this socialisation resulted in a 'splitting' of individuals from their affects which divided corporeality into 'inner and outer physical realms, with the skin forming an increasingly sharp borderline' between a masculine exterior and a feminine interior. It was this border that became central to the armouring of German male bodies, to the hatred of enemy women, and to the depiction of 'good German women' as protected from their polluting selves by strict adherence to images of the 'Pure Mother' and housewife. Fascism, moreover, promised men the 'reintegration' of their split selves through Nazi rituals and symbols suggestive of purity and order.

Theweleit's study focuses on one armoured bodily form and its feminine 'Others', but Ehrenreich (1987) suggests it has broader implications for understanding sexed relationships. Theweleit (1977: 415) shows how the installation of 'dark territories' in men's bodies could stimulate perceptions of women that could be used as a basis for 'subsequent ideological assault'. Women's existence as objects of exchange in Lévi-Strauss's account of peaceful societies breaks down during war (Harstock 1983), and Theweleit implies that men may then experience the 'excess' of the female Other discussed by such theorists as Luce Irigaray with growing dread. While the *Freikorps*'s response to this excess was extreme, it was forged from the 'raw matter' of human bodies, through the caring of mothers themselves, and on a sexual division of labour still relevant for modern society (Theweleit 1977: 329). The male fear of fluidity and boundary crossing appears repeatedly in feminist writing on the anxieties underpinning men's responses to women (Badinter 1980; Grosz 1994). When it comes to women's *own* corporeal socialisation, and to the most influential route through which sexual otherness became a unit idea for feminism, however, we must examine the work of de Beauvoir.

The Second Sex

In *The Second Sex*, de Beauvoir (1949) argues that man has appropriated the status of active, observing *Self*, and designated woman as the passive, observed

Other. This draws on Sartre's (1946) distinctions between Being-For-Itself and Being-In-Itself, and between the Self and the Object (or the Other). Being-In-Itself (*en-soi*) refers to the inert, material existence humans share with the natural world, whereas Being-For-Itself (*pour soi*) refers to the conscious, intentional existence unique to humans (Tong 1989: 196). Sartre's second distinction (between the Self and the Object [or the Other]) is based on the recognition that individual selves often treat others as objects to be used for their own conscious projects. De Beauvoir supplements this distinction by suggesting that woman has histori-cally been constructed as Other (sentenced to a life of immanence) for use by the male Self (able to actively test out opportunities through which he can define his future). Social roles are the primary mechanisms for this process: it is through such roles as wife, daughter and mother that 'men compel [women] to assume the status of the Other', to 'stabilise her as an object and to doom her to immanence' (de Beauvoir 1949). Women's fate involves 'a degradation of existence into the "en soi" – the brutish life of subjection to given conditions – and of liberty into constraint and contingence' (de Beauvoir 1949: liv).

While becoming a woman involves 'apprenticeship' (involving a painful sociali-sation into passive roles, customs and body techniques), de Beauvoir (1949: lv, 34) insists that this socialisation is based on the bodily differences between girls and boys; biological considerations 'play a part of the first rank and consti-tute an essential element' in the situation of women. However, de Beauvoir (1949: 38, 281) also insists that 'Biology is not enough to give an answer to the question … why is woman the *Other*? Women are *created* as Other and this process starts with the constraints characteristic of girls socialisation: sacred authority figures surround and reveal the future for girls, whereas boys are encouraged to 'break away', to discover and project themselves on the world (de Beauvoir 1949: 284–5, 313). When a boy is introduced to violent sports – that teach him how to use his body against 'any attempt to reduce him to the status of an object' – girls are directed to passive activities. These gendered apprentice-ships corporeally damage girls: 'Not to have confidence in one's body is to lose confidence in oneself' and to be vulnerable to attempts to be dominated and 'transcended by others' (de Beauvoir 1949: 348–9).

De Beauvoir analyses the *social* processes surrounding the embodiment of female Otherness. Nevertheless, Tong's (1989: 214) judgment that de Beauvoir was hostile to the female body is shared by many. From childhood to menopause, women's 'troubled bodies' highlight the Being-In-Itself aspect of existence: woman 'has less firmness and less steadiness available for projects that in general she is less capable of carrying out' (de Beauvoir 1949: 36). It may be 'during her periods that she feels her body most painfully as an obscure, alien thing … the prey of a stubborn and foreign life that each month constructs and then tears down a cradle within it'. Women become 'life's passing instrument', absorbed by the burdens of pregnancy including breastfeeding when 'the infant seems to her to be sucking out her strength, her life, her happiness' (de Beauvoir 1949: 30, 29, 535).

This analysis appears to suggest that de Beauvoir validates the taboo against women evident in traditional theories of the creation of society, providing an endorsement rather than a critical analysis of this male vision of sexual difference and female inferiority. More sympathetically, it has been argued that de Beavoir adopts a dual approach to women's Otherness: she examines how women's bodies are *constructed* as immanent Others (and therefore admits the possibilities of change and transcendence through conscious, productive activity), but also views women's bodies as *amenable* to that construction (Hughes and Witz 1997: 49–50). In this context, de Beauvoir (1949: 713) exhorts woman to *leave her body behind*: to engage in conscious productive or artistic activity facilitative of transcendence and resistant to the objectification and exchange characteristic of traditional systems of kinship and taboo.

Our discussions of sexual otherness have centred on Theweleit and de Beauvoir, as they make for productive comparison. While de Beauvoir focuses on apprenticeships in womanhood, Theweleit examines a particularly oppressive form of masculine socialisation. Both relate forms of embodiment to forms of sociality and taboos that position women as the passive objects and (threatening) Others of men. Both examine how the 'raw material' of human embodiment is socially shaped into forms of corporeality recognisably male and female, and both suggest sexed relationships are elementary to the construction of social and moral order. While Theweleit locates social action firmly in the embodied existence of his 'armoured' subjects, however, de Beauvoir proceeds on the basis of the Cartesian division central to Sartre's work. Freedom and action are defined in terms of a conscious existence free from the constraints of emotions and the physical world (Sartre 1946: 28). These different views of sexual otherness are reflected more generally in competing feminist visions of the elementary forms of social and moral life.

3. The elementary forms of social and moral life

With the exception of liberal feminism, which views sexually differentiated action as something that will wither given appropriate legal reform (Williams 1997), the unit idea of sexual otherness is linked in feminist theory to the view that there is an elementary difference between the social and moral capacities, dispositions and actions characteristic of men and women. Nevertheless, while feminists before and after de Beauvoir conceptualised social action as divided along male/female lines (McDonald 1997), there is less agreement about the media through which this action is channelled into unequal outcomes, and the precise character of these outcomes. Sexual apprenticeships mediated social action for de Beauvoir, but other feminists focus on the economy, the household, and ideologies of sexuality as mediators of gendered action. This diversity can be traced in part to 'second wave' feminism in the 1960s and 1970s. In addition to its political ambitions, this feminist movement insisted that malestream knowledge takes into account women's class, status and political affiliations, rather than collapsing them into male norms, but also promoted a variety of specifically female perspectives on social life.

In terms of those malestream perspectives that feminists sought to adapt, Marxist sociologies were based on assumptions about the primacy of the mode of production, but emphasised class rather than gender relations in the productive process. Feminists responded to this during the 1970s by developing forms of Marxist-feminism focused on gender, but sharing Marxism's emphasis on the mode of production. Predominantly concerned with understanding women's oppression by widening notions of (re)production, the household became *the* medium that organised biological reproduction, the socialisation of children, and the reproduction of (male) labour power (Sacks 1974; Vogel 1983; Shelton and Agger 1993; Chafetz 1997). Feminists also sought to write women into other sociological traditions. England (1993) and Chafetz (1997) guide us through this territory. World systems theory, for example, has been extended by feminists to demonstrate how capitalist penetration of 'peripheral' nations by 'core' nations reduces women's status (Ward 1984). Network theory has been widened to suggest that gender-specific networks form in school and develop with increasingly significant social consequences throughout adult life (Smith-Lovin and McPherson 1993), and ethnomethodological accounts expanded to examine the processes involved in 'doing gender' (West and Zimmerman 1987). Feminists even adopted and extended rational choice theory, despite the fact that this form of theory has been criticised for offering an essentially male perspective on human beings (Luker 1984; Gerson 1985; Brinton 1988; Friedman and Diem 1993). To turn to the broader subject of what is elementary to social and moral life, however, three loose groupings of feminist theory illustrate the diversity of feminist theory from 1960 to the start of the twenty-first century.

Radical feminism

In examining the sexed nature of social action, radical feminism prioritises patriarchy over capitalism, sexual over economic relations, and highlights how men control women's bodies through the institutional media of marriage, motherhood and heterosexuality. Radical feminism suggests women possess a unique nature that sets them apart biologically and socially from men, though for them it is men who are perceived to be inherently dangerous to women. As a theory, it has sometimes been analysed as evolving into 'cultural feminism', 'the ideology of a female nature or female essence re-appropriated by feminists themselves to revalidate undervalued female attributes' (Alcoff 1988).[3] These feminisms are closely aligned, both viewing the elementary form of social action as irredeemably divided into (desirable) female and (undesirable) male variants mediated through patriarchal institutions. This institutional context has created a division between women's mediated and estranged experiences of their bodily selves on the one hand, and their essential female nature on the other; patriarchy suppresses women's potential for sensing female values, knowledge and relationships that transcend the oppressions of male dominated society.

This division between men's institutional control of women and women's potential experience of their essential nature is highlighted by Rich (1979) and can be illustrated with reference to motherhood and sexuality. In the case of motherhood, O'Brien (1989: 49) argues that men established an institutional framework predicated on an attempt to gain compensation for their alienation from the reproductive process. Whereas women are involved, body and mind, in reproduction, paternity is for men predominantly an idea. The institutional media of fatherhood and marriage, and the development of the public/private divide, reflect a male attempt to appropriate control of the care and socialisation of children that extends into the management of childbirth. Martin (1989: 146, 61), for example, describes how technology contributes to the sense of estrangement experienced by many women during labour, while others highlight the dangers of men organising reproductive technologies and surrogate motherhood via contractual arrangements (Balsamo 1996; Hartouni 1996).

In the case of sexuality, Mackinnon (1989) argues that the institutionalisation of heterosexuality provides men with another medium of control over women: a control significantly bound up with the legalised violence they have historically exerted in marriage (Dworkin 1981). In this type of feminism, however, women's potential *experience* of their nature cannot be reduced to patriarchal media. Rich (1979) suggests the experience of motherhood can be the most wonderful, celebratory and distinctive aspect of women's nature, while O'Brien (1989: 14) views childbirth as representative of a broader 'unity of knowing and doing' characteristic of female lives. Similarly, the experience of sexuality is understood to be full of liberating possibilities connected to lesbian alternatives to heterosexuality. Daly (1984) defends 'wild' and 'lusty' women who renounce androgyny in favour of radical lesbian separatism. More generally, Rich (1979: 31–2) suggests that while male institutions are oppressive, women have the potential to experience the diffuse, intense sensuality radiating out from clitoris, breasts, uterus as a liberating epistemological resource. This liberation is often associated with a feminist politics of *separatism*, to enable the creation of a social and moral order free of 'masculinist' values (Alcoff 1988). Here, it is heterosexuality that becomes taboo.

Nevertheless, the suggestion by radical feminists that *natural* sexual differences underpin male and female action, and that these differences necessitate separatism, has been criticised. Jaggar (1983, 1984) notes that while radical feminist writings are filled with references to 'the power inherent in female biology' (Griffin 1978), these rule out the possibility of consensual heterosexual relations, and posit unchanging female/male natures at odds with the experiences of many women. Kaplan and Rogers (1990: 209) comment that the women/nature equation has been made by men for thousands of years 'without much evidence of gaining women any more rights or freedoms', while Alcoff (1988) concludes that 'essentialist formulations of womanhood, even when made by feminists, "tie" the individual to her identity as a woman and thus cannot represent a solution to sexism'. Radical feminism has also been criticised as reductionist, ethnocentric and even racist. Certain black feminists, for example, have viewed its 'biological determinism' as 'a particularly dangerous and reactionary basis upon which to build a politic' (Combahee River Collective 1979: 66–9). By associating women's oppression with the universal state of patriarchy, moreover, radical feminism posits an undifferentiated system of oppression insensitive to historical, technological and cultural variation.

Three additional points can usefully be made about this approach. First, radical feminism incorporates a simple inversion of male social orders founded on the domination, marginalisation or exclusion of women. Rather than grappling with the subject of exclusion *per se*, it not only marginalises men in the interests of female solidarity, but also sometimes excludes them completely. The society of harmonious lesbian sociality envisaged by many radical feminists, in fact, has all the hallmarks of what Durkheim (1912) calls a religious cult. Second, radical feminism is not a unitary approach. While radical feminists often claim sexuality can only be expressed in a non-aggressive form within a lesbian relationship, others disagree. Furthermore, the radical feminist Shulamith Firestone (1971) is ambivalent about the natural powers that are understood to characterise women's bodies, and emphasises the capacity of technology to release women from the burdens of reproduction. Third, however, and in spite of these limitations, radical feminism highlights the centrality of the female body to the media that translate male/female action into patriarchal outcomes. If embodiment is central to our ability to intervene in the social world, then institutions and practices that damage women's bodily being are likely to reduce their ability to exercise agency (Shafer and Frye 1986). In highlighting such issues, the development of radical feminism in the 1960s and 1970s 'set the agenda for the women's movement as well as for feminist thought' (Lovell 1995: 310).

Psychoanalytic feminism

Psychoanalytic writings became popular during the latter half of the 1970s among feminists, and attracted substantial followings in the 1980s (Weedon 1987). They offer views of gender identity and action based not simply on the institutional suppression or endorsement of female nature, but on a more complex cultural, interpersonal and symbolic *mediation* of biology (Rubin 1975). Specifically, they focus on how psychic processes are mediated through traditional male/female sex roles or through the linguistic symbolisation of culture. These roles or symbolic media channel and repress childhood experiences to provide a libidinal and mental basis for sexual divisions of labour.

Psychoanalysis views the internalisation of sexual identity as part of a broader developmental process. Freud argued that children 'normally' develop from an undifferentiated, 'polymorphously perverse' sexuality to the adoption of hetero-sexual identities. This takes place as a result of the structuring of the ego through the incest taboo in 'the Oedipal stage', and it is through such mechanisms that children learn to give up desire for their mother and attach it to members of the opposite sex outside the family. Feminists have been critical of the 'phallocen-tric' biological developmental norms characteristic of psychoanalysis (Millett 1970), but developed this approach in two major directions. The first has been referred to as 'maternal feminism', because of its emphasis on the centrality of mothering to development, and was most influential in America through the work of Chodorow.

Chodorow (1978) examines how mother-dominated parenting provides a basis for differentiated sexual selves. Commenting on the masculine domination and oppression of women, Chodorow argues that, far from being exceptional, this is the normal by-product of gendered psychosexual developments mediated by nuclear families in which men rarely engage in childcare. In developing gendered identi-ties, girls do not separate from their mothers but grow into women used to relation-ships based on emotional continuity and communication. The social meaning of masculinity is shielded from boys, however, because of its associations with public sphere, but clearly involves a *break* from the main relationship that dominated their childhood. While mother-child intimacy provides the means by which women grow up, boys must break away from maternal intimacy in order to achieve adulthood.

Chodorow's (1978) thesis suggests that male/female social action is mediated by a domestically located developmental process which produces an enduring gap between masculinity and emotional communication, and between the aspirations and communicative abilities of men and women. While women tend to turn to men for deep emotional relationships, in an adult world in which lesbianism is largely taboo, men are threatened by these relationships. Men's emotional distance, furthermore, draws a new generation of women to motherhood as a means of recreating the 'intense emotional bonds' characteristic of their own upbringing. The outcomes of the processes identified by Chodorow, then, result in fundamental emotional divisions between the sexes (Williams 1993).

Chodorow proposes dual parenting as a solution to this problem (see also Dinnerstein 1977), but her work has been criticised for underestimating the impact of culture, for generalising on the basis of a specific family type, and for neglecting how dual parenting might be detrimental to women (Tong 1989). Nevertheless, Chodorow developed an influential account of how childhood socialisation produces elementary emotional differences between women and men. It informed Gilligan's (1982) suggestion that women developed a relational ethics in comparison with the abstract ethics adopted by men (see also Benhabib 1987), and anticipated certain features of feminist standpoint epistemologies.

The second version of feminist psychoanalysis emerged from critical engagements with the writings of Jacques Lacan, yet shares an affinity with theories of kinship. As Rubin (1975) notes, if theories of kinship explain the enculturation of sex at a social level, psychoanalysis explains the internalisation of gender at an individual level. Lacan (1977) argued that the creation of a conscious human subject from the undifferentiated newly born child occurs through a series of imaginary identifications during which the child apprehends itself as separate from others. Crucial to Lacan is the 'Symbolic Order', the language, symbols and culture of social law represented by the father. If a child is to function socially, it must become proficient within this order, but this order also structures its subjectivity. Specifically, the Symbolic Order 'finalises' the illusion of individuality and sexual identity (via a masculine repression of the dedifferentiated state that characterised the child's early existence), just as systems of taboo have historically affirmed the illusion that women are necessarily objects rather than subjects of exchange. This is the essential insight developed by this version of feminism: women are marginalised, misrepresented, repressed and excluded from the Symbolic. In contrast to Chodorow's argument about the dominance of the maternal female, *masculinity* rather than femininity is represented to children.

Julia Kristeva, Hélène Cixous and Luce Irigaray provide three representatives of this approach. Kristeva accepts that women cannot be represented in the Symbolic, but suggests that a feminine 'semiotic' disrupts cultural order through the intrusion of slips, rhythm, laughter, poetry and meaninglessness. Cixous, in contrast, concentrates on the binary system organising patriarchal thought that places women on the negative side of such divisions as active/passive, culture/ nature and intellect/sensuality. In opposing this phallocentric structure of knowledge, Cixous (1976) coined the term, *écriture féminine*. This female writing challenges patriarchal thought and derives from a specific form of libido. Indeed, Cixous identifies an eternal female essence that, once revealed through writing, has the potential to avoid the mediating power of the Symbolic and transform patriarchy (Duchen 1986: 92; Wenzel 1981: 272).

Irigaray has proved to be perhaps the most influential exponent of feminist psychoanalysis. While de Beauvoir perceived women as Other to men, Irigaray (1977 [1985]) suggests both the subject (or the Self) and the Other are produced by a culture which excludes the feminine altogether: 'woman' is a point of linguistic absence defined as lacking what men have. Nevertheless, Irigaray maintains that female sexuality possesses a libidinal structure different to men's that can be approached by recognising that if man is singular and instrumental, woman is multiple. This multiplicity is evident in women's sensory experiences, and in an autoerotic sensuality manifest in the fundamental difference between the penis and the vagina: 'Woman "touches herself" all the time ... for her genitals are formed of two lips in continuous contact' (Irigaray 1977, 1985: 24, 26, 29). Such comments have been interpreted as revealing the essential female body that forms the basis of Irigaray's writing, but sympathetic commentators suggest they seek simply to challenge the Symbolic by forging descriptions of female sexuality ordinarily excluded from culture (Whitford 1991; Lovell 1995).

Irigaray suggests female desire is 'totally foreign to male desire', and it has been argued that 'the two can only be brought together through a patriarchal repression of the female' (Weedon 1987: 64; Moi 1985: 133). Developing her approach to offer a more positive interpretation of how men and women might relate to each other, however, Irigaray has constructed an 'ethics of sexual difference' offering an alternative vision of sexual relationships. Invoking Descartes's 'first passion', wonder, Irigaray argues that admiration and awe in the face of something unknowable 'ought to be returned to its proper place: the realm of sexual difference'. Here, relations between the sexes can assume a *sacred* quality, and Irigaray uses the term divine to express some of their possibilities. This sense of the divine would allow men and women to retain an autonomy based on their difference, but give them a free space wherein attraction and alliance become possibilities (Irigaray 1984: 124).

Psychoanalysis enabled feminists to explore the complex cultural mediation of sexual otherness and action. In contrast to de Beauvoir's portrayal of woman's 'body in trouble', maternal psychoanalytic feminism identifies positive emotional qualities in women, lacking in men, while Lacanian psychoanalytic feminism *celebrates* sexual difference. Both approaches have critically examined how women are constructed as Other to men in manners which fit them psychically for being objects of exchange (Barrett 1992; Gatens 1992). However, while the maternal feminism of Chodorow identifies possibilities for change, sexual difference remains the only foreseeable outcome for Lacanian-inspired psychoanalytic feminism. Its analysis of the 'Symbolic' (the media responsible for this outcome) has, however, been criticised. Fraser (1997: 384) suggests it turns the complex diversity of culture into 'a monolithic and all-pervasive [order] endowed with an exclusive causal power to fix people's subjectivities once and for all'. Fuss (1990: 12) points out that the view of identity and action associated with the Symbolic is itself based on the fixity of an essential sexual being dividing women from men. Cixous's *écriture féminine*, for example, might purport 'to subvert masculine order and language by writing the feminine libidinal and erotic into the text', but does 'little more than emphasise woman's basic differences – her breasts, womb, or vagina – and the functions unique to these differences – woman as genitrix, daughter or lover' (Wenzel 1981: 272). Feminist psychoanalysis has been criticised, in short, for incorporating a view of sexual identity that reduces gender to universal psychosexual processes based on the body. This 'recreates stereotypes and myths about woman as natural, sexual, biological, and corporal by celebrating her essences' (Wenzel 1981: 272; cf. Moi 1985: 126; Weedon 1987: 46). In this context, how can anatomy ever *not* be destiny?[4] Feminist psychoanalysis might seek to rescue 'woman' from the prohibitions which have surrounded and misrepresented her in male culture, but risks identifying differences which may serve as the basis of renewed taboos and exclusions.

Femininity as fluidity

The 1980s and 1990s witnessed a rise in feminist engagements with social constructionist and deconstructionist theories and sought to develop within a more radical framework previous emphases on otherness. Drawing on the work of Foucault, Lacan and Derrida, feminists added a greater concern with phenomenological issues while also incorporating some notion of sex or gender as elementary to social action. Incorporating at its centre a 'metaphysics of fluidity' (which opposes the binary oppositions and 'ontological fixity' central to male culture with an emphasis on women's embodied experiences of socialisation, menstruation, sexuality, childbirth and lactation), this approach theorises difference via a sensitivity to change and instability. It also emphasises the specific circumstances characteristic of women's lives such as the corporeal 'immersion and repetition' characteristic of caring work (Harstock 1983), and women's responsibility for 'the private realm of need, desire, and affectivity' (Young 1990: 101). While de Beauvoir associated these tasks with a physical immanence detrimental to women's involvement in public life, these contemporary perspectives view immanence *positively* as a medium facilitating social actions that enable and liberate women.

Rethinking female embodiment outside of binary oppositions, in terms of a fluid mode of experience, has been seen as a method that can produce fundamentally new insights. This is because it refuses to apprehend women as always already objectified within male systems of thought: 'Fluids surge and move, and a metaphysic that thinks being as fluid would ... privilege the living, moving, pulsing, over the inert dead matter of the Cartesian worldview' (Young 1990: 193). This metaphysics of fluidity shares an affinity with Irigaray's argument that the feminine is characterised by multiplicity (with 'two lips touching') which dominant philosophical models of ontology as solid cannot appreciate (Irigaray 1985: 111–13).[5] Elizabeth Grosz and Iris Young are influential exponents of this approach.

Grosz views women as fluid, flowing and resistant to male culture and begins with the model of the body as a 'mobius strip' (the inverted three-dimensional figure eight) which suggests flesh and mind flow into each other. She suggests that body image is the flexible, unstable product of the ego's relation between the organism and reality that provides a unity for the senses to interact and produce a coherent world-view (Grosz 1994: 36–43, 66, 99–100). Drawing on Deleuze and Guattari's (1977) notion of the 'Body Without Organs', Grosz conceives body/ image in terms of 'the things it can perform, the linkages it establishes, the transformations ... it undergoes' (Grosz 1994: 164–5). This allows her to highlight how the 'fluidity and indeterminacy of female body parts, most notably the breasts but no less the female sexual organs' are 'confined, constrained, solidified, through ... temporary or permanent means of solidification by clothing or ... by surgery' in male culture (Grosz 1994: 205).

This notion of the fluidity of women is not new: representations of women as limitless flows became popular during the Enlightenment. As Theweleit (1977: 360, 380) notes, critics of the 'increasingly marked atomisation of individuals' in the marketplace portrayed women as nature, emotion and 'transcendence', before the German romantics of the nineteenth century, turned the 'utopian potential' of woman into something quite different where 'the erotic woman becomes the devouring demon'. Grosz, perhaps unwittingly, resurrects this Enlightenment tradition, but it is not just the fluid Other of women's bodies that interests her; she is also concerned with the unstable interior of men's bodies. She asks whether men's concern with bodily integrity might be a move to 'distance themselves from the very kind of corporeality – uncontrollable, excessive, expansive, disruptive, irrational – they have attributed to women (Grosz 1994: 200–3). This resonates with Theweleit's analysis. According to Grosz (1994: 201–2), however, it is *receiving* fluid, rather than fear of fluidity, which heterosexual men cannot bear; a fear bound up with loss of control and transcendence. It is only when men acknowledge the indeterminacy of their own bodily boundaries, she suggests, that they 'will respect women's bodily autonomy and sexual specificity as well'.

Young's (1990) phenomenology of female embodiment also aims to construct a liberating, 'woman-centred experiential voice' via a 'metaphysics of fluids' which refuses the 'metaphysics of objects' implicated in the construction and oppression of women as Other. This opposes the touch-control male mode of engaging with the world with a touch-touched female mode of engagement that blurs the boundaries between self and world and facilitates social action that proceeds on the basis of continuity with experience. As Young (1990: 147–8) argues, 'While feminine bodily existence is a transcendence and openness to the same world, it is an ambiguous transcendence ... that is at the same time laden with immanence'. This ambiguity does not arise because women possess frail 'bodies in trouble', but is the product of socialised and more foundational differences between women and men. Conventional divisions between immanence and transcendence break down when women's embodied experiences are examined (Young 1990: 163); women's fluidity reveals the limitations of those divisions central to male culture which have prohibited women from the role of active subjects.

This metaphysics of fluidity became increasingly popular in the 1990s because of its potential to interrogate sexual difference while leaving aside the precise ontological status of this difference. But this indeterminacy is also problematic. What is the status of women's fluidity? Does the formulation 'femininity as fluidity' resolve the problems of radical and psychoanalytic perspectives? Grosz's (1994) discussions of sexed bodies and sexed relationships suggests not.

Grosz (1994: 188–90) insists she is not forming a new account of the body, but opposes the idea that sexual difference is forged out of undifferentiated bodies. She therefore suggests women and men are indeed different *prior to* their subjection to social forces: the possession of certain genitals 'must play a major role in the type of body imagery one has' (Grosz 1994: 58). Yet Grosz (1994: 203) subsequently denies that women are ontologically more fluid than men: women's corporeality is merely 'inscribed as a mode of seepage' and women 'are represented and live themselves as seepage, liquidity'. The tension between these two statements is side-stepped when Grosz suggests a metaphysics of fluidity might be 'strategic' (we are reminded of her 1995 suggestion that theoretical inconsistency might be the price feminists pay when wanting to prioritise politics). The foundations of Young's analysis are also flexible. 'Ambiguous transcendence' is central, but its origins seem sometimes social, sometimes psychoanalytic, and sometimes associated with states of being such as pregnancy that radical feminists view as essential to female nature.

Each of the theories examined in this section proceeds from the unit idea of sexual otherness. Taken together, they illustrate how feminism has moved from a position of relative certainty about the natural, biological underpinnings of sexual otherness, hidden beneath patriarchal media, to positions that vacillate between viewing sexual action as 'natural' and as 'constructed'. The growing uncertainty about the status of sex and gender in approaches drawing on a metaphysics of fluidity has been accelerated by an increased focus on differences *within* the sexes. Examples of this are evident in studies of race, class and gender (Anderson and Collins 1995), post-colonialism (Mohanty 1988; Spivak 1987), and 'queer theory' (De Lauretis 1991; Seidman 1994). The cumulative impact of these writings has been twofold. First it highlights the diversity and multiplicity of forms of inequality and oppression related to sexual action. Second, it serves to raise doubts about the notion that there is any stable, natural content to 'sexual identity'. As Trinh Minh-Ha (1989: 96) argues, 'Difference is that which undermines the very idea of identity'. This highlights a tension central to feminist theory: is sexual identity determined by the natural bodily bases of sexual otherness (even if its present content is distorted by patriarchal taboos and prohibitions), or is it socially constructed?

4. Sex and gender: are they socially constructed?

Underpinning the discussions in this chapter has been a division central to feminist theory: the sex/gender distinction. Oakley (1972: 16) provided a definitive statement of this distinction as it was understood in the 1960s and 1970s: 'That people are male or female can usually be judged by referring to biological evidence. That they are masculine or feminine cannot be judged in the same way: the criteria are cultural, differing with time and place. The constancy of sex must be admitted, but so must also the variability of gender'.[6] In short, while the 'content' of gender varied across culture and history, the 'container' of sex was thought of as timeless (Delphy 1996: 33). This assumption has been undermined, however, with suggestions that biological definitions of sex consist of genetic, hormonal and physiological indicators whose grouping together under the male/female opposition is a *social* act that varies historically (e.g. Stanley 1984; Kaplan and Rogers 1990; Laqueur 1990; Birke 1992). Far from representing a natural/social division, the sex/gender distinction can be seen as a social/social division.

The idea that both sex and gender are socially constructed suits the deconstructionist tendencies in feminism keen to abolish any 'natural' basis for male/female inequalities. Delphy (1984) and Wittig (1982), for example, interpret the biological as a manifestation of the social which does not require independent analysis as a source of women's oppression but is the creation of an Other within heterosexist discourse which maintains oppression (Fuss 1990: 51). This deconstructionism has also proved problematic for feminists wanting to *maintain* the idea of difference between women and men (Duchen 1986: 41). The women's movement of the 1960s, for example, placed on the political agenda issues related to health, fertility control, abortion and male violence based on the premise that significant differences existed between the sexes which had been ignored by patriarchal society.

This dilemma can be examined via the work of one of the most influential feminists of the 1990s. Critical of the Cartesianism governing de Beauvoir's analysis of the mind as freedom and the (female) body as constraint, Judith Butler (1994, 1990) deconstructs the opposition between the sexual body (as foundational and natural) and normative gender (as product and cultural) by arguing that 'sex', 'body', 'gender' and 'identity' are *equally constructed* by the dominant matrix of heterosexuality. Butler's approach is predicated on the notion that the gendered body is *performative*. This means that 'acts and gestures ... create the illusion of an interior and organising gender core, an illusion discursively maintained for the purposes of the regulation of sexuality within the obligatory frame of reproductive heterosexuality' (Butler 1990: 136). This 'obligatory frame' defines what it is to be Other to men and what it is to excluded from the matrix of heterosexuality. Yet Butler argues that heterosexual identity is as performatively constructed as *any* identity. Drag, for example, 'enacts the very structure of impersonation by which *any gender* is assumed' (Butler 1997: 306). By seeking to make itself appear original and natural, heterosexuality is merely a compulsive and compulsory repetition that can only produce the *effect* of its own originality. The contingency of these effects, however, provides opportunities for *change*. There may be no 'doer behind the deed' able to reclaim an essential humanity, but the repeated actions productive of identity are vulnerable to parody and subversion (Butler 1990: 141–2).

While Butler's (1990) *Gender Trouble* focused on gender as stylised (bodily) performance, her (1993) *Bodies That Matter* focuses on the category of sex. Sex refers to the *discursively constituted* materiality of the sexed body (Butler 1993: 1). Thus, sexed bodies are as constructed as gendered bodies, and Butler's concern with the matter of bodies is actually a concern with the discursive construction and materialisation of bodies. Foucault's writings remain influential (Butler 1993: 10), but Althusser is also used to reveal how bodies are produced as sexed in order for them to engage in gendered doings. Althusser suggests subjects are 'hailed' or 'interpolated' to assume certain positions: ideological and repressive institutions participate in the 'girling' of the infant, a 'founding interpolation', 'reiterated' to produce a 'naturalised effect' which sets boundaries and inculcates norms (Butler 1993: 7–8). Once again, it is the power of discursive authorities to *construct* materiality that interests Butler (1993: 68). Indeed, Butler questions whether feminists need to talk about the materiality of sex and admits 'I began writing this book by trying to consider the materiality of the body only to find that the thought of materiality *invariably moved me into other domains*' (Butler 1993: 29, ix, emphasis added).

Butler's work raises important dilemmas associated with the question 'how far is sexual identity socially constructed?' that are made explicit by two reactions to her thesis. Hughes and Witz (1997: 55–8) are concerned about the occlusion of material bodies in *Gender Trouble*, a study in which gender only really exists through ethereal 'corporeal styles', and suggests she never gets to grips with women's lived experiences. They argue this is partly because Butler loses touch with 'gender' as a distinctive variable that can affect the lived material body. Instead of accusing her of too much constructionism, in contrast, Cealey-Harrison and Hood-Williams (1997) suggest Butler's stated concern for the sexed *materiality* of bodies is a regressive move. While de Beauvoir was unwilling to equate women with their bodies or to regard them as humans labelled 'women' (Cealey-Harrison and Hood-Williams 1997: 108), Butler's early (1990) analysis resolves this tension between materialism and nominalism by turning to social constructionism. What puzzles Cealey-Harrison and Hood-Williams (1997: 107–8), however, is why Butler subsequently continues to distinguish between sex and gender. Far better, they suggest, to recognise that 'sex' is an historical invention, that sex and gender are discursive constructions, and that the sex/gender distinction needs abandoning. This disagreement points us to the continuing difficulties of recovering a sexually other identity and form of social action prior to its distortion through patriarchal media.

5. Concluding comments

References to the materiality of the body inevitably raise the question of whether this involves the return to an analytical focus on a universal, biological phenomenon. This, in turn, would imply a move away from the emphasis on 'heterogeneity, diversity and difference' characteristic of recent feminist thought (Phillips 1992: 11) that suggests there is nothing obdurate in the differences between 'men' and 'women'. Such a continued commitment to essentialist understandings of women and sex/gender relations often tends towards the replication, in an inverted form, of the exclusionary social processes and outcomes associated with patriarchal social orders. As Gilligan's (1982) account of the intrinsic moral characteristics of women and men illustrates, constructions of a 'we' almost always propose a marginalised or excluded 'you' (Collins 1988: 122). Radical separatist forms of feminism, in particular, appear to manifest an interesting case study of such processes rather than a serious challenge to them.

The influence of deconstructionist social theory on contemporary feminism, on the other hand, not only undermines the possibility of a creative engagement with classical sociology, but also actually deprives feminism of a positive subject on which to base any substantive critique of the discipline. The promise of abandoning assumptions about a materially sexed body and the cohesion of 'woman' is held to be that it 'opens out a much richer range of explanatory possibilities' (Cealey-Harrison and Hood-Williams 1997: 113–14), but these possibilities cannot include a morally engaged sociology because it espouses relativism. As Riley (1988) has argued, despite the instabilities associated with woman, and the male/female opposition, abandoning them effectively removes the ground for feminist struggle. In place of the value neutrality feminism has sought to challenge, this theory offers only value relativism.

Standpoint theory has attempted to avoid the extremes of associating all women with a single outlook, or of suggesting that being a woman has no consequences for perceiving the world (Lovell 1996: 336). Nevertheless, the question of '*which* standpoint?' raises, in a different form, the same problems that characterise arguments about the shifting contents and implications of various conceptualisations of 'sex' and 'gender', and broader arguments about the relationship between social orders and embodied predispositions and characteristics. As theorists of race and ethnicity remind us, all women do not share the same experiences or interests, and sometimes these may be diametrically opposed.

Irigaray's (1993) development of the notion of the divine in her work points towards another route out of some of the problems of defining sex and gender. She argues that the *male* God of Christianity has helped men define their gender by allowing them to orient their finiteness by reference to infinity, but women have had no God to act as the limit to and the fulfilment of their gender (Beattie 1997: 170). Consequently, she believes that women need a feminine God. If she is to become woman, if she is to accomplish her female subjectivity, woman needs a God who is a figure for the perfection of *her* femininity (Irigaray 1993: 64). This approach shares with classical sociology an interest in the subjects of transcendence, embodiment and the symbolic power of religion. Nonetheless, while Irigaray's notion of the divine may contain echoes of Durkheim's notion of the sacred as a society's symbolic representation of itself to itself, it suggests a *theological* route for the development of feminist theory. This route, which urges the creation of a new divine order shaped by a metaphysics of embodiment, therefore proposes a radically non-sociological future for feminism. Young's (1990) notions of ambiguous transcendence and a metaphysics of fluidity point in a similar direction.

In conclusion, feminist theories offer valuable corrections to some of the oversights, assumptions and implicit exclusions of earlier generations of sociologists, but the nature of their impact upon the broader theoretical concerns of classical sociology is ambiguous. The argument that classical visions of social and moral life not only ignored women but also implicitly legitimated their subordination to men is an important, if contentious, one. The subsequent development of socio-logical theories that implicitly or explicitly legitimise the marginalisation of *men* from social and moral orders, however, together with relativistic excursions into the more extreme realms of social constructionism, are of more questionable value in terms of any challenge to classical sociological theory. More broadly, however, feminist theories can be understood to manifest a convergence with classical sociology in terms of their interest in issues of embodiment, identity and meaning, and the relationship of these to patterns of social and moral order. This is especially evident in those psychoanalytic studies that, despite their return to metaphysics, seek to develop a system of ethics that is attentive to sexual differ-ences but resistant to the tendency to replace one pattern of exclusion with another. This desire, despite the problems discussed in this chapter, illuminates the continuing importance of feminist theories for reminding sociologists of the social and moral significance of sex and gender in the development of social orders and sociological theories.

Notes

1. There is a tendency within certain forms of feminist writing to 'reject theory' in favour of a focus on women's experiences and narratives about the social world. This disguises the extent to which this is itself a theoretical stance involving the prioritisation of one way of viewing the world over others.

2. It has been claimed that 'feminist' writings explored sexual otherness long before modern the-ories of kinship – early arguments were formulated before the French Revolution (Phillips 1992; McDonald 1997) – even if they shared with them a conviction that male/female relationships were central to the construction of society.

3. Our use of 'radical feminism' is similar to that deployed in a range of feminist writings, but excludes socially- and economically-grounded explanations of women's oppression that sometimes attract the label 'radical' (see Tong 1989; Nicholson 1997). Evans (1995) employs an 'early radical' and strong/weak cultural feminism distinction, while Nicholson's (1997) review of second wave feminisms refers to the emergence of radical feminism in the 1960s and views 'gynocentric feminism' as its partial successor in the 1970s. Gynocentric feminism overlaps with radical feminism but views difference between women and men as sometimes socially shaped (Nicholson 1997). As such we find it analytically clearer to settle on the use of the term we have deployed in this chapter.

4. Gatens (1992) protests that Irigaray and Cixous are interested in the *construction* of women's bodies, that Irigaray's emphasis on women's 'two lips' has nothing to do with a biological founda-tional view of sexuality, and that writers like Moi (1985) who highlight these aspects of her thought misunderstand Irigaray, but Gatens provides no evidence for her assertions, and Irigaray's work is open to diverse interpretations. Even if she is discussing different ways of representing female sexual-ity, the emphasis placed on 'two lips touching' suggests there may be something more foundational to her concerns. Furthermore, even though Irigaray discusses possible avenues open for resistance, these take relatively little note of the *social* circumstances of women's oppression (Tong 1989).

5. Similarly, Cixous identifies water as *the* feminine element, 'containing and reflecting the com-forting security of the mother's womb' (Moi 1985: 117), while Kristeva's emphasis on the semiotic as deriving from pre-Oedipal, undifferentiated human existence also emphasises flux.

6. Delphy (1996) constructed a useful genealogy of the sex/gender distinction traced to the pio-neering anthropology of Mead. Mead (1935) argued that most societies divide human characteristics into a two-fold schema based on reproductive roles, but was predominantly concerned with social divisions and masculine/feminine temperaments. The sociological notion of 'sex roles', in contrast,

developed most significantly from the 1940s to the 1960s. De Beauvoir (1949) was influential, but so too were such figures as Komarovsky (1950), Klein and Myrdal (1956), and Michel (1959) (see Delphy 1996). These latter authors worked within a Parsonian framework, connected roles to the functional needs of social systems, and attributed a status-based, cultural character to male/female divisions rather than the biological basis evident in Mead's work. Subsequent feminist critiques of sex role research emphasised the contingent and *changeable* content of these roles, and it was this critical work that encouraged the elaboration of the biological sex/social gender distinction. Lovell (1996), in contrast, provides us with a distinctive view of the sex/gender trajectory, arguing that it has long been implicit in feminist writings, but was succinctly formulated in 1968 by the psychologist Robert Stoller.

9

'RACIAL' SOCIOLOGY

1. Introduction

In this chapter, we use the term 'racial sociology' to refer to those sociological theories concerned with the contexts, constructions and contents of 'race', and the exclusionary outcomes associated with social actions predicated on the notion of 'racial otherness'. Like conflict and feminist theories, racial sociology highlights the partiality of classical sociological models of social and moral life, although it does this by focusing on processes that produce a *racially* structured social reality. In comparison with these other critiques of the classics, however, racial sociology has a stronger tendency to acknowledge the contingency of its subject matter. 'Race' is rarely seen as an essential, constant and inescapable feature of all human societies: it is a *social construction*, the efficacy and longevity of which is significantly dependent upon other social and economic divisions and inequalities. The fact that racial identities and oppression may be found in medieval, colonial and post-colonial societies testifies to the resilience of these constructions. Nevertheless, the constructed character of race means that this form of sociology tends ultimately to anticipate, or at least hope for, the disappearance of its own subject matter with the elimination of racial conflicts.

If racial sociology highlights the partiality of classical sociology, and focuses on the factors behind the construction of racialised relationships, its relationship to the *general* sociological theories of the classics is an ambivalent one. On the one hand, it challenges their relative neglect of the subject of race, and sometimes implicates them in the modern development of racial oppression, by offering a novel interrogation of the extent to which social orders can also be moral orders. On the other hand, racial sociology can be read as more of a corrective to the classical sociological ambition rather than a complete rejection of earlier accounts of the elementary forms of social and moral life. If race is constructed by other, extra-racial, social, cultural and economic relationships, traditional forms of sociology can continue to provide racial sociology with valuable concepts with which to examine the conditions in which race variously becomes visible, significant and dominant in the operation of social systems.

We have emphasised that sociology arose out of a context where Christian notions of divine order had been overturned, and the relationship between social and moral life rendered problematic. This context is particularly important in relation to the sociology of race. Up to the end of the eighteenth century in Europe, racial differences were commonly seen to be part of God's design for the universe. As Banton (1998: 4) points out, the Biblical story of Noah's curse upon his son Ham, that he must be a servant of servants to his brothers, was used to account for 'the Negro's' blackness, and inferior social standing, even though there is no evidence that Ham was black (see Genesis 10: 25–6). Eighteenth-century biological and evolutionary theories of human development tended to reaffirm much of the Christian doctrine of creation, including the notion of a Biblical curse upon non-white races. This idea might have been increasingly rejected in nineteenth-century social and political and scientific thought, as Christian influence weakened further, but the notion of a hierarchy of races continued to be accepted, though this was now seen in terms of differential patterns of biological inheritance rather than as a manifestation of the divine regulation of human life (Banton 1998: 6). In short, modern science changed the symbolic structure within which racial differences were contained, but continued to express views consistent with those of earlier centuries.

It is in this context that we can understand why classical sociology rejected the notion of race as being of *core* concern to its agenda. Sociology could not be built around a conceptual repertoire that had race at its centre, as it was an exclusionary symbolic construct of the physical sciences. Durkheim and Weber, for example, were strongly opposed to many of the theories of racial differences popular at the time they were writing (Wieviorka 1995: 3). In emphasising the importance of social facts in *The Rules of Sociological Method*, Durkheim rejects religious, philosophical and biological views of race as an important factor in the development of particular types of civilisations, and uses the anti-Semitism of the Dreyfus affair in France to outline a theory of racism as a 'scapegoating' of minorities during periods of moral distress and social malaise (O'Callaghan 1980: 27; Fenton 1980: 153). In this respect, it has been claimed that Durkheim's sociology was important in the dismantling of 'biological race science' (Fenton 1980: 157). Similarly, Weber rejected biological accounts of inherent differences between races to view race relations in terms of the economic conflicts between different social groups (Rex 1980: 121; Wieviorka 1995: 8). Thus, neither Durkheim nor Weber ignored racial divisions and conflicts, but both sought to distance sociology from the claims of evolutionary biologists and any scientific attempt to establish a hierarchy of the races.[1]

This classical sociological view of race as an ideological construct gains some support from the fact that it is now widely accepted that there is no scientific or biological basis for race. Furthermore, in contemporary sociology and anthropology it is now commonly recognised that the concept has only a symbolic or mythological function in relation to group conflicts. Some sociologists follow Durkheim and Weber in preferring to talk of 'racism', a sociological reality, rather than race, a conceptual remnant of previous centuries (Miles 1982, 1993; Wieviorka 1995). Other theorists of race have built upon neo-Marxist analyses of class interests and ideology. Both Miles and the Centre for Contemporary Cultural Studies (1982) have, despite their differences, developed influential paradigms that see race as a social and cultural construct rather than a biological reality, and investigate its significance in relation to inter-group conflict (Solomos and Back 2000: 7–9). While Miles emphasises the significance of social class, the CCCS is heavily influenced by the cultural theory of Stuart Hall. These approaches, like Durkheim's and Weber's opposition to biological race science, have a moral dimension (there is a consensus on the unacceptability of racially structured patterns of social inequality) and express a desire to develop sociological models that facilitate the analysis and, ultimately, the elimination of these inequalities.

The links and continuities between classical sociology, Marxism and contemporary sociologies of race are, however, limited. First, there is a tendency for sociologists of race to reject classical sociology. Back and Solomos's (2000) landmark collection of resources for theorising race and racism, for example, almost totally ignores classical sociology. Durkheim, in passing, is criticised as exemplifying 'colour blind' sociology (Winant 2000: 183), while it is simply noted that John Rex's arguments are drawn to some extent from Weber (Back and Solomos 2000: 102). Indeed, Spivak's (1987: 134) condemnation of sociology's traditional concern with order, which is interpreted as a form of analysis that ultimately applauds a system for its very existence, appears to be representative of a broad rejection of classical theories in contemporary racial sociologies. Second, race, like sex and gender, remains a concept that is more contested than many of those that have been identified as core to the sociological tradition. This contestation is associated with a spiralling multiplication of theoretical accounts of race that has been extended even further through the coupling of accounts of race to theories of ethnicity.[2] Third, while contemporary theorists of race and racism have extended the sociological concern with race, they often fail to follow Durkheim's lead in linking broader racial issues to the specific problem of anti-Semitism (Solomos and Back 2000: 10). Fourth, and this is a point relevant to social rather than strictly sociological views of race, it is possible to identify approaches towards the subject that have reconstructed arguments that were once associated with the biological race science of the nineteenth century. Certain social groupings, such as the Pan African and Black Power movements, have adopted the idea of a homogeneous black culture associated with a unitary geographical place and bodily identity, but inverted its negative implications to view black culture as inherently superior to its white alternative (Gilroy 1993: 190). These developments may exemplify what is at stake in the amnesia of sociology's heritage, but also draw attention to what Solomos and Back (2000) argue is the continuing importance of constructing adequate theoretical models for the socio-logical analysis of race.

This chapter examines racial sociology's attempts to develop such models. Section 2 identifies 'racial otherness' as the term that has developed into the unit idea for this vision of sociology. Section 3 examines several contrasting visions of the elementary forms of social and moral life characteristic of racial sociology. Assimilationist, economist and nationalist approaches do not provide a comprehensive overview of this area, but illustrate something of the variety and development of racial sociology from the late 1940s to the close of the twentieth century. While each approach supplements the idea of 'racial otherness' with the view that social action is racially motivated, they differ on the media through which this action is translated into social outcomes, and on the precise nature of these outcomes. Assimilationist, economist and nationalist approaches are, however, characterised by a tension central to this vision of sociology. The ideas of race as foundational to modernity and the discipline, on the one hand, and as something with no stable, ontological existence of its own, on the other, stand in a potentially uneasy relationship with each other. Section 4 focuses on this tension by examining the ambivalent status of race within racial sociology: an ambivalence that raises the question of whether race is of elementary or secondary theoretical significance. In conclusion, we suggest that racial sociology is indispensable to analysing the moral foundations of modernity, yet serves to supplement rather than to replace the key concerns of classical sociology.

2. Racial otherness

Sociology has often observed how people use familiar images and symbols in order to depict and classify strangers. Symbolic interactionism, for example, has recognised in this process the establishment of the epistemological ground necessary for effective communication. Nevertheless, while the construction of such classifications of others may be a necessary part of everyday life, representations of *racial otherness* invoke the idea of immutable differences that have social and moral consequences. These representations form a significant component of the history of colonial activity, depicting certain territories and peoples as requiring external rule, and racial sociology has critically developed this notion of 'racial otherness' into its unit idea. This confronts classical sociological visions of social and moral order with the accusation that they have been complicit in the marginalisation and oppression of certain racial groups. This complicity is expressed in the belief that they have either been 'colour blind', or have incorporated racist categorisations into their own sociological systems.

The 'Others' of imperial narratives

Western modernity, and its associated systems of academic knowledge, developed alongside a series of imperial conquests. In this context, it is argued, sociology's concern with 'order', with evolutionary narratives, and with categorising societies on the basis of simplified traditional/modern oppositions, overlooks how the foundations of modernity were fractured along *racial* axes (Spivak 1990). As Frederick Douglas and W.E.B. Du Bois argued, the slave trade and plantation production were not 'discrete episodes in the history of a minority', nor 'aberrations from the spirit of modern culture' likely to be overcome by progress, but represented *a central part of the moral history of the Western world* (Gilroy 1993: 42, 70). Parsons's depiction of the development of sociology as converging around a normative view of social order, then, can be seen to rest on the fallacy of historical consensus. This fallacy is evident not only in the imperialist activities of Western nations, but also in the depiction of 'primitive others' common to many products of classical sociology.

Sociology may define itself as 'the science of industrial society' but, as Connell (1997) points out, this overlooks how its early studies constructed an anthropological, evolutionary model of 'man' based on the 'difference between the civilisation of the metropole and an Other whose main feature was its primitiveness' (Connell 1997: 1516–17; Coombes 1994: 109). Echoing the trajectory of academic anthropology, sociology developed in the midst of a political imperialism that identified 'racial otherness' as a resource to be exploited and a problem to be controlled. For example, Herbert Spencer's (1850) theory of evolution developed while the British Empire grew in the nineteenth century. In the period preceding Durkheim's (1893) *Division of Labour*, the French republic conquered Tunisia, fought a war in Indochina, conquered Annam and Tonkin (modern Vietnam), and seized control of Laos and Cambodia (Connell 1997). A further example is provided by Weber's (1894) earliest research looking at the dominant and conquered 'races' resulting from Prussia's imperial conquests in Europe.

This type of argument highlights the background to sociology that is often overlooked, yet tends to ignore the degree to which classical sociologists sometimes engaged critically with such developments. Durkheim, for example, was strongly opposed to Lévy-Bruhl's sharp distinction between modern and primitive mentalities (Fenton 1980: 165). In this respect, Young's (1995: 91) claim that 'modern racism was an academic creation' can too easily be read as a blanket condemnation of classical sociological theory on the basis of the previous products of anthropology and the broader socio-political context in which it developed. We have already noted classical sociology's tendency to marginalize the notion of race within the sociological project, but this can be seen as a reflection of the desire to distance sociology from biological race science as much as it can be interpreted as a manifestation of its 'uncritical racism'. This complicates any simple correlation between sociology and European imperialism, but it does not undermine important aspects of racial sociology's critique of classical theories. If sociology has for much of the twentieth century omitted race from its core concerns, this can only have encouraged visions of normative order that ignore how the foundations of modernity have been dependent on making particular regions and peoples the objects rather than the subjects of international relations. A major goal of racial sociology, in contrast, has been to recover the varied processes through which this objectification and exclusion is accomplished: processes that point towards particular conceptions of the embodied basis of normative social orders.

Embodiment and racial otherness

The symbolic significance of 'black' had a negative, even demonic, character in the medieval Christian West prior to major contact with Africa (Bastide 1968; Jordan 1974). Nevertheless, as this contact grew, the body and skin colour increasingly served to indicate and legitimise an association between blackness and an uncivilised otherness. Black bodies became invested with an animal nature by white colonial powers. Previous images associating black with evil were drawn on, but were also updated within a set of symbols that possessed a particular 'charge' in relation to the fears, the anxieties, the desires, and the repulsions of the day (Schiebinger 1993). These were both explicitly incorporated into political arguments to justify slavery. They provided a symbolic resource that assisted the ability of colonial powers to 'pin a badge of human inferiority on another group and ... make it stick' (Elias 1994: xx), spread throughout colonial societies, and contrasted with normative constructions of whiteness (Frankenberg 1993; Allen 1994).[3]

Theorisations of race in the eighteenth and nineteenth centuries may have shifted the criteria by which people were categorised, but religious narratives were merely replaced with scientific 'discoveries' about evolutionary progress that regarded 'racialised others' as backward, disposable tools of civilisation. European depictions of Asians as 'yellow, melancholy, rigid' and Africans as 'black, phlegmatic, lax', for example, were allied in the nineteenth century to a genetic view of character holding certain 'races' to be civilised and others to be a danger to civilisation (Said 1978: 119). In this respect, Gobineau's (1853–5) *Essay on the Inequality of Races* associates the sexual intermixing of the races with the decline of 'great nations'. The practical application of such theories can be seen in British colonial policies on 'sexual pollution', while Gobineau's writings proved influential among Southern American whites, and may have informed Hitler's programme of genocide (Young 1995).

Writers from Europe and North America categorised Africans as belonging to a different species, or as representing an inferior stage of evolution. By the 1850s, the doctrine of polygenism (the idea that different 'races' originated from different ancestors and represented different species) was widely regarded as the modern scientific view. This opposed the Enlightenment ethos of the 'universal sameness and equality of humanity' and, according to Young (1995: 47, 127), proved so influential that the only effective way for scientists to conceptualise humans as equals was to treat 'racial differences' as manifestations of distinctive evolutionary stages. Visions of racial otherness were also frequently intertwined with connotations of inferior 'sexual otherness'. Thomas (1994) notes that 'Asiatics, and particularly "Hindoos", were regarded as effete or effeminate, as were Polynesians', while Sinha (1995) examines the Victorian ideology of 'effeminate Bengali' men unfit for self-rule. Classifications of 'racial otherness' also became increasingly complex in the United States, where people of 'mixed race', even if they looked white, were not allowed to vote or inherit significant property. Young (1995: 254) details the belief that these people were contaminated by 'dark blood' that could be smelt.

These biologically essentialist visions of 'racial otherness' vary significantly and have been selected with the simple purpose of providing a range of examples of how bodily features have historically been associated with moral and evolutionary differences. In recovering and deconstructing these colonial practices, racial sociology has challenged the conventional sociological vision of an inclusive, normatively based social order. It has also identified the basis on which racially motivated action proceeds: having identified a group as 'racially other' it becomes possible to *act* on the basis of that otherness.

3. The elementary forms of social and moral life

The argument that it is impossible to understand the contemporary world without appreciating the construction of racially motivated action is fundamental to a wide range of past and present sociologists of race. Racial sociology is characterised by considerable diversity, however, in its analysis of the media through which this action is channelled, and in its assessment of the precise social outcomes of these actions. Assimilationism was influential in the mid-twentieth century, economist theories of race developed especially in the 1970s, nationalist perspectives on race were perhaps at their most popular in the 1990s, while each perspective has been modified and adapted in recent writings on race and identity, globalisation and (post)colonialism.

Visions of assimilation

The sociological study of race developed in the mid-twentieth century through the assimilationist concerns of Americans influenced by Robert Park. As Solomos (1993) notes, assimilationism dominated research from the late 1940s to the 1960s and consisted of a functionalist view of society and a definition of the race problem as one of integration. As far as this perspective was concerned, 'racial otherness' became relevant to sociology, and visible to individuals, groups and politicians, only when social actions ascribed an identifiably different immigrant culture 'to the physical traits of a particular social group' (Solomos 1993: 16). Those defined as racial others did not, however, have to remain permanent outsiders but could be assimilated into the values of the established within society.

Park began his career as an academic sociologist at the University of Chicago in 1914, and during the 1920s and 1930s the 'Chicago School' was concerned with the lack of 'effective communication between heterogeneous groups in cities' and how this might fracture the social fabric (Lal 1986: 281). The city constituted 'the natural habitat of civilised man', but contained areas marked by poverty and social problems and populated by immigrant groups. In the absence of appropriate channels of communication, these immigrants could appear alien and threatening to the host population. Communication, then, was the crucial medium of action that could translate the initial identification of cultural and phenotypical differences into accommodation rather than conflict. This assessment was exemplified by Park's landmark study of the immigrant press.

According to Park, the immigrant press serves two vital functions. It preserves a language and maintains contact between 'the home countries and their scattered members in every part of the United States', thus providing a firm base for immigrant life, and it facilitates assimilation by breeding 'new loyalties' from 'old heritages' (Park 1922: 468). During the First World War, for example, foreign language newspapers provided America with 'an effective and necessary means of gaining that understanding and solidarity between the immigrant and native population ... necessary to win' the conflict (Park 1922: 444). Park's (1950: v–vi) conviction that 'accurate and adequate reporting of current events' was important for assimilation rested on the assumption that news did not operate on the isolated individuals, but on the emotional and cognitive attitudes of people *interacting* in group situations (Park 1972: 31). Such interaction occurred in extra-institutional groups that helped bring individuals 'out of old ties and into new ones', facilitated 'a new collective spirit', and maintained social cohesion (Park 1972: 48, 78, 80).[4] These groups were meant to enhance positive relations of interdependence in the modern era, and provided the dynamism informing what Park describes as the 'race relations cycle'. Starting from initial *contact* between people with phenotypical differences interpreted in terms of race, this cycle moved through stages of *conflict, accommodation* and *assimilation* (Park 1950: 150): stages Park believed were 'progressive and irreversible' (Elsner, Jr 1972).

Park's work continues to shape sociological studies of 'race relations', but his focus was on the involvement of immigrants in, and the facilitation by communication media of, 'new relationships' that 'breed new loyalties' (Park 1922: 468). For contemporary theorists of race, this normative outcome is highly iniquitous. Park emphasises that immigrant groups must be prepared to change culturally for assimilation to occur, a process that 'involves the more or less complete incorporation of the individual into the existing moral order' (Park 1972: 141). The implication here is that 'problems will be solved when maximum similarity is achieved with only a rump of cultural difference remaining to provide exotic diversion' (Mason 1995: 2–3). Indeed, Park (1972: 141) suggests that if immigrants maintain a semi-detached relation to the norms of their 'new society', this 'inevitably stimulates in the native a pervasive sense of malaise as if in the presence of something ... always to be a little feared'.

We have focused on the important sociological work of Park, but assimilationism was not a unitary perspective. Kallen (1924), for example, endorsed cultural pluralism and rejected the goal of complete assimilation, while Myrdal (1944) favoured assimilation but was critical of the contradiction between the 'American Creed' of 'high national and Christian precepts', and the 'group prejudice' that characterised white America's behaviour towards black Americans. One of the biggest criticisms levelled against assimilationism, however, was that it applied an analysis based on European immigrants to address the situation of groups characterised by a qualitatively different historical experience (Omi and Winant 1986: 21). In this context, analysts suggested that while effective communication may facilitate the incorporation of certain groups into American society, social actions that identified other groups as radically phenotypically and culturally different resulted in contrasting outcomes. On the one hand, West (1990) noted how European immigrants arrived on American shores seeing themselves as 'Irish' or Sicilian, for example, but found their colour usually did not prevent them from learning they were culturally 'white'. On the other hand, Lloyd Warner (1936) suggested there was an unbridgeable 'caste' barrier between black and white Americans that made assimilation impossible. Even Glazer and Moynihan's (1970: 313) second edition of *Beyond the Melting Pot*, a study that on first publication emphasised how immigrant groups maintained their ethnic identity only because of its political utility, noted the difficulties of assimilation where 'colour is involved'.

The assimilationist approach towards 'race relations' analysed immigrant/native actions predicated on the notion of 'racial otherness' as a temporary obstacle within a wider 'cycle' that had as its outcome cultural homogeneity and social acceptance. The obduracy with which race persisted as a manifestation of cultural difference, however, led an increasing number of theorists to suggest there might be something more fundamental about the construction of 'racial otherness' and its mediation into oppressive social outcomes. Some of these analysts associated racially-motivated action with the economic base of society.

Visions of economic racialisation

Whereas assimilationism views racial action in terms of the ascription of cultural difference to a physically identifiable group, economistic approaches (which draw on Marxist theories of class conflict or Weber's writings on market and status) explain this social action in terms of economic/class/market processes. Action based on prioritising one race over another remains a significant variable for these approaches, but this is a form of action mediated by economic consider-ations that result in outcomes characterised by labour inequalities and economic conflict. Indeed, it is *economic considerations* that constitute the real motive for actions that appear superficially to be based on considerations of race alone.

Economistic approaches can be categorised into variants focusing on *market relations, class conflict*, and the class *stratification/distribution* of resources (Omi and Winant 1986). Market relations perspectives suggest that racially motivated action becomes significant only when individuals are prevented from competing equitably in a free market. Racial discrimination involves practices that ascribe individuals to a racial group which is treated unfairly in the marketplace or which suffers from monopolistic or restrictive practices exercised by other groups of workers or the state (Reich 1981). Laissez-faire policies that appeal to the rational self-interest of actors should, according to this perspective, eventually eliminate racial discrimination (Friedman 1962).

The neo-Marxist work of Robert Miles has, for over two decades, provided some of the most consistent class conflict theories of race (e.g. Miles 1982). Miles sug-gests that capitalist divide and rule strategies and split labour markets may be more or less relevant to racial discrimination depending upon the historical period, industrial sector or economy. In both cases, 'racial otherness' is accepted as a given resource. It is a marker of identity that can serve as a basis for discriminatory actions on the part of the powerful that help produce outcomes conducive to the mainte-nance of relative economic privilege. Nevertheless, there is a different emphasis evident in certain divide and rule and split labour market theories. Starting from the Marxist tenet that capital seeks to maximise the extraction of surplus value, 'divide and rule' theories emphasise how the existence of racial discrimination is used to prevent a unified working class (e.g. Cox 1948; Baran and Sweezy 1966; Reich 1971, 1981; Castles and Kosack 1973; Nikolinakos 1973). Employer dis-crimination against black labour and in favour of white labour in terms of wages, for example, has historically made it less likely for unity to be achieved *across* the working class (Reich 1981). A relatively impoverished black working class also provides a 'reserve army of labour' that can undermine unions, break strikes, and minimise wages. Split labour market theory, in contrast, suggests that it is rational for business to support free market policies in order to reduce wage levels, but that groups of workers are able to effect discrimination. White work-ers in the United States, for example, have historically maintained a labour aris-tocracy that monopolises skilled positions, training and high wage levels (Omi and Winant 1986: 35).

The class stratification/distribution approach toward race is exemplified by Wilson's *The Declining Significance of Race*, one of the most influential studies on the subject published in the last quarter of the twentieth century. Based on a historical analysis of the changing forms of racial subordination, Wilson (1978: 1) argues that 'Race relations in America have undergone fundamental changes in recent years, so much so that now the life chances of individual blacks have more to do with their economic class position than with their day-to-day encounters with whites'. In the pre-industrial period of plantation economy and racial-caste oppression, exploitation was deliberate and overt (characterised by the development and expansion of slavery), and its perpetuation by an elite white 'planter class' easily documented. From the latter half of the nineteenth century through the first half of the twentieth, oppression still exhibited these features, but the era was characterised, especially in the North, by industrial expansion, class conflict and a racial oppression perpetrated by the endeavours of the white working class to eliminate black competition. In contrast, as America entered the second half of the twentieth century, Wilson suggests that many of the traditional barriers facing blacks have been dismantled as a result of the progress made in and after the civil rights era. Once these barriers collapsed, however, new obstacles emerged as a result of structural shifts in the economy.

Global pressures on corporations to maintain their skills base, technological changes that eradicated many skilled jobs, and the proliferation of low wage, casualised jobs in labour intensive industries produced a segmented labour structure (Wilson 1978, 1996a; Danzinger 1996). In terms of the political, economic, and international contexts in which it operates, corporate America cannot afford to discriminate and qualified blacks are moving into corporate jobs in significant numbers (Wilson 1978: 2). At the same time, there is a growing black underclass without the education necessary to profit from such opportunities (Wilson 1978: 2, 15–16).

Wilson (1996b: 567) argues that the contemporary black underclass is the result of economic changes that are not racially motivated, and are outside the control of politicians. This distinguishes the present period of 'race relations' from its antecedents. Competitiveness and equal opportunity policies mean corporate jobs are open to those with appropriate qualifications, while 'recent studies of unemployment in the urban core reveal that blacks do not experience any special employment barriers in the casual, low-paid, and menial jobs of the low-wage sector' (Wilson 1978: 107). Racism may still be endemic in residential areas and private clubs, but in the economic sphere 'class has become more important than race in determining black access to privilege and power' (Wilson 1978: 1). It is no longer racially motivated actions that result in racial inequalities, but actions designed to maximise competitive advantage and social capital that exacerbate social divisions (Wilson 1997, 1999).

Despite their differences, then, these visions of economic racialisation all analyse racially-iniquitous outcomes as a result of the 'functional' needs of capitalism. Race, ultimately, is no more than a convenient, pre-existing construct that the economically privileged use to maintain their position. It is capitalism, rather than racism, that is prioritised as elementary to the structuring of social and moral life. Because of this, these approaches have been criticised for reducing the significance of race to economic criteria (Omi and Winant 1986: 27). Analyses centred on the nation, in contrast, aim to locate racial issues within a broader set of economic, political and cultural processes.

The national construction of otherness

'The nation' has been used to refer variously to people who have never met, yet who belong to the same community, to invoke a shared yet imaginary racial heritage, and to highlight how people born within a country can be labelled as 'outsiders' and 'enemies' on the basis of their supposed possession of a different ancestral, cultural, or biological background (Anderson 1991; Bhabha 1990; CCCS 1982). The difficulty of obtaining a comprehensive and coherent definition of 'the nation' is illustrated by Triandafyllidou's (1998) point that those accounts based on objective indicators of nationhood sit uneasily alongside theories that emphasise the 'irrational, psychological' bonds that enter into the construction of a nation (e.g. Smith 1991).

Despite difficulties in defining the term, the idea of 'the nation' has tended in racial sociology to be associated with an analysis of exclusionary forms of social life that deny membership of a wider community to groups defined as 'racial others'. Miles (1989: 91), for example, notes how the British colony of Australia developed an ideology that 'included the white "races" as acceptable members of the Australian "nation" and simultaneously excluded people of Asian and Pacific origin ... represented as "coloured races"'. This culminated in the 'White Australia' policy in 1901 and the 'racialisation of migration flows' that informed Australia's economic development (Miles 1989: 91; de Lepervanche 1984). Similarly, British immigration policy of the 1960s and 1970s established legislation that excluded potential members of 'the nation' on the basis of their racially designated countries and non-white bodies. That nations appear to be associated with exclusionary social actions is also clear in the frequency with which colonial powers have sought to consolidate their status via military conquest and economic exploitation based on a 'racialised' vision of international relations (Carmichael and Hamilton 1968).

If 'the nation' has been associated with exclusionary social actions, the media through which these actions are channelled involves ideologies and mechanisms associated with *nationalism*. Smith (1991: 73) defines nationalism as the 'ideological movement for attaining and maintaining autonomy, unity and identity on behalf of a population deemed by some of its members to constitute an actual or potential nation', while Kedourie (1992) highlights the emphasis nationalism places upon cultivating the qualities of the established 'we' group in opposition to those held to define that of the outsider 'they' group. As Triandafyllidou (1998: 597) argues, the idea of belonging to a nation 'does not only imply knowing who "we" are but also recognising who are the "others"'. This idea possesses various historical trajectories, but each has provided resources through which 'difference' is searched for, identified, and, in some cases, demonised.

The modern idea of nationalism is usually traced to the nineteenth century. It was in 1882 that Ernest Renan provided a highly influential theorisation of the question 'What is a nation?'[5] Renan incorporated a racial narrative built around Germanic invasions in Europe (from the fifth to the tenth century) alongside an emphasis on the importance of 'will' as a basis for solidarity (evidenced by the French Revolution) (Renan 1882: 9, 11, 19; see also Thom 1990). Anderson (1991) has more recently exposed the preconditions for this 'will' by conceptualising the nation and nationalism as realised through a politically validated *imagination*. The existence of a collective imagination is indispensable if policies informed by nationalism are to be legitimated, because 'members of even the smallest nation will never know most of their fellow members, meet them, or even hear of them' (Anderson 1991: 6, 188). Imaginations of nationhood are not equally effective, though, but are dependent for their realisation on the political validation of certain languages and imaginations over others. Historically, it has been European and American languages that have managed to establish the dominance of their imaginings as a result of the conjunction of print-language and capitalism.

The linguistically informed imaginings residing at the heart of nationalism bring together huge numbers of people but, as we have already noted, also serve to mediate social actions that deny membership of 'the nation' to those constructed as 'racial others'. This has historically resulted in outcomes associated with the creation of established–outsider relations, relations of dominance and subordination in which the dominant group nevertheless remain dependent for their identity on the actions of the dominated (Elias 1994). In seeking to maintain their position, established groups have ruthlessly suppressed non-official languages in particular nations, while language has been a key resource enabling established colonial powers to present themselves as superior and to construct 'racial others' as inferior, uncivilised and lacking the potential to be 'a singular and true political community' (Chatterjee 1993: 224; Bhabha 1985). As Chatterjee (1993: 5) notes, Western print powers have labelled as irrational, primitive and evidence of the need for colonial rule African communities in which oral traditions combine with dance, music and speech as evocations of identity.

These nationalist imaginings may have enabled colonial powers to portray racial others as inferior and in need of colonial rule, but it is worth noting that they did not always assist in the *exercise* of that rule. As Thomas (1994: 15–16) notes, colonial powers used every available means to map the lands and people they occupied, but such efforts 'were frequently accompanied by a kind of despair, which found the space and social entity of the colony to be … constantly untrue to the representations … fashioned of it'. Indeed, effective colonial rule some-times required the *effacement* rather than the enforcement of images of otherness, as illustrated by the British use of south Asian languages in the sub-continent (Thomas 1994: 39). This renders problematic any simple association of race, nationalism and colonialism, and recent scholarship has tended to reinforce this by emphasising that race was a constantly shifting category in the various stages of European colonial expansion (Solomos and Back 2000: 15). More broadly, Mosse (1985) has stressed the temporary, highly contingent, relationship between imperialism and racism.[6]

Each of the approaches examined in this section provide us with distinctive visions of the sociological significance of 'racial otherness'. However, they also illustrate a tension that is central to racial sociology. On the one hand, each of them judges the concept of race to be particularly useful in highlighting inequali-ties and patterns of exploitation. On the other hand, there are evident difficulties in attributing any enduring solidity to the content of 'racial' relationships. Because of its focus on normative consensus, assimilationism creates the impression that, as a sociological category, race is of only secondary significance. It becomes unimportant as immigrant groups are incorporated into an all-embracing social and moral order. The precarious status of race, as a category, is also evident in econo-mistic approaches that view economic processes as the real, underlying causes of racial conflict. Finally, writings on 'the nation' offer thoughtful analyses of the imperialist construction and exploitation of 'racial Others', but questions remain about the validity of these in relation to non-colonial forms of intra-national 'racism'. Despite their differences, then, all these approaches raise the question of whether race is of elementary or secondary sociological importance.

4. Can race be a core sociological category?

The status of race as a sociological category is intimately tied to the question of whether it refers to something that is more structured than structuring. If it refers to a phenomenon, or a series of phenomena, that tends *by itself* to exert a dominant impact on the identities, relationships and actions of individuals and groups, then it is likely to have an elementary significance for the construction and development of social and moral life. If, on the other hand, it is heavily dependent for its appearances and consequences on a configuration of other social phenomena, it is likely to possess an immense significance in some contexts, but little or none in others.

All three of the models considered above imply that race is more structured than structuring, and analyse it in relation to what they regard as more elementary sociological phenomena. Some writers on this subject, such as Miles (1989, 1993), Wieviorka (1995) and Montagu (1997) have suggested that race should be rejected as a core sociological category, and have argued for the complete abandonment of the term in order to concentrate on phenomena deemed to be of more fundamental significance. Others maintain that the analysis of racial issues is of central socio-logical importance while patterns of inequality and exclusion persist, but acknowl-edge that race is not an elementary sociological category in the sense that it must be a core aspect of the sociological study of *all* societies. Rex (1986), for example, argues that the continued existence of race as a marker of social relationships is not to be welcomed: it remains of sociological significance at present but, since the term refers to situations of conflict, inequality and oppression, there is no such thing as good race relations.

In response to these debates about the relative importance of race as a socio-logical category, certain theorists have shifted the ground on which the impor-tance of race should be judged. They have done this by focusing variously on the realm of human *experience* in an era marked by the globalisation of social life, by pursuing a 'postmodern' turn, closely connected to ideas of 'post-colonialism', in theorising race, and by developing a 'post-racial' stance that eschews any reifi-cation of the concept of race. Gilroy's (1993) *The Black Atlantic*, for example, draws on such theories to see race as a social construction, but an enduringly obdurate one, that has exerted a lasting impact upon modern societies. Having rejected essentialist theories of racial difference (be they promoted by white groups, or by groups representing a 'brute pan-Africanism'), Gilroy remains dissatisfied with recent pluralist approaches that view race as an open signifier divided by class, sexuality, gender, age and ethnicity; such approaches are 'insufficiently alive to the lingering power of specifically racialised forms of power and subordination' (Gilroy 1993: 31–2). The problem, as Gilroy sees it, is to develop an approach that does not fix race absolutely, but sees it implicated in an ongoing process of identity construction. In this respect, like a number of other theorists, he utilises the notion of 'diaspora' to explain the shifting character of how 'racial' identity is actually experienced.

Derived from Jewish thought, 'diaspora' denotes 'a network of people, scattered in a process of non-voluntary displacement, usually created by violence or under the threat of violence or death (Gilroy 1997: 328). It contains a systemic element, referring as it does to people who are scattered around a post-colonial state, but Gilroy's analysis allocates priority to human *experience*, rather than structural systems, and he focuses on the many-stranded determinants of experiences that have led to hybrid cultures and identities. Rejecting the notion of a unitary 'racial identity' and the associated idea of 'natural nations' based on singular, primeval forms of culture and consciousness, 'hybridity' signifies ongoing mixing, development and change. Bhabha's (1988: 13) discussion of the term, for example, draws on Bakhtin's analysis of linguistic fusion and applies this to the dialogical situation of colonialism in which cultural change progresses neither in the direction of colonised nor colonisers, but of 'something else besides which contests the terms and territories of both'. Hybridity leads to forms of identity that cut across national frontiers (Bhabha 1990).

'Diaspora' and 'hybridity' have become important concepts within racial sociology as symbols of the unstable and dynamic features of 'racial' identity. Stuart Hall, for example, has constructed a series of analyses based on the argument that while 'black' may have been used by politically oppressed groups to refer to a common marginalisation, black experience is now more generally a diasporic experience (e.g. Hall 1987, 1988, 1996). This reflects global processes of hybridity in which experiences of 'racial' fragmentation have become a defining experience of modernity (Hall 1987: 44). In this context, racial 'identities are never unified', but 'increasingly fragmented and fractured … across different, often intersecting and antagonistic, discourses, practices and positions' (Hall 1996: 4).

Building upon this concern with difference and fragmentation, a number of theorists have pursued a 'postmodern' turn in the analysis of race. Rattansi and Westwood's (1994) collection, for example, suggests that contemporary manifestations of race reflect a proliferation of fast changing forms of racism and racial identities in the context of new forms of global dislocation, economic recession, and a general sense of social and psychic crisis within modernity. These writings tend to be closely associated with the mutually interdependent identities of colonisers and colonised in a world where most of the former colonies of Western imperial powers have gained formal independence (Rattansi 1997: 440–81). While their work overlaps with theorists of nationhood, the proponents of this postmodern turn lean much more heavily on the likes of Foucault, Derrida and Lacan, and adopt a highly deconstructive approach towards previous analyses of race. Their work also tends to be less empirically and historically informed than many of its antecedents, even though its proponents acknowledge that highly generalised concepts such as postmodernism and post-colonialism can provide 'only the most general framework of analysis' (Rattansi 1997: 491).

The work that perhaps most directly challenges the idea that race can be a core sociological category, however, is Gilroy's *Between Camps: Nations, Cultures and the Allure of Race*. Gilroy (2000: 43, 334) is concerned that theorists of race may have contributed to the reification of racial differences, and argues that the oppositional identities constructed around the old 'visual signatures of race' are best let go along with the notion that corrective or compensatory inclusion in modernity should supply the dominant theme of critical theories of race. In their place, Gilroy (2000: 17) urges that more attention be paid to the future possibilities of a 'planetary humanism', a 'radically non-racial humanism' that is concerned primarily with 'the forms of human dignity that race thinking strips away'.

It might be said that such analyses revitalise racial sociology by linking the subject of race to broader theoretical accounts of the contingency and fragmentation of contemporary identities, or to the future possibilities that might transcend the particularities previously associated with race. Alternatively, the deconstructive implications of these same studies might be interpreted as marking the exhaustion of racial sociology as a *distinctive* sociological enterprise. In this regard, Anthias and Yuval-Davis (1992: 2) have insisted on reinstating race as central to the analysis of modernity, and argue that an overemphasis on contingency and multiplicity risks emptying this concept of meaning, of 'fail[ing] to provide the axis upon which phenomena of race depend'. What they are concerned about is the further downgrading of race within the sociological project, and the deconstruction of the moral impetus behind racial sociology. If there is nothing substantive about race, if it is just another signifier in the postmodern, post-colonial interplay of hybrid subjectivities, then the sociological study of the subject loses any substantive theoretical basis on which to challenge social and moral orders, and sociological conceptualisations of them.

It has been suggested that debates such as these can be seen as defining the outer limits of what it is possible for theory to accomplish, and that they point to the importance of empirical research that covers the specific contexts in which racial categories gain specific meanings if we are to move beyond apparently intractable theoretical problems (Solomos and Back 1996). In this view, if flux, change and fragmentation really do characterise 'racialised' identities and relationships in the (post)modern world, then it is vital to investigate these issues empirically if theoretical analysis is to remain accurate and relevant. From the point of view of Anthias and Yuval-Davis (1993), this is unsatisfactory, however, as empirical research into race, racism or racialised identities is surely pointless without a clear idea of what these terms actually mean. This criticism redirects our attention to the contested nature of the concept of race, and to its unresolved status within sociology.

5. Concluding comments

This chapter has highlighted different conceptualisations of racial otherness, competing models of the role of race in relation to elementary forms of social and moral life, and the unresolved tension about the status of race in sociology. In the light of these, it can be argued that racial sociology appears to exemplify the contemporary fragmentation of the discipline and, in terms of some of its criticisms of the racist formulations of classical theory, the amnesia afflicting much contemporary sociology. More positively, racial sociology makes two valuable contributions to the development of sociology, both of which can be contextualised within the key concerns of classical sociology. First, it draws attention to the power of symbols in the shaping of power relationships between competing social groups. Second, it offers a particularly challenging analysis of the gap that can exist between social orders and moral imperatives.

In relation to the first of these, what the work of both Durkheim and Weber makes clear, and what is implied in most of the studies examined in this chapter, is that the sociological significance of race is primarily *symbolic*. It is possible, in fact, to articulate the central concerns of racial sociology in terms central to classical sociology by conceptualising race, at its most general level, as a *symbol of (dis)association*. Adapting Halbwach's (1941) discussions of memory, we might say that individuals construct and reconstruct the symbols they use under the pressure of society: society invests symbols with particular meanings, but these reflect its own divisions, conflicts and patterns of inclusion and exclusion. The meaning of race as a symbol of (dis)association is not naturally given, then, but invokes traditions of social and national belonging that are invented or imagined (Hobsbawm 1983; Anderson 1991). These traditions are often invoked as a result of political pressures to racialise economic or other problems in order to transport responsibility away from governing powers and towards groups marginalised from the centres of a social system (e.g. CCCS 1982; Omi and Winant 1986). Colour represents one of the more frequent symbols or 'tribal labels' used to distinguish groups from each other, and these are instrumental in the 'cognitive maps' people construct of situations (Mitchell 1956; Epstein 1978; Banks 1995).

Symbols are not simply cognitive, however. Durkheim (1912) noted the close relationship between the human body and patterns of collective symbolisation. Building on Durkheim's work, Douglas (1970, 1966) suggests that the body provides us with the most readily available analogy of the social system and helps people conceive of the societal dimensions of such issues as risk and pollution, conflict and control, social class and race. When there is a perceived or actual threat to the social system, there is likely to be intensified concern about the integrity of the individual body and its conformity to social norms, and a reaction against groups perceived as posing a threat to these norms.[7] Said (1978) provides one example of how physical appearance was implicated in this signification of power when discussing the young retirement age for British administrators in India. By retiring at fifty-five, no Oriental was ever allowed to see a Westerner as he aged and degenerated, just as no Westerner needed ever to see himself, mirrored in the eyes of the subject race, as anything but a vigorous, rational, everalert young Raj. In highlighting such policies, racial sociology illustrates how the body has served as a vital and enduring source of these symbols, even if its contemporary malleability suggests that it is an increasingly precarious container for naturalistic markers of difference (Shilling 1993; Gilroy 2000).

In re-articulating the central concerns of racial sociology in the terms of the basically classical conceptualisation of race as a symbol of (dis)association we can see the value of much racial sociology. It demonstrates how what might appear to be a 'consensual' social system can operate at the expense of groups designated as 'others' and how, in these circumstances, race becomes an important social variable reflecting fractured or divided social systems. Nevertheless, as a symbol of (dis)association, race is vitally important in some contexts, but clearly less so in others. This helps explain Durkheim's and Weber's contextualisations of race within broader sociological patterns and processes: their unit ideas of the sacred and rationalisation are understood to embrace *all* societies, unlike racial otherness, which is specific only to certain social contexts. Thus, if racial sociology makes an important contribution to the development of the discipline, it is in offering an important corrective to the tendency to marginalize race too readily rather than any promise of a radical reconstruction of the sociological ambition.

If racial sociology draws attention to the power of symbols in shaping the relationships between competing social groups, it also offers a significant contribution to the consideration of the relationship between social and moral orders. Its analyses of race in European and American history help us understand how notions of divine order, that saw racial differences as part of God's design for the universe, established a racially structured conception of social life that was incorporated in the secular models of the modern world. It therefore highlights how any sense of empathy or any burden of responsibility for others was limited by the symbolic codification of embodied characteristics into particular races, so that black bodies became marginalised within, or seen as threats to, the creation and maintenance of (white) social orders. Its arguments in this respect may relate to the historical development of the West, but it challenges the classical theorists to remember that social and moral orders are not necessarily synonymous, and that sociology has an important role in illuminating the gulf that can exist between them and the oppression of certain groups that this gulf allows. Durkheim and Parsons were particularly forgetful in this respect. Contemporary sociological analyses of the symbolic mechanisms of racism, such as that of Wieviorka (1995), continue this pattern of confronting sociologists with the moral consequences of their conceptions of social order, and therefore exemplify the continuing importance of this form of sociology. Indeed, it is interesting how current debates in this area, many of which appear to be converging around the issue of 'living with difference', question the capacity of social systems to even tolerate, let alone facilitate, cultural diversity. What racial sociology offers to the discipline is not so much its reconfiguration in terms of a core variable of race, but an important reminder of the social and moral issues that have been significant to sociology from the start. It demonstrates that the moral foundations of social orders have historically possessed exclusionary foundations, and that constructions of race have been one of the most flexible symbolic means by which the real basis of these foundations have been obscured.

Notes

1. Even Comte, who believed that different races had different brains, developed no conclusions from this that affected his vision of social and moral order.

2. Even when race is dropped from analysis, as too contested a term to be analytically productive, associated concepts take its place as a way of highlighting the oppression people confront when attributed with supposedly immutable physical or genetic characteristics. As Solomos (1993) summarises, the term *racism* was linked to the rise of Nazism and refers to ideas and practices defining one racial or ethnic group as superior or inferior to others. It continues to be a key term even if Banton (1998) wants its use to be confined to describing the 'scientific racism' characteristic of nineteenth-century Europe. *Institutional racism* refers to systemic practices that result in unequal outcomes between 'races' irrespective of the motivations behind the policies or laws under examination (Sivanden 1982). *Racialisation*, in contrast, signifies the ideological processes through which social relations become viewed as 'race relations' distinguished by the different physical and biological features of human groups (Miles 1993). Omi and Winant, for example, explore how the racial category 'black' developed with the consolidation of slavery. By the end of the seventeenth century, 'Africans whose specific identity was Ibo, Yoruba, Fulani, etc., were rendered "black" by an ideology of exploitation based on racial logic – the establishment and maintenance of a "colour-line"' (Omi and Winant 1986: 64).

Social scientific interest in *ethnicity* can be traced to anthropological explorations of non-Western cultures in the nineteenth century, but it was in the second half of the twentieth century that the term became used in a manner familiar to contemporary sociologists. As Banks (1995) explains, it was during this period that Frederick Barth and his colleagues (1969) analysed the geographical and cultural *boundaries* marking out ethnicities, that the 'Manchester School' focused on *urbanisation* and *colonialisation* in Africa (e.g. Gluckman 1940; Mitchell 1956; Cohen 1969; see also Epstein 1978), and that 'Soviet ethnos theory' focused on the *stable core of ethnicity* they held to persist among a people irrespective of economic change (e.g. Bromley 1974, 1980). 'Ethnicity' was invested with a certain stability of meaning in the 1960s and 1970s that enabled theorists to view it as a cultural counterpart to the more biological connotations of race. Before the 1970s ended, however, 'ethnicity' was recognised as 'a term still on the move' that could no longer serve unproblematically as the identifier of (potentially malleable) cultural differences (Glazer and Moynihan 1975: 1; Banks 1995). As Rex (1986: 16) notes, the content of the term was questioned at the same time many academics stopped using race to refer to any enduring mark of physical difference. Both 'ethnicity' and race were seen as social constructs that shed more light on people's *attitudes* toward a particular group than on the actual cultural or physical identity of that group. In this context, Blu (1980) and Ardener (1989) questioned the term's continued validity, while Banks (1995: 190) ends his study with the damning conclusion that 'ethnicity' is too vague and simplistic a term to yield analytical insights.

3. Thomas (1994: 72) notes that the ancient Greeks used 'barbarian' to describe those not sharing in the civilised life of the *Polis*. McGrane (1989) separates constructions of 'Others' into the monstrous inhabitants of remote regions in the medieval era, the non-Christians of the Renaissance, the mentally ignorant Others of the Enlightenment, and the 'primitives' of nineteenth-century evolutionary narratives. Pre-Enlightenment Others were often conceptualised in religious terms as people who might be saved through conversion. Post-Enlightenment conceptions, in contrast, often placed this hierarchy on a scientific basis that, according to Thomas (1994), consolidated and accentuated this Otherness.

Although they did not have the power to turn their observances of difference into oppressive relations, Hibbert (1984) suggests that skin colour was one of the features that Africans found most noticeable about the physical appearance of Europeans. Furthermore, the pejorative associations linked to 'racially Other' bodies have not always been unambiguously negative. Varying representations of blackness, for example, accompanied the expansion of the ancient Graeco-Roman empire into Africa (Snowden 1970, 1983; see also Stepan 1982). The association of colour, bodies and (dangerous) Others was, however, central to the French and British traditions of *Orientalism*; a collective notion identifying 'us' Europeans as against all 'those' non-Europeans of the East (Said 1978: 7). This had its roots in the opposition of an emergent feudal Christian Europe to the existence and dominance of Islam close to and within its boundaries during the Middle Ages, but continued to characterise European ideas of 'foreignness' for some time thereafter (Daniel 1975). Gustave Flaubert's vision of the East as an antidote to the banality and greyness of bourgeois life, for example, is characterised by 'gorgeous colour' associated with 'exciting spectacle instead of humdrum routine': colours that flow through an emotional, non-rational, sensual part of the world which offers 'the freedom of licentious sex' (Said 1989: 187, 190). This may appear more positive than equating blackness with sin, but still portrayed an Other as 'irrational', 'depraved' and 'fallen' compared with the European 'rational', 'virtuous' and 'normal' (Said 1978: 40).

4. Park's analysis of the constructive, as well as the deconstructive, elements of groups explicitly rejects Le Bon's association of collective behaviour with intense irrationalism (Elsner Jr 1972: xix), but nevertheless associates the Public with mind and the Crowd with emotions. *Public* interaction allows discussion, debate and criticism, and allows individual interests to emerge against a common background (Part 1972). *Crowds*, in contrast, suppress individuality in favour of collective emotions. The capacity to participate in a Crowd is dependent on the ability to feel and empathise, whereas the ability to think and reason is required for entry into the Public. It is in this context that news and media are vital for Park, promoting 'group stability by providing common understandings, regulating competition, coordinating the division of labour, and assuring intergenerational continuity' (Elsner Jr 1972: xxiii). News provides a basis for common focus of attention and action, while more expressive forms of communication, incorporated in such media as film or art characteristic of a social system, also assist in the assimilation of different cultures.

5. While some writers identify the origins of nationhood at a far earlier period than the nineteenth century (Hastings 1997), Banks (1995: 125) argues that prior to this time European states consisted of a small band of administrators, landlords and clerics. These may have made deals with other states and fought with them, but there seems to have been no idea that people shared an identity or shared anything in common beyond allegiance to a monarch.

6. In an approach that can be seen to complement the notion of nationalist imaginings, certain writers have focused on the state as the central power involved in differentiating people on the basis of race. Goldberg (1993), for example, traces the state's role in breaking down resistance to colonisation, in using racial categories to reinforce colonial rule, and views race as a political category that has been vital to the classification and prioritisation of people's capacity to exercise autonomy. Goldberg (1993: 151) argues that race has been used to achieve an erasure of people 'in the name of a universality that has no place for them'.

7. While emphasising the stubborn corporeal referent in race, however, it is important to note Miles's (1989: 71) reminder that since only certain physical characteristics are held to designate races in particular circumstances, 'we are investigating not a given, natural division of the world's population, but the application of ... specific meanings to the totality of human physiological variation'. The capacity of these meanings to be varied should be clear from our previous discussions of sex and gender: the breaking of social taboos and boundaries is often expressed in sexual as well as racial terms, while it is no accident that these variables overlap and intersect in those groups most marginalised or oppressed within a society.

10

RATIONAL SOCIOLOGY

1. Introduction

During the last quarter of the twentieth century much sociology has not only tended to reject the notion that society constitutes an overarching normative order, but has also fragmented into a series of competing, often mutually exclusive visions of social and moral life. A few theories sought to reconceive of 'society' and 'morality' by establishing new totalising syntheses, but the likes of neo-functionalism were generally seen as adding to the proliferation of sociological perspectives rather than providing a solid basis for the discipline's unification. In this context 'rational choice theory' (a theory whose roots lie in eighteenth-century utilitarianism but which re-established itself in the 1950s under the title 'exchange theory') developed into a highly influential and radical attempt to reconstruct sociology. The promise of rational choice theory was that it could unify warring schools of thought: it represented a 'paradigm setting theory' that could inform 'fine grained and effective social science work' (Favell 1996: 298). The cost associated with rebuilding sociology along these lines was not only abandoning the sociological ambition, rejecting 'society' and 'morality' as primary objects of study, but also dispensing with the idea that *any* vision of 'the social' could constitute a foundational referent for analysis.

In disregarding the discipline's traditional object of study, rational choice theory's key assumption is that methodological, ontological and moral primacy be accorded to the notion of the utility maximising, 'rational' individual. As a consequence, Parsonian notions of values as transpersonal phenomena are rejected in favour of a focus on the individual as either unaffected by social norms or, at the most, as a generator of norms. Such a vision of the actor might not be entirely accurate, rational choice theory admits, but its proponents believe that it captures the most significant thing about how people act most of the time and therefore allows for the construction of sophisticated and *testable* theories (Abell 1996).[1]

This project has its roots in the Enlightenment belief that society is created by rational individuals. Drawing on the utilitarian tradition of economics to propose the leanest possible theoretical model for sociology, rational choice theory has no significant place for race, class, or gender (Neitz and Mueser 1997: 107). More radically, it rejects classical sociology in favour of neoclassical economic conceptions of individual, rational action. This is clear in the work of George Homans, a figure whose writings in the 1950s and 1960s influenced recent versions of rational choice theory. He argues that the 'social system' is a myth, that 'structures' never do anything, and that sociology's unit of analysis should be the actions of individuals engaged in processes of preference-maximising exchange.

In this context, a rational actor is one 'who chooses the course of action that has the highest position in his or her preference ordering' (Scott 1995: 79). Rational choice theory not only rejects Parsons's 'overemphasis' on the structural features of social systems (Homans 1964), but also seeks to match the explanatory scope and synthesising ambitions of classical theory (Münch 1992: 137; Young 1997). Social contexts and structures, values, beliefs, habits, emotions, and religious choices have all been explained as products of rational, individual, utility maximisation.

The inclusion of 'economic man' into sociology entails the subordination of *homo sociologicus* to *homo economicus*. While the former approximates to the 'norm oriented conformer', the latter represents 'an all-informed, strongly consumption oriented maximiser' (Lindenberg 1990). In Durkheim's time opposition to *homo economicus* was integral to the project of establishing sociology, yet rational choice theory sides with economics in its attempt to reconstruct sociology. James Coleman (1990: 40) is one of the most important exponents of rational choice theory. He offers a total theory of 'society' and a new theoretical and methodological agenda for sociology, and associates his work with that of Thomas Hobbes and Adam Smith. Gary Becker's (1986: 113) uncompromising vision of rational choice theory also traces this 'economic approach to human behaviour' back to Smith, and views Jeremy Bentham as a particularly significant figure. This is because Bentham formulated systematically the view that all human behaviour is governed by the 'pleasure–pain' calculus that stimulates individuals to act in an instrumentally rational manner in order to achieve their desired ends.[2]

Becker's (1986) work has been characterised as the pinnacle of this approach's 'economic imperialism' (Goldthorpe 1998: 175), and provides a clear statement of the key assumptions of this perspective. For Becker, *all* human behaviour can be explained through an economic approach emphasising the 'expected utility' individuals seek to gain from undertaking rational actions. The choice of marriage partner, for example, is a form of utility maximisation in a sexual marketplace (Becker 1986). Consistent with this approach, social order is understood simply as the *aggregation* of the actions of rational individuals (Scott 1995: 86; Iannaccone 1997). While some rational choice theories are more attentive than Becker to the constraints upon individual action imposed by the choices of other actors, they still maintain that social phenomena are explicable in terms of the rational choices of individuals rather than in terms of norms, values or structures (Coleman 1990; Bohman 1991; Abell 1991).

If Becker's work provides us with a clear statement of the bolder claims made by this theory, rational choice theories can be categorised into 'strong' and 'weak' versions. The most significant difference here is that 'strong' versions suggest individuals act consistently in relation to their 'objectively rational' self-interest (Becker 1986). Weak versions hold only that individuals act consistently in relation to 'subjectively rational' beliefs about their self-interest (Abell 1996): beliefs that may be distorted as a result of the situation they are formed in and by the limited knowledge of those who hold them. Other variations in rational choice theories concern whether individual intentions and/or actions are deemed to be rational, whether individuals maximise or 'satisfice' their self-interest, whether rational action is the same as self-interested action, and whether rational action is a general or special theory of action. These variations are blended together in various ways, but we concentrate on the stronger versions of this approach that present the greatest challenge to traditional sociology. Sociology has long accepted the validity of the notion of rational action, but the wholesale reconstruction of its theories along the line of rational choice is a radical departure from its traditions.

The chapter progresses as follows. Section 2 explores the meaning of 'rationality', the 'unit idea' of this approach, while Section 3 explicates the elementary form of 'social' life underpinning rational choice theory. *Utilitarian action* (action directed toward maximizing self-interest) is foundational to rational choice theory. Utilitarian action is mediated through the choices of rational *individuals*, and results in outcomes which are simply the *aggregate* effects of such choices. The notion of aggregation rejects the possibility that the outcomes of individual actions add up to more than their parts. It rejects the possibility, for example, that individual actions might produce emergent moral systems that socialise people into non-rational forms of action. Rational choice theory depends heavily, then, on assumptions about the *stability*, as well as the dominance, of utility-maximising rationality. Despite its emphasis on rationality, however, rational choice theory has not avoided completely the subject of norms. In examining the foundations of exchange, for example, Homans (1961) added the normative idea of 'distributive justice' to his focus on rational action. Section 4 examines the tension that arises when rational choice theory addresses the relationship between rational interests and social norms, and asks whether rational choice theory ultimately relies on a non-rational, normative commitment to the idea of the rational actor.

2. Rationality

The difference between rational choice and much traditional sociological theory is stark: while the former is 'rationalist-individualist', the latter is more usually 'non-rational-collectivist' (Coleman and Fararo 1992: xviii). Furthermore, while sociology has analysed rationality in a variety of ways, rational choice theory has defined 'rationality' more narrowly, while using it to explain a far greater range of phenomena (Bohman 1991). This narrow definition involves the idea that people act consistently to *maximise the realisation of their preferences*, whatever these may be. Individuals are seen as seeking to maximise their 'expected utility' (Coleman 1986), 'private benefits' (Hardin 1997), 'cost–benefit ratios' (Frey 1997), rent (Tollison 1997), or money income (Opp 1989; Zafirovski 1999: 48).

This lean, economistic definition of rationality aims to avoid what Lukes (1970: 207) suggests is the 'untold confusion and obscurity' caused by sociological uses of the term.[3] Its implications for the conception of individual action will be examined in the next section, but we focus now on three dimensions of the rational choice treatment of 'rationality' that differentiate it from traditional sociological theory. These can be demonstrated with reference to Mauss's analysis of gift exchange, Weber's typology of action, and sociological analyses of crowd behaviour. The comparison with Mauss shows how rational choice theory holds that rationality *produces*, rather than being defined by, social relationships. The comparison with Weber highlights how it is defined *unidimensionally*, rather than heterogeneously, in order to facilitate the *construction of testable hypotheses*. The comparison with sociological analyses of crowd behaviour reveals how this vision of the discipline explains as *rational*, forms of action traditionally described as non-rational or irrational.

The rationality of exchange

Rational choice theories sometimes appear under such labels as 'game theory', which we examine later, and 'exchange theory' (Abell 1991). Exchange theory describes the attempt by writers such as Homans, Blau, and Olson to incorporate economic models of the market into explanations of human interaction. According to this approach, utility-maximising exchanges are guided by rationality, rather than normative factors, and produce social relationships rather than being shaped by them. Patterns of exchange do not derive from the pre-contractual foundations of solidarity, but emerge as individuals seek to maximise their interests. Sociality and solidarity (as well as the norms, values, and structures associated with them) are *secondary* phenomena arising from rationally interacting individuals.

The difference between this account of rationality and traditional sociological accounts can be illustrated with reference to the status of exchange in Marcel Mauss's work. Mauss (1950) was significant in the development of sociology as well as anthropology. He sought to refute the rationalist idea that utility maximisation explains action, by exploring 'the gift' as a foundational expression of sociability. According to Mauss, the apparently voluntary character of gift exchange disguises how it derives from the creation and sustenance of allegiances between families, clans, and tribes. These allegiances encompass gift exchange within a complex series of moral obligations and rules. Even in modern societies characterised by the apparent domination of economic rationalism, Mauss (1950: 26, 63) emphasised that the emotional values arising from gift exchange can represent the consolidation and creation of bonds between people. The 'non-utilitarian' character of Christmas gifts, for example, sometimes has a sentimental value far greater than their economic value (Solnic and Hemenway 1996). The refusal to acknowledge obligations associated with gifts is, therefore, a denial of friendship rather than a calculation dependent on utility maximisation (Mauss 1950: 11). As Douglas (1992: 158) notes, 'The theory of the gift is a theory of human solidarity'.

Modalities of rationality

Rational choice theory's treatment of 'rationality' is also distinctive in defining it as a *unidimensional*, rather than a multiple, phenomenon. Rationality involves means–end rational action concerned with maximising the realisation of preferences. While Weber's analysis of rational action has been viewed as 'prototypical' of the kind of sociology advocated by this approach (Olson 1965: 104;

Coleman 1979: 82; Stinchcombe 1986), this ignores Weber's argument that different modalities of action follow from different forms of rationality (Levine 1998). Weber made a distinction between instrumental means–ends rationality, that is central to rational choice theories, and a value-rational orientation where individuals act in relation to transcendent values. Actions prompted by duty, honour, beauty, and a religious calling, for example, encourage individuals to act out convictions regardless of their costs and benefits and could never be regarded as instrumentally rational. Weber also discussed forms of social action – traditional and affectual action – that could not be reduced to the means–ends schema, and argued in his essay, 'Science as a Vocation', that habit and impulse predominate over rational action.

Weber's account of the various modalities of rationality tends to be neglected by rational choice theorists in favour of a unidimensional model. This places great emphasis on Weber's (1968: 6) suggestion that it is possible for sociologists to identify what rational action would have been in any situation: identifying action informed by limited knowledge or emotions as a 'deviation from the line of conduct which would be expected on the hypothesis that the action were purely rational'. Some rational choice advocates, for example, view value-rationality as merely instrumental-rationality in disguise, rejecting the idea that ideals can stimulate individuals to pursue goals regardless of their cost (Spickard 1998: 104; Stark 1997: 6–7). Others make a distinction between 'subjectively' and 'objectively' rational action (Boudon 1996), but proceed to evaluate the former in relation to the latter. The Hoppi rain dance, for instance, may not actually cause rain to fall but is subjectively rational action in periods of drought because it is a ritual people *believe* will bring rain.

Rational choice theory's narrow definition of rationality also contributes to its goal of *constructing testable hypotheses*. If humans act rationally, then social theory can be seen as a series of testable propositions about the causation of aggregate phenomena. Coleman (1990) evaluates Weber's Protestant ethic thesis in these terms, criticising its 'defective' account of the causal linkages between Calvinism and the spirit of capitalism. Such an interpretation of *The Protestant Ethic*, however, is at odds with Weber's own view of theory. As Mouzelis (1995: 35) points out, Coleman ignores Weber's own insistence that he is examining an 'elective affinity' between a religious ethic and capitalism, and is not identifying causally-determinant linkages.

These differences between Weber and rational choice theorists show that the latter work with a narrower definition of rationality and a more scientistic vision of theory. Rational choice theorists are concerned with means–ends rational action, and insist theoretical speculations be 'hardened up' into testable propositions. Weberian sociology and rational choice theory, in other words, represent fundamentally different approaches to the discipline.

Rationality and 'social contagion'

Rational choice theory seeks to explain apparently emotional actions (such as those indicated by Weber's notion of charismatic action) as instances of rational action. Coleman, for example, examines events that critics suggest rational choice theory cannot cope with, such as stock market panics and wars borne out of impulsive acts (Scheff 1992: 102), and insists 'much of what is ordinarily described as non-rational or irrational is merely so because the observers have not discovered the point of view of the actor, from which the action *is* rational (Coleman 1990: 18).

Coleman's (1979: 86) account of the 'social contagion' that appears to spread in crowd situations is particularly significant as it offers a rationalistic account of a recurring object of theoretical analysis. Gustave Le Bon's analysis of the irrationality of crowds, for example, was influential in psychology and political theory, while Durkheim (1912) viewed group life as an irreducibly effervescent social phenomenon. Coleman, in contrast, argues that crowds, riots, and mob behaviour can all be understood in terms of rational choices, and examines what can happen when there is smoke in a crowded theatre and someone yells 'Fire!'. Coleman observes that this situation is sometimes followed by 'collective panic' and sometimes by orderly exit. Why? He argues that both outcomes are products of rationality, and that it is only rational choice theory that can explain which outcome predominates (Coleman 1979: 86).

In opposing the idea that 'escape panics' (Brown 1965) are shaped by emotional factors, Coleman introduces the idea of 'control transference'. What appears to be 'social contagion' can best be understood as the rational decisions of individuals to *transfer to others* control of a particular situation. If people follow the actions of others in rushing out of a burning theatre, for example, it is the result of a rational calculation to transfer control of what to do to others. In such situations, individuals assess their chances of survival if they act in certain ways, by taking into account the potential actions of others (Coleman 1979: 87). It is the *aggregation* of these choices that determine whether most individuals file out of the theatre in an orderly way, or whether individuals rush out.

If rationality produces social relationships and is defined unidimensionally in rational choice theory, Coleman's rational action analysis of 'crowd behaviour' provides us with a third example of what differentiates this approach from traditional sociology. Coleman recognises that crowds manifest a collective form of action no member would engage in alone, but resists any Durkheimian tendency to attribute an inherent dynamism to these groups. They merely offer certain resources for the rational decision-maker. 'Race riots', for example, are dependent for Coleman on a collective density of persons, but also on individuals calculating the consequences of acting together. Crowds, in short, are the consequences of rational calculations of self-interest. They come into being when enough people calculate they would provide sufficient advantage for the possible costs of participation to be worthwhile risks.

3. The elementary forms of social and moral life

Having analysed its unit idea, we now examine the elementary forms of social and moral life underpinning this vision of sociology. *Utilitarianism* constitutes the elementary form of action underlying rational choice theory, as illustrated by its interpretation of even socially 'contagious' panics and crowd behaviour in terms of self-interested calculations. Utilitarianism is mediated through *individual* actions, while the outcomes of such actions are conceptualised simply as aggregation effects. These visions of what is elementary to 'social life' are complemented by a moral commitment to the individual rational actor as the basic unit of sociology.

Utilitarian action

Rational choice theory assumes that action seeks to maximise rewards and minimise costs. Homans (1961: 61), for example, theorised the relation between costs and rewards in terms of calculations of 'profit' likely to ensue from particular actions (Scott 1995: 78). Coleman and Fararo (1992: xi) suggest the distinctive element of rational choice is the concept of *optimisation*. They argue that social actors engage in processes of optimisation, sometimes expressed as maximising utility and sometimes as minimising cost, and postulate that actors will choose actions likely to produce the 'best' outcome in terms of the satisfaction of self-interest. 'Profit' and 'optimisation' are not the only terms used to describe utilitarian action. What Coleman calls 'optimisation', Becker calls 'maximisation'. It is Bentham's 'pleasure–pain' calculus that forms the core of what Becker (1986: 110) calls the 'stable preferences' that are directly related to the 'maximising behaviour' of humans.

The idea that individuals act to maximise the realisation of their preferences has been applied to a huge range of sociological concerns. Such is Becker's (1986: 116) commitment to a strict rational choice model of utilitarian action that he explains even death in terms of rational choices. All deaths can be understood as 'suicide' in the sense that life could have been prolonged if individuals had chosen to act in ways that maximised their longevity (Becker 1986: 116). A further example of the rational choice approach is provided by religion. Sociologists traditionally associated rational action with secularisation, yet religious affiliation remains high in contemporary America. In seeking to explain this, Stark and Bainbridge (1987) begin from the conventional rational choice principle that action is the outcome of reward seeking. They then note that certain rewards are not only scarce but beyond the reach of mortal actors, and explain religion in terms of its function as a 'compensator' for unobtainable goals such as immortality.[4] Individuals choose a religion that provides them with the promise of the afterlife just as they would seek to achieve other desired ends (Stark 1997: 7).

The individual: the medium of rational action

If utilitarianism describes the form of action elementary to this vision of sociology, it is a form of action mediated through the *individual*. Rational choice theory is methodologically individualist, rejecting Durkheim's argument that the unit of sociological explanation is the 'social fact'. It is individuals, not collectivities, that undertake actions (Abell 1992: 189) and these individuals are perceived as 'rational egoists' (Zafirovski 1999). Rational choice theory accepts that sociology is ultimately concerned with social phenomena, but insists analysis must start with individual actions (Elster 1989a: 13). As Coleman (1990: 2, 503) argues, 'the elementary actor is the wellspring of action, no matter how complex are the structures through which action takes place'. This methodological individualism is not compromised when theorists such as Coleman examine 'corporate actors', such as businesses and trade unions. This is because corporate actors are not considered elementary units of social action, even though they are understood to act in a highly purposive manner reminiscent of rational individuals, but are explained in terms of their constituent parts: individuals.

This methodological individualism is complemented by an ontological individualism (Wrong 1994: 199). To talk of the 'sovereignty' of natural individuals, as Coleman does, implies a commitment to individuals as prior to, and more fundamental than, collective structures. It also coexists with a *normative* individualism. Coleman, for example, assesses the legitimacy of corporate actors in terms of how far they respect the 'sovereignty' of the rational individual (Coleman 1990: 531; Mouzelis 1995: 31).

The priority accorded to rational individuals raises a number of potential problems. First, 'strong' versions of rational choice theory often confine their attentions to the rationally *acting* individual, eschewing concern with the interior of the actor, even when neoclassical economists have pointed out that 'economic man need not be conceived of as a pure egoist' (Keynes 1955: 128; Zafirovski 1999: 49). When this concern with action is supplemented, it tends only to involve the actor's *cognitive* functions.[5] Olson (1965: 61), for example, argues that erotic, psychological, and moral motivations should be excluded from analysis: what matters is the rational exercise of self-interest. Second, for rational choice theorists interested in motivation, there is the methodological problem of how to ascertain that the rationale the analyst attributes to the individual's actions exist in the mind of that individual rather than solely in the theory of the analyst (Hollis 1987: 187–8). Third, rational choice theories concerned with intentional action tend not only to assume people have rational reasons for acting, but that these reasons actually motivate actions. This overlooks the possibilities that individuals may have a rational reason for acting but fail to act, and may sometimes perform actions for which they have no reasons (MacIntyre 1970: 117). Fourth, the normative commitment to the rational individual calls into question whether rational choice theory can itself be justified on rational grounds. Fifth, arguments about maximising behaviour tend to rule out preference indifference or rapid preference changes on the part of the individual, and make the problematic assumption that actors have a 'perfect knowledge' in order to achieve their goals (Goldthorpe 1998: 170).

These problems have stimulated further refinements of rational choice theory. In terms of the possible difference between individual intent and action, Becker (1986: 112) suggests individuals (whom he terms 'decision units') *may not be conscious* of seeking to maximise their rewards, but that this is what they are doing. Individuals are utility maximisers, then, regardless of their intentions and regardless of the strong emotions that might appear to motivate them. In this view, action is not necessarily consciously purposeful but *unconsciously* purposeful. As Bohman (1991: 75) suggests, however, this search for unconscious maximising motives and market mechanisms displaces the rational actor from the centre of analysis, and compromises the claims of those rational choice theories that assume reasons cause actions.

Other rational choice theorists have dealt with the 'limited knowledgeability' of actors by working with a notion of 'subjective' rather than 'objective' rationality. They suggest that individuals act according to what they perceive to be in their self-interests, even if they cannot possibly have all the knowledge necessary to calculate what that self-interest might actually be (Goldthorpe 1998: 171). Boudon's (1996, 1998) 'cognitivist model' of rational choice theory develops this notion of subjective rationality, focusing on how individuals can hold, and act on, 'mistaken' beliefs. Boudon acknowledges that such beliefs may have little to do with objectively rational utility maximisation, but attacks explanations that associate them with affective or emotional influences. Subjectively rational beliefs are based instead on the limited cognitive resources of actors: on what actors *believe* to be rational instead of what *actually* is rational.

Despite such qualifications, however, rational choice theory still confronts the criticisms that human preferences are neither stable nor as readily identifiable as is assumed in this theory (Tversky et al. 1988: 383). The very notion, indeed, of stable preferences faces the problem that certain goals can be mutually contradictory. The contradiction between the pursuit of wealth and the maintenance and pursuit of status, for example, is vividly evident in Adam Smith's explanation of the decline of the aristocracy and in Veblen's analysis of conspicuous consumption, yet there is nothing in rational choice theory to suggest individuals cannot hold both preferences.

By identifying the individual as the medium for this utilitarianism, rational choice theory either focuses on individual *action*, a focus which assumes the embodied preconditions and disregards the psychological preconditions of action, or widens its concerns by accepting individuals may act on a mistaken view of their self-interest. The former option is justified on the basis of its being an 'adequate' model of the actor for explanatory purposes, the latter on the basis that theorists are in a privileged position to know the interests of individuals.

Aggregation: the outcome of rational action

In line with its methodological individualism, rational choice theory insists that the *outcomes* of action are simply 'aggregation effects'. This goes further than Spencer, who recognised an 'individuality of aggregate' transcendent of component units (Zafirovski 2000: 556), and returns to the Hobbesian conception of the relationship between individual and society: a compound (society) can only be understood in relation to the things of which it is compounded (individuals) (Bohman 1991: 148–9; Hindess 1988). As Abell (1996: 259) argues, 'The maxim of no emergent distinctions is central' to rational choice theory: 'there are no macro distinctions without micro distinctions'. This requires theorists to analyse the social outcomes of individual actions through progressively higher levels of aggregation. From households, to groups, to entire religious markets, what is understood as 'social' is simply the 'equilibria' emerging from aggregation patterns (Iannaccone 1997: 26).

Most rational choice theory recognises that a focus on social outcomes as simply the aggregation effects of rational individual actions needs supplementing by accepting that individuals act *strategically* by taking account of the choices of other people. One of the best-known illustrations of this is 'the Prisoner's Dilemma', one example of 'game theory'. In the 'Prisoner's Dilemma' two suspects are questioned separately about a joint crime and have to decide, independently, whether to confess or remain silent. The legal context for these decisions is such that if suspects A and B remain silent, both go free; if both confess they receive a medium prison sentence; if A confesses and B does not, then A will get a short sentence while B will receive a long sentence. The assumption made by rational choice theory is that both suspects will confess, and receive a medium sentence, as neither can trust the other to remain silent. It would be irrational to remain silent, as one faces the possibility of a long prison sentence.

The 'Prisoner's Dilemma' has been used to highlight the sophistication of rational choice theory's account of the strategic choices which lead to aggregate outcomes. It has also been interpreted as showing the limits of rational decision-making, as revealing the value of co-operation over rational choice, and as representative of the difficulties this theory has in explaining co-operative action (Hardin 1982; Sen 1986; Barnes 1995). As Parfit (1986) notes, the supposedly rational confessions of suspects earn them prison sentences. If they had co-operated, trusted each other and remained silent, they would have gone free.

If rational choice theory's focus on 'aggregation effects' creates problems in explaining co-operation, it also raises the difficulty of accounting for other collective phenomena. Given the high numbers of people involved in sustaining an institution that provides collective goods and/or services, why should a single rational individual incur the costs associated with joining or supporting that institution if they still stand to receive its benefits? Scott (1995: 87) employs a common example of this when noting that, in terms of rational choice theory, it is difficult to explain why individuals join trade unions. Rationally, an individual must calculate that his/her participation in a union involves costs, but will hardly alter the union's bargaining power. If the individual can still benefit from the union's strength without joining (e.g. in terms of bargaining increased pay awards), it makes no rational sense for the individual to join. The paradox arising from this, however, is that if every individual acted 'rationally', the aggregate outcome would be the collapse of the union and its power.

This type of paradox is referred to as the 'free rider problem'; a problem that has led many political theorists to follow Olson in arguing that coercion is necessary in order to encourage co-operative action (Tuck 1979), or to follow Iannaccone (1997) in emphasising the importance of imposing costs on those who free ride. Such sanctions might enable rational choice theory to explain the persistence of collective organisations. Nevertheless, it still has problems in explaining collectivities when these conditions do not exist. Furthermore, empirical research suggests people 'free ride' far less than rational choice theorists assume (Marwell and Ames 1981; Dawes 1980; Edney 1980). Many people do join unions, for example, even when they would receive the benefits of a higher bargained wage outside the union. Indeed, even sympathetic critics of rational choice theory have noted evidence that shows humans act in ways that place the interest of others above their own self-interest (Mooney Marini 1992: 35; see Staub 1978). Zafirovski (1999: 92), for example, cites a study of the Dutch Peace Movement in the 1980s in which the 'free rider problem' did not impede movement mobilisation. Cases such as these, in which people refuse to 'free ride', constitute an unavoidable problem for rational choice theories. This theory allows no real room for acting altruistically or in order to achieve collective interests, as individuals are always assumed to act self-interestedly.[6] Sociological research, in contrast, suggests that a variety of additional factors prompts people to engage in social institutions and society. Furthermore, as Zafirovski (1999: 81) notes, even rational choice theorists have admitted that social order would collapse if a large proportion of people started to act as the rational choice model suggests.

Coleman (1990: 301) has provided an ambitious attempt to address this problem. First, he claims self-interests do not necessarily result in *selfish* actions. Rational action, in other words, is not necessarily 'egotistical', as individuals can act in ways that give themselves satisfaction through giving satisfaction to others (Scott 1995: 76). Joining an already existing union, then, may be rational for an individual because it provides him or her with the satisfaction of satisfying other union members. Second, Coleman (1990: 301, 503) seeks to extend the explanatory power of rational choice theory by suggesting that outcomes of rational actions are not simply 'aggregations' but can be viewed as 'emergent phenomena': networks of enablement and constraint that form a context for individual action. Rational individuals, in other words, have to reflexively engage with resources and events around them that they have only limited control over. In this context, joining a union might constitute a rational decision for an actor who judged that although they might gain from free riding in the short-term, union membership offered a degree of security in the long run. Recognising the paradox of free riding, which could lead to the ending of a union, this actor has decided to make a rational, longer-term investment in a resource that may assist self-interest.

Coleman (1990: 302) refers to such emergent phenomena as forms of 'social capital'. Social capital constitutes a collective asset for individuals seeking to maximise their self-interest. In the case of students, for example, the family and its relations with the community and school constitute a form of social capital. Other examples of social capital cited by Coleman include the *comités d'action lycéen* of the French student revolt of 1968, and the workers' cells of tsarist Russia advocated by Lenin. These groups constituted resources for individuals, aiding them in moving from individual protest to organised revolt.

This rational choice 'solution' to problems concerning collectivities has not satisfied everyone. Mouzelis (1995: 34) criticises Coleman's notion of emergent social phenomena, suggesting it simply recognises that individuals' rational choices have to take account of the rational choices of others. Broader contextual issues, however, such as *historical* circumstances, are ignored in favour of 'logico-deductive' generalisations about rational decisions. In other words, Coleman still reduces macro-level phenomena into the micro-level actions of individuals seeking to maximise their self-interest. This has prompted the criticism that rational choice theory is characterised by 'institutional unrealism or non-institutionalism' in that 'individuals are expected to do too much and institutions too little' (Zafirovski 1999: 88). One example of this is that there is no social creativity at a collective level other than that legitimised by the interests of the individuals involved. In fact, Coleman's analysis of the 'network of inter-actions' that produce particular social outcomes tends to replicate the aggregation model endorsed by Becker despite his stated recognition of 'emergent pheno-mena'. The analysis of 'panic situations' discussed earlier, for example, clearly expresses the idea that responses to dangerous situations are *aggregate* outcomes dependent on how the choices of individuals add up (Coleman 1979: 88). Fararo (1996: 28) makes the point that where social bonds appear in Coleman's work, they do so in the context of 'social capital' *already available* to the actor. The bonds are *given* and we receive no satisfactory explanation of their creation. Nevertheless, Coleman's analysis of strategic decisions at least recognises the often complex patterns of interaction that generate aggregate outcomes.

In this section we have seen how rational choice theorists go to considerable lengths in order to argue that collective phenomena, which appear to reflect com-munal interests, actually arise on the basis of individuals acting to maximise their rational self-interests. Collective social phenomena cannot be accounted for with reference to historical events that make certain outcomes more likely than others. Neither can such phenomena be explained as the result of communal norms. Instead, and despite the *ad hoc* riders with which rational choice theory supple-ments its formulations, social outcomes are simply an *aggregation* of utility-maximising individual actions.

4. Norms and interests

Rational choice theory neglects or marginalizes a variety of factors central to socio-logy. These include socialisation, values, normative influences, the extent to which action takes place within a socially structured set of opportunities, and the role of emotionally motivated actions (Mooney Marini 1992: 34). Partly as a result of its anti-Parsonian vision of sociology, rational choice theory has been particularly keen to reject explanations of action based on the internalisation of norms (Sciulli 1992: 161; Homans 1950). Nevertheless, it has rarely been able to dispense with normative factors in their entirety, and tends at some point to encounter either individual behaviour or social phenomena that cannot be described as rational and appear, at least initially, to be non-rational and normative.

This rational/non-rational opposition introduces us to a major tension within this vision of sociology. Where they appear within rational choice theory, norms have either to be argued away as insignificant and outside the scope of this theory, or integrated into a rationalist analysis. In this context, 'stronger' versions of rational choice theory often come across a particular problem. The more they seek to apply the category of the 'rational' to diverse areas of social life, the more they have difficulties accounting for the residual category of the 'non-rational' (Joas 1996: 146). So, how does rational choice theory cope with this issue?

Some rational choice approaches analyse norms as rational phenomena. While Parsons viewed rational action as shaped by norms, strong versions of rational choice theory view 'norms' as outcomes of individual rational actions (Coleman 1990; Iannaccone 1997). Norms, in other words, are another way of referring to the utilitarian preferences of individuals or the aggregation of individual actions and do not constitute a residual category. Weaker versions of rational choice theory, in contrast, view norms as providing the context in which individuals undertake rational choices and actions (Boudon 1998). Hayek (1967: 172), for example, argues that markets are like complex games that involve rule following. This imputes a greater role for normative elements. Finally, some rational choice theorists, in a move which compromises the distinctiveness of this theory, suggest normative action coexists with rational action and even acknowledge that norms can shape what counts as rational action (Sherkat 1997). Indeed, Elster (1989a) argues that rational calculation and normative commitment are *complementary* parts of the development of social action (Scott 1995: 91).

The tension between norms and interests in rational choice theories, and the different ways theorists attempt to resolve it, is evident at the levels of individual actions and 'irrational' social outcomes. This is clear in two highly influential versions of rational choice theory: Coleman's relatively 'strong' vision of rational choice theory, and Elster's weaker approach that seeks to incorporate more traditional sociological concerns.

Rational actions, norms and the individual

Coleman analyses norms as outcomes of utility-maximising individual actions. Unlike certain rational choice theorists, he accepts that norms are legitimate objects of analysis. However, norms do not enter into an individual's choices or actions because individuals are 'norm-free self-interested persons'. It is only by starting with rational individuals, indeed, that we can see how normative expectations come to be developed and maintained (Coleman 1990: 31).

Norms are created and maintained when rational individuals, in interaction with others, realise that observing certain 'rules' of behaviour will advance their interests (Coleman 1990: 242). Sanctions that seek to enforce norms are developed for similar reasons. Drawing on Elias's discussion of etiquette, for example, Coleman argues that individuals voluntarily commit themselves to all sorts of restrictive codes and sanctions in order to benefit from belonging to a status group differentiated from the masses (Coleman 1990: 258). Thus, rational individuals develop norms when they calculate they will benefit from relinquishing control over certain areas of social life. Although norms mean that individuals give up the right to control certain of their own actions, they calculate that the control over other people's actions provided by normative rules may be to their advantage in the long run (Coleman 1990: 288). Norms, in other words, are co-ordinating mechanisms that arise when individuals judge them to be beneficial to their interests (Bohman 1991: 95, 166).

Coleman, like Durkheim and Parsons, views norms as reflecting social consensus. He departs from traditional sociological theory, nonetheless, in insisting that they represent a *contractual* consensus rooted in rational choices. When Coleman (1990: 243) deals with the internalisation of norms by individuals, for example, he is particularly keen to emphasise that sanctions applied by individuals to their own actions can only be assessed in relation to this rational, interactional network of utility maximisation. At all times, the normative features of society can be traced back to the self-interests of individuals. Norms are rational, not non-rational phenomena.

This account of the development of norms appears to provide us with a powerful alternative to Parsonian explanations and mitigates, to some extent, the accusation that Coleman always views social bonds as given. As Fararo (1996: 282) notes, however, this explanation sounds most feasible for 'conscious attempts to institute normative ideas in a group' and less so for the unconscious internalisation of standards that become norms without anyone explicitly intending this to happen. Furthermore, Coleman's account coexists in a somewhat uneasy relationship with the idea that humans possess stable preferences. Adhering to norms, after all, constitutes a trade off between the freedom to act in certain ways (a situation that might reduce the chances of realising certain preferences), and the expectation that shared norms might restrict the behaviour of others (a situation that might increase the chances of realising other preferences). Coleman (1990: 517), however, suggests that the acceptance of norms means that individuals create a broader range of stable preferences, allowing for a greater realisation of one's total preferences than would otherwise occur.

There remains a problem for this strong vision of rational choice theory when it confronts normative actions that cannot be reduced to utility-maximising decisions. This is most obvious in the case of altruistic action, but is also evident in cross-cultural research. In the former case, theorists such as Coleman frequently suggest that altruistic and other non-utilitarian forms of action are self-interested rational actions in disguise. This argument rests on a massive conflation, however, involving the complete collapse of those actions and areas of social life Weber regarded as value-based into means–ends rationality. It also contradicts the evidence of experiments in laboratory conditions that suggest social values such as fairness, altruism and revenge are evident in people's tendencies to interact in line with what has been called a 'fairness equilibrium' (Babcock and Loewenstein 1997; Camerer 1997; Zafirovski 1999). In the case of cross-cultural research, rational choice theory remains centred on conceptions of the 'rational individual', and ignores how culture may affect the meaning of this notion (Mouzelis 1995: 37; Douglas and Ney 1998). Various critics have noted the existence of cultures in which any attempt to analyse action in terms of individuals seeking to maximise self-interest is manifestly absurd (Crespi 1992: 16–17). Anthropological accounts of non-Western societies make it clear that communities exist where the rational, self-interested, maximising individual of rational choice discourse would be viewed as 'mad' rather than as expressing anything 'natural' (Crespi 1992).

Rather than acknowledging that such examples pose fundamental problems for rational choice theory, strong rational choice theories maintain their commitment to the notion of rationality as a category that transcends cultural differences. This encourages the idea that individuals and communities can have a mistaken (non-rational) view of their own (rational) actions and orientations. Many sociologists would accept this view, given sufficient evidence, but would remain uncomfortable with a position that shielded itself from all criticism. This view also leads to the breathtaking conclusion that when people fail to behave in the way rational choice theorists expect them to, there is something wrong with these people rather than with the theory. For example, when Coleman (1990: 504) discusses certain non-rational actions of individuals that resist his interpretation of them as 'masked' rational actions, he refers to them as a 'malfunctioning of the actor'! The foundations of 'strong' versions of rational choice theory are finally revealed: a normative view of the actor as someone who *should* behave rationally. Elster (1990: 20) characterises such dogmatism as hyperrational: certain rational choice theories exhibit an irrational belief in the power of reason.

Elster (1989a) constructs a contrasting theory of the relationship between rational action and norms through a weaker version of rational choice theory. He argues that individuals do not merely take account of social norms in the rational calculation of the costs and rewards of particular actions, but develop an *emotional attachment* to norms, often of an unconscious sort, so that their infringement can result in feelings of shame, guilt, embarrassment, and personal inadequacy. In contrast to many rational theorists, then, Elster attempts to explain collective action as a mixture of selfish and normative, rational and emotional factors, interacting and snowballing beyond the individuals involved (Elster 1989a: 186–7). Contrary to Coleman's straightforward focus on interests as productive of norms, Elster suggests interests can be *transformed* by norms and other non-rational factors in three ways.

First, rational interests can be shaped by the socially structured processes surrounding education. Learning, for Elster, is not simply a process of the individual accumulating information about their rational interests, but a social phenomenon influenced by friends, family, community, and other emotional ties. Basil Bernstein's (1970) research into linguistic codes, for example, suggests there is interaction between family structures, social outlook and education which structures people's view of the world and their interests in that world. Second, rational interests can also be shaped by acts of *seduction* in which individuals are enticed into trying something they might initially find objectionable but subsequently come to acquire as a preference. This can be seen as an alteration of preferences arising out of temptation, passion, or even coercion rather than a rational expression of individual interest (Elster 1979). Third, people may possess rational preferences but may act in ways which contradict these preferences and which reflect instead the greater influence of cultural norms. In applying Elster's work to the sociology of religion, for example, Sherkat (1997: 67) argues that many Black Americans join Churches and participate in religious activities that have no place in their rational preferences. The reason they, and many white Americans, display such religiosity is because they do not wish to disrupt the norms of the community in which they are members.

Elster's work is a notable attempt to broaden the applicability of rational choice theory to traditional sociological phenomena. Whether it actually transcends problems central to rational choice approaches, however, is debatable. Bohman (1991: 166) questions whether Elster's account of social norms is really a rational choice one at all. Mouzelis (1995), in contrast, argues that Elster does not go far enough in integrating cultural factors into his analysis. He has criticised as arbitrary Elster's account of the differences between individual, rational 'interests' and collective, non-rational 'norms': Elster (1989b: 98) simply assumes that rationality is a universal feature of what it is to be human, irrespective of cultural influences. In other words, Elster does not follow through the logic of his suggestion that the emotional power of norms can shape interests to the conclusion that *rationality itself* might just be one cultural norm.

Rational actions, norms and collective outcomes

Coleman's and Elster's treatments of rational and non-rational action also highlight the challenge confronting this theory when it seeks to account for social outcomes that do not appear to reflect the actions of rational individuals: outcomes that might be described as 'irrational'.

For Weber, 'rational' capitalism could be explained in terms of its origins in the 'irrational' impulses of Calvinism. Rational choice theorists, in contrast, start with individual rationality but acknowledge that the aggregation of actions and interactions arising from rational individuals, or, in Coleman's case, the 'emergent phenomena', cannot always be termed 'rational'. The recognition of 'irrational' outcomes might be seen as a problem for rational choice theory. If rational actions resulted in collectively 'irrational' outcomes, then truly rational actors would surely change their behaviour to prevent such outcomes from reoccurring. As they frequently do not, then surely the rational actor is a myth?

Coleman rejects such criticism by suggesting that 'irrational' outcomes of rational actions reveal 'the problematic character of social order' rather than an inaccuracy in his model of the actor (Coleman and Fararo 1992: xiv). He has discussed this in relation to how it is that, in an election, individuals can make a rational choice about whom to vote for that may result in an 'irrational' outcome and 'irrational' policies for most of those concerned. Coleman (1979: 79) argues that rational choice theory remains useful in such circumstances, as it predicts that rational persons will react to such an irrational outcome by attempting to use 'outside resources', such as money or power, to obtain the outcomes they want and thereby circumvent the irrationalities of an electoral system. In other words, individuals' rational choices involve a strategic engagement with issues of power, money, and hierarchy in order to maximise the realisation of self-interest in 'hostile' situations.

In contrast to some forms of rational choice theory, Coleman's argument on this point acknowledges that rational choices are not exercised in a social or cognitive vacuum. Nevertheless, given the emphasis rational choice theories place on the knowledgeability of social actors, is it not problematic to assume individuals will carry on making rational choices when the outcomes of their choices carry on being irrational? In the case of elections, for example, to suggest that individuals try to circumvent the irrationalities of electoral outcomes by means other than voting sidesteps a more immediate conclusion: if they were reflexive about the outcomes of their actions then 'rational' people might not vote at all.[7] The fact that Coleman focuses on what rational actors do after having voted (yet again?), only to discover they have helped produce an irrational outcome (yet again?), raises the suspicion that the rational actor at the heart of this theory is unreflexive about whether their behaviour really is rational. More seriously, it also raises the possibility that the actor depicted by rational choice theory does not exist.

Interestingly, Elster's (1983: 24) greater attention to non-rational phenomena leads him to argue that the *action* of voting appears to be more important than voting *outcomes*. This argument falls outside a strong rational choice theory, but has a long sociological pedigree. Parsons (1960), for example, draws on Durkheim in interpreting voting as a ritual evocation of solidarity.

Elster's work includes a focus on the unintended consequences of rational action and, as we have stated, recognises normative and emotional modes of behaviour as well as rational action. His discussion of Ulysses's behaviour, for example, highlights how people can impose forms of coercion upon themselves in order to prevent their future actions from being affected by emotions that would sabotage earlier intentions (Elster 1979). This weaker vision of rational choice theory also makes it easier to recognise the irrational outcomes of even rational actions. Norms, Elster argues, are not outcome oriented but are internalised and acquire a compulsive character that can result in social outcomes at variance with individual intentions (Scott 1995).

We have suggested that rational choice theory confronts a tension when it seeks to explain the relationship between rational and non-rational actions and outcomes. This tension has prompted different responses. Some theorists restrict their explanatory ambitions by ignoring the residual category of the non-rational or normative, a move that removes from analysis many issues that have preoccupied sociology. Others interpret the non-rational, or normative, as outgrowths of rationality, thereby extending the scope of rational choice theory. Finally, others have diluted the distinctiveness of rational choice theory by incorporating into it non-rational, normative factors ordinarily associated with traditional sociology. The first two of these responses betray a normative commitment to the rational individual. This is clear in the rational choice argument that social outcomes must be judged in terms of whether they allow for the realisation of rational individual interests. This normative commitment to what is essentially an economistic view of the individual raises the question of whether rational choice theory can be accepted as a form of sociological theory.

5. Concluding comments

Sociology has traditionally worked with an anthropologically informed vision of the individual whose thought and bodily habits and actions are moulded, to a greater or lesser extent, by social relationships, processes and structures. In this context, action has been conceptualised as motivated not just by rational self-interest, but also by prestige and status considerations (Veblen, Weber), by interpersonal ties (Simmel), by cultural capital (Bourdieu), by morality (Durkheim, Parsons), by transcendental ideals (Weber, Parsons), and by ideological factors (Marx, Mannheim) (Zafirovski 1999). Rational choice theory's conception of individuals as rational, optimising actors, then, can be seen as a peculiarly unsocial view of social beings. In responding to the 'over-socialised' individual of Parsonian sociology, it has gone to the polar extreme and proposed, as an elementary form of social and moral life, an individual that is judged to be 'malfunctioning' when he or she fails to act as a 'norm-free' rationalist. As Wrong (1994: 199) expresses it, rational actors are not treated as people who have life-historical, biographical factors shaping their identities and development. For Mouzelis (1995: 29), this view of rational actors is simply inaccurate. People do not always operate in this utilitarian way and, if they sometimes do, this is behaviour into which they have been socialised. If rational behaviour really is inherent and not learned, then, as Barnes (1995: 35) suggests, small babies presumably lie in their cots making rational decisions about whether to cry for their mothers, opt for some language development, or seek to improve their motor skills.

Some rational choice theorists are more sensitive to such criticisms than others. Becker (1986) dismisses them, but Elster (1986) views rational choice models of human behaviour as 'ideal types' rather than rounded accounts of human action. Coleman and Fararo (1992) also distinguish the *real* nature of action from the *usefulness* of their analytical model. Nonetheless, if humans do not generally engage in the kind of rational decision process the theory assumes then we might expect to find some much tighter boundaries than presently exist around the explanatory limits of rational choice theory.

In addition to making a distinction between the real nature of action and the explanatory utility of a particular model, Coleman provides another defence of the rational choice view of the individual that rests on biological determinism. Coleman argues that utility maximisation reflects the 'primary needs' of the human organism that, over time, developed from an animal desire to maintain survival to a cognitive 'superstructure' of other interests. These other interests, however, can still be traced back to these central needs (Coleman 1990: 516): they are not the responsibility of society or culture but reflect the fundamentally unchanging nature of the human organism. Opposing this view of the biologically determined self-interested individual, however, Douglas and Ney (1998: 39) accuse such rationalist formulations as 'naturalising' the theory of the market within the physiology of the individual. As Zafirovski (1999: 78) argues, there is something peculiarly reductionist about a theory which subsumes under 'utility optimising behaviour' the very different actions of making and spending income to improve one's own material comfort, for example, and giving one's income away to others and thereby becoming impoverished.

This naturalisation of the market not only problematises the notion of the *social* actor, but sociology's other traditional concern with 'society' and 'culture'. In the case of society, Alexander (1984) argues that by emphasising the properties and actions of individuals, rational choice theory empties the already existing society into which we are born of its ontological and explanatory significance. Favell (1996) points out that this can only work analytically by assuming an identity between individuals and collective 'structures' (so that when one analyses individuals one is already taking into account the influence of collective structures). However, this consensus and stability among individuals in the social world is *at the very least* absent in situations of flux and rapid social change. Emptying society of its significance also presupposes the very power of legal contract that has long been recognised as providing the basis on which economic behaviour can proceed (Durkheim 1893). As Archer (1995: 251) notes, what sociology is confronted with in this theoretical model 'is the desperate incorporation of all emergent and aggregate social properties into the individual'. When rational choice theory does turn its attention to society, in contrast, it presupposes that it can be analysed as a product of economic rationality. This extension of cost–benefit analysis to even non-market based institutions, however, has come under criticism from economists as well as sociologists for being inattentive to differences in how these institutions work (Yaeger 1997).

Similar problems are evident with regard to the rational choice account of 'culture'. Ironically, the rationalist, utilitarian view of humanity became influential in Western societies at a time when different cultures, with very different views of what it is to be human, were being discovered and studied in early forms of anthropology and sociology (Crespi 1992). The distinction between 'objective' and 'subjective' rationality, for example, was evident in the early development of anthropology: Tylor and Frazer used it to interpret 'primitive' magic (Evans-Pritchard 1965). Other cultures may have their own view of what is rational, it was often suggested, but we know they hold mistaken, irrational beliefs. Such approaches towards cross-cultural study have generally been discredited, principally because they reduce cultural diversity into a specifically Western model of 'objective rationality', but they are resurrected by rational choice theory in its evaluation of both Western and non-Western cultures.[8] Culture, like society, is an epiphenomenon, reducible to the aggregate outcomes of the actions of rational individuals (Carruthers and Espeland 1991).

We have seen in previous chapters how visions of conflict, feminist and 'racial' sociology reject the idea that society can be described as an overarching, normative order. Rational choice theory goes further than these, and replaces 'society' and 'morality' with the notion of rational, utility-maximising individuals. Any structure/agency tension more or less vanishes in favour of the generative power this approach accords to the individual. As Archer (1995: 250) suggests, rational choice theory constitutes an under-constrained, under-socialised picture of the individual that 'makes no allowance for inherited structures, their resistance to change, the influence they exert on attitudes to change, and … the delineation of agents capable of seeking change'. The residual, shifting category of the 'non-rational', and the fact that rational choice theories ultimately concede that many social outcomes are 'irrational', reflect the problematic nature of this simplification.

In conclusion, if the resurrection of *homo economicus* provides a basis on which to construct a radically different vision of sociology, then it is a vision of the discipline that no longer recognises its traditional referents and has abandoned the sociological ambition in favour of a revitalised utilitarianism. In fact, rational choice sociology often appears even more utilitarian, economistic and individualistic than contemporary neoclassical economics itself (Zafirovski 1999). From this point of view, although it has found many devotees amongst contemporary sociologists, it is hard to avoid the assessment that it is essentially anti-sociological (Harrod 1956; Keynes 1972: 276). In Durkheim's time, the opposition to such reductive, rationalist individualism was 'part and parcel of the business of establishing the discipline of sociology' (Barnes 1995: 14), and there is a strong case for arguing that this remains true of its continued development. While this form of theory may seek to resurrect the 'dead hand' of Benthamite utilitarianism, however, its inability to avoid 'normative' issues calls into question the viability and extent of its challenge to classical sociology. The explicit incorporation of normative elements into 'weak' forms of rational choice theory, and the implicitly normative value attached to the maximising individual, direct our attention to the failures of the rational choice approach in its own terms. More positively, this reliance on norms expresses an implicit convergence with the classical theories of writers such as Durkheim and Parsons, despite its claims to the contrary (Zafirovski 2000). From this point of view, rational choice sociology continues to make some sort of contribution to the pursuit of the sociological ambition, albeit in a largely implicit, flawed and contradictory manner.

Notes

1. In other words, they suggest that they are not claiming that each individual always acts 'rationally', but that if you apply the rational choice model in attempting to explain their actions, then it is able to comprehend wider patterns of social behaviour (Coleman and Fararo 1992: xi). The validity of rational choice as a social theory is therefore unaffected by whether individuals really act rationally or not, since predictions and analyses developed on this assumption still turn out to be true (Coleman 1990: 506; see also Iannaccone 1997).

2. Levine (1995: 149) has suggested that Parsons underestimated the extent to which affective factors also played a part in the philosophy of figures such as Bentham, alongside the attention to the individual's rational maximisation of self-interest, though Becker's (1986) endorsement of Bentham as a seminal proponent of rational choice continues this selective reading of Bentham's ideas. Similarly, while rational choice theory can be interpreted as a revival of Spencer's individualistic utilitarianism, this ignores the fact that 'for Spencer society's emergence and persistence are contingent on observing certain social norms and values by the individuals' (Zafirovski 2000: 556).

3. This specific understanding also attempts to circumvent anthropological considerations of the impact of culture upon 'rationality', and avoids the fundamental anthropological question of whether rationality is itself a Western concept.

4. Although Stark and Bainbridge avoid any speculation about the truth or falsity of religious beliefs, a compensator is, as Collins (1997b: 164) points out, an *imaginary* reward that is a substitute for unavailable earthly rewards. Stark and Bainbridge also have difficulty explaining why rich, successful people who attain much of what life has to offer should still seek religious compensators, and why, historically, it is the relatively affluent who have been the most ardent supporters of religion (Collins 1997b: 169)

5. In economics, utilitarian approaches emphasise the *cognitive* aspects of human action, in terms of the actor's capacity to draw upon knowledge and information, and to calculate the most rational courses of action in terms of the furtherance of self-interest (Scott 1995: 74). Homans's approach was more behavioural, eschewing assumptions about subjective states of mind. For Homans, 'rationality' was not a conscious strategy so much as a learned response (Scott 1995: 75). In contrast, the later theories of Blau (1964) and Cook (1977) offered more cognitive models of human action, as did the theories of Coleman (1973, 1990) and Boudon (1996, 1998). In all these versions of rational choice, however, the rational individual is the starting point, and the centre, of sociological analysis.

6. Coleman (1990: 274–5) rejects the idea that free riding is universal because he is conscious of those social actions which cannot be accommodated within such a notion, though he does not explain how this rejection can be accommodated to the idea that all individuals seek to maximise benefits and minimise costs. Noting the patriotic fervour that leads people to volunteer for military duty in times of war, the dangerous missions of terrorists acting on behalf of what they regard as a public good, and a range of other self-sacrificing activities by individuals involved in political and religious movements, he notes that in such cases the rewards gained by these individuals do not seem to outweigh the costs incurred. He calls this an 'excess of zeal' which, though diametrically opposed to free-riding, nevertheless has the same rational choice origins: individuals calculate that the reward of helping others to satisfy *their* interests will help offset the immense costs involved in the individual pursuing

his/her own interests. How a direct link between rational calculation and such excessive zeal can be established remains obscure, however, and Coleman excludes the possibility that armies, terrorist groups, and religious communities might provoke forms of emotional fervour that override rational calculation.

7. An alternative view is that people might vote for reasons other than simple utility maximisation, such as class, tribal, or ethnic loyalties that have more to do with an emotional identification with a group and the power of norms to shape the preferences of individuals. In Coleman's view, however, such an 'irrational' form of action might constitute a 'malfunctioning' of the social actor since it contradicts his commitment to the 'norm-free' individual actor as the elementary unit of social life.

8. As Collins (1997b: 163) notes, rational choice approaches to religion are often explicitly anti-Durkheimian and anti-Parsonian, and focus on motivated, self-interested individuals, to the detriment of any detailed concern with the dynamics of social solidarity.

11

POST/MODERN SOCIOLOGY

1. Introduction

One of the most visible symptoms of the contemporary fragmentation of sociology has been the discipline's proliferating, partial, idiosyncratic and creative engagement with postmodern developments in philosophy and literary criticism, architecture, art, linguistics and cultural theory. If sociology grew out of an intellectual context where 'the problem of order' was a key concern following the decline of medieval notions of divine order, these theoretical engagements appear to mark the exhaustion of this concern. In place of traditional analyses of normative order, and in contrast to rational choice theory's commitment to the utility-maximising individual, these analyses are concerned with the *end* of classical conceptions of society, history, space, culture, progress, truth and the individual. They include attempts to construct a new sociology freed from 'anachronistic' concerns with societies (Urry 2000), analyses of gendered identities liberated from the restrictive binary oppositions that order 'heterosexist' conceptions of social selves (Butler 1990), constructions of transformative politics based on new social movements (Nicholson and Seidman 1995), interrogations of the experience of a world whose contours and spaces are more compressed yet more fluid and unstable than ever (Harvey 1989), and attempts to reinstate morality into a sociology freed of its canonical shackles and ready to address the realities of the twenty-first century (Lemert 1995).

The task of clarifying those philosophies and theories that have informed these sociological developments is a complex one, as the notion of the 'postmodern' is one of the most flexible and imprecise concepts in the social sciences. The diverse traditions and theories it draws on frequently constitute an uneasy alliance, but Featherstone (1991) has usefully identified a 'family of terms' associated with this notion. The 'postmodern' itself can be held to signal an *epochal shift* from modern social orders to new forms of social life that have their own distinct organising principles, while 'postmodernité' refers to the *experience* of this shift. 'Postmodernisation', in contrast, refers to the social and cultural *processes* through which social life is transformed, while 'postmodernism' signifies the opposition to the modern expressed in a variety of artistic, philosophical and theoretical forms.[1] This clarification is useful, yet in practice these terms are frequently interpreted in 'confusing and interchangeable ways' and do not help us understand the arguments of particular theorists (Featherstone 1991: 11). Commentators continue to raise doubts about whether the terms associated with postmodernity are used to refer to an idea, a cultural experience, a social condition, or a combination of all three (Lyon 1999: 6).

What we can say about the more sophisticated *sociological* engagements with these disparate ideas is that their criticisms and reformulations of the discipline, and conceptions of the contemporary era, also display *ambivalence* towards certain features of postmodern theory. Daniel Bell's (1974) theory of post-industrial society, for example, has been one source of inspiration for sociology's engagement with postmodern ideas. While suggesting that classical conceptions of society were outdated, however, Bell's concern with technical efficiency, citizenship and welfare represent a development rather than a dismissal of the discipline's traditional concerns. Similarly, many contemporary sociologists seek to combine and mix postmodern ideas with a continued concern for issues such as human experience, social relationships and identities, liberty and justice, rather than remaining entirely within the parameters of 'the text' or of a deconstructive methodology. This ambivalence is prefigured by the radical critic C. Wright Mills who is responsible for the first explicit discussion of the postmodern within social theory (Smart 1996a: 398). Mills (1959: 184) used the term during his evaluation of the grand narratives of liberalism and socialism as inadequate descriptors of 'the world and ourselves', yet maintained his concern with radical social criticism.

Even when they reject out of hand classical sociological conceptions of modernity, sociological engagements with notions of postmodernity often display a renewed concern with what Maffesoli (1996) has called 'the logics of social attraction', and the moral outcomes of these 'logics' in a context marked by diversity and reflexivity. This is reflected in their concerns for such matters as 'inhumanity' (Lyotard 1991; Tester 1995), social ambivalence (Selznick 1992; Stivers 1994; Smart 1996b), and 'postmodern ethics' (Bauman 1993). These moral concerns provide another link between classical sociologies and those contemporary forms that claim to have transcended or rejected them.

It is this ambivalence towards certain features of postmodern theory, as well as to classical sociology, that explains why we use the term *post/modern* sociology in this chapter. Post/modern sociology signifies a hybrid vision of sociological analysis that engages with the idea that we now live in a postmodern world, yet which sometimes rejects this conclusion in favour of the idea that 'postmodernity' marks the extension of certain aspects of modernity at the expense of others. As such, post/modern sociology is an umbrella term referring to theories that adopt certain features of postmodern thought extensively, as well as to those that subsume them with other forms of theory.

The broad range of post/modern perspectives is evident, for example, in Jameson's (1991) and Harvey's (1989) analyses of the experience of postmodern culture and spaces, in Bauman's (1992a: 193) account of the chaos, indeterminacy and ambivalence of postmodern society, in Giddens's (1991) suggestion that the contemporary Western era is characterised by chronic reflexivity and doubt, in Lash and Urry's (1987) vision of disorganised capitalism, in Featherstone's (1991) study of contemporary consumer culture, in Crook et al.'s (1992) overview of the 'phase shift' characterising contemporary societies, and in Robertson's (1992) analysis of globalisation processes. Each of these works has drawn on postmodern themes in order to articulate a sense of the collapse of modern social and cultural orders, yet none accepts in their entirety the philosophical and literary sources of postmodern thought.

This depiction of post/modern sociology may appear to make the task of this chapter impossibly broad, yet it is narrowed somewhat by the fact that these visions of sociology often share certain assumptions. Post/modern sociologies tend to accept there has been a proliferation of centrifugal social and cultural (if not always economic) processes that make it unfeasible to talk about overarching normative orders. These processes – which are interpreted and expressed in different ways through the use of such terms as globalisation, flows and networks, reflexivity, and hyper-reality – have produced such diversity and difference that traditional concepts of 'society', 'social order' and 'identity' are judged to warrant condemnation. This is justified, it is suggested, because classical sociological concerns with overarching social and moral orders came to be associated with 'totalising' attempts to dominate nature and human beings, and with political projects that deny, and even seek to destroy, differences between peoples and nations. Any newly envisaged conception of sociology, in contrast, needs to account for the complex and fluid configurations of peoples and identities that actually characterise the current era.

This chapter proceeds as follows. Section 2 identifies the post/modern engagement with theoretical conceptions of the 'end of the social' as the unit idea of this sociology. Post/modern sociology does not always accept this idea that there exists no stable social or cultural reality that forms the referent of social analysis, yet frequently draws on its major sources in order to reformulate classical conceptions of social life. Section 3 examines the elementary forms of 'social' and moral life underpinning post/modern sociology by focusing on the work of Anthony Giddens and Zygmunt Bauman. This introduces an inevitable selectivity to this chapter, but their writings reflect the two dominant sociological responses to postmodern writings. Both are concerned with individual action, mediated through reflexivity, which is productive of discrete life-worlds that must be understood against broader social processes. Nevertheless, while Giddens argues that recent social and cultural changes represent the *intensification* of certain features of modernity and seeks to identify a basis on which a reconstructed 'social' may be built, Bauman speaks of the *end* of modernity and seeks to remove the moral individual from the degenerating effects of the modern social fabric.[2] Section 4 analyses a major tension within postmodern sociology. The self/other relationship emerges in place of conventional conceptions of 'the social' within post/modern sociology. It is the 'foundation' of morality in a world supposedly without foundations, yet is frequently bereft of broader supports. It is even lacking in the social emotions that Simmel identified as solidifiers of interactional forms. In concluding, we focus on the transcendental features of certain post/modern sociologies in order to examine whether these analyses may unintentionally be resurrecting a quasi 'religious sociology'.

2. The end of the social?

The abolition of overarching conceptions of 'the social' within postmodern thought has a number of roots and is expressed in different ways. Common to each of them, though, is a concern to divorce their analyses of those phenomena they regard as structuring or characterising human life from classical conceptions that conflate the social with society. In this respect, *post-structuralism* and *nihilism* have proved particularly influential resources. They are not the only traditions to have informed what Eagleton (1996: 21) has referred to as 'bizarrely heterogeneous' attempts to deconstruct conventional notions of the social, however, and two other trends have featured prominently in post/modern sociology. The first draws on radical political economy in viewing postmodernism as the *cultural counterpart* of late capitalism: a counterpart that has decentred people's experiences of life at the same time it has globalised economic forms and processes. The second draws on theological themes in suggesting that postmodernity involves a *re-enchantment* of the atomised and fragmented existence of individuals living through the exhaustion of modernity. These sources and features of postmodern thought have very different implications for whether human subjects are portrayed as determined by forces outside their control, or as able to glide between identities in the absence of modern constraints.

Post-structuralism has its origins in structuralism. While structuralism can be traced to Durkheim's (1912) concern to analyse forms of knowledge as reflections of underlying patterns in social and cultural life, it was developed by Lévi-Strauss into a concern with the structures of the human mind, and by Saussure into a concern with the structures inherent within language. Post-structuralism, and some of the deconstructive perspectives that emerged from this perspective, developed this approach within a much more explicit anti-humanist framework. They suggested that the ways in which humans speak about the world creates the world, yet that this speech is itself determined by discourses based on exclusions and differences. The post-structuralist and deconstructive features of the work of Lyotard, Derrida and Lacan, for example, suggest that neither society nor the subject have any meaning other than that created arbitrarily within language, and that 'reality' is characterised by indeterminacy, instability and the impossibility of agreed meaning (Rorty 1992; Bertens 1995: 6; Lyon 1999: 19).

Post-structuralism was an important influence on postmodernism, and the two perspectives now overlap. Post-structuralism not only conceptualises the 'social' as an artifice directly comparable to the religious artifice of divine order, but insists that the 'metanarratives' of reason, progress and liberation that informed much classical sociology are bereft of ultimate foundations. Lyotard's (1984: 17) definition of the postmodern as 'incredulity towards metanarratives', for example, provides us with an influential adaptation of post-structuralist themes. Lyotard argues that the 'social' has been fractured into atomised 'language games', and he does this by focusing on the decomposition of 'science' into bodies of competing opinions, and on the ways in which computer technologies make 'performativity', the efficiency and productivity of systems, more important than issues of intrinsic value (Lyon 1999: 17). Foucault's (1970, 1971, 1972) analyses of the construction and the instability of the discourses that constituted the object 'man' in the human sciences, and the repressive dimensions of those liberational discourses associated with modernity, further exposes the contingent foundations that underpin modern knowledge, moralities and conceptions of the rational, autonomous subject.

If one source of postmodern thought to have influenced sociology is post-structuralism, another draws on radical political economy in viewing post-modernism as a form of culture. The view that postmodernism is the *cultural counterpart of late capitalism* is one of the more conservative forms of postmodern thought, in that it views the ending of classical conceptions of 'the social' as caused by the economy and confined to the cultural sphere. As developed by the likes of Jameson (1991) and Harvey (1989), it has nevertheless exerted a major impact on post/modern sociology. Jameson suggests that the late, multi-national form of capitalism is associated with commodification processes that have saturated the social world. This has given rise to a postmodern culture that is experienced as internally referential and destructive of previous social spheres. As all areas of social life become subjected to the judgments of exchange value, there is an erasure of those norms and morals that once guided social relationships. This erasure of qualitative difference, which is a feature of commodification processes as anticipated by Simmel, facilitates the emergence of a culture able to express everything in terms of a proliferation of depthless signs. In this context, there is a tendency for individuals to experience social life as one-dimensional and as having been eclipsed by the pervasiveness of a playful and shallow postmodern culture. Harvey (1989) makes an analogous argument insofar as he identifies the movement from Fordist to flexible forms of production as having accentuated a compression in people's experience of time and space, and as responsible for the postmodern condition.

Jameson and Harvey show how postmodern thought can be harnessed to radical political economy, yet their analyses also suggest the continuing importance of post-structuralism. Linguistic models of social life can be justified not because they are accurate scientific representations of the world, but because contemporary societies 'offer the spectacle of a world … saturated with messages and information, whose intricate commodity network may be seen as the very proto-type of a system of signs' (Jameson 1972; Anderson 1998: 67). In contemporary societies, then, there is a close affinity between linguistics as a method and a systemised and hyper-real culture in which the experience of space and time is massively compressed and from which there seems no escape.

Post-structuralism and the view of postmodernism as culture have both influenced sociological studies of the contemporary era, yet also tend to minimise the importance and freedom of the individual subject. Two contrasting sources of postmodern thought, however, have the effect of rescuing the subject as a significant actor.

Nihilism has exerted an important influence on the context in which postmodern analyses developed. As David Lyon (1999: 7) suggests, the emergence of the idea 'postmodernity' can be contextualised within a shift in Western ideas from 'Providence', to 'Progress', to 'Nihilism'. Bauman (1992a: xvii), for example, equates the 'sinister warning' of Dostoyevsky that if there is no God then everything is permissible, with 'the no less sinister premonition of Durkheim: if the normative grip of society slackens, the moral order will collapse'. As Baudrillard (1990: 186) expresses it, Nietzsche grappled with the death of God, but we now have to deal with the death of politics, history and 'the social'. The distinction between representation and the real has collapsed, and humans now exist in a world in which all is 'simulacra'. This means that there is now no conceivable secular grounding for redemption from individual and collective discontents, since all hopes and all Utopias have proved illusory. There is now no promise, as there was for Nietzsche, of a Dionysian re-empowerment of humanity (Wernick 1992: 67). In this context, all forms of knowledge, truth and meaning simply become competing discourses. Moral impulses are exercised, if at all, through individual discretion or impulses in a context marked by pluralism, relativism and chronic uncertainty (Bauman 1991).

Nihilism seems to offer little hope for the subject but, as Nietzsche's analysis of morality illustrates, it can also be seen as freeing humans from the constraints of debilitating systems of thought in order that they may fulfil their potential. If traditional certainties and hopes have been destroyed, people are free to create their own goals, ethics and relationships in a radically new era. What Vattimo (1992) refers to as an 'accomplished nihilism', for example, highlights the possibility of a postmodern liberation and emancipation based on an embrace of contingency, and a positive response to the fluctuating experiences of familiarity and strangeness.

Having stripped the world of stable structures and meanings, postmodern thought also sometimes draws on theological themes in suggesting that a *re-enchantment* of the bleak landscapes that populate their analyses is occurring. Baudrillard's work, for example, is characterised by a strong dose of nihilism, yet insofar as he understands himself to be a 'metaphysician' or 'moralist', he aligns himself with the Jesuits of the Counter-Reformation. Despite accepting the 'death of God', these Jesuits sought to use the glittering, seductive images of the baroque to offer the promise of redemption. Similarly, Baudrillard seems to advocate a strategy of immersion in the seductive 'simulacra' of the hyper-real. He knows that behind the images there is no truth or meaning, but is nevertheless suspended between 'a playfully immoral stoicism and the hope that something redemptive may yet appear' (Wernick 1992: 69).

This expression of hope regarding the possibilities open to the human subject, in an analysis that appears to deny the validity of such expression, points to a 'submerged religious paradigm' within postmodern theorising (Turner 1990: 10). This is nowhere clearer than in its frequent insistence that we *celebrate* the differences between and within people that we are left with after the deconstruction of modern orders, narratives and subjects. Other versions of this religious dimension of postmodern thinking appear in Maffesoli's (1996) vision of the current age as one characterised by the rebirth of effervescent forms of sociality and a new 'ethic of aesthetics', and in Bauman's (1993: 33) attack on modernity's attempt to eliminate difference and mystery, and the valorisation of the moral subject. Dean's (1997: 225) account of postmodern sociality shares this concern, and provides a clear example of how postmodern thought can endorse the idea of 'self-actualising individuals moving within and between loose aggregations'.

The post-structuralist and nihilistic sources of postmodern thought, and its contrasting concerns with culture and re-enchantment, are often clearly incompatible, and have not been important for all the writers who have been influential within this theoretical movement. Furthermore, their contradictory emphasis on the *determination* of the subject and the subject *freed* from traditional constraints and able to glide between subject positions has been a target of criticism (Eagleton 1996: 28). Nevertheless, some of the most creative and influential sociological engagements with postmodern thought have focused on this concern for individual freedom within the multiple structural determinations of a new age. This provides the context in which a vision of the elementary forms of social and moral life can be found within post/modern sociology. The writings of Giddens and Bauman, in particular, engage with postmodern themes in offering us contrasting visions of what the individual is and of how people now live in a world significantly different from that envisaged within classical sociology. Giddens (1990) recognises postmodernity as a cultural response to the experience of living in a world which seems to be like riding a 'juggernaut out of control'. The term for him signifies a form of utopian thinking about a future characterised by post-scarcity and multi-layered democratic processes, while *high modernity* more accurately describes the intensification of certain features of modernity that mark the contemporary era. Bauman (1993), in contrast, interprets postmodernity as 'modernity without illusions': it coexists with, yet also challenges, central features of the modern world and provides for the possibility of a resurfacing of the moral impulses of individuals.

3. The elementary forms of social and moral life

Post/modern sociologies take from postmodern thought their concerns with the contingency, fragility and arbitrariness of human life, but tend to modify the deconstructive and nihilistic features of this thought by locating individual action and identity at the basis of their vision of social life. While they share this feature with rational choice theory, they differ from this vision of the discipline by suggesting that individual action is mediated by reflexivity and results in the pluralism of different 'life-worlds'.

Individual action
Giddens and Bauman seek to rescue a place for individual action but take seriously the postmodern idea that the autonomous, self-constituting subject of modernity has fragmented under the impact of a 'mediatised' and 'consumerised' mass society (Kellner 1992; Jameson 1983). While this 'schizoid, nomadic' fragmentation is celebrated by postmodern theorists such as Deleuze and Guattari (1997) and Kroker and Cook (1986), however, post/modern sociologists such as Giddens and Bauman prefer to take this condition as the starting point for reconstructing a more coherent vision of the individual in their accounts of social action (Kellner 1992: 144).

Giddens (1991: 35) begins from 'the premise that to be a human being is to know, virtually all of the time, in terms of some description or another, both what one is doing and why one is doing it'. Rather than associating this knowledge-ability of humans with 'rationality', however, Giddens suggests it is based on individuals acquiring in their formative years a sufficient sense of 'ontological security'. This provides individuals with a basic 'security system': a sense that the natural and social worlds are as they appear to be, and the capacity to 'bracket out' anxieties and fears that might otherwise obstruct social action.

The theoretical supports for this conception of the individual are psychological rather than sociological. While, for Lyotard and Baudrillard, the fragmentation of the self has social and cultural origins in the postmodernisation of Western societies, Giddens views it is a general psychological factor with which all individuals have to cope, but one which has *intensified* in the current era. Drawing on Laing (1965) and Winnicott (1965), Giddens (1991: 53–4) interprets fragmentation in terms of ontological insecurity. This term refers to 'existential threats' to an individual's sense of self and reality: threats that are normally 'filtered out' through an early 'inoculation' against them by parents who nurture in children a 'basic trust' in their environment. It is the successful acquisition of ontological security that enables individuals to acquire both 'practical consciousness' (tacit modes of awareness and competence sedimented in bodily capacities and habits), and to develop 'discursive consciousness' (what actors are able to articulate about the social contexts in which they live). This ontological security also enables individuals to construct a sense of self in a world that no longer bestows traditional identities on people but which requires them to construct their own biographical narratives. The chaotic and fast changing experience of the contemporary era, however, means that individuals can never entirely escape the potentially ontologically destabilising sense of biographical discontinuity, chronic uncertainty, and the awareness of risks so overwhelming that action becomes problematic.

Bauman's vision of the post/modern individual is quite different. His 'postmodern ethics' accepts that the subject may be a fragmented, mutable phenomenon. Thus, he employs the terms postmodern 'nomads', 'vagabonds' and 'tourists' in order to capture the transience and fragmentation of postmodern subjects, and to contrast these with what he characterises as the 'Protestant pilgrims' of modernity (Bauman 1993: 35). Nevertheless, Bauman also engages with Kant's emphasis on the 'mystery of morality inside me' in suggesting that there still exists a moral impulse inherent within the individual. In doing this, he follows Lévinas's (1991) argument that the relationship between self and other is characterised by an unconditional, pre-social *being for the other*. As Bauman (1993: 35) argues, it 'is the primal and primary "brute fact" of moral impulses, moral responsibility, moral intimacy that supplies the stuff from which the morality of human cohabitation is made'. This unconditional commitment to the other is *pre-social*, and the ethical rules and demands that may or may not be placed upon individuals by a society are therefore irrelevant to any assessment of the degree to which an individual's actions are 'moral' (Bauman 1993: 51).

Bauman and Giddens provide us with two contrasting post/modern visions of the individual. Bauman posits the individual's sensual, emotional body as a bulwark against the immoral, rationalising processes of totalising social orders: processes that ultimately have the power to distort and diminish the moral potentialities of human beings. He is fundamentally concerned with the *moral individual* in an analysis that is radically opposed to traditional French sociological conceptions of the subject that are unable to speak of the 'non-social or pre-social' features of human being other than in terms of them constituting the raw material for social processing (Bauman 1992a). Giddens, in contrast, examines early social processes of caring as compensating for natural fears of loss and desertion, and as providing the individual with the practical and discursive knowledge that enables them to intervene in, and make a difference to, the social world. While Bauman is concerned with the moral individual, Giddens provides us with a model of the ontologically secure individual as an instrumental *doer*.

The medium of reflexivity

Bauman's and Giddens's conceptions of the subject are very different, yet both theorists suggest that reflexivity has become a major mediator of action in the contemporary era. The major difference between them is that while Giddens analyses this reflexivity in terms of the *opportunities* it provides for individuals' personal growth, and for establishing private and public forms of dialogical democracy, Bauman associates its mediating effects with a *blunting* of the moral impulse and a distancing of people from the moral consequences of their actions.

Giddens argues that the reflexive monitoring of action has acquired a unique significance in the high modern era. While pre-modern contexts constrained reflexivity as a result of the emphasis they placed on tradition, community and religion, thought and action are continually reflected back on each other within the contemporary era. This reflexive relation between thought and action occurs at the level of both institutions and individual self-identity (Giddens 1990: 37–8).

At the *institutional* level, social organisations have been 'disembedded' from their local contexts and become 'abstract systems'. These abstract systems are organised across 'indefinite tracts of time-space', operate on the basis of 'symbolic tokens' such as money that are highly liquid carriers of value, and are driven by expert 'knowledges' such as science and medicine (Giddens 1991: 18). The abstract and 'all-encompassing' nature of these systems means that they have to be reflexively maintained and also encourage the further spread of reflexivity. This spreading of reflexivity occurs because, while individuals have to live within economic, political and legal abstract systems, they cannot escape knowing them as environments of risk. As the capacity of these systems to control the natural and social environments increases, so too do the disasters they can precipitate (Beck 1992: 22). The mass production and regulation of food, for example, has in recent years been accompanied by a series of health concerns involving BSE, salmonella and genetically modified food. Similarly, advances in genetic engineering and animal to human transplants have raised fears of cross-species infection and disease.

At the *individual* level, Giddens suggests that individuals confront the world through the medium of reflexive thought in their private as well as their public lives. His notions of the 'pure relationship' and 'confluent love' exemplify the importance he places on reflexivity within the intimate sphere. The pure relationship 'is a key environment for building the reflexive project of the self' (Giddens 1991: 186–7). Its inherently fragile, transient character is indicative of the broader 'until-further-notice' character of reflexively defined projects. These close personal ties are no longer rooted in economic or moral systems, but are 'free-floating' in the sense that they are entered into, and maintained, only for the benefits they offer to individuals (Giddens 1991: 89).[3] 'Confluent love' therefore has no independent value, but is simply a 'codifying force' for organising the competing, reflexively determined pursuit of emotional and sexual satisfaction by the individuals involved. Issues of mutual trust, the amounts of time and energy invested in the relationship, and the achievement of satisfactory levels of emotional intimacy, are all subject to endless reflexive scrutiny and negotiation (Giddens 1991: 95–7).

This thoroughgoing institutional and individual reflexivity is associated with the 'future-oriented' character of high modernity which means all beliefs, values, social practices, and forms of knowledge can be altered, revised or abandoned in the light of reflexive adaptations to changed circumstances. High modernity, in fact, is identifiable with 'chronic' reflexivity. This reflexivity has undermined Enlightenment metanarratives, as well as traditional narratives, yet represents the *intensification* of certain features of modernity rather than its supercession by a postmodern era (Giddens 1990: 39, 51; see also Beck 1992).

Bauman agrees with Giddens's vision of the contemporary era as a self-reflexive world. As he puts it 'self reflection', 'monitoring the outcome of past action', re-evaluating situations and the adequacy of means and purposes, and re-assessing one's values and strategies 'have replaced to great extent the deterministic push of tradition both on the organisational and the individual level' (Bauman 1992a: 90). Bauman, like Giddens, also associates these conditions with 'the absence of a single *authoritative* standpoint from which unambiguous and universally binding pronouncements can be made' (ibid.), and recognises that individuals reflexively reconstruct their engagements with other people on the basis of their own ongoing concern with self-identity. At this point, however, similarities between these theorists cease.

For Bauman (1989), the abstract systems that dominate daily life, and that have increased the extent to which action is mediated through reflexive reconsiderations, have also blunted people's pre-social moral impulses and removed them from the moral consequences of their actions. Bauman suggests, for example, that these systems enable experts to escape responsibility for their behaviour (Bauman and Tester 2001). At a personal level, this blunting of morality is illustrated by the 'experimental, fragmentary and episodic togetherness' that characterises the 'until-further-notice' relationships talked of by Giddens. These relationships are associated with an 'aesthetic space' in which individuals encounter each other as objects of enjoyment with no (or very few) strings attached. The moral consequences of our choices and actions appear to disappear into a game of solitaire that can be evaluated as narcissistic and inherently anti-social (Bauman 1993: 178–9). The amoral subjects that have come to populate the contemporary era are exemplified by Bauman's typification of contemporary individuals: the vagabond and the tourist are concerned with their own interests and possess little grasp of the notions of moral proximity and moral responsibility (Bauman 1993: 142).

Life-world outcomes

In evaluating the social outcomes of the reflexively mediated action characteristic of the high modern era, Giddens (1991: 214) suggests that while politics in modernity was largely concerned with *emancipation* and *life chances* it is now centred on a *lifestyle* politics of self-actualisation. Where emancipatory politics was concerned with the elimination of oppression, exploitation and inequality, lifestyle politics is focused only on the promotion of self-actualisation (Giddens 1991: 215). This means that the categories of the social, political and moral, which used in modernity to refer to overarching collective orders, have become sites for the interplay of the reflexive life projects of individuals. Contemporary politics needs to recognise this, he suggests, by eschewing the goal of implementing policies designed to reflect common needs and life-courses in favour of maximising the opportunities of individuals for planning their own lives (Giddens 1998).

The preponderance of lifestyle politics does not herald the eclipse of moral issues from a wider, public life, but it does mean that these issues are placed there as a result of individual engagements with their own identities. Even global problems about the exploitation of nature gain their public salience only in relation to the lifestyle choices of individuals (Giddens 1991: 224–5). This emphasis on lifestyle politics is associated with pluralism and relativism in terms of those moral issues that do emerge in public agendas. Nevertheless, Giddens (1991: 226) attributes this lifestyle politics with the capacity for 'remoralising' daily life. In this respect, he draws attention to surveys that claim to show how 'younger generations today are sensitised to a greater range of moral concerns than previous generations were' (Giddens 1998: 36).

The competing life-worlds that emerge from lifestyle politics can be reconciled through reflexive dialogue in which individuals come to a better understanding of difference and otherness. Those occasions on which individuals negotiate and renegotiate their needs and wants in private relationships, indeed, provide a valuable example of 'dialogical democracy' which Giddens (1991: 231; 1994: 252–3) suggests can inform abstract systems and lead ultimately to the establishment of 'universal ethical principles' and 'universal values'. This expresses great faith in the ability of individuals to reflexively negotiate their relationships with others, and holds out the promise of a world where individual life-worlds are held together within a reflexively constituted web of shared values. Thus, instead of having their lives shaped by extant norms, Giddens imparts reflexive actors with the capacity to create and recreate a social and moral fabric. His promulgation of a set of 'Third Way' values, that understands public life in terms of the nurturing and protection of individual lifestyle choices and opportunities, is a reflection of this faith in individuals: values such as 'no rights without responsibilities', 'equality', 'freedom as autonomy' and 'cosmopolitan pluralism' express the idea that a democratic, post-traditional social fabric can be reflexively constituted by, and in the interests of, individuals (Giddens 1998: 66).

Bauman, like Giddens, associates the contemporary era with a plurality of life-worlds. As he puts it, 'the main feature' of postmodernity is 'the permanent and irreducible *pluralism* of cultures' (Bauman 1992a: 102). Bauman also agrees with

Giddens that lifestyle politics has emerged as a major outcome of reflexively mediated action in the contemporary era. In contrast to Giddens, Bauman (1993: 225) is more ambivalent about this development, and has even associated it with genocide and the trampling on individuals and their consciences in the name of the 'Grand Idea of Emancipation'. The interpersonal forms that emerge from this politics of individualism are 'made-up' communities, akin to Kant's aesthetic communities, that are brought into being, and maintained, only by individuals exercising their reflexively constituted choices. Thus, 'pure relationships' and other forms of contemporary sociality such as 'neo-tribalism' are further mani-festations of the 'dissolution of the obligatory in the optional' (Bauman 1993: 238). Contrary to Giddens's focus on the dynamism of the new lifestyle politics, Bauman evaluates this as a sham, concealing the narrow interests of self-obsessed individuals in the language of global concerns. In this context, moral issues tend to be compressed into the notion of 'human rights', but what this really means is 'the right to be left alone' (Bauman 1993: 243).

Bauman's (1998b: 77) discussion of the 'new poor', for example, focuses on how 'the moral question of defending the poor against the cruelty of their fate' has been replaced with the ethical question of defending the rights of 'decent people' to be protected from the potential assaults of the poor. The resurgence of a thoroughly secularised 'work ethic' reinforces this moral neglect of the less for-tunate: 'moral empathy' for the poor, if it comes into existence at all, can only be bestowed if they pass the 'eligibility test' of a manifest will to work, even though there may be no work for them to do (Bauman 1998b: 78). For Giddens (1994: 195), on the other hand, the poor do not present a moral challenge necessitating any redistribution of wealth, but a stimulus to further *self-development* amongst the more affluent sections of society: people who have been more or less con-stantly 'out of work' 'come to have a knowledge about a life that doesn't have paid work as its centre or as its main motivating influence'. This knowledge can enrich the life experiences of the rich, who tend to work too much. In making this 'reciprocal lifestyle contribution', the poor are likely to find greater employment opportunities as the affluent work less. From this point of view, the moral problem identified by Bauman can be eliminated through reflexive lifestyle choices. For Bauman (1998b: 94), however, the chances of this happening can be compared to the survival chances of 'snowball in hell'.

If Bauman is critical of Giddens's vision of high modernity, he also sees more positive potentialities in the present postmodern milieu. The postmodern features of the current age have freed moral issues from the dictates of reason, and the modern social projects that accompanied them, and therefore have the potential to awaken the individual moral consciences anaesthetised by modernity (Bauman 1993: 247). In this respect, Bauman seeks to avoid the moral relativism implied in many accounts of the 'end of the social' by suggesting that the rejection of universal ethical norms need not mean the rejection of notions of ultimate value. The moral conscience of the individual, which Bauman believes to be an innate property of human beings, persists as the basis upon which human cohabitation is made possible. The morally ambivalent character of the current age is reducible, therefore, to the tension between this moral basis and the amoral pluralism stimulated by reflexive choices. The postmodern challenge to the grand projects of modernity still has the potentiality to make individuals aware of this basis, even though the reduction of the social to a proliferation of lifestyle choices makes the exercise of this wisdom problematic (Bauman 1993: 248–50).

In assessing Giddens's and Bauman's respective visions of the elementary forms of social life, it is fair to say that Bauman has a sociological account of the characteristic features of postmodern societies (the aesthetic space of the tourist's life-world), and a philosophical conception of the inherent characteristics of human beings (the capacity for unconditional and infinite moral responsibility). These characteristics have been subdued in the current era that stands opposed to the moral potentialities of human beings. There is no conception of this tension in Giddens's work: his conception of human beings focuses on their inherent capacities for the reflexive awareness he believes to be an essential characteristic of high modernity. Consequently, while there may be difficulties in achieving any sort of moral consensus in a world marked by the relativism of competing, reflexively constituted life-worlds, these can be worked through reflexively (Giddens 1991: 231).[4]

These post/modern visions have very different implications for sociology. For Giddens (1991), the notion of 'postmodernity' is a cultural response to the difficulties of living in a 'high modern' context. This acknowledges social and cultural changes, but sees them as being directed towards further modernisation, not postmodernisation. Consequently, sociology, itself a modern phenomenon, must reorient itself to these changes, but not embrace the relativism of postmodern theorising. Bauman (1992a) shares some of Giddens's arguments concerning the extension of certain aspects of modernity, but believes that a new 'postmodern' social condition is upon us. This condition requires that sociologists renounce the legislative role they have traditionally assumed in legitimising normative systems that anaesthetise 'natural' moral impulses, and adopt an interpretive role that seeks to enhance understanding between individuals and communities. Nevertheless, Bauman's rejection of the relativism that appears to signal the 'demise of the ethical' within certain postmodern philosophies, and his exploration of the processes through which people come to act in an amoral way towards others, show that he is not so far removed from the classical sociological ambition as he might initially appear to be.

4. The self/other tension

Bauman and Giddens provide contrasting visions of sociology that signal a break with classical conceptions of society and social action. In doing this, however, Giddens's emphasis on dialogue, and Bauman's emphasis on moral propensities towards the other, involve a massive shrinking of sociology's traditional concern with social and moral life to the self/other relationship. This self/other relationship occupies an important general place in post/modern sociology, yet also highlights a central tension in this approach to the discipline. How is it that individuals are able to transcend themselves and relate to others in the absence of normative orders? Bauman and Giddens may cite pre-social impulses or reflexive dialogue, but are these sufficient to bind together flesh and blood individuals supposedly bereft of wider collective supports?

Classical sociology has at its core a concern with the social transcendence of individuals into a wider community. Classical theorists differ widely as to what it is that facilitates this social transcendence. Durkheim identifies a collective effervescence that welds people together through the symbolic power of the sacred, for example, while Simmel talks of an impulse towards sociality and the creation of social emotions that serve to bind individuals into interactional forms. Nevertheless, they commonly recognise that the very existence of society is dependent on social phenomena that have the power to turn individual humans into socialised, morally responsible people. In the post/modern sociologies of Giddens and Bauman, however, there is no *social* transcendence, or transcendent reshaping, of the self. It is this feature of their work, and that of other post/modern writers, that raises most acutely the question of whether these visions of the discipline are sociological visions at all.

Giddens's view of self/other relations represents an individualism that is antithetical to all conceptions of transcendence, loss or unconditional joining of self with others. Genuine moral phenomena can only emerge through the negotiations of reflexive selves within 'pure relationships' and the extension of such embryonic 'dialogical' forms of democracy. Giddens's conception of intimacy is one in which individuals open themselves up to the other, rather than merge with another, and the archetypal high modern individual is one who embarks on a quest for self-growth and enrichment, and the reordering of his or her biographical narrative in line with their reflexively constituted vision of self-identity (Shilling & Mellor 1996). It is no accident that it is *therapy*, rather than religion, that Giddens identifies as the resource on which individuals draw in making their way through the complexities and contingencies of high modern life. It is this expert system, involving an individual getting to know *themselves* and maximising their *own* autonomy, that is most closely associated with the reflexive project of self central to all aspects of individuals' encounters with others.

Bauman also maintains a focus on the individual and on his or her engagement with an 'other', if for very different reasons. His view of individual moral selves, that cannot be dissolved into an all-embracing 'we', represents an inversion of the Durkheimian concept of morality as something that is social in the sense that it transcends individuals (Bauman 1993: 47). This conflation of the moral into the social inevitably temporalises and localises all standards of valid knowledge, since everything that is meaningful is socially produced (Bauman 1993: 87). Instead, Bauman follows Lévinas (1991) in arguing that the relationship between self and other is not characterised by reciprocity or any reflexive monitoring of costs and benefits, but by an unconditional *being for* the other. This unconditional commitment to the other is pre-social: Bauman's defence of the moral is, therefore, an attack on classical notions of 'the social'. Thus, when he denies sociology's concern with 'universality' it is not to endorse relativism, only to defend moral impulses from social attempts to turn them into ethical codes. Similarly, when he criticises sociology's concern with 'foundations' it is to deny that morality has a social cause. Morality starts and ends when individuals transcend themselves in the face of the other (rather than the 'person' of the other, as that would imply a social relationship) (Bauman 1993: 12–13, 73). This is not, however, a social transcendence: individuals remain individuals during and after their encounter with the other. This brute fact of individual existence is perhaps at its starkest in Bauman's (1992b) much neglected study of the encounter with death. The collective and social acts of love and procreation are all doomed to failure as projects against death. The moral individual, in contrast, displays a willingness to die, *as an individual*, for the other.

These conceptions of the self/other relationship shrink sociology's concern with 'the social' to the individual's relationship with other individuals. Furthermore Giddens's reflexive negotiations and Bauman's moral impulses are perhaps too fragile bases on which these relations can be consolidated. Giddens's subjects are able to be reflexive negotiators because the inertial drag of traditional habits, customs and obligations has supposedly been lifted from their shoulders (Giddens 1990: 102). Bauman's (1993: 33; 1998a) vision of self/other relations, in contrast, is underpinned by a notion of 're-enchantment' and a strong religious dimension. When Bauman (1993: 74) confronts his readers' incredulity towards his views of the pre-social moral propensities of individuals, he draws on the Biblical analogy of Cain's shrugging off the inquisition of God. His work is clearly marked by a very strong sense of moral responsibility and duty, but the question of where these come from, and his faith in its presence in other people despite evidence to the contrary, remain problematic.

The weak sociological basis for self/other relations is common to a range of post/modern thought. Recent theorists of sexuality and gender have drawn creatively on postmodern trends but frequently end up endorsing an individualism that is not so far removed from the writings of Giddens and Bauman as might first be apparent. The concern to deconstruct the category of 'woman', for example, has resulted in an emphasis on 'multiple genders'. The logical consequence of this, however, is to trace gender difference to the individual: a regress that removes any common gender ground for sociality other than that which might be provided by some 'pure relationship' based on negotiation. The mechanisms involved in gender identity politics, in contrast, entail a *construction* of a group based on individuals' shared social position or sexual attributes. The basis on which this group is forged, however, can be seen as arbitrary; it is dependent upon the individual possessing a pre-social, quasi-religious impulse of *being for* particular others.

Seidman has identified a related individualism at the heart of dominant forms of queer theory. He talks of the contemporary era as one in which a solidarity 'built around the assumption of a common identity and agenda' has 'given way to social division; multiple voices often speaking past one another' (Seidman 1995: 117). Queer theory has been a major contributor to this development in its treatment of homosexuality and heterosexuality as cultural figures or categories of knowledge (Sedgwick 1985). Queer theory is characterised by an eagerness to deconstruct the binary oppositions on which sexual identities are based. It frequently struggles, however, to impart to sexual identities any positive content and neglects those institutional conditions that could help social groups actually deconstruct the dominant 'heterosexual matrix' and establish alternative forms of sociality. As Seidman (1995: 135) argues, despite its critique of methodological individualism, queer theory is often left celebrating individual difference and diversity without providing any ethical guidelines that could inform alternative relationships and guard against the abuse of power within these relationships. The individual is left alone – with all their uniqueness and able to celebrate a possible multiplication of pleasure zones – yet without any reliable grounds on which to enter with others into dyads, groups or wider communities.

5. Conclusion

The underlying individualism of certain forms of post/modern sociology appear to mark the end of the classical sociological concern with 'the problem of order', and a major shrinkage in the scope of traditional conceptions of social and moral life, at least with regard to those found in the French tradition. Giddens and Bauman continue to offer particular conceptions of these forms, but it is possible to raise the question of whether these remain *sociological* visions.

In Giddens's case, the actions of ontologically secure individuals produce, through the medium of reflexivity, a plurality of life-worlds as a social outcome. This model of social life is not dissimilar to that of the rational choice theorists in several senses. First, sociological analysis focuses initially on individuals, and the conceptualisations of the media through which actions are mediated are inextricably related to the initial formulation of the inherent characteristics of those individuals ('reflexivity' or 'rationality'). Second, the social outcomes of each basically follow an 'aggregation' model. The reflexive actions of individuals remain the basic unit of analysis for Giddens, and their actions 'add up' to produce particular social outcomes. 'Pure relationships', for example, come into being and exist only in so far as the reflexive choices and actions of the individuals concerned add up in a way that makes the relationship viable. Thus, if rational choice theory is ultimately non-sociological in the sense that it pays no attention to inherently social dynamics that reshape individual lives, a similar criticism can be levelled at Giddens.

Bauman endorses postmodern philosophising about the 'end of the social', and tends to eschew the term 'social life' for that of human cohabitation (Bauman 1993: 248). This is because of his concern about those modern conceptualisations of the social he believes to have repressed innate moral capacities. Nevertheless, his reflections on the dangers of people being strangers to each other, of resisting real intimacy, imply a normative vision of what is elementary to human cohabitation (Bauman 1993: 149). Modernity's repression of moral proximity is, for him, inextricably related to its promotion of a social order where people live in the constant company of strangers: people with whom they have no real connection (Bauman 1993: 159). His critique of the dismantling of the Welfare State, which institutionalised notions of shared responsibility and a commonality of fate, also reflects his sense of what human cohabitation should be, in contrast to what it is at the present (Bauman 1993: 243; 1998b: 93). While modern social orders distance people from the moral consequences of their actions, Bauman remains determinedly concerned with how a morally responsible and individually driven form of human co-habitation can come about. This is the promise of the postmodern condition: 'it restores to agents the fullness of moral choice and responsibility while simultaneously depriving them of the comfort of the universal guidance that modern self-confidence once promised' (Bauman 1992c: xxii).

This vision of desirable human cohabitation is not, however, an unambiguously sociological one. While Bauman (1995: 284) may occasionally imply that a revitalised social life may reinvigorate moral responsibilities, this contradicts his general writings on the social and on communitarianism (Bauman 1996: 89). Instead, Bauman ultimately adopts a philosophical/theological commitment to the idea that human being is a being for the other. If sociology originally had the problem of filling the 'God-shaped' hole left by the decline of notions of divine order, Bauman's modification of the scope of the classical sociological ambition reintroduces, via Lévinas, questions concerning God's relationship to social life. It has to be said that the subject of 'God' remains problematic in his work, and is effectively reduced to obeying one's conscience (Lévinas 1981, 1991). The work of Lyotard and Derrida also struggles with this subject in a somewhat ambiguous fashion (Foshay 1992; Lyon 1999: 106). The fact that this subject is introduced at all is significant, however, and raises questions about the limits of postmodern theorising. Far from having abandoned all foundations, this religious dimension to postmodern theory has been interpreted as suggesting that at the end of all the deconstruction of language, meaning and knowledge lies not nihilism but God: the ultimate foundation and metanarrative (Rose 1992: 46).

In conclusion, post/modern sociologies suggest that the wheel of social reflection has turned full circle. Having rejected the utilitarian focus on the rationally maximising individual actor, the individual once more becomes the focus of analysis in Giddens's vision of a fluid and reflexive world in which anything is possible. Alternatively, while Nietzsche may have grappled with the death of God, postmodern engagements with the death of politics, history and modern ideas of 'the social', resurrect the idea of God in their reflections upon human life and destiny.[5] It would be an exaggeration, however, to say that post/modern sociologies amount to a simple rejection of the sociological ambition. In Bauman's work, in particular, a creative engagement with philosophical notions of 'the end of the social' stimulates a thoughtful exploration of the nature of moral impulses and actions, and a critical assessment of the tension-filled relationship between moral concerns and modern social orders. This not only expresses a continuity with Weber's vision of modernity, but manifests a certain convergence, in broad terms, with classical concerns about the relationship between social life and moral life. Post/modern sociologies, then, return us to classical sociological problems, even though they sometimes offer resolutions to them that are only ambiguously 'sociological'. Viewed in this light, their promise of a radical reconstruction of the discipline is a highly problematic one, reflecting contradictory attitudes to classical sociological thought. More positively, such developments suggest that, despite appearances to the contrary, the sociological ambition has not yet had its day.

Notes

1. According to Featherstone (1991: 30), although the term 'postmodernism' was first used by Federico de Onis in 1934 to describe a reaction against modernism, and the term 'postmodernity' was first coined to designate a new cycle in Western civilisation by Toynbee in 1947, these may have first come to the attention of sociologists in the 1980s with the debate between Habermas and Foucault. This 'debate', largely conducted by third parties, centred on Habermas's vision of modernity as an 'incomplete project' aimed at liberation, and his criticisms of Foucault and Derrida for what he saw as their relativistic accounts of social and cultural realities. Habermas equated the linguistically oriented character of this post-structuralism with an implicit social and political 'conservatism' in the sense that it viewed the modern as just another set of discourses to be deconstructed (Featherstone 1991: 31).

2. We concentrate on Giddens and Bauman not only because they have had a particularly significant influence upon contemporary sociology, but because they aim to move beyond the classical sociological tradition in their analyses of 'high' or 'post'-modernity. Unlike Bauman, Giddens is not generally classified as a theorist of postmodernity, and formulated his theory of 'high modernity' as an alternative to the notion that we no longer live in a world whose contours are essentially modern. The significant influence of postmodern ideas on his notion of social life, however, provides a good illustration of the sociological ambivalence towards this form of thought, and a justification for our use of the term 'post/modern' rather than 'postmodern' sociology.

3. This perceived lack of anchorage in broader social conditions no doubt explains why so many of the theoretical supports for Gidden's arguments come from therapists rather than sociologists.

4. Aside from the issue of how satisfactory Giddens's account of 'traditional' societies is, it can also be noted that he is loath to acknowledge any evidence of the limits of reflexivity. His discussion of the apparent resurgence of religion in advanced modernity as evidence of 'tribulations of the self' arising from the extension of reflexivity, and therefore the reflexive reconstruction of religious traditions to enhance the life-projects of individuals, show his determination not to acknowledge any end to the process of reflexive modernisation, and contrasts with Bauman's (1993) and Maffesoli's (1996) accounts of the 're-enchantment' of Western societies.

5. Aside from Lévinas, the work of Jacques Derrida, Luce Irigaray, Julia Kristeva, and Hélène Cixous have all marked themselves off from the more nihilistic tendencies of postmodern thought through the engagement with what can be called the broadly theological potentialities of the decline of modernity (Ward 1998; see Wyschogrod 1990).

12

CONCLUSION

This book has examined the emergence, development and contemporary state of sociology as a subject that is centrally concerned with studying the relationship between social life and moral life. We have emphasised the convergences of sociological forms in this respect, yet classical and post-classical explorations of this relationship clearly possess a different character. In sociology as a whole, of course, it is possible to minimise these differences by focusing on contemporary writings that have been built on classical traditions, such as symbolic interactionism and neo-functionalism. Nonetheless, this would seriously underestimate the challenges to, and reconstructions of, the discipline that have been posed by feminist, rational choice, post/modern and other theories that possess a more ambivalent relationship to the sociological heritage. Post-classical theories may converge with their classical antecedents in their concern with the relationship between social and moral life, but their conceptions of these phenomena represent a narrowing of the scope of this ambition. This narrowing is not wholly negative, however, as it has involved the recovery of peoples and experiences marginalised within, and sometimes omitted from, classical sociology. The promise of dialogue, therefore, is that sociology may return to a more encompassing, genuinely inclusive, pursuit of the sociological ambition.

For classical theorists, the sociological ambition was to develop theoretical and methodological models that could illuminate the social and moral dimensions of the human condition. By focusing on the *social* contexts that constrain, shape, or constitute the parameters within which human experience and destiny is shaped, sociology aimed to surpass theology, philosophy, and other systems of thought in its elucidation of what human life has been, what it is now, and what it might be in the future. This is particularly evident in the work of Comte, a figure with as good a claim as anyone to be the founder of the discipline. For him, sociology was not only to be at the pinnacle of the sciences, but was to replace Christianity as a new 'Religion of Humanity', to offer an account of the entire history and future of human development, and to increase the moral content of social orders. In Durkheim's work too, the ultimately social category of the 'sacred' comes to have a fundamental, permanent significance for the shaping of human life and moral sensibilities. From the German tradition, both Simmel and Weber developed accounts of the processes through which humanity's moral capacities can be understood in terms of their complex, often conflictual, relationship to patterns of social life. For Parsons, who sought to combine elements of both French and German traditions, as well as other strands of sociological thought, even advanced forms of capitalism could be understood in terms of the circulation of values that underpin the segmented character of the social system. Classical sociology's ambition, and its deep concern regarding the human condition, was manifest in these bold, visionary models of the elementary forms of social and moral life.

Post-classical sociology's relationship to this ambition has been ambiguous. From one point of view, it has sought to *expand* classical notions of social and moral life by focusing on the general sociological significance of such issues as 'conflict' or 'gender', and on how these have been marginalised within the classics. On the other hand, these attempts have either fallen back on classical models as the result of tensions within their own analyses, so that 'conflict' theorists turn out to be theorists of 'consensus' after all, or they have ended up shrinking the scope of the social and moral to the extent that general human concerns and problems become lost in atomised life-worlds or new patterns of exclusion and marginalisation. Along the way, many of those categories introduced to illuminate the weakness or failures of classical sociology, such as 'gender', 'race' or 'postmodernity', become so contested, or resistant to theoretical clarification, that even many of their own advocates end up being uncertain about their general ontological status or sociological value. Rational choice theory, for all its apparent confidence, is not entirely free of such uncertainty either: its bold claims concerning the analytical value of its theoretical models are not always matched by a confidence that human beings really are, and behave, as these models imply. Taken together, it can be said that such post-classical forms of sociology frequently lack the breadth of the ambition, and the theoretical coherence, of the classics in terms of the development of a morally concerned, human-centred sociology.

This criticism is not made with the intention of denigrating the sociological value of these forms in other respects. We have made it clear that many of them make a significant contribution to the development of the sociological project. With regard to gender, for example, it is undeniable that the classical theorists were men of their time and that the marginal status of women in their sociologies can be understood to reflect, and even reinforce, broader patterns of marginalisation. While all of them were more interested in, and even sympathetic to, what are now termed 'feminist' concerns than they are often given credit for, their lack of a systematic incorporation of gender issues into general sociological models of social and moral life is a significant weakness. Similarly, one of the most powerful contributions 'racial' sociology has made to the discipline is to reveal the constructed nature of race as an oppressive artefact that has been central to the reproduction of iniquitous social orders. This was often overlooked by the tendency of classical sociology to reject 'race' as an important theoretical tool. The challenge of these theories is that they can offer an important opportunity to expand, rather than contract, the scope of the sociological imagination. If that opportunity has not always been taken, however, it may be due, in part, to the widespread amnesia concerning sociology's classical heritage. In pursuing our exploration of post-classical sociologies, and encountering references to the 'misogynist', 'colour-blind' classical theorists as well as to a broader series of complaints about them based on other uncritically received ideas, it was hard not to wonder if many of these writers had ever read the classics. Rational choice theory's attempts to resuscitate the corpse of utilitarianism, buried by Durkheim at the end of the nineteenth century, and the simplistic association of classical sociology with limited features of 'industrial society' made by certain types of post/modern sociology, seem to us further evidence of this amnesia.

In particular, it can be said that the fashionable desire to reject the classical notion of 'society' ignores the considerable flexibility, and imaginative power, of its classical use, ranging from Simmel's dyad to the concerns of Comte and Durkheim with the society of humanity. A creative, open-minded reassessment of the classics and how they relate to contemporary sociological concerns can revitalise the sociological 'imaginary' in this respect. Maffesoli (1996), for example, who could hardly be called a conservative figure, roots his conceptualisation of 'postmodern tribalism' in Durkheim's analyses of sociality, religion, and moral community. This study is of interest as a creative use of a classical theorist in relation to a phenomenon, 'postmodernity', that is often understood to render classical sociology redundant. It is also significant, however, as a pointer towards the reconstruction of a greater coherence within the discipline. If the spiralling fragmentation of sociology in recent years is really to be reversed, it will take such a willingness to look closely at the discipline's classical contents before arguing for their abandonment, and a readiness to be open to the idea that there may be patterns of convergence concerning classical and contemporary concerns.

Our focus in this book on those conceptualisations of elementary forms of social and moral life that can be drawn out of very diverse traditions illuminates a major instance of sociological convergence. Despite their apparent ambivalence, and even hostility, towards the generality of the classical sociological ambition, conflict, feminist, 'racial', rational, and post/modern sociologies can all be interpreted as offering their own implicit conceptualisations of the elementary forms of social and moral life. It is notable that even those post/modern sociologies focused on the so-called 'end of the social', and indirectly or directly the end of sociology, tend to return to some of the basic problems that confronted the classical theorists. Bauman's work, for example, is marked by a deep thoughtfulness about the relationship between social life and moral life, even though, as we have argued, his route through some of the problems associated with this relationship reflects his rejection of certain aspects of the classical tradition. Indeed, for all the talk of abandoning 'meta-narratives', embracing heterogeneity and fragmentation, and slinging the 'dead white males' of classical theory into the trashcan of the imperialist, Euro-centric past, the post-classical sociologies examined in this book have, at root, some very similar goals to the classics. If the goal of understanding the relationship between social life and moral life can be described as *the* sociological ambition, then contemporary sociology can be only enriched through addressing it *directly*, through a creative engagement with the classics, and recovering some of the boldness and coherence that characterised sociology in its earlier incarnations. In this respect, a number of opportunities for dialogue, and challenges that need to be addressed, can be noted.

With regard to the French classical tradition, represented here by Comte and Durkheim, there are certain areas of analysis where dialogue could be particularly important. The 'conflict', 'feminist' and 'racial' sociologies discussed in Part II of this book reject what they see as the classical inattention to social divisions, exclusions and patterns of marginalisation, but share with them a concern for the *group basis* of social and moral life. While Durkheim suggested that diverse groups are united by their common 'homo duplex' nature, and by the processes through which individuals are forged into collectivities, these post-classical forms tend to narrow their focus to particular social groupings. This reflects a sense that Durkheim's 'humanity' is really 'the middle class' or 'men' or 'white people', so his sociological analysis is not as general as it claims to be. Rather than seeking to develop more *generally* inclusive models of analysis, however, the focus on 'marginalised' social groupings tends to encourage the development of new exclusionary models. Feminists, for example, concentrate on women rather than humanity in general, but not only have to face questions about the degree to which the notion of 'women' is a social construct or a reflection of inherent characteristics marking them out from 'men' as a social group, but also have to deal with the question of whether the tendency to associate women with moral community can be expanded to include men. In some cases, as we have seen, this results in a sectarianism that narrows the scope of the social and the moral, and therefore makes no significant contribution to the sociological study of exclusion in general. Reading classical and post-classical theories together, it is clear that the former certainly needs to take more account of issues such as gender, but the latter needs more frequently than at present to broaden its horizons beyond particular groups. It is notable that when this happens, as in some of the developments we discussed in the chapter on conflict sociology, the classical theories can prove valuable contemporary resources.

Opportunities for dialogue can also be noted with regard to the German tradition of sociology, represented here by Simmel and Weber. In highlighting the weaknesses of this particular focus on the (interacting) individual, post-classical sociology has often suggested that the likes of Weber unjustifiably universalise male forms of social action that prize rationality over affectivity, promoting a masculine vision of the heroic, independent personality over the multiple interdependencies that necessarily characterise human existence. Contemporary theories have clearly not, however, jettisoned a sociological focus on the individual. In terms of those we examined in Part II of this book, this focus is most prominent in rational choice theory and in post/modern sociology. What these theories often lack, however, in comparison with the classical theorists, is a sense of the tensions between individual capacities, the broad existential and embodied parameters of human life, and the social contexts through which life is shaped and experienced. Rational choice theory, as we have argued, is at times so inattentive to social contexts it has little claim to the title 'sociology'. Post/modern sociology also often eschews recognition of even those forms or social emotions that Simmel associated with the stabilisation of the dyad. The work of Giddens, for all its talk of the constraints of 'globalised reflexivity', is ultimately centred on a therapeutic vision of creative individuals reflexively constituting their own life-worlds, with little sense of the general frustrations, limitations and struggles of human social experience. This, after all, is a form of sociological theory where children are seen as a source of 'inertial drag' on the reflexive life projects of their parents! Without succumbing to the deep pessimism of the German classical tradition, and with the acknowledgement that the world may indeed be more complex than in the time of Weber and Simmel, such analyses of contemporary societies would surely benefit from an engagement with the human breadth of their analyses, and their insights into the difficulties of an authentic social and moral existence.

Parsons, of course, sought to unite the work of Durkheim, Weber and others by suggesting that they converged in their pursuit of the sociological ambition. They did this in the close association they made between voluntaristic action and normative order. For all the problems with Parsons's interpretation of his socio-logical antecedents, his attempt to explain how individual actions can result in moral social orders also provides an important resource for dialogue. This is particularly the case for those post-classical theories that have still to explain the mechanisms that can enable morally-informed relationships to be extended beyond particular social groups.

There are, of course, a number of recent developments within contemporary sociology that engage in the type of dialogue with classical sociology we are advocating in this book, though they have tended to focus on particular theorists. The rise of neo-functionalism in the 1980s by Alexander (1998) and others, for example, provides a totalising approach to the study of social and cultural systems based on a development of Parsons's work. Similarly, Robertson (1992) developed an approach towards globalisation that provides us with a neo-Parsonian focus on how the cultural understanding of economic developments can serve to steer them in a particular direction. These issues, Robertson suggests, were foreshadowed by classical sociological concerns with the universal, 'global', dimensions of human experience, and are themselves informed by the attempts of individuals and societies to render life, death, and other human absolutes morally meaningful. A series of other classically grounded syntheses and developments appeared during the 1980s and 1990s that sought to rescue and reinterpret the foundations of sociology within analyses designed to address the realities of the contemporary era (Giddens 1984; Bourdieu 1984; Bourdieu and Waquant 1992; Archer 1988, 1995; Collins 1993; Mouzelis 1995). Characteristic of such analy-ses was an attempt to reconcile or realign within a single framework the opposi-tions and dualisms – such as action and structure, subject and object – that had traditionally characterised different forms of sociology.

These developments appear to reject the fragmentation that has characterised much post-classical sociology, yet have not yet managed to reverse the divisions that continue to characterise the discipline. This is partly because the resurrec-tion of sociologies such as neo-functionalism has been seen as yet one more option for the discipline, among a plurality of others. It must also be noted that while these developments have sought to refocus sociology on general concep-tualisations of social life and social systems, they are not all centrally concerned with the moral dimensions that have traditionally characterised the discipline. A prime example of this can be found within the work of Norbert Elias, a figure who has presented sociology with an agenda that is radically different from its traditional forms.

To interpret such developments as providing us with a return to the classical agenda would, then, provide a misleading picture of the overall state of sociology. As we emphasised earlier, it is only by considering the likes of feminist, 'racial', rational choice, and post/modern theories that we appreciate how strongly the discipline has been challenged and substantively reconstructed in recent decades. These are the sociological forms that are, perhaps, doing most to shape the future development of the discipline at present, though with varying degrees of success and varying degrees of value.

If we are to look towards a more creative, coherent and ambitious future for sociology then Comte, Durkheim, Simmel, Weber and Parsons make thoughtful, helpful guides, though these figures have their limitations too, and sociology should build on some of the developments of the post-classical tradition to supplement the critical engagement with the insights of these classical authors. In this respect, and in the light of our discussions in this book, we can reject two broad approaches to sociology, both of which are indicative of limited horizons, and endorse a third, based on the need for contemporary sociologists to engage in a creative dialogue that brings classical resources to bear on contemporary problems.

First of all, sociology should not be reduced to a conduit for the complaints of a series of sectarian groupings. Particular forms of sociological theory may have long possessed connections with social movements but, as writers such as Seidman (1994) argue, there is an obvious danger for any analysis to be constrained and confined by the historically and culturally specific parameters of such groups. We might be 'men', 'women', 'black' or 'white', but we are all human beings subject to certain embodied constraints and potentialities, to certain existential dilemmas, and to the challenges of social and moral life. These are all affected, to varying degrees, by issues such as gender, but the classical sociologies discussed in this book demonstrate that they are not reducible to such issues. Indeed, a key part of the sociological ambition has always included examining how collectivities translate issues of ultimate concern and common destiny, such as death and the meaning of life, into social norms and socially patterned ethical dilemmas facing *all individuals*.

The fact that post-classical sociology for so long eschewed this general interest can be seen as symbolising a narrowing of the scope of the sociological ambition. Evidence for this can be found in post-classical sociology's relative neglect of religion. It is notable that in Part I of this book, religion occupies a central place in the work of each classical theorist. None of these theorists was 'religious' in any conventional sense, but all of them saw in religious phenomena a socially significant attempt to grapple with issues of meaning, identity and moral concern. In the French tradition, religion's social significance is fundamental and permanent, regardless of the vitality of particular historical religions. In the German tradition, the future for religion is bleak, but this is representative of a broader limitation of human capacities and potentialities in modern societies. In each case, the social and moral dimensions of human experience are intimately tied to religion. For post-classical sociology, on the other hand, religion tends to be of only marginal significance, symbolising the relative neglect of issues of common concern and destiny in favour of a narrower focus on factors that distinguish humans from each other. On the other hand, the recent return of theological themes in certain forms of contemporary theory can be interpreted as evidence of a return to the consideration of some of the broader parameters of human experience. Bauman's work during the 1990s, for example, has an implicitly theological dimension, drawing heavily on the philosophy of Lévinas where 'God' is a significant absence/presence. This neo-theological route through problems relating to social and moral life is indicative of a broader post/modern tendency, also evident in the work of writers such as Irigaray and Derrida. What is notable about this tendency, however, is that in returning to the notion of 'God' it tends to abandon the specifically sociological character of the classical engagements with religion, where religious phenomena are analysed in relation to social processes. The classical analysis of religion, in contrast, while open to a creative dialogue with theology, is nonetheless clear about its own disciplinary concerns and foci.

Despite our firm endorsement of the contemporary importance and value of the classics, however, a second option for sociology that we reject is the simple return to what has been identified and endorsed as the 'conservative' agenda of the discipline. The engagement with the classics should be critical. How could it not be, since they are so diverse, and so often critical of each other? Furthermore, it would be ludicrous to argue that the classical theorists have provided definitive models for sociology that cannot be improved upon over time, and cannot benefit from the critical interpretations of analysts attentive to issues that were ignored, unimportant, or unheard of when the classical texts were written. Our argument is that when sociologists ask themselves the question 'What is sociology?' they might find themselves lost in a labyrinth of competing discourses, ideologies, and theories. A critical engagement with the classical theorists who did so much to shape the discipline's development, particularly with respect to their attempt to grapple with social and moral issues, can help make sense of what sociology has been, and continues to be. A creative and illuminating link between past and present can be established, and the future progress of the discipline made more secure.

In advocating the value of a dialogue between classical and post-classical sociology, then, we endorse Levine's (1995: 326) desire to see creative inquiry replace 'wasteful polemics', and for coherence to overcome fragmentation as a way of refuelling the sociological ambition. It is our argument that a dialogue centred on a common concern with the elementary forms of social and moral life forms the basis for this creativity and coherence. This dialogue cannot take place, however, if those contemporary sociologists who continue to exhibit a lack of interest in the classical theorists are not persuaded to look beyond their immediate concerns towards the broader sociological horizons that characterised the earlier development of the discipline. Sociology needs to recover a sense of the ambition evident in the classics, and to reassess how this ambition could enhance and develop contemporary theories and methods that embrace the recognition that we exist as one human species with common needs in a single world. In the light of our discussions in this book, the current rejection of the 'grand narratives' that characterised earlier sociologies looks premature: a comprehension of the complexity of social realities does not legitimise the turning of fragmentation and incoherence into sociological virtues. It is also clear that some of the most vociferous advocates of abandoning grand narratives need to look more closely at their own theories: it is in post/modern theory, for example, that 'God' (surely *the* grand narrative) reappears amidst all the fragmentation and diversity.

In conclusion, the diverse sociological visions examined in this study may appear to exemplify the fragmentation of the sociological project but they also manifest a convergence around analysing the interaction between social life and moral life. This convergence is often more implicit than explicit, and sometimes firmly denied, but it is there all the same. Many forms of post-classical sociology have not only failed to address this interaction as directly and systematically as the classical theorists, however, but have often effectively reduced the scope of social and moral life even though this may have been contrary to their original intentions. In consequence, while many of these sociologies offer some important correctives to the classical traditions, they often operate within more restricted horizons than their forebears. By re-engaging with the classics through an acknowledgement of their continuities with key aspects of these earlier sociological visions, and by addressing the omissions of these works, however, it is possible to reconstruct a more ambitious and inclusive sociological project. We hope that this book has made a small contribution to the development of this re-engagement, and to the revitalisation of the sociological ambition.

BIBLIOGRAPHY

Abbinnett, R. 1998. *Truth and Social Science*. London: Sage.

Abell, P. 1991. 'Introduction' to P. Abell (ed.), *Rational Choice Theory*. Aldershot: Elgar.

Abell, P. 1992. 'Is rational choice theory a rational choice of theory?', in J. Coleman and T. Fararo (eds), *Rational Choice Theory*. London: Sage.

Abell, P. 1996. 'Sociological theory and rational choice theory', in B.S. Turner (ed.), *The Blackwell Companion to Social Theory*. Oxford: Blackwell.

Abercrombie, N., Hill, N. and Turner, B.S. 1980. *The Dominant Ideology Thesis*. London: Allen and Unwin.

Abrams, P. 1972. 'The sense of the past and the origins of sociology', *Past and Present*, 55: 18–32.

Adorno, T. et al. 1950. *The Authoritarian Personality*. New York: Harper.

Adorno, T. 1966. *Negative Dialektik*. Frankfurt: Suhrkamp.

Adorno, T. 1975. 'Culture industry reconsidered', *New German Critique*, Vol. 6.

Adriaansens, H.P.M. 1980. *Talcott Parsons and the Conceptual Dilemma*. London: Routledge and Kegan Paul.

Albrow, M. 1970. *Bureaucracy*. London: Pall Mall Press.

Alcoff, L. 1988. 'Cultural feminism vs. Poststructuralism: The identity crisis in feminist theory', *Signs*, 13(3): 405–36.

Alexander, J.C. 1983. *Theoretical Logic in Sociology*, Vol. 3: *The Classical Attempt at Theoretical Synthesis: Max Weber*. Berkeley: University of California Press.

Alexander, J.C. 1984. *Theoretical Logic in Sociology*, Vol. 4: *The Modern Reconstruction of Classical Thought: Talcott Parsons*. London: Routledge.

Alexander, J.C. 1988. *Durkheimian Sociology: Cultural Studies*. Cambridge: Cambridge University Press.

Alexander, J.C. 1998. *Neofunctionalism and After*. Oxford: Blackwell.

Alexander, J.C. and Colomy, P. 1998. 'Neofunctionalism today: Reconstructing a theoretical tradition', in Alexander, J.C. *Neofunctionalism and After*. Oxford: Blackwell.

Allen, T.W. 1994. *The Invention of the White Race*, Vol. 1: *Racial Oppression and Social Control*. London: Verso.

Amos, V. and Parmar, P. 1984. 'Challenging imperial feminism', *Feminist Review*, 17: 3–20.

Anderson, B. 1991. revised edition. *Imagined Communities*. London: Verso.

Anderson, M and Collins, P. (eds) 1995. *Race, Class and Gender: An Anthology*. Belmont, CA: Wadsworth.

Anderson, P. 1998. *The Origins of Postmodernity*. London: Verso.

Andreski, S. 1974. 'Introduction', in S. Andreski (ed.), *The Essential Comte*. London: Croom Helm.

Anthias, F. and Yuval-Davis, N. 1992. *Racialized Boundaries*. London: Routledge.

Archer, M. 1988. *Culture and Agency: The Place of Culture in Social Theory*. Cambridge: Cambridge University Press.

Archer, M. 1995. *Realist Social Theory. The Morphogenetic Approach*. Cambridge: Cambridge University Press.

Ardener, E. 1989. *The Voice of Prophecy and Other Essays*. Oxford: Blackwell.

Aron, R. 1965. *Main Currents in Sociological Thought*, Vol. I. London: Weidenfeld and Nicolson.

Aron, R. 1967. *Main Currents in Sociological Thought*, Vol. II. London: Penguin.

Arthur, C. 1970. 'Editor's introduction', in K. Marx and F. Engels, *The German Ideology*. London: Lawrence and Wishart.

Babcock, L. and Loewenstein, G. 1997. 'Explaining bargaining impasses: The role of self-serving biases', *Journal of Economic Perspectives*, 11(1): 109–26.

Badinter, E. 1980 [1987] 'Maternal indifference', in T. Moi (ed.), *French Feminist Thought. A Reader*. Oxford: Basil Blackwell.

Balsamo, A. 1996. *Technologies of the Gendered Body: Reading Cyborg Women*. London: Duke University Press.

Banks, M. 1995. *Ethnicity: Anthropological Constructions*. London: Routledge.

Banton, M. 1977. *The Idea of Race*. London: Tavistock.

Banton, M. 1998. *Racial Theories*. Cambridge: Cambridge University Press.

Baran, P. and Sweezy, P. 1966. *Monopoly Capital: An Essay on the American Economic and Social Order*. Harmondsworth: Penguin.

Barnes, B. 1995. *The Elements of Social Theory*. London: UCL Press.

Barth, F. (ed.) 1969. *Ethnic Groups and Boundaries: the Social Organisation of Cultural Difference*. London: Allen and Unwin.

Barrett, M. 1992. 'Words and things: materialism and method in contemporary feminist analysis', in M. Barrett and A. Phillips (eds), *Destablizing Theory. Contemporary Feminist Debates*. Cambridge: Polity.

Bastide, R. 1968. 'Colour, racism and Christianity', in J. Franklin (ed.), *Colour and Race*. Boston: Houghton Mifflin.

Bataille, G. 1938 [1988]. 'The Sorcerer's Apprentice', in Hollier, D. *The College of Sociology, 1937–39*. Minnesota: University of Minnesota Press.

Bataille, G. 1973 [1992]. *Theory of Religion*. New York: Zone.

Baudrillard, J. 1990. *Cool Memories*. London: Verso.

Baudrillard, J. 1993. *Symbolic Exchange and Death*. London: Sage.

Bauman, Z. 1989. *Modernity and the Holocaust*. Cambridge: Polity.

Bauman, Z. 1991. *Intimations of Postmodernity*. London: Routledge.

Bauman, Z. 1992a. *Legislators and Interpreters*. Cambridge: Polity.

Bauman, Z. 1992b. *Mortality, Immortality and Other Life Strategies*. Cambridge: Polity.

Bauman, Z. 1993. *Postmodern Ethics*. London: Routledge.

Bauman, Z. 1995. *Life in Fragments*. Cambridge: Polity.

Bauman, Z. 1998a. 'Postmodern religion?', in P. Heelas (ed.), *Religion, Modernity and Postmodernity*. London: Routledge.

Bauman, Z. 1998b. *Work, Consumerism and the New Poor*. Buckingham: Open University Press.

Bauman, Z. and Tester, K. 2001. *Conversations with Zygmunt Bauman*. Cambridge: Polity.

Beattie, T. 1997. 'Carnal love and spiritual imagination', in J. Davies and G. Loughlin (eds), *Sex These Days*. Sheffield: Sheffield Academic Press.

Beauvoir, S. de 1949 [1993]. *The Second Sex*. London: Everyman.

Beck, U. 1992. *Risk Society. Towards a New Modernity*. London: Sage.

Becker, G. 1986. 'The economic approach to human behaviour', in J. Elster (ed.), *Rational Choice*. Oxford: Blackwell.

Bell, D. 1962. *The End of Ideology: The Exhaustion of Political Ideas in the Fifties*. New York: Free Press.

Bell, D. 1974. *The Coming of Post-Industrial Society*. New York: Basic Books.

Bell, D. 1979. *The Cultural Contradictions of Capitalism*. London: Heinemann.

Bell, V. 1999. 'Historical memory, global movements and violence. Paul Gilroy and Arjun Appadurai in conversation', *Theory, Culture & Society*, 16(2): 21–40.

Bellah, R. 1967. 'Civil religion in America', *Daedalus*, 96: 1–21.

Bellah, R. 1970. *Beyond Belief*. New York: Harper and Row.

Benhabib, S. 1987. 'The generalized and the concrete other: The Kohlberg–Gilligan Controversy and feminist theory', in S. Benhabib and D. Cornell (eds), *Feminism as Critique*. Cambridge: Polity.

Bendix, R. 1959. *Max Weber. An Intellectual Portrait*. London: Methuen.

Bendix, R. 1964. *Nation Building and Citizenship*. New York: Wiley.

Benedict, R. 1983. *Race and Racism*. London: Routledge and Kegan Paul.

Berger, J. 1991. 'The linguistification of the sacred and the delinguistification of the economy', in A. Honneth and H. Joas (eds), *Communicative Action: Essays on Jürgen Habermas's The Theory of Communicative Action*. Cambridge: Polity.

Berger, P.L. 1967. *The Sacred Canopy*. Doubleday: New York.

Berghe, P.L. Van der 1967. *Race and Racism*. New York: Wiley.

Bergson, H. 1912. *Creative Evolution*. London: Macmillan.

Bergson, H. 1935. *The Two Sources of Morality and Religion*. London: Macmillan.

Berlin, I. 1979. *Against the Current. Essays in the History of Ideas*. London: Hogarth.

Bernstein, B. 1970. 'Social class differences in communication and control', in Brandis, W. and Henderson, D. *Social Class, Language and Communication*. London: Routledge.

Bertens, H. 1995. *The Idea of the Postmodern: A History*. London: Routledge.

Bhabha, H. 1985. 'Signs taken for wonders: Questions of ambivalence and authority under a tree outside Delhi', *Critical Inquiry*, 12(1).

Bhabha, H. 1988. 'The commitment to theory', *New Formations*, 5: 5–23.

Bhabha, H. 1990. 'DissemiNation: Time, narrative and the margins of the modern nation', in Bhabha, H. (ed.), *Nation and Narration*. London: Routledge.

Binns, D. 1977. *Beyond the Sociology of Conflict*. London: Macmillan.

Birke, L. 1992. 'In pursuit of difference: scientific studies of women and men', in G. Kirkup and L.S. Keller (eds), *Inventing Women. Science, Technology and Gender*. Cambridge: Polity.

Blau, P.M. 1964. *Exchange and Power in Social Life*. New York: John Wiley.

Blauner, R. 1972. *Racial Oppression in America*. New York: Harper and Row.

Blu, K. 1980. *The Lumbee Problem: the Making of an American Indian People*. Cambridge: Cambridge University Press.

Bobbio, N. 1979. 'Gramsci and the conception of civil society', in C. Mouffe (ed.), *Gramsci and Marxist Theory*. London: Routledge and Kegan Paul.

Bohman, J. 1991. *New Philosophy of Social Science: Problems of Indeterminacy*. Cambridge: Polity.

Bologh, R. 1990. *Love or Greatness. Max Weber and Feminist Thinking – A Feminist Inquiry*. London: Unwin Hyman.

Bonacich, E. 1972. 'A theory of ethnic antagonism: the split labor market', *American Sociological Review*, 37: 547–59.

Bottomore, T. and Frisby, D. 1990. 'Introduction', in Simmel, G. 1907. *The Philosophy of Money*. Edited by T. Bottomore and D. Frisby. London: Routledge.

Boudon, R. 1996. 'The "cognitivist model": a generalised "rational choice model"', *Rationality and Society*, 8: 123–50.

Boudon, R. 1998. 'Social mechanisms without black boxes', in P. Hedström and R. Swedenberg (eds), *Social Mechanisms: An Analytical Approach to Social Theory*. Cambridge: Cambridge University Press.

Bourdieu, P. 1984. *Distinction*. London: Routledge and Kegan Paul.

Bourdieu, P. and Wacquant, L.J.D. 1992. *An Invitation to Reflexive Sociology*. Chicago: University of Chicago Press.

Boyne, R. and Rattansi, A. (eds) 1994. *Postmodernism and Society*. London: Macmillan.

Brinton, C. 1930. 'The revolutions', *Encyclopaedia of the Social Sciences*, Vol. 1. New York: Macmillan.

Brinton, M. 1988. 'The social-institutional bases of gender stratification: Japan as an illustrative case', *American Journal of Sociology*, 94: 300–34.

Bromley, Y. (ed.) 1974. *Soviet Ethnology and Anthropology Today*. The Hague: Mouton.

Bromley, Y. 1980. 'The object and the subject-matter of ethnography', in E. Gellner (ed.), *Soviet and Western Anthropology*. London: Duckworth.

Brown, R. 1965. *Social Psychology*. New York: Free Press.

Brubacker, R. 1984. *The Limits of Rationality. An Essay on the Social and Moral Thought of Max Weber*. London: Allen and Unwin.

Brubaker, R. 1985. 'Rethinking classical theory', *Theory and Society*, 14(6): 745–75.

Bryant, C.G.A. 1990. 'Tales of innocence and experience: developments in sociological theory since 1950', in C.G.A. Bryant and H.A. Becker (eds), *What Has Sociology Achieved?* London: Macmillan.

Butler, J. 1990. *Gender Trouble*. London: Routledge.

Butler, J. 1993. *Bodies That Matter*. London: Routledge.

Butler, J. 1994. 'Gender as performance: an interview with Judith Butler', by P. Osborne and L. Segal, *Radical Philosophy*, 67 (Summer).

Butler, J. 1997. 'Imitation and gender subordination', in L. Nicholson (ed.), *The Second Wave. A Reader in Feminist Theory*. New York: Routledge.

Caillois, R. 1950. *L'homme et le sacré*. Paris: Gallimard.

Camerer, C. 1997. 'Progress in behavioural game theory', *Journal of Economic Perspectives*, 11(4): 167–8.

Carby, H. 1982. 'White woman listen! Black feminism and the boundaries of sisterhood', in CCCS (eds), *The Empire Strikes Back. Race and Racism in '70s Britain*. Hutchinson: London.

Carmichael, S. and Hamilton, C. 1968. *Black Power: The Political Liberation in America*. Boston: Cape.

Carruthers, B. and Espeland, W. 1991. 'Accounting for rationality: Double entry bookkeeping and the rhetoric of economic rationality', *American Journal of Sociology*, 97(1): 31–69.

Cassirer, E. 1951. *The Philosophy of the Enlightenment*. Princeton, NJ: Princeton University Press.

Castles, S. and Kosack, G. 1973. *Immigrant Workers and Class Structure in Western Europe*. London: Oxford University Press.

Cealey-Harrison, W. and Hood-Williams, J. 1997. 'Gender, bodies and discursivity: A comment on Hughes and Witz', *Body & Society*, 3(4): 103–18.

Centre for Contemporary Cultural Studies 1982. *The Empire Strikes Back. Race and Racism in 70s Britain*. London: Hutchinson.

Chafetz, J.S. 1997. 'Feminist theory and sociology: Underutilised contributions for mainstream theory', *Annual Review of Sociology*, 23: 97–120.

Chatterjee, P. 1993. *The Nation and Its Fragments. Colonial and Postcolonial Histories*. Princeton, NJ: Princeton University Press.

Chodorow, N. 1978. *The Reproduction of Mothering. Psychoanalysis and the Sociology of Gender*. Berkeley: University of California Press.

Cixous, H. 1976. 'The laugh of the medusa', *Signs*, 1(4): 875–93.

Cladis, M. 1992. *A Communitarian Defense of Liberalism*. Stanford, CA: Stanford University Press.

Classen, C. 1993. *Worlds of Sense. Exploring the Senses in History and Across Cultures*. London: Routledge.

Cohen, A. 1969. *Customs and Politics in Urban Africa: A Study of Hausa Migrants in Yoruba Towns*. London: Routledge and Kegan Paul.

Coleman, J.S. 1973. *The Mathematics of Collective Action*. London: Heinemann.

Coleman, J.S. 1979. 'Rational actors in macrosociological analysis', in R. Harrison (ed.), *Rational Action. Studies in Philosophy and Social Science*. Cambridge: Cambridge University Press.

Coleman, J.S. (ed.) 1986. *Individual Interests and Collective Action*. Cambridge: Cambridge University Press.

Coleman, J.S. 1990. *Foundations of Social Theory*. Cambridge, MA: Belknap/Harvard University Press.

Coleman, J.S. and Fararo, T.J. 1992. 'Introduction', in J.S. Coleman and T.J. Fararo (eds), *Rational Choice Theory: Advocacy and Critique*. London: Sage.

Collins, P.H. 1997. 'Defining black feminist thought', in L. Nicholson (ed.), *The Second Wave. A Reader in Feminist Theory*. New York: Routledge.

Collins, R. 1974. 'Reassessments of sociological history: the empirical validity of the conflict tradition', *Theory and Society*, 1: 147–78.

Collins, R. 1975. *Conflict Sociology*. New York: Academic Press.

Collins, R. 1986a. *Weberian Sociological Theory*. Cambridge: Cambridge University Press.

Collins, R. 1986b. *Max Weber. A Skeleton Key*. London: Sage.

Collins, R. 1988. 'The Durkheimian Tradition in Conflict Sociology', in J.C. Alexander (ed.), *Durkheimian Sociology: Cultural Studies*. Cambridge: Cambridge University Press.

Collins, R. 1993. 'Emotional energy as the common denominator of rational action', *Rationality and Society*, 5(2): 203–30.

Collins, R. 1997a. 'A sociological guilt trip: comment on Connell', *American Journal of Sociology*, 102(6): 1558–64.

Collins, R. 1997b. 'Stark and Bainbridge, Durkheim and Weber: theoretical comparisons', in L.A. Young (ed.), *Rational Choice Theory and Religion: Summary and Assessment*. New York: Routledge.

Collins, R. and Makowsky, B. 1978. *The Discovery of Society*. New York: Random House.

Combahee River Collective 1979 [1997]. 'A black feminist statement', in L. Nicholson (ed.), *The Second Wave. A Reader in Feminist Theory*. New York: Routledge.

Comte, A. 1853a. *The Positive Philosophy of Auguste Comte*, Vol. I: Translated by Harriet Martineau. London: John Chapman.

Comte, A. 1853b. *The Positive Philosophy of Auguste Comte*, Vol. II. Translated by Harriet Martineau. London: John Chapman.

Comte, A. 1858. *The Catechism of Positive Religion*. Translated by Richard Congreve, London.

Comte, A. 1875–7. *Système du politique positive ou Traité du sociologie instituant la religion de l'Humanité*, 4 Vols, Paris: Au Siège de la Société Positiviste (translated as *System of Positive Polity*, 1973, New York: Hill).

Connell, R.W. 1997. 'Why is classical theory classical?', *American Journal of Sociology*, 102(6): 1511–57.

Connerton, P. 1976. 'Introduction', in *Critical Sociology. Selected Readings*. Harmondsworth: Penguin.

Cook, K.S. 1977. 'Exchange and power in networks of inter-organisational relations', *American Sociological Review*, 43: 721–39.

Cooley, C. 1918. *Social Process*. New York: Scribner's Sons.

Coombes, A.E. 1994. *Reinventing Africa. Museums, Material Culture and Popular Imagination*. New Haven, CT: Yale University Press.

Coser, L. 1956. *The Functions of Social Conflict*. London: Routledge and Kegan Paul.

Coser, L. 1967. *Continuities in the Study of Social Conflict*. New York: Free Press.

Coser, L. 1971. *Masters of Sociological Thought. Ideas in Historical and Social Context*. New York: Harcourt Brace Jovanovich.

Coser, L. 1977. 'Georg Simmel's neglected contributions to the sociology of women', *Signs, Journal of Women in Culture and Society*, 2: 869–76.

Cox, O.C. 1948. *Caste, Class and Race: A Study in Social Dynamics*. New York: Doubleday.

Craib, I. 1984. *Modern Social Theory*. Brighton: Wheatsheaf.

Crespi, F. 1992. *Social Action and Power*. Oxford: Blackwell.

Crook, S., Pakulski, J. and Waters, M. 1992. *Postmodernization*. London: Sage.

Cruze, H. 1984. *The Crisis of the Negro Intellectual*. New York: Quill.

Csikszentmihalyi, M. 1975. *Beyond Boredom and Anxiety: The Experience of Play in Work and Games*. San Francisco: Jossey-Bass.

Dahrendorf, R. 1959. *Class and Class Conflict in Industrial Society*. London: Routledge and Kegan Paul.

Daly, M. 1984. *Pure Lust. Elemental Feminist Philosophy*. Boston: Beacon.

Daniel, N. 1975. *The Arabs and Medieval Europe*. London: Longman.

Danziger, S.H. and Gottschalk, P. 1995. *America Unequal*. Cambridge, MA: Harvard University Press.

Dawe, A. 1978. 'Theories of social action', in T. Bottomore and R. Nisbet (eds), *A History of Sociological Analysis*. London: Heinemann.

Dawes, R.M. 1980. 'Social dilemmas', *American Psychological Review*, 31: 169–93.

Dayan, D. and Katz, E. 1988. 'Articulating consensus: the ritual and rhetoric of media events', in J.C. Alexander (ed.), *Durkheimian Sociology: Cultural Studies*. Cambridge: Cambridge University Press.

Dean, M. 1997. 'Sociology After Society', in D. Owen (ed.), *Sociology After Postmodernism*. London: Sage.

DeJean, J. 1997. *Ancients Against Moderns: Culture Wars and the Making of a Fin de Siècle*. Chicago: University of Chicago Press.

Delanty, G. 1997. Habermas and occidental rationalism: The politics of identity, social learning and the cultural limits of moral universalism', *Sociological Theory*, 15(1): 30–59.

De Lauretis, T. 1991. 'Queer theory and lesbian and gay sexualities: An introduction', *Differences*, 3: iii–xviii.

Deleuze, G. and Guattari, F. 1977. *Anti-Oedipus*. New York: Viking.

Delphy, C. 1984. *Close to Home. A Materialist Analysis of Women's Oppression*. London: Hutchinson.

Delphy, C. 1996. 'Rethinking sex and gender', in L. Adkins and D. Leonard (eds), *Reconstructing French Feminism: Commodification, Materialism and Sex*. Lewes: Falmer.

Dijkstra, S. 1992. *Flora Tristan: Feminism in the Age of George Sand*. London: Pluto.

Dinnerstein, D. 1977. *The Mermaid and the Minotaur: Sexual Arrangements and Human Malaise*. New York: Harper Colophon Books.

Douglas, M. 1966. *Purity and Danger*. London: Routledge and Kegan Paul.

Douglas, M. 1970. *Natural Symbols*. London: Routledge.

Douglas, M. 1992. *Risk and Blame. Essays in Cultural Theory*. London: Routledge.

Douglas, M. and Ney, S. 1998. *Missing Persons: A Critique of Personhood in the Social Sciences*. Berkeley: University of California Press.

Du Bois, W.E.B. 1903 [1989]. *The Souls of Black Folk*. New York: Bantam.

Ducassé, P. 1939. *Essai sur les origines intuitives du positivisme*. Paris: F. Alcan.

Duchen, C. 1986. *Feminism in France. From May '68 to Mitterand*. London: Routledge and Kegan Paul.

Durkheim, E. 1893 [1984]. *The Division of Labour in Society*. London: Macmillan.

Durkheim, E. 1895 [1982]. *The Rules of Sociological Method*. Edited by S. Lukes, translated by W.D. Halls. London: Macmillan.

Durkheim, E. 1897 [1952]. *Suicide*. London: Routledge.

Durkheim, E. 1898a. Représentations individuelles et représentations collectives. *Revue de métaphysique et de morale*, 6: 273–302.

Durkheim, E. 1898b [1963]. 'Incest: The nature and origin of the taboo', in E. Durkheim and A. Ellis, *Incest*. New York: Lyle Stuart.

Durkheim, E. 1899 [1974]. 'Concerning the Definition of Religious Phenomena', in W.S.F. Pickering (ed.), *Durkheim on Religion*. London: Routledge and Kegan Paul.

Durkheim, E. 1912 [1995]. *The Elementary Forms of Religious Life*. Translated by Karen E. Fields. New York: Free Press. (French text: *Les formes élémentaires de la vie religieuse*. Paris: Le Livre de Poche (Librarie Générale Française)).

Durkheim, E. 1914 [1974]. Le Dualisme de la nature humane et ses conditions sociale. *Scientia*, 15: 206–21 (trans. The dualism of human nature and its social conditions. In R.N. Bellah (ed.), *Emile Durkheim on Morality and Society*. Chicago: University of Chicago Press).

Dworkin, A. 1981. *Pornography: Men Possessing Women*. New York: Pedigree.

Eagleton, T. 1996. *The Illusions of Postmodernism*. Oxford: Blackwell.

Edney, J.J. 1980. 'The commons problem: Alternative perspectives', *American Psychologist*, 35: 131–50.

Ehreneich, B. 1987. 'Foreword' to K. Theweleit, *Male Fantasies*, Vol. 1: *Women, Floods, Bodies, History*. Cambridge: Polity.

Eisenstadt, S.N. 1968. *Max Weber on Charisma and Institution Building*. Chicago: University of Chicago Press.

Elias, N. 1939 [2000]. *The Civilizing Process*. Oxford: Blackwell.

Elias, N. 1977. *What is Sociology?* London: Hutchinson.

Elias, N. 1985. *The Loneliness of the Dying*. Oxford: Blackwell.

Elias, N. 1989 [1996]. *The Germans*. Cambridge: Polity.

Elias, N. 1991. *The Symbol Theory*. London: Sage.

Elias, N. 1994 'Introduction: A theoretical essay on established and outsider relations', in *The Established and the Outsiders*. London: Sage.

Elsner, Jr H. 1972. 'Introduction' to R.E. Park, *The Crowd and Other Essays*. Chicago: University of Chicago Press.

Elster, J. 1979. *Ulysses and the Sirens*. Cambridge: Cambridge University Press.

Elster, J. 1983. *Sour Grapes: Studies in the Subversion of Rationality*. Cambridge: Cambridge University Press.

Elster, J. 1986. 'Introduction', in J. Elster (ed.), *Rational Choice*. Oxford: Blackwell.

Elster, J. 1989a. *Nuts and Bolts for the Social Sciences*. Cambridge: Cambridge University Press.

Elster, J. 1989b. *The Cement of Society: A Study of Social Order*. Cambridge: Cambridge University Press.

Elster, J. 1990. 'When rationality fails', in K.S. Cook and M. Levi (eds), *The Limits of Rationality*. Chicago: University of Chicago Press.

England, P. 1993. *Theory on Gender. Feminism on Theory*. New York: Aldine de Gruyter.

Epstein, A.L. 1978. *Ethos and Identity: Three Studies in Ethnicity*. London: Tavistock.

Evans, J. 1995. *Feminist Theory Today. An Introduction to Second Wave Feminism*. London: Sage.

Evans-Pritchard, E. 1965. *Theories of Primitive Religion*. Oxford: Clarendon.

Fararo, T.J. 1996. 'Foundational problems in theoretical sociology', in J. Clark (ed.), *James S. Coleman*. London: Falmer.

Favell, A. 1996. 'Rational choice as grand theory: James Coleman's normative contribution to social theory', in J. Clark (ed.), *James S. Coleman*. London: Falmer.

Featherstone, M. 1991. *Consumer Culture and Postmodernism*. London: Sage.

Featherstone, M. 1995. *Undoing Culture. Globalization, Postmodernism and Identity*. London: Sage.

Fenton, C.S. 1980. 'Race, Class and Politics in the Work of Emile Durkheim', in *Sociological Theories: Race and Colonialism*. Paris: Unesco.

Ferguson, H. 1992. *The Religious Transformation of Western Society*. London: Routledge.

Firestone, S. 1971. *The Dialectic of Sex*. London: Jonathan Cape.

Flacks, R. and Turkel, G. 1978. 'Radical sociology: the emergence of neo-Marxian perspectives in US sociology', *Annual Review of Sociology*, 4: 193–238.

Foshay, T. 1992. 'Resentment and apophasis: the trace of the other in Levinas, Derrida and Gans', in P. Berry and A. Wernick (eds), *Shadow of Spirit: Postmodernism and Religion*. London: Routledge.

Foucault, M. 1970. *The Order of Things*. London: Tavistock.

Foucault, M. 1971. *Madness and Civilisation*. London: Tavistock.

Foucault, M. 1972. *The Archaeology of Knowledge*. London: Tavistock.

Frankenberg, R. 1993. *White Women, Race Matters: The Social Construction of Whiteness*. London: Routledge.

Fraser, N. 1997. 'Structuralism or pragmatics', in L. Nicholson (ed.), *The Second Wave. A Reader in Feminist Theory*. New York: Routledge.

Freud, S. 1950. *Totem and Taboo*. London: Routledge and Kegan Paul.

Frey, B. 1997. 'The public choice of international organisations', in D. Mueller (ed.), *Perspectives on Public Choice. A Handbook*. Cambridge: Cambridge University Press.

Friedman, M. 1962. *Capitalism and Freedom*. Chicago: University of Chicago Press.

Friedman, D. and Diem, C. 1993. 'Feminism and the pro(rational-) choice movement: rational choice theory, feminist critiques and gender inequality', in P. England (ed.), *Theory on gender. Feminism on Theory*. New York: Aldine de Gruyter.

Frisby, D. 1981. *Sociological Impressionism: A Reassessment of Georg Simmel's Social Theory*. London: Heinemann.

Frisby, D. 1992. *Simmel and Since*. London: Routledge.

Frisby, D. 1985. 'Georg Simmel: First sociologist of modernity', *Theory, Culture & Society*, 2(3): 49–67.

Frisby, D. 1994. *Georg Simmel*. London: Fontana.

Fromm, E. 1956. *The Sane Society*. London: Routledge and Kegan Paul.

Fuss, D. 1990. *Essentially Speaking: Feminism, Nature and Difference*. London: Routledge.

Gane, M. 1983a. Durkheim: the sacred language. *Economy and Society*, 12(1): 1–47.

Gane, M. 1983b. Durkheim: woman as outsider. *Economy and Society*, 12(2): 227–70.

Gane, M. 1995. 'Unresolved Comte', *Economy and Society*, 24(1): 138–49.

Gatens, M. 1992. 'Power, bodies and difference', in M. Barrett and A. Phillips (eds), *Destabilizing Theory. Contemporary Feminist Debates*. Cambridge: Polity.

Gay, P. 1973. *The Enlightenment: An Interpretation*. 2 Vols. London: Wildwood House.

Geras, N. 1983. *Marx and Human Nature*. London: Verso.

Gerth, H.H. and Mills, C.W. 1948. 'Introduction' to *From Max Weber: Essays in Sociology*. London: Routledge and Kegan Paul.

Gerson, J.M. 1985. 'Boundaries, negotiation, consciousness: reconceptualising gender relations. *Sociological Problems*, 32: 317–31.

Giddens, A. 1981. *The Class Structure of Advanced Societies*. London: Hutchinson.

Giddens, A. 1984. *The Constitution of Society*. Cambridge: Polity.

Giddens, A. 1990. *The Consequences of Modernity*. Cambridge: Polity.

Giddens, A. 1991. *Modernity and Self-Identity*. Cambridge: Polity.

Giddens, A. 1994. *Beyond Left and Right*. Cambridge: Polity.

Giddens, A. 1998. *The Third Way. The Renewal of Social Democracy*. Cambridge: Polity.

Gilligan, C. 1982. *In a Different Voice. Psychological Theory and Women's Development*. Cambridge, MA: Harvard University Press.

Gilroy, P. 1993. *The Black Atlantic. Modernity and Double Consciousness*. London: Verso.

Gilroy, P. 1997. 'Diaspora and the detours of identity', in K. Woodward (ed.), *Identity and Difference*. London: Sage.

Gilroy, P. 2000. *Between Camps: Nations, Cultures and the Allure of Race*. London: Penguin.

Girard, R. 1972 [1997]. *La Violence et le sacré*. Paris: Editions Bernard Grasset (trans. *Violence and the Sacred*. Baltimore: Johns Hopkins University Press).

Glass, D. 1954. *Social Mobility in Britain*. London: Routledge and Kegan Paul.

Glazer, N. and Moynihan, D.P. 1970 [2nd edn]. *Beyond the Melting Pot*. Cambridge, MA.: MIT Press.

Glazer, N. and Moynihan, D.P. 1975. *Ethnicity: Theory and Experience*. Cambridge, MA: Harvard University Press.

Gluckman, M. 1940 [1958]. *Analysis of a Social Situation in Modern Zululand*. Manchester University Press.

Gluckman, M. 1956. *Custom and Conflict in Africa*. Oxford: Blackwell.

Gluckman, M. 1963. *Order and Rebellion in Tribal Africa*. London: Cohen and West.

Gobineau 1853–5. *Essai sur l'inégalité des races humaines*. Paris: Firmin-Didot.

Goffman, E. 1969. *The Presentation of Self in Everyday Life*. Harmondsworth: Penguin.

Goldberg, D.T. 1993. *Racist Culture*. Cambridge: Blackwell.

Goldthorpe, J. 1972. 'Class, status and party in modern Britain', *European Journal of Sociology*, 13.

Goldthorpe, J.H. 1998. 'Rational action theory for sociology', *British Journal of Sociology*, 49(2): 167–92.

Gough, I. 1979. *The Political Economy of the Welfare State*. London: Macmillan.

Gouhier, H. 1988. *La Philosophie d'Auguste Comte*. Paris: Vrin.

Gouldner, A. 1955. 'Metaphysical pathos and the theory of bureaucracy', *American Political Science Review*, 49: 496–507.

Gouldner, A. 1970. *The Coming Crisis of Western Sociology*. London: Heinemann.

Gouldner, A. 1980. *The Two Marxisms. Contradictions and Anomalies in the Development of Theory*. London: Macmillan.

Gramsci, A. 1971. *Selections from the Prison Notebooks*. Tr. and ed. Q. Hoare and G.N. Smith. London: Lawrence and Wishart.

Griffin, S. 1978. *Women and Nature: The Roaring Inside Her*. New York: Harper and Row.

Grosz, E. 1994. *Volatile Bodies. Toward a Corporeal Feminism*. Bloomington: Indiana University Press.

Habermas, J. 1981a [1984]. *The Theory of Communicative Action*, Vol. 1 (trans. T. McCarthy). London: Heinemann.

Habermas, J. 1981b [1987]. *The Theory of Communicative Action*, Vol. 2 (trans. T. McCarthy). Cambridge: Polity.

Habermas, J. 1982. 'A Reply to My Critics', in J.B. Thompson and D. Held (eds), *Habermas: Critical Debates*. London: Macmillan.

Habermas, J. 1985. 'Modernity – an incomplete project', in H. Foster (ed.), *Postmodern Culture*. London: Pluto.

Hacker, A. 1961. 'Sociology and ideology', in M. Black (ed.), *The Social Theories of Talcott Parsons*. Englewood Cliffs, NJ: Prentice-Hall.

Haines, V.A. 1987. 'Biological and social theory: Parsons's evolutionary theme', *Sociology*, 21(1): 19–39.

Halbwachs, M. 1941, 1952 [1992]. *On Collective Memory*. Edited, translated and with an introduction by L.A. Coser. Chicago: University of Chicago Press.

Hall, S. 1987. 'Minimal selves', in *Identity: The Real Me*, ICA Document 6.

Hall, S. 1988. 'New ethnicities', *Black Film British Cinema*, ICA Document 7: 27–31.

Hall, S. 1996. 'Introduction: Who needs "identity"', in S. Hall and P. du Gay (eds), *Questions of Cultural Identity*. London: Sage.

Hamilton, P. 1992. 'The Enlightenment and the birth of social science', in S. Hall and B. Gieben (eds), *Formations of Modernity*. Cambridge: Polity.

Hardin, R. 1982. 'Collective action as an agreeable – prisoners' dilemma' in B. Barry and R. Hardin (eds), *Rational Man and Irrational Society*. London: Sage.

Hardin, R. 1997. 'Economic theories of the state', in D. Mueller (ed.), *Perspectives on Public Choice. A Handbook*. Cambridge: Cambridge University Press.

Harrod, R. 1956. *Towards a Dynamic Economics*. London: Macmillan.

Harstock, N. 1983. 'The feminist standpoint', in S. Harding and M. Hintikka (eds), *Discovering Reality*. Dordrecht: Reidel.

Hartouni, V. 1996. *Making Life Make Sense: New Technologies and the Discussion of Reproduction*. Minneapolis: University of Minnesota Press.

Harvey, D. 1989. *The Condition of Postmodernity*. Oxford: Blackwell.

Hastings, A. 1997. *The Construction of Nationhood*. Cambridge: Cambridge University Press.

Hawkins, M. 1999. 'Durkheim's Sociology and Theories of Degeneration', *Economy and Society*, 28(1): 118–37.

Hayek, F. von 1967. *Studies in Philosophy, Politics and Economics*. London: Routledge and Kegan Paul.

Hayek, F. von 1973. 'The principles of a liberal social order', in F. von Hayek (ed.), *Studies in Philosophy, Politics and Economics*. London: Routledge and Kegan Paul.

Hegel, G.W.F. 1821 [1967]. *The Philosophy of Right*. Oxford: Oxford University Press.

Heilbron, J. 1995. *The Rise of Social Theory*. Minneapolis: University of Minnesota Press.

Held, D. 1980. *Introduction to Critical Theory: Horkheimer to Habermas*. Berkeley: University of California Press.

Hennis, W. 1988. *Max Weber: Essays in Reconstruction*. London: Allen and Unwin.

Herberg, W. 1956. *Protestant, Catholic, Jew*. New York: Doubleday.

Hertz, R. 1922 [1994]. *Sin and Expiation in Primitive Societies*. Trans. Robert Parkin. Oxford: British Centre for Durkheimian Studies.

Hertz, R. 1973. 'The pre-eminence of the right hand', in R. Needham (ed.), *Right and Left*. Chicago: University of Chicago Press.

Hibbert, C. 1984. *Africa Explored*. Harmondsworth: Penguin.

Hindess, B. 1988. *Choice, Rationality and Social Theory*. London: Unwin Hyman.

Hobbes, T. 1651 [1957]. *The Leviathan*. Ed. M. Oakeshott. Oxford: Oxford University Press.

Hobsbawm, E. 1983. 'Introduction: inventing traditions', in E. Hobsbawm and T. Ranger (eds), *The Invention of Tradition*. Cambridge: Cambridge University Press.

Hollier, D. 1988. *The College of Sociology, 1937–39*. Minneapolis: University of Minnesota Press.

Hollis, M. 1987. *The Cunning of Reason*. Cambridge: Cambridge University Press.

Holmwood, J. 1996. *Founding Sociology? Talcott Parsons and the Idea of General Theory*. London: Longman.

Holton, R. 1996. 'Has class analysis a future? Max Weber and the challenge of liberalism to Gemeinschaftlich accounts of class', in D.J. Lee and B.S. Turner (eds), *Conflicts about Class*. London: Longman.

Homans, G. 1950. *The Human Group*. New York: Harcourt Brace.

Homans, G. 1961. *Social Behaviour: Its Elementary Forms*. London: Routledge and Kegan Paul.

Homans, G. 1964. 'Bringing Men Back In', *American Sociological Review*, 29: 808–18.

Honneth, A. 1987. 'Critical theory', in A. Giddens and J. Turner (eds), *Social Theory Today*. Cambridge: Polity.

Horowitz, I.L. 1993. *The Decomposition of Sociology*. Oxford: Oxford University Press.

Hughes, A. and Witz, A. 1997. 'Feminism and the matter of bodies: From de Beauvoir to Butler', *Body & Society*, 3(1): 47–60.

Huxley, T.H. 1869. 'On the physical basis of life', *Fortnightly Review*, V.

Iannaccone, L.R. 1997. 'Rational choice: framework for the scientific study of religion', in L.A. Young (ed.), *Rational Choice Theory and Religion: Summary and Assessment*. New York: Routledge.

Ingram, J.K. 1901. *Human Nature and Morals According to Auguste Comte*. London: Adam and Charles Black.

Irigaray, L. 1977 [1985]. *This Sex Which is Not One*. Trans. C. Porter with C. Burke. New York: Cornell University Press.

Irigaray, L. 1984 [1987]. 'Sexual difference', in T. Moi (ed.), *French Feminist Thought*. Oxford: Blackwell.

Irigaray, L. 1993. 'Divine Women', in *Sexes and Genealogies*. New York: Columbia University Press.

Jacquard, A. and Pontalis, J.-B. 1984–5. 'Entretien: une tête qui ne convient pas', *Le Genre humain*, No. 11.

Jaggar, A. 1983. *Feminist Politics and Human Nature*. New Jersey: Rowman and Allenheld.

Jaggar, A. 1984. 'Human biology in feminist theory: sexual equality reconsidered', in C. Gould (ed.), *Beyond Domination*. New Jersey: Rowman and Allenheld.

James, S. 1997. *Passion and Action. The Emotions in Seventeenth-Century Philosophy*. Oxford: Clarendon.

Jameson, F. 1973. 'The vanishing mediator: narrative structure in Max Weber', *New German Critique*, 1: 52–89.

Jameson, F. 1983. 'Postmodernism and the consumer society', in H. Foster (ed.), *Postmodern Culture*. London: Pluto.

Jameson, F. 1991. *Postmodernism or the Cultural Logic of Late Capitalism*. Durham, NC: Duke University Press.

Janssen, J. and Verheggen, T. 1997. 'The double center of gravity in Durkheim's symbol theory: bringing the symbolism of the body back in', *Sociological Theory*, 15(3): 294–306.

Jay, N. 1992. *Throughout Your Generations Forever*. Chicago: University of Chicago Press.

Joas, H. 1996. *The Creativity of Social Action*. Cambridge: Polity.

Jones, R.A and Kibbee, D.A. 1993. 'Durkheim, language and history: a pragmatist perspective', *Sociological Theory*, 11: 152–70.

Jordan, W. 1974. *The White Man's Burden*. Oxford: Oxford University Press.

Kalberg, S. 1980. 'Max Weber's types of rationality: cornerstones for the analysis of rationalizing processes in history', *American Journal of Sociology*, 85(5): 1145–79.

Kallen, H. 1924. *Culture and Democracy in America*. New York: Boni and Liveright.

Kant, I. 1784 [1970]. 'An answer to the question: "What is the Enlightenment?"', in H. Reiss (ed.), *Kant's Political Writings*. Cambridge: Cambridge University Press.

Kant, I. 1797 [1985]. *Foundations of the Metaphysics of Morals*. London: Macmillan.

Kaplan, G. and Rogers, L. 1990. 'The definition of male and female. Biological reductionism and the sanctions of normality', in S. Gunew (ed.), *Feminist Knowledge, Critique and Construct*. London: Routledge.

Kasler, D. 1988. *Max Weber: An Introduction to his Life and Work*. Cambridge: Polity.

Kedourie, E. 1992. *Nationalism*, 4th edn. Oxford: Blackwell.

Kellner, D. 1992. 'Popular culture and the construction of postmodern identities', in S. Lash and J. Friedman (eds), *Modernity and Identity*. Oxford: Blackwell.

Keynes, J.N. 1955. *The Scope and Method of Political Economy*. New York: Kelley and Millman.

Keynes, J.M. 1972. *Essays in Persuasion. The Collected Writings*, Vol. IX. London: Macmillan.

Kilminster, R. 1998. *The Sociological Revolution. From the Enlightenment to the Global Age*. London: Routledge.

Klein, V. and Myrdal, A. 1956. *Women's Two Roles: Home and Work*. London: Routledge and Kegan Paul.

Komarovsky, M. 1950. *Common Frontiers of the Social Sciences*. Glencoe, IL: Free Press.

Kontos, S. 1994. 'The world disenchanted and the return of gods and demons', in A. Horowitz and T. Maley (eds), *The Barbarism of Reason. Max Weber and the Twilight of Enlightenment*. Toronto: University of Toronto Press.

Kroker, A. and Cook, D. 1986. *The Postmodern Scene*. New York: St Martin's Press.

Lacan, J. 1977. *Ecrits: A Selection*. trans. A. Sheridan. New York: W.W. Norton.

Laing, R.D. 1965. *The Divided Self*. Harmondsworth: Penguin.

Lal, B.B. 1986. 'The "Chicago School" of American sociology, symbolic interactionism, and race relations theory', in J. Rex and D. Mason (eds), *Theories of Race and Ethnic Relations*. Cambridge: Cambridge University Press.

Laqueur, T. 1990. *Making Sex*. Cambridge, MA: Harvard University Press.

Lasch, C. 1979. *The Culture of Cynicism. American Life in an Age of Diminishing Expectations*. New York: W.W. Norton.

Lash, S. and Urry, J. 1987. *The End of Organised Capitalism*. Cambridge: Polity.

Lassman, P. and Velody, I. with Martins, H. (eds) 1989. *Max Weber's Science as a Vocation*. London: Unwin Hyman.

Le Bon, G. 1895 [1975]. *Psychologie des Foules*. Paris: Presses Universitaires de France.

Lechner, F.J. 1991. 'Parsons and modernity: An interpretation', in R. Robertson and B.S. Turner (eds), *Talcott Parsons: Theorist of Modernity*. London: Sage.

Le Doeuff, M. 1987. 'Women and philosophy', in T. Moi (ed.), *French Feminist Thought*. London: Blackwell.

Lehmann, J.M. 1993. *Deconstructing Durkheim*. London: Routledge.

Lehmann, J. 1994. *Durkheim and Women*. Lincoln: University of Nebraska Press.

Lemert, C. 1995. *Sociology After the Crisis*. Boulder, CO: Westview.

Lemert, C. 1998. 'Series Editor's Preface', in J.S. Alexander, *Neofunctionalism and After*. Oxford: Blackwell.

Lepervanche, M. de 1984. *Indians in a White Australia*. Sydney: Allen and Unwin.

Lerner, M. 1957. *America as a Civilization*. New York: Simon & Schuster.

Lévinas, E. 1981. *Otherwise than Being, or Beyond Essence*. trans. A. Lingis. The Hague: Martinus Nijhoff.

Lévinas, E. 1991. *Entre nous: Essais sur le penser l'autre*. Paris: Grasset.

Levine, D. 1971. 'Introduction', in *Georg Simmel On Individuality and Social Forms*. Chicago: University of Chicago Press.

Levine, D. 1980. *Simmel and Parsons: Two Approaches to the Study of Society*. New York: Arno.

Levine, D. 1991a. 'Simmel as educator: On individuality and modern culture', *Theory, Culture & Society*, 8(3): 99–117.

Levine, D. 1991b. 'Simmel and Parsons reconsidered', in R. Robertson and B.S. Turner (eds), *Talcott Parsons. Theorist of Modernity*. London: Sage.

Levine, D. 1995. *Visions of the Sociological Tradition*. Chicago: University of Chicago Press.

Levine, D. 1998. 'Putting voluntarism back into a voluntaristic theory of action', for the session 'Theorising Subjects and Agents', XIV World Congress of Sociology.

Levine, D., Carter, E.B. and Gorman, E.M. 1976. 'Simmel's influence on American Sociology, I & II', *American Journal of Sociology*, 81(4–5): 813–45, 1112–32.

Lévi-Strauss, C. 1961. *The Elementary Forms of Kinship*. London: Eyre and Spottiswoode.

Lévi-Strauss, C. 1966. *The Savage Mind*. London: Weidenfeld and Nicolson.

Lévy-Bruhl, L. 1903. *The Philosophy of Auguste Comte*. London: Swan Sonnenschein and Co.

Lidz, V. 1982. 'Religion and cybernetic concepts in the theory of action', *Sociological Analysis*, 43(4): 287–305.

Lidz, V. 1991. 'The American value system: A commentary on Talcott Parsons's Perspective and Understanding', in R. Robertson and B.S. Turner (eds), *Talcott Parsons. Theorist of Modernity*. London: Sage.

Lindenberg, S. 1990. 'Homo Socio-economicus: the emergence of a general model of man in the social sciences', *Journal of Institutional and Theoretical Economics*, 146: 727–48.

Lockwood, D. 1956. 'Some remarks on the social system', *British Journal of Sociology*, 7: 134–46.

Lockwood, D. 1992. *Solidarity and Schism: 'The Problem of Disorder' in Durkheimian and Marxist Sociology*. Oxford: Clarendon.

Loewith, K. 1982. *Max Weber and Karl Marx*. London: Allen & Unwin.

Lovejoy, A. 1942. *The Great Chain of Being*. Cambridge: Harvard University Press.

Lovell, T. 1996. 'Feminist social theory', in B.S. Turner (ed.), *The Blackwell Companion to Social Theory*. Oxford: Blackwell.

Luker, K. 1984. *Abortion and the Politics of Motherhood*. Berkeley: University of California Press.

Lukes, S. 1970. 'Some Problems about Rationality', in B.R. Wilson (ed.), *Rationality*. Oxford: Blackwell.

Lukes, S. 1973. *Émile Durkheim: His Life and Work*. London: Allen Lane/Penguin Press.

Lukes, S. 1982. 'Introduction' to S. Lukes (ed.), *The Rules of Sociological Method and Selected Texts on Sociology and its Method*. London: Macmillan.

Lundby, K. 1997. 'The web of collective representations', in S.M. Hoover and K. Lundby (eds), *Rethinking Media, Religion, and Culture*. London: Sage.

Lyon, D. 1999. *Postmodernity*, 2nd edn. Buckingham: Open University Press.

Lyotard, J-F. 1984. *The Condition of Postmodernity*. Manchester: Manchester University Press.

Lyotard, J-F. 1991. *The Inhuman. Reflections on Time*. Stanford, CA: Stanford University Press.

McDonald, L. 1997. 'Classical social theory and women founders', in C. Camic (ed.), *Reclaiming the Sociological Classics*. Oxford: Blackwell.

McGrane, B. 1989. *Beyond Anthropology: Society and the Other*. New York: Columbia University Press.

MacIntyre, A. 1970. 'The idea of a social science', in B.R. Wilson (ed.), *Rationality*. Oxford: Blackwell.

Mackinnon, C. 1989. *Towards a feminist Theory of the State*. Cambridge, MA: Harvard University Press.

McLellan, D. 1980. *The Thought of Karl Marx*. London: Macmillan.

McLellan, D. 1985. 'Marx's concept of human nature', *New Left Review*, 149: 121–4.

McLellan, D. 1987. *Marxism and Religion*. London: Macmillan.

MacRae, D.G. 1974. *Weber*. London: Fontana.

Maffesoli, M. 1996. *The Time of the Tribes*. London: Sage/TCS.

Manuel, F.E. 1962. *The Prophets of Paris*. Cambridge, MA: Harvard University Press.

Marcuse, H. 1964. *One Dimensional Man*. Boston: Beacon.

Marshall, T.H. 1950. *Citizenship and Social Class*. Cambridge: Cambridge University Press.

Martin, E. 1989. *The Woman in the Body*. Milton Keynes: Open University Press.

Martín-Barbero, J. 1997. 'Mass Media as a Site of Resacralisation of Contemporary Cultures', in S.M. Hoover and K. Lundby (eds), *Rethinking Media, Religion, and Culture*. London: Sage.

Marwell, G. and Ames, R.E. 1981. 'Economists free ride, does anyone else?', *Journal of Public Economics*, 15: 295–310.

Marx, K. 1844 [1975]. 'The economic and philosophical manuscripts of 1844', in *Karl Marx Early Writings*. Harmondsworth: Penguin.

Marx, K. 1848 [1968]. 'Manifesto of the communist party', in *Marx/Engels. Selected Works in One Volume*. London: Lawrence and Wishart.

Marx, K. 1849 [1968]. 'Wage, labour and capital', in *Marx/Engels. Selected Works in One Volume*. London: Lawrence and Wishart.

Marx, K. 1906. *Capital*, Vol. I. London: Lawrence and Wishart.

Marx, K. 1956. *Selected Writings in Sociology and Social Philosophy*. Eds T. Bottomore and M. Rubel. New York: McGraw-Hill.

Marx, K. 1972. *Capital*, Vol. III. London: Lawrence and Wishart.

Marx, K. 1973. *Grundrisse*. Harmondsworth: Penguin.

Marx, K. and Engels, F. 1846 [1970]. *The German Ideology*. London: Lawrence and Wishart.

Mason, D. 1995. *Race and Ethnicity in Modern Britain*. Oxford: Oxford University Press.

Mauss, M. 1904–5 [1973]. *Sociologie et anthropologie*. Paris: Presses Universitaires de France.

Mauss, M. 1936 [1992]. 'Letter to S. Ranulph', in M. Gane (ed.), *The Radical Sociology of Durkheim and Mauss*. London: Routledge.

Mauss, M. 1950. *The Gift: Forms and Functions of Exchange in Primitive Societies*. London: Cohen and West.

Mead, M. 1935. *Sex and Temperament in Three Primitive Societies*. New York: Morrow.

Mellor, P.A. 1998. 'Sacred contagion and social vitality: collective effervescence in *Les formes élémentaires de la vie religieuse*', *Durkheimian Studies/Études Durkheimiennes*, 4: 87–114.

Mellor, P.A. and Shilling, C. 1997. *Re-forming the Body: Religion, Community and Modernity*. London: Sage.

Melucci, A. 1996. *Challenging Codes: Collective Action in the Information Age*. Cambridge: Cambridge University Press.

Meštrović, S.J. 1994. *The Balkanization of the West. The Confluence of Postmodernity and Post-communism*. London: Routledge.

Meštrović, S.G. 1997. *Postemotional Society*. London: Sage.

Mészáros, I. 1970. *Marx's Theory of Alienation*. London: Routledge and Kegan Paul.

Mészáros, I. 1985. *The Power of Ideology*. New York: Harvester Wheatsheaf.

Michel, A. 1959. *Famille, Industrialisation, Logement*. Paris: Centre National de Recherche Scientifique.

Milbank, J. 1990. *Theology and Social Theory. Beyond Secular Reason*. Oxford: Blackwell.

Miles, R. 1982. *Racism and Migrant Labour*. A Critical Text. London: Routledge and Kegan Paul.

Miles, R. 1989. *Racism*. London: Routledge.

Miles, R. 1993. *Racism after 'Race Relations'*. London: Routledge.

Millett, K. 1970. *Sexual Politics*. Garden City, NY: Doubleday.

Mills, C. Wright. 1951. *White Collar. The American Middle Classes*. Oxford: Oxford University Press.

Mills, C. Wright. 1956. *The Power Elite*. New York: Oxford University Press.

Mills, C. Wright. 1959. *The Causes of World War Three*. London: Secker and Warburg.

Mills, C. Wright. 1970. *The Sociological Imagination*. Harmondsworth: Penguin.

Minh-ha, T.T. 1989. *Woman, Native, Other*. Bloomington: Indiana University Press.

Mitchell, C. 1956. *The Kalela Dance: Aspects of Social Relationships Among Urban Africans in Northern Rhodesia*. Manchester: Manchester University Press.

Mohanty, C. 1988. 'Under western eyes. Feminist scholarship and colonial discourses', *Feminist Review*, 30(Autumn): 61–88.

Moi, T. 1985. *Sexual Textual Politics. Feminist Literary Theory*. London: Routledge.

Mommsen, W. 1974. *The Age of Bureaucracy, Perspectives on the Political Sociology of Max Weber*. New York: The University Library.

Montagu, A. 1997. *Man's Most Dangerous Myth: The Fallacy of Race*. London: Sage.

Mooney Marini, M. 1992. 'The role of models of purposive action in sociology', in J.S. Coleman and T.J. Fararo (eds), *Rational Choice Theory*. London: Sage.

Morris, B. 1987. *Anthropological Studies of Religion*. Cambridge: Cambridge University Press.

Moscovici, S. 1993. *The Invention of Society*. Cambridge: Polity.

Mosse, G.L. 1985. *Toward the Final Solution: A History of European Racism*. Madison: University of Wisconsin Press.

Mouzelis, N. 1995. *Sociological Theory: What Went Wrong?* London: Routledge.

Münch, R. 1992. 'Rational Choice Theory. A Critical Assessment of Its Explanatory Power', in J.S. Coleman and T.J. Fararo (eds), *Rational Choice Theory*. London: Sage.

Myrdal, G. 1944. *An American Dilemma: The Negro Problem and Modern Democracy*. New York: Harper.

Nedelmann, B. 1991. 'Individualization, exaggeration and paralysation: Simmel's three problems of culture', *Theory, Culture & Society*, 8: 169–93.

Neitz, M.J. and Mueser, P.R. 1997. 'Economic man and the sociology of religion: a critique of the rational choice approach', in L.A. Young (ed.), *Rational Choice Theory and Religion: Summary and Assessment*. New York: Routledge.

Nicholson, L. (ed.) 1990. *Feminism/Postmodernism*. London: Routledge.

Nicholson, L. (ed.) 1997. *The Second Wave. A Reader in Feminist Theory*. New York: Routledge.

Nicholson, L. and Seidman, S. 1995. *Social Postmodernism. Beyond Identity Politics*. Cambridge: Cambridge University Press.

Nielson, J.K. 1991. 'The political orientation of Talcott Parsons', in R. Robertson and B.S. Turner, (eds), *Talcott Parsons. Theorist of Modernity*. London: Sage.

Nietzsche, F. 1872 [1993]. *The Birth of Tragedy*. Harmondsworth: Penguin.

Nietzsche, F. 1887 [1994]. *On the Genealogy of Morality*. Edited by K. Ansell-Pearson. Cambridge: Cambridge University Press.

Nikolinakos, M. (1973) 'Notes on an economic theory of racism', *Race: A Journal of Race and Group Relations*, 14: 365–81.

Nisbet, R. 1966 [1993, 2nd edition]. *The Sociological Tradition*. New Brunswick, NJ: Transaction.

Oakley, A. 1972. *Sex, Gender and Society*. London: Temple Smith.

Oberschall, A. 1978. 'Theories of social conflict', *Annual Review of Sociology*, 4: 291–315.

O'Brien, M. 1989. *Reproducing the World*. Boulder, CO: Westview.

O'Callaghan, M. 1980. 'Introductory Notes' to *Sociological Theories: Race and Colonialism*. Paris: Unesco.

O'Connor, J. 1973. *The Fiscal Crisis of the State*, New York: St Martin's Press.

Olson, M. 1965. *The Logic of Collective Action*. Cambridge, MA: Harvard University Press.

Omi, M. and Winant, H. 1986. *Racial Formation in the United States*. London: Routledge and Kegan Paul.

Opp, K-D. 1989. *The Rationality of Political Protest. A Comparative Analysis of Rational Choice Theory*. Boulder, CO: Westview.

Orema, D. and Klandermas, B. 1994. 'Why social movements support sympathizers don't participate: Erosion and nonconversion of support. *American Sociological Review*, 49(5): 703–22.

Ossowski, S. 1956. 'La vision dichotomique de la stratification sociale', *Cahiers Internationaux de Sociologie*, Vol. 20.

Ossowski, S. 1963. *Class Structure in the Social Consciousness*. London: Routledge and Kegan Paul.

Outhwaite, W. 1994. *Habermas: A Critical Introduction*. Cambridge: Polity.

Owen, D. 1997. 'The postmodern challenge to sociology', in D. Owen (ed.), *Sociology After Post-modernism*. London: Sage.

Parfit, D. 1986. 'Prudence, morality, and the prisoner's dilemma', in J. Elster (ed.), *Rational Choice*. Oxford: Blackwell.

Park, R.E. 1922. *The Immigrant Press and Its Control*. New York: Harper.

Park, R.E. 1950 [1964]. *Race and Culture*. Glencoe, IL: Free Press.

Park, R.E., Burgess, E. and McKenzie, R. 1925 [1967]. *The City*. Chicago: University of Chicago Press.

Park, R.E. 1972. *The Crowd and the Public and other Essays*. Chicago: The University of Chicago Press.

Park, R.E. and Burgess, E.W. (eds) 1921. *Introduction to the Science of Sociology*. Chicago: University of Chicago Press.

Parsons, T. 1937 [1968]. *The Structure of Social Action*. New York: Free Press.

Parsons, T. 1951 [1991]. *The Social System*. London: Routledge.

Parsons, T. 1959 [1983]. 'The school as a social system', in B. Cosin and M. Hales (eds), *Education, Policy and Society*. London: Routledge and Kegan Paul.

Parsons, T. 1960. *Structure and Process in Modern Societies*. New York: Free Press.

Parsons, T. 1961. 'The contribution of psychoanalysis to social science', *Science and Psychoanalysis*. 4: 28–38.

Parsons, T. 1962. 'Comment on "The oversocialised conception of man" by Dennis Wrong', *Psychoanalysis and Psychoanalytic Review*, 10: 322–34.

Parsons, T. 1964. *Essays in Sociological Theory*. Revised Edition. New York: Free Press.

Parsons, T. 1966a. 'Religion in a modern, pluralistic society', *Review of Religious Research*, 7(3): 125–46.

Parsons, T. 1966b. *Societies: Evolutionary and Comparative Perspectives*. Englewood Cliffs, NJ: Prentice-Hall.

Parsons, T. 1967a. *Sociological Theory and Modern Society*. New York: Free Press.

Parsons, T. 1967b. 'Durkheim's Contribution to the Theory of Integration of Social Systems', in *Sociological Theory and Modern Society*. New York: Free Press.

Parsons, T. 1969. *Politics and Social Structure*. New York: Free Press.

Parsons, T. 1970. 'On building social system theory: A personal history', *Daedalus*, 99(4): 826–81.

Parsons, T. 1971a. 'Evolutionary universals in society', in A.R. Desai (ed.), *Essays on Modernization of Underdeveloped Societies*. Bombay: Thacker Spink.

Parsons, T. 1971b. 'Value-freedom and objectivity', in O. Stammer (ed.), *Max Weber and Sociology Today*. Oxford: Blackwell.

Parsons, T. 1978. *Action Theory and the Human Condition*. New York: Free Press.

Parsons, T. 1981. 'Revisiting the classics throughout a long career', in B. Rhea (ed.), *The Future of the Sociological Classics*. London: Allen and Unwin.

Parsons, T. 1982. 'American values and American society', in L. Mayhew (ed.), *Talcott Parsons on Institutions and Social Evolution*. Chicago: University of Chicago Press.

Parsons, T. 1991. 'A tentative outline of American values', in R. Robertson and B.S. Turner (eds), *Talcott Parsons. Theorist of Modernity*. London: Sage.

Parsons, T., Bales, R.F. et al. 1955. *Family, Socialization and Interaction Process*. Glencoe, IL: Free Press.

Parsons, T. and Shils, E. 1962. *Toward a General Theory of Action*. Cambridge, MA: Harvard University Press.

Phillips, A. 1992. 'Universal pretensions in political thought', in M. Barrett and A. Phillips (eds), *Destablizing Theory. Contemporary Feminist Debates*. Cambridge: Polity.

Pickering, M. 1993. *Auguste Comte: An Intellectual Biography*, Vol. I. Cambridge: Cambridge University Press.

Pickering, M. 1997. 'A new look at Auguste Comte', in C. Camic (ed.), *Reclaiming the Sociological Classics*. Oxford: Blackwell.

Pickering, W.S.F. 1984. *Durkheim's Sociology of Religion*. London: Routledge and Kegan Paul.

Porter, R. 1990. *The Enlightenment*. Basingstoke: Macmillan.

Portis, E.B. 1973. Max Weber's theory of personality', *Sociological Inquiry*, 48(2).

Preuss, K.Y. 1904. 'Der Unsprung der Religion und Kunst', *Globus*, 86: 321–89.

Radcliffe-Brown, A.R. 1952. *Structure and Function in Primitive Societies*. London: Cohen and West.

Rattansi, A. 1997. 'Post-colonialism and its discontents', *Economy and Society*, 26(4): 480–500.

Rattansi, A. and Westwood, S. (eds) 1994. *Racism, Modernity and Identity*. Cambridge: Polity.

Rawls, A. 1996. Durkheim's epistemology: the neglected argument. *American Journal of Sociology*, 102(2): 430–82.

Ray, L. 1993. *Rethinking Critical Theory: Emancipation in the Age of Global Social Movements*. London: Sage.

Reedy, W.J. 1994. 'The historical imaginary of social science in post-Revolutionary France: Bonald, Saint-Simon, Comte', *History of the Human Sciences*, 7(1): 1–26.

Reich, M. 1971. 'The economics of racism', in D.M. Gordon (ed.), *Problems in Political Economy*. Lexington, MA: Heath.

Reich, M. 1981. *Racial Inequality*. Princeton, NJ: Princeton University Press.

Renan, E. 1882 [1990]. 'What is a nation?', in H.K. Bhaba (ed.), *Nation and Narration*. London: Routledge.

Rex, J. 1961. *Key Problems of Sociological Theory*. London: Routledge and Kegan Paul.

Rex, J. 1973. *Race, Colonialism and the City*. London: Routledge and Kegan Paul.

Rex, J. 1980. 'The theory of race relations: a Weberian approach', in *Sociological Theories: Race and Colonialism*. Paris: Unesco.

Rex, J. 1981. *Social Conflict*. London: Longman.

Rex, J. 1986. *Race and Ethnicity*. Milton Keynes: Open University Press.

Rex, J. 2000. 'Race relations in sociological theory', in J. Solomos and L. Back (eds), *Theories of Race and Racism*. London: Macmillan.

Rich, A. 1979. *Of Woman Born*. New York: W.W. Norton.

Richman, M. 1995. 'The sacred group. A Durkheimian perspective on the College de sociologie (1937–39)', in C. Bailey Gill (ed.), *Bataille. Writing the Sacred*. London: Routledge.

Riesman, D. 1950. *The Lonely Crowd*. New Haven, CT: Yale University Press.

Riley, D. 1988. *Am I That Name? Feminism and the Category of 'Women' in History*. New York: Macmillan.

Ritzer, G. 1992. *Sociological Theory*. New York: McGraw-Hill.

Ritzer, G. 1996. *Classical Sociological Theory*. New York: McGraw-Hill.

Robertson, R. 1991. 'The central significance of "Religion" in social theory: Parsons as an epical theorist', in R. Robertson and B.S. Turner (eds), *Talcott Parsons: Theorist of Modernity*. London: Sage.

Robertson, R. 1992. *Globalisation*. London: Sage.

Robertson, R. and Turner, B.S. 1991. 'An introduction to Talcott Parsons', in R. Robertson and B.S. Turner (eds), *Talcott Parsons: Theorist of Modernity*. London: Sage.

Rocher, G. 1974. *Talcott Parsons and American Sociology*. London: Nelson.

Rock, P. 1979. *The Making of Symbolic Interactionism*. London: Routledge.

Roediger, D.R. 1991. *The Wages of Whiteness*. London: Verso.

Rorty, R. 1992. 'Cosmopolitanism without emancipation: a response to Lyotard', in S. Lash and J. Friedman (eds), *Modernity and Identity*. Oxford: Blackwell.

Rose, G. 1992. 'Diremption of Spirit', in P. Berry and A. Wernick (eds), *Shadow of Spirit*. London: Routledge.

Rubin, G. 1975. 'The traffic in women', in R. Reiter (ed.), *Toward an Anthology of Women*. New York: Monthly Review Press.

Sacks, K. 1974. 'Engels revisited: women, the organization of production and private property', in M.Z. Rosaldo and L. Lampere (eds), *Women, Culture and Society*. Stanford, CA: Stanford University Press.

Said, E.W. 1978. *Orientalism. Western Conceptions of the Orient*. Harmondsworth: Penguin.

Sartre, J.P. 1946. *Existentialism and Humanism*. London: Methuen.

Savage, S.P. 1981. *The Theories of Talcott Parsons. The Social Relations of Action*. London: Macmillan.

Scharff, R.C. 1995. *Comte After Positivism*. Cambridge: Cambridge University Press.

Scheff, T.J. 1992. 'Rationality and emotion: homage to Norbert Elias', in J.S. Coleman and T.J. Fararo (eds), *Rational Choice Theory*. London: Sage.

Schelsky, H. 1956. 'Gesellschaftlicher Wandel', *Offene Welt*, 41.

Schiebinger, L. 1993. *Nature's Body: Gender in the Making of Modern Science*. New York: Beacon.

Schoenfeld, E. and Meštrović, S.G. 1991. 'From the sacred collectivity to the sacred individual: The misunderstood Durkheimian legacy', *Sociological Focus*, 24(2): 83–92.

Schwanenberg, E. 1971. 'The two problems of order in Parsons' theory: An analysis from within', *Social Forces*, 49: 569–81.

Sciulli, D. 1992. 'Weaknesses in rational choice theory's contribution to comparative research', in J.S. Coleman and T.J. Fararo (eds), *Rational Choice Theory*. London: Sage.

Scott, J. 1995. *Sociological Theory: Contemporary Debates*. Aldershot: Edward Elgar.

Sedgwick, E. 1985. *Between Men: English Literature and Homosocial Desire*. New York: Columbia University Press.

Seel, M. 1991. 'The two meanings of 'communicative' rationality: remarks on Habermas's critique of a plural concept of reason', in A. Honneth and H. Joas (eds), *Communicative Action: Essays on Jürgen Habermas's The Theory of Communicative Action*. Cambridge: Polity.

Seidman, S. 1994. 'The end of sociological theory', in S. Seidman (ed.), *The Postmodern Turn*. Cambridge: Cambridge University Press.

Seidman, S. 1995. 'Deconstructing queer theory', in L. Nicholson and S. Seidman (eds), *Social Postmodernism. Beyond Identity Politics*. Cambridge: Cambridge University Press.

Seidman, S. 1998. *Contested Knowledge*. Oxford: Blackwell.

Selznick, P. 1992. *The Moral Commonwealth*. Berkeley: University of California Press.

Sen, A. 1986. 'Behaviour and the concept of preference', in J. Elster (ed.), *Rational Choice*. Oxford: Blackwell.

Shafer, C. and Frye, M. 1986. 'Rape and respect', in M. Pearsall (ed.), *Women and Values*. California: Wadsworth.

Shelton, B. and Agger, B. 1993. 'Shotgun wedding, unhappy marriage, no-fault divorce? Rethinking the feminism–marxism relationship', in P. England, *Theory on Gender. Feminism on Theory*. New York: Aldine de Gruyter.

Sherkat, D.E. 1997. 'Embedding religious choices: preferences and social constraints into rational choice theories of behaviour', in L.A. Young (ed.), *Rational Choice Theory and Religion: Summary and Assessment*. New York: Routledge.

Shilling, C. 1993. *The Body and Social Theory*. London: Sage.

Shilling, C. and Mellor, P.A. 1996. 'Embodiment, structuration theory and modernity: mind/body dualism and the repression of sexuality', *Body and Society*, 2(4): 1–15.

Shils, E. 1965. 'Charisma, order, and status', *American Sociological Review*, 30: 199–213.

Simmel, G. 1898 [1997]. 'A contribution to the sociology of religion', in J. Helle (ed.), *Essays on Religion*. New Haven, CT: Yale University Press.

Simmel, G. 1903a [1971]. 'The Metropolis' in D. Levine (ed.), *Georg Simmel On Individuality and Social Forms*. Chicago: University of Chicago Press.

Simmel, G. 1903b [1997]. 'On the salvation of the soul', in J. Helle (ed.), *Essays on Religion*. New Haven, CT: Yale University Press.

Simmel, G. 1904 [1997]. 'Religion and the contradictions of life', in J. Helle (ed.), *Essays on Religion*. New Haven, CT: Yale University Press.

Simmel, G. 1907 [1990]. *The Philosophy of Money*. Edited and with an introduction by Tom Bottomore and D. Frisby. London: Routledge.

Simmel, G. 1908a [1971]. 'The problem of sociology', in D. Levine (ed.), *Georg Simmel on Individuality and Social Forms*. Chicago: University of Chicago Press.

Simmel, G. 1908b [1971]. 'How is society possible?', in D. Levine (ed.), *Georg Simmel on Individuality and Social Forms*. Chicago: University of Chicago Press.

Simmel, G. 1908c [1971]. 'Subjective culture', in D. Levine (ed.), *Georg Simmel on Individuality and Social Forms*. Chicago: University of Chicago Press.

Simmel, G. 1908d [1971]. 'Group expansion and the development of individuality', in D. Levine (ed.), *Georg Simmel on Individuality and Social Forms*. Chicago: University of Chicago Press.

Simmel, G. 1909 [1997]. 'Fundamental religious ideas and modern science: an inquiry', in J. Helle (ed.), *Essays on Religion*. New Haven, CT: Yale University Press.

Simmel, G. 1910 [1971]. 'Sociability', in D. Levine (ed.), *Georg Simmel on Individuality and Social Forms*. Chicago: University of Chicago Press.

Simmel, G. 1911a [1968]. 'On the concept and the tragedy of culture', in G. Simmel, *The Conflict in Modern Culture and Other Essays*. trans. P. Etzkorn. New York: The Teachers College Press.

Simmel, G. 1911b [1997]. 'The problem of religion today', in J. Helle (ed.), *Essays on Religion*. New Haven, CT: Yale University Press.

Simmel, G. 1912 [1997]. 'Religion', in J. Helle (ed.), *Essays on Religion*. New Haven, CT: Yale University Press.

Simmel, G. 1914 [1997]. 'Rembrandt's religious art', in J. Helle (ed.), *Essays on Religion*. New Haven, CT: Yale University Press.

Simmel, G. 1918a [1971]. 'The conflict in modern culture', in D. Levine (ed.), *Georg Simmel on Individuality and Social Forms*. Chicago: University of Chicago Press.

Simmel, G. 1918b [1971]. 'The transcendent character of life', in D. Levine (ed.), *Georg Simmel on Individuality and Social Forms*. Chicago: University of Chicago Press.

Simmel, G. 1950. *The Sociology of Georg Simmel*. trans. K. Wolffe. Glencoe, IL: Free Press.

Simmel, G. 1955. *Conflict and The Web of Group-Affiliations*. New York: Free Press.

Simon, W.M. 1963. *European Positivism in the Nineteenth Century*. London: Kennikat Press.

Sinha, M. 1987. 'Gender and imperialism: colonial policy and the ideology of moral imperialism in late nineteenth-century Bengal', in M. Kimmel (ed.), *Changing Men. New Directions in Research on Men and Masculinity*. Newbury Park, CA: Sage.

Sinha, M. 1995. *Colonial Masculinity*. Manchester: University of Manchester.

Sivanden, A. 1982. *A Different Hunger: Writings on Black Resistance*. London: Pluto.

Skarga, B. 1974. 'Le coeur et la raison, ou les antinomies du système de Comte', *Les études philosophiques*, 3: 383–90.

Smart, B. 1993. *Postmodernity*. London: Routledge.

Smart, B. 1996a. 'Postmodern social theory', in B.S. Turner (ed.), *The Blackwell Companion to Social Theory*. Oxford: Blackwell.

Smart, B. 1996b. 'Facing the body in Goffman, Levinas and the subject of evidence', *Body and Society*, 2(2): 67–8.

Smart, B. 1998. *Facing Modernity: Ambivalence, Reflexivity and Morality*. London: Sage.

Smith, A.D. 1991. *National Identity*. Harmondsworth: Penguin.

Smith, D. 1987. *The Everyday World as Problematic: A Feminist Sociology*. Boston: Northeastern University Press.

Smith-Lovin, L. and McPherson, J.M. 1993. 'You are who you know: A network approach to gender', in P. England (ed.), *Theory on Gender. Feminism on Theory*. New York: Aldine de Gruyter.

Snowden, F.M. 1970. *Blacks in Antiquity: Ethiopians in the Greco-Roman Experience*. Cambridge, MA: Harvard University Press.

Snowden, F.M. 1983. *Before Colour Prejudice: The Ancient View of Blacks*. Cambridge, MA: Harvard University Press.

Solnic, S. and Hemenway, D. 1996. 'The deadweight loss of Christmas: comment', *American Economic Review*, 86(5): 1298–1305.

Solomos, J. 1993. *Race and Racism in Britain*, 2nd edn. London: Macmillan.

Solomos, J. and Back, L. 1996. *Racism and Society*. Basingstoke: Macmillan.

Solomos, J. and Back, L. 2000. 'Introduction: theorising race and racism', in J. Solomos and L. Back (eds), *Theories of Race and Racism*. London: Macmillan.

Sorokin, P. 1966. *Sociological Theories of Today*. New York: Harper and Row.

Spencer, H. 1850 [1972]. 'The social organism', in J.D.Y. Peel (ed.), *On Social Evolution*. Chicago: University of Chicago Press.

Spickard, J.V. 1998. 'Rethinking religious social action: What is "rational" about rational-choice theory?', *Sociology of Religion*, 59(2): 99–116.

Spivak, G.C. 1987. *In Other Worlds. Essays in Cultural Politics*. New York: Methuen.

Spivak, G.C. 1990. *The Post-Colonial Critic. Interviews, Strategies, Dialogues*. Edited by S. Harasym. London: Routledge.

Stanley, L. 1984. 'Should "sex" really be "gender" – or "gender" really be "sex"?', in R. Anderson and W. Shurrock (eds), *Applied Sociological Perspectives*, London: Allen and Unwin.

Stark, R. 1997. 'Bringing theory back in', in L.A. Young (ed.), *Rational Choice Theory and Religion: Summary and Assessment*. New York: Routledge.

Stark, R. and Bainbridge, W.S. 1987. *A Theory of Religion*. New York: Peter Lang.

Stark, R. and Bainbridge, W.S. 1996. *Religion, Deviance and Social Control*. London: Routledge.

Staub, E. 1978. *Positive Social Behavior and Morality*. London: Academic Press.

Stein, M. 1960. *The Spirit of Community*. Princeton, NJ: Princeton University Press.

Stepan, N. 1982. *The Idea of Race in Science: Great Britain 1800–1960*. London: Macmillan.

Stinchcombe, A.L. 1986. 'Reason and rationality', *Sociological Theory*, 4: 151–66.

Stivers, R. 1994. *The Culture of Cynicism*. Cambridge: Blackwell.

Strenski, I. 1997. *Durkheim and the Jews of France*. Chicago: University of Chicago Press.

Synnott, A. 1991. 'Puzzling over the senses: from Plato to Marx', in D. Howes (ed.), *The Varieties of Sensory Experience: A Sourcebook in the Anthropology of the Senses*. Toronto: University of Toronto Press.

Swingewood, A. 1991. *A Short History of Sociological Thought*. Basingstoke: Macmillan.

Tenbruck, F. 1980. 'The problem of thematic unity in the works of Max Weber', *British Journal of Sociology*, 31(3): 316–51.

Tester, K. 1995. *The Inhuman Condition*. London: Routledge.

Theweleit, K. 1977. *Male Fantasies*, Vol. 1: *Women, Floods, Bodies, History*. Cambridge: Polity.

Theweleit, K. 1978. *Male Fantasies*, Vol. 2: *Male Bodies: Psychoanalysing the White Terror*. Minneapolis: University of Minnesota Press.

Thom, M. 1990. 'Tribes within nations: the ancient Germans and the history of modern France', in H.K. Bhabha (ed.), *Nation and Narration*. London: Routledge.

Thomas, N. 1994. *Colonialism's Culture. Anthropology, Travel and Government*. Cambridge: Polity.

Thomas, P. 1913. *A Religion of this World. Being a Selection of Positivist Addresses*. London: Watts and Co.

Thompson, K. 1976. *Auguste Comte: The Foundation of Sociology*. London: Nelson.

Tijssen, L. van Vucht 1991. 'Women and objective culture: Georg Simmel and Marianne Weber', *Theory, Culture & Society*, 8: 203–18.

Tiryakian, E. 1995. 'Collective effervescence, social change and charisma: Durkheim, Weber and 1989'. *International Sociology*, 10(3): 269–81.

Toby, J. 1977. 'Introduction: Parsons's theory of societal evolution', in T. Parsons, *The Evolution of Societies*. Englewood Cliffs, NJ: Prentice-Hall.

Tollison, R. 1997. 'Rent seeking', in D. Mueller (ed.), *Perspectives on Public Choice: A Handbook*. Cambridge: Cambridge University Press.

Tonelli, G. 1997. 'The "weakness" of reason in the Age of Enlightenment', in R.H. Popkin, E. de Olaso and G. Tonelli (eds), *Scepticism in the Enlightenment*. Dordrecht: Kluwer.

Tong, R. 1989. *Feminist Thought. A Comprehensive Introduction*. London: Routledge.

Touraine, A. 1995. *Critique of Modernity*. Oxford: Blackwell.

Triandafyllidou, A. 1998. 'National identity and the other', *Ethnic and Racial Studies*, 21(4): 593–612.

Tuck, R. 1979. 'Is there a free-rider problem, and if so, what is it?', in R. Harrison (ed.), *Rational Action. Studies in Philosophy and Social Science*. Cambridge: Cambridge University Press.

Turner, B.S. 1986. 'Simmel, rationalization and the problem of money', *Sociological Review*, 34: 93–114.

Turner, B.S. 1990. *Theories of Modernity and Postmodernity*. London: Sage.

Turner, B.S. 1991a. 'Preface to the new edition', in H.H. Gerth and C.W. Mills (eds), *From Max Weber: Essays in Sociology*. London: Rouledge.

Turner, B.S. 1991b. 'Preface to the new edition', T. Parsons, 1951, *The Social System*. London: Routledge.

Turner, B.S. 1991c. *Religion and Social Theory*. London: Sage.

Turner, B.S. 1996a. *For Weber*. London: Sage.

Turner, B.S. 1996b. 'Introduction to the second edition', *The Body and Society*. London: Sage.

Turner, J.H. 1987. 'Analytical theorizing', in A. Giddens and J.H. Turner (eds), *Social Theory Today*. Cambridge: Polity.

Turner, J.H. and Maryanski, A.R. 1988. 'Is "neofunctionalism" really functional?', *Sociological Theory*, 6: 110–21.

Turner, V. 1969. *The Ritual Process. Structure and Antistructure*. London: Routledge.

Turner, V. 1976. 'Ritual, tribal and Catholic'. *Worship*, 50(6): 504–26.

Turner, V. 1977. 'Variations on a theme of liminality', in Sally F. Moore and Barbara G. Myerhoff (eds), *Secular Ritual*. Amsterdam: Van Gorcum.

Tversky, A., Sattath, S. and Slovic, P. 1988. 'Contingent weighing in judgment and choice', *Psychological Review*, 95: 371–84.

Ullmann-Margalit, E. 1977. *The Emergence of Norms*. Oxford: Oxford University Press.

Urry, J. 2000. *Sociology Beyond Societies*. London: Routledge.

Vattimo, G. 1992. *The Transparent Society*. Cambridge: Polity.

Vogel, L. 1983. *Marxism and the Oppression of Women*. New Brunswick, NJ: Rutgers University Press.

Wallerstein, I. 1991. 'The French revolution as a world-historical event', in F. Feher (ed.), *The French Revolution and the Birth of Modernity*. Berkeley: University of California Press.

Wallerstein, I. 1996. 'Social science and contemporary society', *International Sociology*, 11(1): 7–25.

Ward, G. 1998. 'Kenosis and naming: beyond analogy and towards allegoria amoris', in P. Heelas (ed.), *Religion, Modernity and Postmodernity*. London: Routledge.

Ward, K. 1984. *Women in the World System: Its Impact on Status and Fertility*. New York: Praeger.

Warner, W.L. 1936. 'American caste and class', *American Journal of Sociology*, 42: 234–7.

Warner, W.L. 1959. *The Living and the Dead*. New Haven, CT: Yale University Press.

Warner, W.L. 1963. *Yankee City*. New Haven, CT: Yale University Press.

Watts Miller, W. 1996. *Durkheim, Morals and Modernity*. London: UCL Press.

Weber, M. 1894 [1989]. 'Developmental tendencies in the situation of East Elbian rural labourers', in K. Tribe (ed.), *Reading Weber*. London: Routledge.

Weber, M. 1904–5 [1991]. *The Protestant Ethic and the Spirit of Capitalism*. London: Harper Collins.

Weber, M. 1915 [1991]. 'Religious rejections of the world and their rejections', in H.H. Gerth and C. Wright Mills (eds), *From Max Weber: Essays in Sociology*. London: Routledge and Kegan Paul.

Weber, M. 1919a [1991]. 'Politics as a vocation', in H.H. Gerth and C. Wright Mills (eds), *From Max Weber*. London: Routledge.

Weber, M. 1919b [1991]. 'Science as a vocation', in H.H. Gerth and C. Wright Mills (eds), *From Max Weber*. London: Routledge.

Weber, M. 1949. *The Methodology of the Social Sciences*. New York: Free Press.

Weber, M. 1951. *The Religion of China*. New York: Free Press.

Weber, M. 1958. *The City*. New York: Free Press.

Weber, M. 1968. *Economy and Society*. 2 vols. Berkeley: University of California Press.

Weber, M. 1975. *Roscher and Knies: The Logical Problem of Historical Economics*. trans. Guy Oakes. New York: Free Press.

Weber, Marianne 1975. *Max Weber: A Biography*. New York: Wiley.

Weedon, C. 1987. *Feminist Practice and Poststructuralist Theory*. Oxford: Blackwell.

Wenzel, H.V. 1981. 'The text as body/politics: An appreciation of Monique Wittig's writings in context', *Feminist Studies*, 7(2): 264–87.

Wernick, A. 1992. 'Post-Marx: theological themes in Baudrillard's America', in P. Berry and A. Wernick (eds), *Shadow of Spirit: Postmodernism and Religion*. London: Routledge.

West, C. 1990. 'The new cultural politics of difference', in R. Ferguson, M. Gever, T. Minh-ha, and C. West (eds), *Out There: Marginalisation and Contemporary Cultures*. Cambridge. MA: MIT Press.

West, C. and Zimmerman, D. 1987. 'Doing gender', *Gender and Society*, 1: 125–51.

Whitehead, A. 1925. *Science and the Modern World*. New York: Macmillan.

Whitford, M. 1991. 'Introduction', in M. Whitford (ed.), *The Irigaray Reader*. Oxford: Blackwell.

Wiener, N. 1948. *Cybernetics. Or Control and Communication in the Animal and the Machine*. New York: Wiley.

Wieviorka, M. 1995. *The Arena of Racism*. London: Sage.

Williams, C. 1993. 'Psychoanalytic theory and the sociology of gender', in P. England (ed.), *Theory on Gender. Feminism on Theory*. New York: Aldine de Gruyter.

Williams, W.W. 1997. 'The Equality crisis' in L. Nicholson (ed.), *The Second Wave. A Reader in Feminist Theory*. London: Routledge.

Wilson, W.J. 1978. *The Declining Significance of Race. Blacks and Changing American Institutions*. Chicago: University of Chicago Press.

Wilson, W.J. 1996a. *When Work Disappears*. New York: Alfred K. Knopf.

Wilson, W.J. 1996b. 'When work disappears', *Political Science Quarterly*, 111(4): 567–95.

Wilson, W.J. 1997. 'Toward a broader version of inner city poverty', in K. Erikson (ed.), *Sociological Visions*. Lanham, MD: Rowman.

Wilson, W.J. 1999. 'When work disappears. New implications for race and urban poverty in the global economy', *Ethnic and Racial Studies*, 22(3): 479–99.

Winnicott, D.W. 1965. *The Maturation Process and the Facilitating Environment*. London: Hogarth.

Winant, H. 2000. 'The theoretical status of the concept of race', in J. Solomos and L. Back (eds), *Theories of Race and Racism*. London: Macmillan.

Wittig, M. 1982. 'The category of sex', *Feminist Issues*, (Fall): 63–8.

Wolff, K.H. 1960. *Emile Durkheim, 1858–1916: A Collection of Essays, with Translation and Bibliography*. Columbus: Ohio State University Press.

Wright, E.O. 1985. *Classes*. Cambridge: Polity.

Wright, T.R. 1986. *The Religion of Humanity. The Impact of Comtean Positivism on Victorian Britain*. Cambridge: Cambridge University Press.

Wrong, D. 1961. 'The oversocialized conception of man in modern sociology', *American Sociological Review*, 26(2): 183–92.

Wrong, D. 1970. 'Introduction: Max Weber', in D. Wrong (ed.), *Max Weber*. Englewood Cliffs, NJ: Prentice-Hall.

Wrong, D.H. 1994. *The Problem of Order: What Unites and Divides Society*. Cambridge, MA: Harvard University Press.

Wyschogrod, E. 1990. *Saints and Postmodernism*. Chicago: University of Chicago Press.

Yaeger, L. 1997. 'Austrian economics, neoclassicism, and the market test', *Journal of Economic Perspectives*, 11(4): 153–66.

Young, I.M. 1990. *Throwing Like a Girl and Other Essays in Feminist Philosophy and Social Theory*. Bloomington: Indiana University Press.

Young, L.A. 1997. 'Introduction', in L.A. Young (ed.), *Rational Choice Theory and Religion: Summary and Assessment*. New York: Routledge.

Young, R.J.C. 1995. *Colonial Desire. Hybridity in Theory, Culture and Race*. London: Routledge.

Zafirovski, M.Z. 1999. 'What is really rational choice? Beyond the utilitarian concept of rationality', *Current Sociology*, 47(1): 47–113.

Zafirovski, M.Z. 2000. 'Spencer is dead, long live Spencer: individualism, holism and the problem of norms', *British Journal of Sociology*, 51(3): 553–79.

Zeitlin, I.M. 1981. *Ideology and the Development of Sociological Theory*. Englewood Cliffs, NJ: Prentice-Hall.

Index